Dear David,

May this new year bring you all wonderful things, - health happiness and love!

Love
Lisa

Rosh Hashanah
Readings

Also edited by Rabbi Dov Peretz Elkins
and published by Jewish Lights

Yom Kippur Readings:
Inspiration, Information and Contemplation

Rosh Hashanah

Readings

INSPIRATION
INFORMATION
CONTEMPLATION

Edited by Rabbi Dov Peretz Elkins

With Section Introductions from
Arthur Green's *These Are the Words*

JEWISH LIGHTS Publishing
Woodstock, Vermont

For my seven precious grandchildren—
Ari and Mia, Emma, Leila and Elan, Mollie and Arthur
—with great love.

Rosh Hashanah Readings:
Inspiration, Information and Contemplation

2006 First Printing
© 2006 by Dov Peretz Elkins

Library of Congress Cataloging-in-Publication Data
Rosh Hashanah readings : inspiration, information, and contemplation / edited by Dov Peretz Elkins ; with section introductions from Arthur Green's These are the words.
p. cm.
Includes bibliographical references.
ISBN-13: 978-1-58023-239-5 (hardcover)
ISBN-10: 1-58023-239-6
1. Rosh ha-Shanah—Meditations. I. Elkins, Dov Peretz. II. Green, Arthur, 1941– These are the words. Selections. III. Title.
BM695.N5M67 2006
296.4'315—dc22

2006015173

10 9 8 7 6 5 4 3 2 1
Jacket design: Tim Holtz
Jacket art: S-29, "Akedah VI," 1970 original color serigraph by Shraga Weil. Published by the Safrai Fine Art Gallery, Jerusalem, Israel. Copyright Safrai Gallery.

Manufactured in the United States of America

Published by Jewish Lights Publishing
A Division of LongHill Partners, Inc.
Sunset Farm Offices, Route 4, P.O. Box 237
Woodstock, VT 05091
Tel: (802) 457-4000   Fax: (802) 457-4004
www.jewishlights.com

Contents

v

Introduction

My respect for Judaism grows each year, but never more than on Rosh Hashanah when the theme is *teshuvah*. Rabbi Avraham Yitzhak Kook, late Chief Rabbi of Eretz Yisrael (d. 1935), defined *teshuvah* as the potential for personal growth. The unparalleled notion that a human being should devote the most important religious-holiday period of the year to inner spiritual reflection and moral growth continues to both amaze and elate me.

When I decided to study for my doctorate in pastoral counseling, I discovered the writings of humanistic psychologists Carl Rogers, Abraham Maslow, Erich Fromm, Margaret Mead, Roberto Assagioli, Will Schutz, and many others. It did not take long for me to realize that I was attracted to these thinkers so strongly because they reflected the basic philosophy of traditional Judaism. The silver thread that runs through the Torah, the biblical prophets, and rabbinic masters and later Judaism, is that there is enormous potential for spiritual and psychological growth in every human being. The Midrash says that every blade of grass has an angel that whispers to it, "Grow, grow!" So there is such an angel that tells us every Rosh Hashanah, "Grow, grow!" You have the power to change and become the person God meant you to be. When we come to High Holy Day services, we need to be aware of our own divine power to be a better person. Rabbi Nachman of Breslov taught: If we are not better tomorrow than we are today, why have a tomorrow?" This is humanistic psychology at its best, and it is ancient, medieval and modern Judaism at its best. This is the meaning of Rosh Hashanah, and it makes so much sense to me to let a sweet sample of all the "growers" of the world—prophets, saints, sages, psychologists, poets—join together in an anthology like this to tell us in one voice: "Grow, grow!"

There has been a great deal of writing and discussion in Jewish circles about *tikkun olam*—changing the world, redeeming society and improving the lot of God's creatures. To this vital religious notion has been added similar thought about *Tikkun Mishpahah*—improving relationships, family life, child-rearing and strengthening of the bonds of commitment among those connected to each other by ties biological or legal.

A third area of *tikkun* ("fixing," "repairing") is *tikkun nafshi*—fixing the soul, the spirit, the God-given inner core of humanity that drives everything we think and do. Rosh Hashanah deals with all of these, with its three basic sections of the *Musaf* service—*Malkhuyot* (God Is Sovereign), *Zikhronot* (God Remembers) and *Shofarot* (God will bring the Messiah with the proclamation of the Shofar). We pray, sing, reflect and contemplate the meanings of the birth and re-birth of our world, the memories of our sacred history, and the proclamation of the coming of God's sovereignty when the world will be One, and God's Name One. The *Alenu* doxology, written originally for the Rosh Hashanah *Musaf* service, embodies all of these *tikkunim*—change, growth and repair of our world, our communities, our families and our souls.

No religious ideology or civilization has been so spiritually and emotionally intelligent in the area of the need for personal growth and corporate redemption. I learned much from my teachers from early childhood through adulthood. One of the host of penetrating insights that has stayed with me while pursuing my doctoral studies in human growth and development (part of pastoral counseling) was the definition of psychotherapy as "the unfinished business of growing up." When Mahatma Gandhi was asked what he thought of Western civilization he said it is such a wonderful idea that we ought to try it. And Rabbi Mordecai M. Kaplan once wrote that humans are not born civilized, they must be taught to be civilized. There is no system, religion, philosophy or educational program that helps us grow up and be civilized better than does Judaism.

In what other body of literature, ideas and rituals does one find more ways to discover sea-changing ideas such as personal and community renewal, intimate love, personal responsibility, compassion for others, the importance of memory, the need for quiet, the indispensable need for private and public prayer, and, in the words best enunciated by Rabbi Abraham Joshua Heschel, moral grandeur and spiritual audacity?

Readers who found meaning and inspiration from the companion to this volume, *Yom Kippur Readings*, will find complementary ideas in this anthology. It has been said that Rosh Hashanah deals with repentance and regret, while Yom Kippur moves on to forgiveness, pardon and renewal. In this collection you will discover some of the deeper meanings of prayers like *U'Netaneh Tokef,* the blowing of the shofar, God's sovereignty, the robust power of "I'm sorry." Those who study this collection will find a wide variety of important components of Jewish civilization: Scriptural readings about our Founding Parents, the deeper meanings of faith and trust, and other similar ideas upon which our intellectual, spiritual and moral world rest.

Neither Rosh Hashanah nor Yom Kippur are days of sadness or mourning. Each has its own celebratory flavor and direction. The optimistic view of human nature expressed on Rosh Hashanah, that we are creatures made in the Divine Image and are not unalterably destined to be tomorrow what we are today, exposes to us the potential for leaps of *tikkun* in all aspects of our lives. Yom Kippur, with its fasting, self-flagellation through beating our breasts, wearing the white *kittel* we are some day to don in the coffin, exposes to us an image of seriousness about life, yet never gives up the cheerful hope that life is an opportunity for renewal and not a crawling through the mud of regret.

As in *Yom Kippur Readings*, it is our intention to offer the lay and scholarly public a variety of stimulating thoughts and ideas that will make of these holiest of days a period of sacred time that is ever more memorable and influential in our daily lives. This two-volume set of High Holy Day readings and reflections will help worshipers gain more depth from the Days of Awe, and give prayer leaders a renewed sense of responsibility in leading their flocks to a higher pitch of feverish absorption in the wealth of words lovingly spun by our ancestors who strove for the perfection of their soul and a closer sense of God in their daily lives. It is our hope that these two collections will heighten the anticipation of those who use it for preparation during the month of Elul, and will expand the horizons of those who take the books to synagogue to peer into a page when a certain passage does not lift them to the heights they were hoping for.

One of the uses of a collection such as this is to stimulate your thinking to pursue similar ideas in other places. Reading the works of people like the ancient Jewish sages, modern rabbis, poets and philosophers through the ages who come from all faiths and traditions may bring one to explore other writings of these same creative spirits. It is no small pleasure for an anthologist to join in one volume the thoughts and artistry of people like the prophet Jeremiah, midrashic and Talmudic sages, together with more recent teachers and writers like Rabbi Yisrael Meir HaKohen Kagan, Martin Buber, Ernest Hemingway, Rabbi Avraham Yitzhak Kook, and modern spiritual leaders like Rabbis Arthur Green, Reuven Kimelman, Kenneth L. Cohen, Nina Beth Cardin, Irwin Kula, Abraham J. Twerski, Bonnie Koppell, Rami Shapiro, and others like them. Just seeing their names is an education: knowing who are some of the leading contributors to human moral education in past and present centuries.

May this new collection help bring Israel closer to God, and God closer to Israel, and thereby make the world a better place for all God's children.

Rabbi Dov Peretz Elkins

OPENING MEDITATIONS AND THOUGHTS

Hasidic sources speak of an "inward point" that lies hidden, waiting to be discovered. That point is the presence of God implanted within this world, especially within each person. Our task is to discover that point and to expand it, making it the very center of the way we see both ourselves and others. As we do so, our vision of the world is transformed and we may catch a glimpse of the entire natural order radiant with a supernatural presence that glows from within.

RABBI ARTHUR GREEN, *THESE ARE THE WORDS*

1

L'Shanah Tovah

When we wish each other a *shanah tovah,* a good year, we think of the
Hebrew word *shanah,* or year, and extend greetings for a good year.
But the Hebrew root *shin, nun, heh* has another meaning as well, from
the verb *le-shanot,* to change. Further, the same root, *shin, nun, heh,*
also denotes repetition, as in the name of the fifth book of the Torah,
Mishneh Torah, the repetition of the Torah.

In other words, a *shanah tovah,* a good year, is a year of *le-shanot,*
of change, of doing things differently and better. And it also denotes a
year of repetition, of relearning all the old lessons that our tradition of
truth and wisdom has been teaching us for many centuries.

Shanah is a unique word. And may the new *shanah* be a unique
year, one in which there is both repetition of the old, and change for
the better.

Rabbi Dov Peretz Elkins

A New Year

With the New Year, we have a chance for newness within our hearts, a
newness that can change the course of our lives. But change is often
frightening, and sometimes we are not sure that we are indeed ready
for it. "What will this new heart be like?" we wonder. "How will this
purified heart change the persons we are?" "Will the very structure of
our lives change as our spirits are renewed?" So much uncertainty
comes with change. As we stand at the threshold of a New Year, we
pray for the valor to face uncertainty, the courage to truly change what
needs to be changed, and the faith to welcome the new spirit that is
within us.

Rabbi Leila Gal Berner

A Fresh Start

It's the beginning of a new year. We have examined our deeds, made
amends, and been renewed. But recovery and spiritual renewal do not
come quickly or easily. Repentance, *teshuvah,* is hard work. That's
really why when we finally—after the long hot summer—get to Rosh

Hashanah we call it a New Year, because through honest repentance we are given the opportunity to begin life anew and get a fresh start on the year, and our lives.

While Tishrei is actually the seventh month of the Hebrew calendar, it leads the year nevertheless. The symbol for the month is a scale, reflecting the balance that the month gives our lives. And so with it we begin counting, continuing to keep our lives in balance one day at a time—from the awe-filled days of Rosh Hashanah and Yom Kippur through the harvest of self-searching at Sukkot and the rejoicing of our relationship with God on Simchat Torah.

During the entire month, we are absorbed by the fall holidays. Powerful moods to begin a year, reflections of a life of the spirit. The Gaon of Vilna taught us: "Each day should be a new experience. Each day we have the opportunity of a fresh start. A person who has made *teshuvah* is like a newborn child."

Rabbi Kerry M. Olitzky

A Clean Heart

Hide Your face from my sins,
And blot out all my iniquities.
Create for me a clean heart, O God;
And renew a steadfast spirit inside me.
Cast me not away from Your presence;
And do not take Your holy spirit from me
Restore to me the joy of Your saving presence;
And let a willing spirit uphold me.
Then will I teach transgressors Your ways;
And sinners will return to You
The sacrifices of God are a broken spirit;
A broken and a contrite heart, O God, You will not despise.

Psalms 51:11–15, 19

The Future

This is what we are about: We plant seeds that one day will grow. We water seeds already planted, knowing that they hold future promise. We lay foundations that will need further development. We provide yeast that produces effects beyond our capabilities. We cannot do everything and there is a sense of liberation in realizing that. This enables us to do something and to do it very well. It may be incomplete, but it is a beginning, a step along the way, an opportunity for God to enter and to do the rest. We may never see the end results, but that is the difference between the master builder and the worker. We are workers, not master builders, ministers not messiahs. We are prophets of a future not our own.

Archbishop Oscar Romero

Those Who Err Are Closest to God

Every human being is tied to God by a rope. If the rope breaks, and is later fixed with a knot, that individual is connected ever closer to God than if there never were a break in the rope. Thus, errors, mistakes and failures have the potential of drawing us even closer to God.

Hasidic teaching

Standing in Our Defense

A person's true defense attorneys are repentance and good acts *(teshuvah u-ma-asim tovim)*. Even if 999 witnesses testify against a person, and only one speaks in the defense, she is acquitted....

And even if the testimony of that one witness is 999 parts against, and only one part in favor, she is acquitted.

Adapted from Talmud, Shabbat 32a

Teshuvah—A Creative Process

Rabbi Kalonymous Kalmish Shapira, the Rebbe of the Warsaw Ghetto, wrote on Rosh Hashanah 5702/1941 (Esh Kodesh):

> The time for repentance is Rosh Hashanah, the time of the creation of the world, because repentance—the essence of which is committing to worship God from now on—is also a form of creating (from *Esh Kodesh*).

Teshuvah is a kind of creativity. As a creative act, it is not a simple return. *Teshuvah* is a return forward, a return to something that never was, a return to a new creation.

We return to who we have always been, and are meant to be, but have not yet become. We return to growth and possibility that have lain dormant within us and not yet flourished, much as a sculpture lies hidden within a brute block of stone. That is the sense in which *teshuvah* is a creative act.

That is why the process of *teshuvah,* as painful and even humiliating as it can be, is in fact very joyous and hopeful. It is a creative process in which we imitate God and become partners with God in the work of creation. And what are we creating? Ourselves.

Rabbi Jan R. Uhrbach

A New Year—Turning Stone into Light

Arthur Waskow has pointed out that inside the walls of the Old City near the Jaffa Gate, there is an ancient block of stone. It is a very busy place, and most people rush by. But if you stop and look closely you can see carved on that stone, the letters "LEG X." That stone is a relic of Titus' Tenth Roman Legion, the legion which destroyed Jerusalem and our Temple almost two thousand years ago.

Recently something most interesting has happened to that block of Roman stone. It has been recycled and now serves as the base for a homely ordinary street lamp. Waskow observes, "Giving light: a strange renewal of the old Menorah. And a strange reversal of the Arch of Titus: where the Arch turned the light from the Menorah into stone, this street lamp turns the stone back into light. Light to live by."

That is the eternal task of our people—to keep turning stone back into light. And that is what this Rosh Hashanah, the birthday of the world comes to tell us. A new year has been born and is waiting to be shaped by us into a season of healing, for ourselves and those we love, but not only for them.

D.P.E.

Three Lessons about the High Holy Days from the Musar Movement

Rabbi Samuel Chiel notes three important teachings from the Musar Movement of the nineteenth century that we would do well to keep in mind at the beginning of this sacred ten-day period.

Rabbi Israel Salanter, founder of the Musar Movement, taught these lessons:

1. "Even while you are absorbed in concern and trepidation about the Day of Judgment, you are not free to violate the prohibition against stepping on another person's toes."

In the small European shtetl, while daveners swayed and shuckled, Reb Yisrael wanted them to make sure that fulfilling their own needs did not preclude being sensitive to the needs of others.

2. "When you have to make a decision, ask yourself: 'How would I decide if it were *N'eilah* on Yom Kippur?'" During these next ten days, try to capture some of the more precious moments, and seal them in your spiritual memory, to recall them all throughout the year when making significant decisions.

3. "People begin to do *teshuvah* during the days of *Selihot*. The more devout people begin even earlier, during the month of Elul. But in my personal view, it is possible to begin even earlier: one should begin to do *teshuvah* immediately after *N'eilah* on Yom Kippur."

If you do not feel quite ready for this high holy day period (and who, truly, is totally ready?), then next week, after Yom Kippur, begin to prepare for Rosh Hashanah next year, so during the entire year you will ready yourself for these incomparable days!

D.P.E.

A Blessing

Berakhot 17a
Eruvin 54a

May your eyes sparkle with the light of Torah,
and your ears hear the music of its words.
May the space between each letter of the scrolls
bring warmth and comfort to your soul.
May the syllables draw holiness from your heart,
and may this holiness be gentle and soothing
to you and all God's creatures.
May your study be passionate,
and meanings bear more meanings
until Life itself arrays itself to you
as a dazzling wedding feast.
And may your conversation,
even of the commonplace,
be a blessing to all who listen to your words
and see the Torah glowing
on your face.

Danny Siegel

Forgive Your Neighbors

Forgive your neighbors for their wrongdoings
And then your sins will be forgiven when you pray.
Should one person cherish anger against another,
And then ask for healing from God?
Does that person have no mercy for a person like themselves,
And yet pray for personal sins?

Ben Sira 28:2–4

Where Are You, God? (Before *Ma Tovu*)

God, where are You?

Where do I find You?

Where do You Live?
You have no address.

The Universe is filled with Your glory.

You live in every mountain
and in every valley
and on the busy boulevard outside.

You live in the beautiful riot of many colors
of the Indian summer;
... and You live in my Soul.

You have no need for
an earthly address.

And yet ...

We have built for You a special building—
beautiful, dignified, majestic;
intimate, warm and friendly.

For whom then did we build it?

For You *and* us.

For our conversations together.

For Your glory, God,
and for *our* humble need.

We should be talking to You—
when we see You in the beautiful sunrise,
when we see You in the innocent smile of a child,
when we see You in a person's kind deed.

But we forget ...

So we built this building.
We come here and remember to talk to you.

With the Psalmist, we say the *Ma Tovu:*

> "Through Your abundant kindness
> I come into Your house.
> Reverently I worship You
> in Your holy Sanctuary.
> I love the habitation of Your house,
> the place where Your glory dwells."

Rabbi Noah Golinkin

Hold On to What Is Good

> Hold on to what is good,
>   Even if it is a handful of earth.
> Hold on to what you believe,
>   Even if it is a tree which stands by itself.
> Hold on to what you must do,
>   Even if it is a long way from here.
> Hold on to life,
>   Even if it is easier letting go.
> Hold on to the hand of your neighbor,
>   Even when we are apart.

Native American Prayer

How We Become Wise, How We Change

The following story speaks for itself, in giving us insight into the process of growing wisdom and performing *teshuvah*:

After a long, hard climb up the mountain, the spiritual seekers finally found themselves in front of the great teacher. Bowing deeply, they asked the question that had been burning inside them for so long: "How do we become wise?"

There was a long pause until the teacher emerged from meditation. Finally the reply came: "Good choices."

"But, teacher, how do we make good choices?"

"From experience," responded the wise one.

"And how do we get experience?"

"Bad choices," smiled the teacher.

D.P.E.

Prayer for a Happy New Year

May you be blessed with good neighbors who are there for you when you need them, and who are not around too much when you don't need them.

May the clothing styles of yesterday come back so I can wear all that stuff that I don't have the heart to throw away.

Let Nehru jackets, and bell-bottom trousers, and slim ties, and Hawaiian prints become fashionable for men again, so that I can be in style again.

And may empire waistlines, and muumuus, and granny skirts come back for women.

After all, why should those foreigners—Armani, Gucci, Versace and Borsini dictate what we wear?

Instead may those great American Jewish designers ... Poly and Ester, reign supreme, and may they bring back those wonderful stretch leisure suits, and sun bonnets and high button shoes, which are no longer seen anywhere, except maybe in Century Village.

May the expressions "you know," and "like," and "whatever" be retired.

And may those old-fashioned expressions: "thank you," "pardon me," "after you," and "you look lovely," come back into use instead.

May we sing songs that are singable, that have lyrics that are understandable, and may we not have to wear earplugs when our children play music in their rooms.

In this new year that now begins, may your hair, your teeth, your facelift and your stocks not fall. And may your blood pressure, your cholesterol and your mortgage interest rate not rise.

May the world enjoy a year that is free of hurricanes, earthquakes, fires, drought, and political speeches, which produce the most wind of all.

May you have a spouse, or a child or a friend, or a grandchild, who loves you, even though they really know you. And may you learn that giving love away freely without strings is the surest way of receiving it in return.

And, in the darkest moments of this new year, and there will be some dark moments, may you remember that you are not alone, that God is with you, and that God loves you, that is why He made you just a little bit lower than the angels.

May your insurance pay whatever your doctor charges, without insisting on any further investigation, and may the IRS accept whatever you pay, without insisting on any further investigation too.

May your children or your grandchildren receive a good report in school.

And may you receive a good report too, from your dentist, from your ophthalmologist, from your dermatologist, from your cardiologist, from your gastroenterologist, from your podiatrist, from your urologist, and ultimately, from your God.

May there be peace this year between the Jews of Israel and the Arabs, and may there also be peace between the Jews of Israel, which sometimes seems much more difficult to achieve.

May your bank statement and your budget both balance, and may they both include generous amounts for charity.

May we discover evidence of civilized life on Mars this year, and, more important, may we discover evidence of civilized life, here on Earth.

May you receive a letter from a long lost friend, and a kiss from a long indifferent spouse or child. and may you see a smile on the face of your doorman, your mailman, and when you look in the mirror, every day.

May you feast your eyes often in this new year on green trees, on blue waters, and best of all, on the happy face of a grandchild, whom you have just embraced.

May we keep rage off of the freeways, and out of the workplace, and out of our homes, and direct it instead at racism, at poverty and at all the evils that we politely tolerate.

May we learn in this new year that what really counts the most is not the years but the days, not the machines we have in our lives, but the people we have in our lives, not how much we can accumulate but how much we can share, and with whom.

May you have enough to give you contentment, and may you have enough left over, so that you can be generous.

May the telemarketers not call you during dinner time, and instead, may you receive calls, from long lost friends, and from new ones too.

Rabbi Jacob Pressman

A Prayer for Life

Source of all life, we pray for life. Bless us, once more, with a year of life so that we may be privileged to complete the year we have just begun.

Despite the burdens and the heartbreaks, the pains and perils, we want to live; we ask to be inscribed in the Book of Life.

But even as we pray that years may be added to our lives, we ask, too, that true life may be added to our years.

May the new year be for us a time for enhancing the quality of our lives, enriching their content, deepening their meaning.

Help us to keep our minds alive. May we be open to new ideas, entertain challenging doubts, reexamine long-held opinions, nurture a lively curiosity, and strive to add to our store of knowledge.

Help us to keep our hearts alive. May we develop greater compassion, be receptive to new friendships, sustain a buoyant enthusiasm, grow more sensitive to the beauty which surrounds us.

Help us to keep our souls alive. May we be more responsive to the needs of others, less vulnerable to consuming greed, more attentive to the craving for fellowship, and more devoted to truth.

Help us to keep our spirits alive. May we face the future with confidence, knowing that every age has its unique joys and satisfactions, each period in our lives a glory of its own.

Help us to keep our faith alive. May we be sustained by the knowledge that You have planted within us life eternal and have given us the power to live beyond our years.

Whether our years be few or many, help us to link our lives to the life of our people and to our eternal faith.

Rabbi Sidney Greenberg

God's Boxes

I have in my hands two boxes
Which God gave me to hold.
He said, "Put all your sorrows in the black box
And all your joys in the gold."

I heeded God's words, and in the two boxes
Both my joys and sorrows I stored.

But though the gold became heavier each day
The black was as light as before.
With curiosity, I opened the black,
I wanted to find out why,
And I saw, in the base of the box, a hole
Which my sorrows had fallen out by.
I showed the hole to God, and mused,
"I wonder where my sorrows could be."
God smiled a gentle smile and said,
"My child, they're all here with me."
I asked why God gave me the boxes,
Why the gold and the black with the hole?
"My child, the gold is for you to count your blessings. The
    black is for you to let go."

Author Unknown

Spiritual Flutterings

We read in Bereshit (Genesis 1:2), in the Story of Creation, *ruah elohim mirahefet al p'nei ha-mayim*. This is typically translated as: "a wind
from God hovered (or swept) over the face of the water." The word
that is translated as hovered or swept is *mirahefet. Mirahefet* is a word
of ancient Hebrew poetry. It is rarely found in Torah, but we do read
it in Deuteronomy (32:11) where *mirahefet* refers to a mother eagle
beating her wings in place, over the nest of her young, in order to feed
them. And so I translate *mirahefet* as "fluttering." So that *ruah elohim
mirahefet al p'nei ha-mayim* is better understood as "a wind from God
fluttered over the face of the water."

Because each of us is created *b'tzelem elohim*, in the unique image
of God, each of us has our own deep and internal *mirahefet*; our own
spiritual fluttering. All spiritual yearning begins in the wordless flut-
terings/*mirahefet* of our souls. Because *mirahefet* at its core is wordless, no matter what language we speak, we spend our lives trying to
attach words to our own deep internal spiritual fluttering.

Communally, as we approach every New Year we both celebrate
the beginning of the new year and review the past. Yet individually,
depending on our current physical, emotional, or spiritual state, we
may look forward to the fullness of this coming year or we may not. We

may look at the past year as filled with promise or we may not. Certainly there are some years we have looked forward to and some years we were glad to end.

No matter what our framework for any particular year, we are always filled with wordless yearning, *mirahefet*, that flutters in us and seeks to be articulated. Part of our spiritual task at any time, and certainly at the turn of the new year, is to listen to the *mirahefet* that soul-flutters, to pay attention to its own unique patterns in each of us, to attempt to give it expression, and allow words—as best they can—to settle in so that we can let ourselves and others know the wisdom that our spiritual flutterings can give

May this New Year give us enriching spiritual flutterings.

Rabbi Eric Weiss

Getting Rid of the Mud

We have a custom at weddings. Before you go to the wedding canopy, there is the veiling of the bride. At the veiling of the bride, I usually gather together all the blood relatives into a room, to ask them each to forgive each other, because it's impossible to grow up in a family, with siblings and parents, without having some secret anger. And you don't want people to have to go into the next phase of life with all this karmic load. So that is why bringing in those people is so important. That way they can forgive each other and really bless each other. It is a very powerful thing.

On one occasion, a young girl was present while we were doing this forgiveness, and she wanted to know how to do it. I tell you, it was a wonderful thing that she asked this question. She really wanted to know how to do it. It was as if nobody had ever shown her how to do forgiving. So I said to her, "Could you imagine that you have a beautiful shiny white dress on, and here comes this big clump of mud and dirties it? You would want to clean it off, wouldn't you?" "Oh, yes," she said. "Could you imagine then, instead of the mud being on the outside on your dress, the mud is on your heart?" "Uh huh." "And being angry with people and not forgiving them is like mud on your heart." "I sure want to get rid of that," she said. "OK, how are you going to go about doing that?" I suggested that she close her eyes, raise up her hands in her imagination, and draw down some golden light and let it flow over that mud on her heart until it was all washed away. In this way she really understood forgiving.

Do you understand how important it is, just as with this child, to respond decently when somebody says, "You ought to ... ," and starts giving you advice and you want to say, "I've been trying to do it myself. You don't have to scold me—show me how to do it"?

This is the issue in all spiritual direction work.

Rabbi Zalman Schachter-Shalomi

What Being Jewish Means to Me

I remember: as a child, on the other side of oceans and mountains, the Jew in me would anticipate Rosh Ha-Shanah with fear and trembling.

He still does.

On that Day of Awe, I believed then, nations and individuals, Jewish and non-Jewish, are being judged by their common creator.

That is still my belief.

In spite of all that happened? Because of all that happened?

I still believe that to be Jewish today means what it meant yesterday and a thousand years ago. It means for the Jew in me to seek fulfillment both as a Jew and as a human being. For a Jew, Judaism and humanity must go together. To be Jewish today is to recognize that every person is created in the image of God and that our purpose in living is to be a reminder of God.

Naturally, I claim total kinship with my people and its destiny. Judaism integrates particularist aspirations with universal values, fervor with rigor, legend with law. Being Jewish to me is to reject all fanaticism anywhere.

To be Jewish is, above all, to safeguard memory and open its gates to the celebration of life as well as to the suffering, to the song of ecstasy as well as to the tears of distress that are our legacy as Jews. It is to rejoice in the renaissance of Jewish sovereignty in Israel and the reawakening of Jewish life in the former Soviet Union. It is to identify with the plight of Jews living under oppressive regimes and with the challenges facing our communities in free societies.

A Jew must be sensitive to the pain of all human beings. A Jew cannot remain indifferent to human suffering, whether in other countries or in our own cities and towns. The mission of the Jewish people has never been to make the world more Jewish, but to make it more human.

Elie Wiesel

Lines to My Son

In spite of everything, we have made you one of us.
From desire came the covenant,
from memory the gravity of our purpose.
Even from your first moments
you are more than yourself.
At times, perhaps, a child of Warsaw or Canaan
sleeping in a cold apartment or a goatskin tent.
Mesmerized by Sabbath flames,
You could be staring at a mote-filled beam
that spills from a hidden pane
Or
gazing at a clay lamp that lights the wilderness.
Without clothing or speech or even a haircut,
I see you
As vanished sisters saw their little one.
And when you smile at me, I know the joy they knew.
But when you cry, I sometimes hear the small voices of miss-
    ing lads,
so far away and inconsolable
that I must love you all the more for them.
Child, when I look upon your round and heavy-lidded face
your fine and slightly curling mane,
I know with fear and pride that you are
one of us.
Before words, before rituals,
we have conceived our past into your flesh,
And I read it from your face
like a sentence or a psalm.

Lynn Levin

The Promise of This Day

> Look to this day,
> For it is life,
> The very life of life.
> In its brief course lie all
> The realities and verities of existence,
> The bliss of growth,
> The splendor of action,
> The glory of power—
> For yesterday is but a dream,
> And tomorrow is only a vision.
> But today, well lived,
> Makes every yesterday a dream of happiness
> And every tomorrow a vision of hope.
> Look well, therefore, to this day.

Sanskrit Proverb

A Meditation for the New Year

In the twilight of the vanishing year, I lift my heart to You, O God.

I give thanks for all the blessings which fill my life with joy, for the love of family and support of friends, for the comfort others have given me in difficult moments, and for the privilege of life that You have granted me.

Now the time of repentance and renewal has come. These Days of Awe provide me with moments to meditate on the meaning of my life, on the worth of my deeds, and upon the regrets that mock my noblest intentions. No human being lives without failures. No year passes without its disappointments, its sorrows, its sins.

On this eve of the New Year, awaken me to the wisdom of my faith and people. Let these sacred days remind me that life is Your precious gift and that You have called me to Your service. You have made me in Your image, a fragile soul empowered with goodness and truth, justice and love.

So turn me to You now. Open the gates of the New Year, and grant to me, to my loved ones, my people, and all peoples, life and health, contentment and peace.

From the Wilshire Boulevard Temple
High Holy Day prayer book

The Month of Elul: Preparing for the Days of Awe

*T*efillah or "prayer" is the living heart of Jewish faith, the daily out-pouring of the soul before God. This flow of human emotion may come in the form of joyous exultation or desperate plea. Both are part of the complex and universal phenomenon of prayer. Prayer expresses itself directly in the language the heart knows best. Sometimes it is given expression in words spoken aloud, while at other times prayer is beyond words, the speechless call of the innermost self.

RABBI ARTHUR GREEN, *THESE ARE THE WORDS*

Opening to the New Year

At this time of year, we often read the Song of Moses in *parashat Haazinu*. In the Torah scroll, the Song has a unique presentation. A wide, blank space cuts each line in two, so that the clauses line up on either side of the space like tribes assuming formation, like the banks of the river Israel is soon to cross. It is as if the draw of what was, and the tug of what must be, pull at the poem's very integrity, and open up its center.

The song is a beautiful, sometimes difficult, tangle of history and foresight: the tale of love, betrayal, punishment, estrangement and reconciliation between God and Israel. At this point in Israel's story, a time of suspense, the Song uses its poetry to suspend time. It becomes a kind of bridge spanning past and future, and so helps its listeners, and its orator Moses, to move forward and move on.

In this way, the Song works like the *Yamim Noraim*. In these days of focus and attention, we try to open at the center, like the Song, in order to ask the deep questions and to perform the significant deeds that are part of *teshuva*. To help, we have liturgy that retells, in different ways, the Song's basic storyline of wondrous beginnings, human failing, and divine forgiveness.

It is customary to visit the cemetery at this time of year. I have read that women used to bring candlewick with them. Walking the length of family plots, unwinding the wick, they would return and make the extra-long candles needed to provide light at synagogue for the holidays. Their practical task reminds me of the spiritual work of these *Yamim Noraim,* and of the Song's accomplishment: taking careful measure of the past, and using it to enlighten the future.

We begin the cycle of Torah reading about separation and division in the first *parasha, Beresheet*. Here, in the penultimate *parasha,* the focus is on connection and repair. Let us, in these days, try to embrace present, past and future. As we move forward and move on, let us form a bridge to the new year, to one another, and beyond.

Elizabeth Leiman Kraiem

A *Shanah Tovah*

What's the difference between wishing someone "Happy New Year" and wishing someone a *"Shanah Tovah"*? When we say "happy new year," we evoke images of revelers drinking champagne, laughing and dancing—a party atmosphere. What comes to mind when we ask for a *"shanah tovah,"* a good year? Certainly, an image of sobriety and concern. What might make this a good year? Our attention is drawn to more fundamental concerns—health, family life, education and professional development.

As Americans we are guaranteed "life, liberty and the pursuit of happiness," and pursue it we do. As we enter into the new year, it behooves us to shift our focus from the desire for a happy year, to a deeper appreciation of what might make this a good year.

I am reminded of the *Peanuts* cartoon strip, in which Charlie Brown asks, "Sometimes I wonder if I even know what it would take to make me happy." Snoopy responds by throwing a ball—"Here, get the ball." He seems mystified when Charlie Brown is still despondent in the final frame—"That usually works with dogs."

Sometimes I think we all feel like Charlie Brown, wondering what it would take to make us feel happy. Leo Rosten addressed the issue of what is happiness, writing, "Ask an American mother what she wants most for her child. The chances are she will reply: 'To be happy.' But there was a time when what we most wanted, for our children or ourselves, was to amount to something. What is this myth, 'happiness,' that has bamboozled so many of us? And what is this idiotic thing, 'fun', which so many chase after? Where people once said 'Good-bye' they now say, 'Have fun' ... I know of nothing more demeaning than the frantic pursuit of 'fun.' No people are more miserable than those who seek desperate escapes from the self, and none are more impoverished, psychologically, than those who plunge into the strenuous frivolity of night clubs.... The word 'fun' comes from the medieval English 'fol'—meaning fool.

"Where was it ever promised to us that life on this earth can ever be easy, free from conflict and uncertainty, devoid of anguish and wonder and pain? ... The purpose of life is not to be happy. The purpose of life is to matter, to be productive, to have it make some difference that you lived at all. Happiness, in the ancient, noble sense, means self-fulfillment—and is given to those who use to the fullest whatever talents God or luck or fate bestowed on them. Happiness, to me, lies in stretching, to the farthest boundaries of which we are capable, the resources of the human mind."

Rabbi Bonnie Koppell

The Binding of Isaac and the Binding of You and Me

With Rosh Hashanah coming in a few weeks, it is a good time to think about some of its important lessons. The High Holy Days are a time to evaluate our relationship with important people in our lives. We ask their forgiveness, they ask ours, and if there is regret for past faults and insensitive acts (Tradition calls them "sins"), we lend forgiveness to others, and they to us.

Rosh Hashanah is also a time to think about our relation with our Tradition, with Judaism. It is the Jewish New Year, and a time to reexamine where we stand with regard to the faith/culture/civilization we call Judaism. Those hearing these words have already taken significant steps toward solidifying their Jewish connections by joining a synagogue, coming to religious worship, and doing many other Jewish things in our lives.

Take a few moments—even a few hours—to think about and discuss your Jewish values and priorities with your loved ones and intellectual sparring partners. How can you deepen and strengthen your Jewish ties and commitments in the coming year?

Perhaps that is why we are bidden to hear the sound of the Shofar each morning for thirty days during the month of Elul, before Rosh Hashanah, as well as on the New Year itself. The Talmud, in tractate "Rosh Hashanah" (16a), tells us: "Rabbi Abahu said: Why do we use the horn of a *ram* on Rosh Hashanah? Because the Blessed Holy One is saying to us: If you blow a horn from a ram before Me on Rosh Hashanah, I will be reminded of the act of ultimate faith performed by Avraham when he was ready to carry out my demand, even though a ram was eventually sacrificed in place of Yitzhak. The merit of Avraham will reflect merit on you, his descendants. In fact, when you blow the Shofar, and I remember the Binding (Hebrew: *Akedah*) of Yitzhak I will attribute to you the merit of having bound (Hebrew: *akad-tem*) yourselves to me.

As we begin to blow the Shofar each morning, from the first day of the Hebrew month of Elul, let's begin to think about how we bind ourselves to God. About our Jewish boundaries, the ties that bind us to our Jewish past. Let's think of how our ritual lives can be enriched and enhanced with more song, custom, prayer and ceremony. Let's think of how we can give ourselves to more Jewish causes (Israel, Jewish education, the synagogue), and how being Jewish can help bind and tie us to the needs of humanity (the environment, the needs of our community, the eradication of poverty and injustice).

Rabbi Dov Peretz Elkins

Are We Wise Enough to Change Our Minds?

Taking spiritual stock is one of the most revered customs during the High Holy Day period. *Heshbon Ha-Nefesh* (examining the soul) is an honored and significant custom in Judaism.

When we are involved in a national debate as to the meaning of the Constitution of the United States, and about who are the most authentic interpreters of the Constitution, it is good to listen to the words of Benjamin Franklin, who, on the final day of the constitutional Convention, had this to say:

> Mr. President, I confess that there are several parts of the Constitution which I do not at present approve, but I am not sure I shall never approve them: For having lived long, I have experienced many instances of being obliged by better information or fuller consideration, to change opinions even on important subjects, which I once thought right, but found to be otherwise. It is therefore that the older I grow, the more apt I am to doubt my own judgment, and to pay more respect to the judgment of others.

Those of use who are too closed-minded to hear the opinions of those around us might do well to listen carefully to Mr. Franklin's words. It is not a bad sermon for those of us who have gathered here today to participate in *Heshbon Ha-Nefesh,* and to claim to have a true desire to change for the better in the year, to come.

Rabbi Dov Peretz Elkins

The Days of Awe—or the Daze of Ah?

The period before the *Yamim Noraim,* the Days of Awe, is carefully orchestrated. The rabbis did not intend for us to be plunged into this important time without preparation. They built it in ever intensifying stages which remind us that these critical days are coming.

Throughout the month of Elul we sound the shofar. In the days before Rosh Hashanah we gather for penitential prayers, *selichot.* During the Ten Days of Repentance, the ten days between the two holidays, we add special requests for life and blessing to our prayers. All these are designed as a "spiritual warm-up."

The sentiment that this entire period should evoke in us was inadvertently provided to me by a student. While lecturing on the theology of this period, I noticed that he had written at the top of his notes: the *Daze of Ah.* I was unsure whether to chastise him for not having done the readings or give him extra credit for offering this insight. For this is exactly how we should approach this time: in a *Daze of Ah,* a daze of wonderment at the opportunity that has been given to us.

Most of us never achieve this stage. We are like people who have been told that the last scene of *Hamlet* is the most riveting and only show up for that scene. We fail to understand what the fuss is about. We parachute into the *Yamim Noraim.* This period is the April fifteenth of the Jewish year, yet I spend more time preparing my taxes than preparing my soul.

The Hafetz Hayim says we would never appear before a king without thinking through precisely what we were going to say, yet here most of us are without having given the *Yamim Noraim* consistent and serious thought.

Dr. Deborah E. Lipstadt

It Is Never Too Late

The last word has not been spoken,
the last sentence has not been written,
the final verdict is not in.
It is never too late
to change my mind,
my direction,

to say no to the past
and yes to the future,
to offer remorse,
to ask and give forgiveness.
It is never too late
to start over again,
to feel again
to love again
to hope again....

Rabbi Harold M. Schulweis

How "High" Are the High Holidays?

Rosh Hashanah and Yom Kippur have, for a long time now, been called the High Holidays or the High Holy Days. This is not a term known in traditional sources, which speak of the entire ten-day period we are about to enter as the *"Yamim Nora'im,"* the "Days of Awe."

Why do we call them "High" holidays? Why *are* they "high"? What do they have to do with height? Are there "low" Holidays?

A joker would pun and say the spelling is wrong: they are the "Hi" Holidays. On two or three days, Jews who haven't seen each other all year gather in synagogues and temples to say "Hi!"

Others, borrowing from the hip elements of contemporary culture and lingo, tell us that Rosh Hashanah and Yom Kippur are indeed times when we can—or even should—get high. Not through chemicals or magical mantras but with a *mahzor*, a *minyan*, and meditation on the nature of our journey through this world.

I have learned not to be dismissive of either of these "explanations." For those to whom prayer does not come easily and for whom the ideas, language, and symbols of these days are, at best, problematical, what could be wrong with investing them with a social, if not a religious, focus? Something good, I believe, accrues when we get out of the confines of our selves and come together with other Jews, sitting with them in community and re-connecting with the words (however remote from our consciousness) and melodies (however unfamiliar) of our people.

Similarly, for those who are open to or ready for religious experience, and who are undeterred by performance auditoriums, unfamiliar tunes, and the trappings of mass worship, why not utilize Rosh Hashanah and Yom Kippur as opportunities to transcend the boundaries of mundane consciousness so often constricted by the pressures of our daily regimen?

Either way, fastening onto the "high" in these holidays can help us look upward even as we look inward. Rosh Hashanah and Yom Kippur can allow us to articulate, or re-articulate, to our selves our loftiest aspirations and capacities. As we sit through the services, perhaps we will be able to tap into the reservoir of spirit and sensitivity and concern for others, be they fellow Jews or all members of the human family, that I believe is inherent in every human heart.

We owe it to our selves and to the world to try. May these forthcoming High Holidays be elevating to everyone.

Rabbi James S. Diamond

Do We Really Want to Change?

A woman proudly hung on her mantelpiece a needlework plaque that said "Prayer Changes Things." A few days later, the plaque was missing from its place. The woman asked her husband if he had seen it. "I took it down, I didn't like it," her husband replied.

"But why?" the woman asked. "Don't you believe that prayer changes things?" "Yes, I honestly do," her husband answered. "But it just so happens that I don't like change, so I threw it away."

None of us like change. Sure, we will mouth many prayers during the holy days but few of us really intend that these prayers will either begin a process of change or reflect a changing lifestyle. Some of us are happy with our lives and see no reason to change. Others of us, who are unhappy with our lives, may not have the necessary courage to make the changes needed to orient our goals with the goals of the Holy One.

But we live in a time where many are disconnected to the source of enduring values. Values that we assumed were societal standards have been tossed aside. During this High Holy Day season, we need to muster the courage to face our lives honestly and to overcome our fear of the unknown. We need to reconnect ourselves to the moorings of Jewish tradition and return to a life informed by God's teachings. When we do offer the words of the ancient prayers, let those prayers help us return to God, challenge us to resolve to be better, and help us not fall into the trap of repeating the mistakes that we have made.

Rabbi Eric M. Lankin, DMin

The Meaning of Elul

The 40-day period beginning with Rosh Hodesh Elul and ending at the final shofar blast of Yom Kippur is considered by tradition as the 40-day period Moses spent receiving the second set of Tablets containing the Ten Commandments. As you recall, Moses broke the first set of tablets when he returned to the Israelite camp and found many of them celebrating their worship of the golden calf (Exodus 32).

Rebbe Nachman of Bratslav teaches that in this 40-day period, which culminates with Yom Kippur, Moses opened up the path of *teshuvah* for us to emulate each year. Just as he neither ate nor drank anything on Mount Sinai, so do we fast on Yom Kippur. Just as he and the people had to atone for sinning, so do we need to atone in order to possess the Torah once again.

And, most importantly, just as something that was broken in anger could not be repaired but needed to be re-originated, so too do we need to—while preserving what we have, to our shame, broken—rebuild our lives from the ground up. And it will be sufficient to make our lives into tablets that carry the words of the living God.

Rabbi David Bockman
(adapted from Breslov Research Institute)

Elul

Once, during the holy season of Rosh Hashanah and Yom Kippur, the Hasidic master Rabbi Levi Yitzhak of Berditchev, paused in his devotions and looking at his disciples with sad, tear-laden eyes, remarked, "What a funny world it is that we live in these days. There was a time, you know, when Jews would be scrupulously honest in the market place and be the most outrageous liars in the synagogue. These days, however, everything is reversed. The Jews are surprisingly honest in synagogue, but in the streets and market places, I'm ashamed to tell you."

"But rabbi," his followers asked, "why are you so distressed. How can it be bad if Jews are telling the truth in synagogue?"

"I'll tell you why I'm distressed," answered Levi Yitzhak. "In days gone by, Jews were known for their honest dealings. They took the words of Torah seriously. Their 'yes' was always a 'yes' and their 'no' was always a 'no.' They had honest weights and fair measures. Yet, on the Days of Awe they would fervently recite the confessional prayers declaring that they had lied, cheated, swindled and dealt dishonestly. This was a lie. Everyone knew that truth and faithfulness were the lamps lighting their way.

"But these days, the reverse takes place. In the streets and in the market place, the world of commerce and social interaction, they lie and cheat, but when they come to synagogue, they, sadly, profess the truth" (adapted from Martin Buber, *Tales of the Hassidim, Early Masters*, p. 230).

The Days of Awe are rapidly approaching. We are now in the month of Elul, the month of repentance that precedes Rosh Hashanah. Soon we will be in synagogue for the High Holidays and we might ask ourselves if Levi Yitzhak's words refer to us. Where do we tell the truth and where do we lie?

We know that we can live the truth of our faith in our daily lives. We are able to bear witness to our commitment to God and our heritage by the way we interact with each other and our world. All our pious devotions, our concerns with ritual details, our deep identification with the Jewish people and tradition, our profound journeys of spiritual self-discovery mean very little if we do not conducted ourselves in the spirit of truth and honesty.

These are important values for all aspects of our lives but they are central to our working lives. We all work hard. We spend so much of our time making a living. We put in many hours, sometimes too many hours, at our jobs and professions. A very good part of our day is spent at work. Though we may wish to be someplace else and long for more time with family and friends, our working hours can be spiritually precious. They provide us with many opportunities to express our deepest values.

Rabbi Lewis John Eron

Moving Time

I like to tell this story a lot. Maybe you've heard it. I was on the subway once when I saw a man who looked totally exhausted sitting across from me. I watched him struggle to stay awake, watched him as he anxiously peered out the window at a stop to see if he had missed his. It took me a while, but I figured out why he was so tired. His shirt had the name of his company on it: "Time Movers." No wonder he was exhausted! He had spent his day moving time!

Time movers. I wonder what they do, and how they do it. Think about it: if you could move time, how would you do it? Would you move time in a way that is different from the way we currently experience it? Would you make time move faster or slower? (After all, doesn't time fly when you're having fun?) Would you move your time to a different age altogether, like the seventeenth century or the twenty-fifth century?

I wanted to wake the Time Mover, to ask him how he does what he does, and to seek his advice on how I could learn his technique. Unfortunately, such things just are not done in New York. With the exception of the Time Movers, the rest of us live in time which can't be moved. Life has really just two tenses: past and future. We are in the constant flow between the two, every moment is either about to happen or has slipped by. We experience time each moment as it comes, each day as we live it, each week, etc.

Rosh Hashanah takes the concept of holiness in time one step further. It marks the passage of a complete Jewish year. Rosh Hashanah begs the question: If you can't move time, what have you done with the time since last Rosh Hashanah? What have you done with the hundreds of thousands of minutes, the nearly 8,500 hours, the 350-odd days, the fifty or so weeks since last Rosh Hashanah? Have you lived these times to your fullest? Rosh Hashanah asks us to begin a process of examining how we lived our time, and how we will use our own time in the future.

Rosh Hashanah is the Jewish time to reflect on how we have used our time as a nation, as a people, as human beings. Think back and list all of the things which have happened this year in human history. And what has happened this year in your own life? What really made you proud? Where did you find your *nachas*—your sources of joy? What were the challenges you faced? How did you do with those challenges? What remains undone, unexamined, unapproached? Who was sick, who is sick, who has recovered? What were your major life-changes of this year, and what became more comfortable for you in its ongoing reliability? Think of two moments in the last year which made your heart sing, and two moments that made your soul ache.

Rosh Hashanah is the moment of transition between what was and what will be. We begin today to look at our lives over the past year, and start considering for the year to come. How do we want it to be? In what ways do we have to change in order for the desires of our hearts to happen? What needs to be done to undo the things we have done that were wrong? How can we prevent them from happening next year? During the next days we will be in limbo between how we lived our lives in 5764, and how we will live our lives in 5765. We have ten days to think about it. We have ten days not to move time but to change how we move through time.

The rabbis teach us that we should live each day of our lives as though it were our last day, because, in reality, we never can know. Live each day fully, one day at a time, live time fully, for each moment could be our last.

This Rosh Hashanah, may we all be blessed beneath the wings of shehinah, God's Holy presence, with the strength and courage to face our failures, to own our weaknesses, and may we find the help, the security, the compassion we all seek. May we look at our time, forgive ourselves and commit to the changes that we must make to move peacefully through time, rather than to move time. May we be blessed with that which is truly precious and therefore most holy—time.

Rabbi H. Rafael Goldstein

The Confessions of Elul

It was a dark, cloudy, *Selihot* evening, the Saturday night prior to Rosh Hashanah, the beginning of the last week of the month of Elul. Not a star could be seen. On this cold and heavy early fall night, the entire village was gathered in the synagogue for the penitential prayers. The plaintive voice of the cantor and the soul-bending exhortations of the rabbi so moved the worshipers, that one by one they came up trembling and confessed their sins. This one admitted to missing the morning worship. That one confessed to eating forbidden foods. Another confessed to smoking on the Sabbath. And so on throughout the congregation. The darkened heavens captured their darkened spirits.

Finally, Joseph, the grocer, came forward, humble and ashamed. He felt over burdened by his sense of sinfulness. He felt that each sin his friends and neighbors confessed could be his own. With a broken spirit, he shuffled up to the front of the synagogue and sighed, "Dear God, please forgive me for neglecting my studies, for avoiding your house, for my lazy observance. I was so busy with making a way for myself and my family. I did not always keep the Sabbath or follow the dietary laws, but please remember, that I always made payroll and that I kept my scales honest and my measures exact.

At that moment, the clouds parted and the late-night stars twinkled through the synagogue's windows and all returned home with a new sense of resolve.

That night, at least, and, hopefully, for many more, truth and faithfulness lit Joseph's path.

Rabbi Lewis John Eron

Psalm 27:4 " … Dwell in the House of the Lord All the Days of My Life"

King David said: " … that I may dwell in the house of the Lord all the days of my life, to behold the beauty of the Lord, and to frequent God's temple" (Psalms 27:4). There is an apparent contradiction here. "Dwell" has a sense of permanency about it but "to frequent" implies a measure of transience.

King David's desire was to dwell in the house of the Lord on a permanent basis all the days of his life, but since permanent dwelling can be tainted with a suspicion of habit and routine, he further requested "to frequent." A person who comes to visit frequently has a taste of something new each time. And so King David's request was to be a permanent resident in the house of the Lord, but with a level of constant renewal as though he were visiting frequently, as though he were coming to visit anew, God's temple.

Rabbi Simcha Raz

Demanding God's Presence

What are we really asking God for, in this season of uncertainty? The prayer we say most often during the *Yamim Noraim,* is not *Unetaneh Tokef,* but Psalm 27, the psalm for the Days of Awe. We read it every day starting with the month of Elul, and we read it until *Hoshanah Rabbah.* When you read it, it isn't immediately clear why we are reading this psalm right now, as it deals neither with creation or with *teshuvah,* neither God's mercy nor God's justice. And yet by reading this now, by placing it in the liturgical context of the season of forgiveness, we make a very interesting demand of God. Rather than demanding an accounting of God, the way indeed that God does of us, we demand God's presence in our lives. We demand God to be a source of strength when all else fails. We ask God not to be ignored.

Psalm 27 begins with a statement of perfect faith in God: God is my light and my savior, whom shall I fear?" Even in the face of nameless enemies, God is on the psalmist's side and his faith remains strong. Then, the psalmist falters. The thing he most asks for is to dwell in God's presence always: "One thing I ask of Adonai ... to live in the house of God all the days of my life." Rather than God's protection being a result of personal faith, the psalmist knows that being in God's presence will serve as a shield from the terrors that surround. God's presence brings safety and shelter. Finally, the psalmist explains why this demand has come. He has been abandoned by those closest to him, and he does not want God to do the same. One feels the pain of the psalmist: why is God hiding? The psalmist cries: "Do not hide your face from me, do not thrust aside your servant in anger."

The psalm ends with a different kind of statement of faith: "Mine is the faith that I surely will see Adonai's goodness in the land of the living." Even though the psalmist has yet to see God's presence, he has to see an answer to the evil in the world. The one constant that remains is the hope that God is listening. What is left, is hope that God is present, that God has responded to the one demand the psalmist actually feels he can make of God.

We, like the psalmist, don't need answers from God. Maybe, even, we would not accept what we heard. But we have a demand on God's presence. In the face of uncertainty in our own lives, what God owes us is not answers, but it is also not speeches out of whirlwinds. We desire to feel the presence of God, to dwell in the house of God all the days of our lives. The psalm is a message of hope, the hope expressed when our relationship with God is unclear. As God demands repentance from us, we have a response. We can't know what God is writing on the page in the book of life, but we can ask for God not to desert us no matter what the outcome. We need God's presence in our lives now. It's our basic right as God's creations.

Rachel Kahn-Troster

Meditation on Psalm 27

For my father and my mother have abandoned me, but THE LIVING ONE shall take me in. Everything human is imperfect and finite—even my parents—who were to me as gods when I was a young child. As I mature, I realize that only in sensing my connection to the ground of being and becoming, the perfect and infinite, can I ever fully feel safe.

Were it not for my belief that I'll behold God's goodness in the land of life.... This line is a fragment—the beginning of a thought stranded in mid-air which I refuse to complete. I don't want to put into words or visualize a life without faith. It would be like the end of the verse—an empty chasm.

Rabbi Sheila Peltz Weinberg

Selihot Meditation

Dear God, Ruler of the Universe,

We are gathered together at this hour to ask forgiveness from You ... for the many misdeeds we performed and for the many deeds we neglected. We address You in humility. We are humbled by Your power, by the mind-boggling forces of nature which produce this earth ... carried aloft in space and traveling thousands of miles an hour, and yet this earth appears stationary to us. We are in awe of the beauty and order of this universe ... the precise orbits of planets, stars, and galaxies ... the dependable changes of seasons, the grandeur of mountains, oceans, and continents, the complex yet systematic structure of the smallest micro-organisms and pieces of matter.

Who are we to address You? And yet You have bidden us to come to Synagogue at this hour to ponder the meaning of our lives ... to take responsibility for our failures ... to share our individual pain ... but mollify it since we stand together with our community.

We are Your creations, under Your control, and yet You have fashioned us with free choice, independent thoughts, and independent actions which can defy Your will. In striking contrast to an ordered universe you have created humans ... capable of poetry that inspires and enhances life ... but we are also capable of destroying beauty and cruelly ending life.

Yet in Your inimitable way O Lord You have created this world and called it good and very good ... because You know the good that man can achieve if we direct our efforts to follow Your law.

You focus Your attention on us, the Jewish people at this hour to listen to the sacrifice of our humbled hearts pour out confessions to You.

We cannot comprehend how in this vast, limitless universe with myriad stars and solar systems that at this moment You have chosen to listen to us ... unless we realize that You are *HaRahaman,* the All Merciful One.

You desire that we return unto You ... that we turn inward and examine our deeds, not because You long to punish us ... but because You wish to forgive us and have us be reconciled with You.

Why do You love human beings so? Why do You so patiently await our return unto You?

Are not the celestial beings more pleasing to You? Are they not dependable like the orbits of the planets ... programmed for goodness and to sing Your praise?

Yet You desire our songs and poetry. You prefer our frail voices and freedom ... because when we return to You we do so out of choice. We are not robots, controlled by others to follow commands and demands. We are created with free will.

We are able to choose between blind impulse and moral conscience. We are capable of concern and compassion or insensitivity and perverseness.

You have risked man's inhumanity in order to pray for man's godliness.

Like human lovers who choose to care and caress and risk pain and rejection, You love us and pray that we will be faithful in our love for You. And when we fall short of our potential greatness ... you lovingly await our return ... and willingly accept our sincerely spoken word and performed worthy deed as apology and atonement.

Your prophet Hosea taught us, "And I will betroth you to Me forever, and I will betroth you to Me in righteousness, in justice, and in loving kindness, and compassion. And I will betroth you to Me in faithfulness and you shall know the Lord."

May we learn to recognize this year, Your love for us and so be moved to return to you in love.

Amen.

Rabbi Gershon Johnson

Selihah—Forgiveness

God is primarily a forgiving God. The theme of the *Selihot* service speaks of the mightiest attributes of God—and we sing the attributes—"*Adonai Adonai, El rahum v'hanun,* forgiving wrongdoing, transgression and sin." The Israelites rebel against God and do not want to enter the Promised Land and God wants to destroy them. But Moshe challenges God, and Moshe says: Pardon the iniquity of this people according to the greatness of your mercy, as you have forgiven this people, from Egypt until now. And HaShem says to Moshe, *Salahti Kid'varekha,* I have pardoned according to your word.

These words of forgiveness by God become the central theme of the entire high holydays. Because of God's forgiveness the Jewish people, despite its shortcomings, exists to this very day.

This religious insight is relevant for the world in which we live. So often we read stories of forgiveness in the news. I vividly remember how the Pope forgave Ali Mehmet who shot him in Rome. It raised tremendous controversy. So often we read in the news how families forgive murderers. And on 9/11, there were stories in the press of how families of victims forgave the perpetrators of the horrendous crimes.

What is in back of this concept of forgiveness that on first blush seems to destroy the concept of any Justice in the world? Psychological studies are showing that it is better to forgive than to be forgiven. I found a story that explains this.

Years ago, an idealistic California college student won a Fulbright Scholarship to travel to South Africa to assist the anti-apartheid movement; she went there, and was murdered by a black mob during a riot. After years of grief, her parents quit their upper-middle-class California jobs and moved to South Africa to try to complete the work their daughter started.

Eventually the parents met two of their daughter's killers. The two men, who have been pardoned, try to atone for their crime by doing public service for a foundation the parents established in their daughter's name. The parents forgave the two killers and they became friends, and the young men now address the mother as "Mom."

Isn't that hard to fathom? Few among us could be so forgiving. The student must have been an exceptional person to inspire her parents to transform their lives in her memory. Her parents must be exceptional as well, to be capable of such acts. But their experience is an unusually dramatic example of a rule that applies to everyone: that forgiveness is good not just for the person who is forgiven, but also for the person who forgives.

Traditionally, we think of forgiveness as a blessing extended to the transgressor, easing her conscience; the person who does the forgiving is seen as engaged in a gallant self-sacrifice. In this view, the forgiven person benefits while the forgiver gains nothing. But what if forgiveness is just as important for the person who forgives as for the person forgiven? What if it's in our self-interest to forgive, because we will be better off?

Consider that once the murder happened, the young woman was gone: nothing could bring her back!! Her parents might have allowed their lives to be burned up in hatred for the people who committed the crime. Instead, they forgave. The sorrow of their loss will never go away. But forgiving the killers left the family better off.

Today, her parents are leading constructive lives as part of the great South African reconciliation effort. They keep their daughter's spirit alive as a living memory, and they feel hope rather than anger. Strictly from the standpoint of their own self-interest, the parents are better off than if they had refused to forgive.

Is this a one-of-a-kind situation? Hardly. There are psychological research studies that show that being a forgiving person is essential to happiness. Even when someone wrongs you, feeling anger or hatred only causes life to descend into misery and resentment: You are the one who suffers, not the person you're angry at. Forgiving, on the other hand, lifts the burden. When Moshe taught us to forgive those who sin against us, when he made God forgive a people that deserved to be destroyed by the prevailing justice, Moshe was giving practical down-to-earth life advice. *Selihot*, forgiveness, introduces, is a prelude to, the New Year.

Author Unknown

A *Selihot* Ritual: Changing Our Torah Mantles as We Change Ourselves

Prior Preparation

We suggest using this ritual at the beginning of your *Selihot* service:

For each Torah mantle you will be changing, select two individuals. One person will serve as reader, the other as the Torah holder during the ceremony. Remove all the silver from each Torah in advance. Leave it in the ark or some other easily accessible place. Replace the silver at the end of the ceremony. Following the opening responsive reading, the cantor begins to lead the congregation with a *niggun* and the first two participants come forward. One takes the Torah out; the other reads the selected text. Then together, they change the mantle. Continue this pattern until all mantles have been changed. The *niggun* should continue until the end of the ritual. Six readings are provided below. Based on the number of Torahs you have, you may wish to combine, rearrange, or edit the readings.

The Ritual

It is the middle of the night. We Jews have gathered to begin the Days of Awe.

Selihot means "apologies." Have we made our apologies? Have we stood face-to-face with those we have wronged during the year or in years past? Have we told them, "I am sorry"? Have we forgiven those who have approached us with contrition? If not now, when? Now is the time for *teshuvah*—repentance from the heart, turning and changing. Now is the time to let go of the past and move into the future with a clean and pure heart. Each year on *Selihot* we prepare our souls for the High Holy Days, when we will judge ourselves and when G-d will judge us. On *Selihot* we also prepare our sanctuary. To help us change and reach toward holiness, we change our Torah covers and bimah clothes to white ones in order to signify purity and sanctity. Tonight we will witness this change together.

> As the Torah covers go from dark to white,
> So may our motives and our actions
> Change from greed to generosity,
> From selfishness to compassion,
> From fear to faith,
> And from indifference to righteousness

Niggun/Reader 1

"Just as the hand, held before the eye, can hide the tallest mountain, so can the routine of everyday life keep us from seeing the vast radiance and the secret wonders that fill the world" (Chasidic saying, eighteenth century).

Niggun/Reader 2

"G-d does not want to be believed in, to be debated and defended by us, but simply to be realized through us" (Martin Buber, twentieth century).

Niggun/Reader 3

"In Psalm 109 we read, 'I am prayer.' There are three rungs on this ladder. The third best is to talk about prayer. The second best is to pray. Best of all is to be prayer" (Rabbi Chaim Stern, twentieth century).

Niggun/Reader 4

"Days are scrolls: Write on them what you want to be remembered" (Bachya Ibn Pakuda, eleventh century).

Niggun/Reader 5

"Rabbi Akiva said: How greatly G-d must have loved us to create us in the image of G-d. Yet even greater love did G-d how us in making us conscious that we are created in the divine image" (Mishnah).

Niggun / Reader 6

"Do not imagine that character is determined at birth. We have been given free will. Any person can become as righteous as Moses or as wicked as Jereboam. We ourselves decide whether to make ourselves learned or ignorant, compassionate or cruel, generous or miserly. No one forces us, no one drags us along one path or the other. We ourselves, by our own volition, choose our own way" (Maimonides, twelfth century).

Niggun / Reader 7

"We do not choose to be born. We do not choose our parents. We do not choose our historical epoch, the country of our birth or the immediate circumstances of our upbringing. We do not, most of us, choose to die, nor do we choose the time or conditions of our death. But within all this choice of choicelessness, we do choose how we will live; courageously or in cowardice, honorably or dishonorably, with purpose or in drift. We decide what is important and what is trivial in life. We decide that what makes us significant is either what we do or what we refuse to do. But no matter how indifferent the universe might be to our choices and decisions, these choices are ours to make. We decide. We choose. And as we decide and choose, so are our lives formed" (Joseph Epstein).

Niggun / Reader 8

"At a time when the Temple does not exist and we have no altar for atonement, we have only *Teshuvah*. *Teshuvah* atones for all transgressions (against God). Even one who has sinned all his life and has only turned at the end, nothing of wickedness is remembered of him, as it is said, 'And as for the wickedness of the wicked, he shall not stumble thereby in the day that he turneth from his wickedness'" (Ezekiel 33:12) [Maimonides].

Rabbi Valerie Lieber

BEGINNING OUR SEARCH FOR WORDS AND PRAYERS

The *mahzor* is a prayer book for holiday use, especially for Rosh Hashanah and Yom Kippur. A *mahzor* will include special *piyyutim* or liturgical poems recited on the holiday, as well as additional readings appropriate for study and reflection on that particular day. In a traditional *mahzor,* these will include chapters of the Mishnah in which the particular holiday is discussed.

The term *mahzor* comes from a verb meaning "return," which refers to the cycle of holidays that brings us back to the beginning of each year. *Mahzorim* have been printed in many versions and often incorporate local customs of various Jewish communities.

RABBI ARTHUR GREEN, *THESE ARE THE WORDS*

Prayer for Rosh Hashanah Evening

Oh God, we are humbled before Your Unknowable Perfection for we are so small and our flaws are so large. As we stand poised to celebrate Your creation of the world we ask You, in Your never failing mercy, to remember the promise you made to Abraham and Sarah, to Isaac and Rebekah and to Jacob, Leah and Rachel.

Please God, imbue all the leaders of this world with strength of character and with wisdom just as you did for Jacob and Esau on the banks of the Jabbok River. Give those who can bring peace the power of voice so that even the deafest among us can hear words of peace. Spread over all humanity a steadfast desire to make peace with one another, a peace that stands firm even against the shadow of evil that never ceases to exist in this imperfect world.

Grant us clarity of vision and purity of heart to know the difference between haughtiness and dignity so we may live side-by-side in peace with all nations. Hear the weeping heart of our People and spare them from the agony of the wickedness of those who want to rule over us like the Pharaoh of Egypt. Let not another life be taken by anyone in Your Name or that of false gods.

Please God, Who awes us with might and justice and mercy, give us the fortitude and wisdom to protect Your Chosen People, without hardening our hearts like the hardened hearts of our foes, lest we become like them. In this New Year, we pray that we may find mercy in Your eyes. Spare all of humanity the pain of war. Please God, Who holds the power of the universe above us all, grant us peace on this day and forever.

Author Unknown

Seek Adonai When God May Be Found, Call Upon Adonai When God Is Near

This biblical verse is often quoted during the High Holy Day season. From the first of Elul until the end of Yom Kippur, we feel God's presence even more than we do at other times. This is indeed the time when God is near, when Adonai can be found, more than during other times.

Is not God everywhere, all the time? True, but God's presence is felt more deeply during the month of Elul, and during the *Aseret Y'mai Teshuvah*. At these times God's nearness is more powerfully felt. Yet, the question arises, Why should God's presence be more strongly felt at any one time of the year, more than another?

The late Rabbi Milton Steinberg, the famous spiritual leader of Manhattan's Park Avenue Synagogue in the 1940s, once taught that in our spiritual lives there are moments when God's presence is very deeply felt, and other times, when God seems to be absent. God's nearness is fluctuating, he said. We cannot expect to feel God's presence with the same passion and feeling in the same way in every single moment of our lives.

This is only natural. The spiritual life, like all aspects of our lives, ebbs and flows. If we know that, and understand that God is sometimes near, and sometimes far, sometimes easily "found" and sometimes not-so-easily found, then we will recognize that it is up to us to seek God during those precious moments when we can sense God's immanence and take advantage, as best we can, of those special, sacred moments.

A poem by James Kavanaugh reflects the same thought:

A Conversation

"Are you there, God?"
    She asked prayerfully.
"Sometimes,"
    He answered carefully.
"Do you care, God?"
    she asked faithfully.
"Not always,"
    He said playfully.
"But, you do believe, God?"
    she asked persistently.
"At times," He replied.
    "But not consistently."

Rabbi Dov Peretz Elkins

Silence as Prayer

Søren Kierkegaard writes of prayer, "To pray is not to hear oneself, but it is to be silent, and to remain silent, to wait, until the one who prays hears God." Elsewhere in his works we read, "When all around thee is solemn silence ... and when there is silence within thee, then thou dost apprehend, and apprehend with the emphasis of inward-ness, the truth of the saying, 'Thou shalt love the Lord thy God and him only shalt thou serve,' and thou dost apprehend that it is thou alone in the whole world, thou who art alone in the environment of solemn silence, so alone that every doubt, and every objection, and every excuse, and every evasion, and every objection, and every ques-tion, in short, every voice, is reduced to silence in thine own inward being, every voice, that is to say, every other voice but God's, which about thee and within thee talks to thee by means of the silence." I suppose after that introduction I should just sit down and be quiet!

I do believe that this is ultimately what we all want in prayer, in our heart of hearts we want to hear God's voice speak to us ... directly and unmistakably.

I don't believe that God speaks to us directly. I do believe, as Kierkegaard writes, that silence is an essential element of worship. The *Amidah*, the standing, silent prayer at the center of our service, is the answer to that need.

The *Amidah* is known as *Ha-Tefilah*, the prayer, par excellence. The words of the *Siddur* are there to inspire us, to uplift our souls and to suggest images to our minds. They guide us to consider a broad range of concerns and ensure that we will encounter important values on a daily basis.

This should never be seen as detracting from the value of private, personal prayer. During the time of the *Amidah*, I would highly encourage you to formulate your heartfelt concerns according to your own words or methods, and offer them up to God as your prayer for Rosh HaShanah. Meditation is a time-honored Jewish tradition. This time of silence is a priceless gift.

When the service formally continues, you do not have to sit down immediately if you would like to remain standing. Don't be intimi-dated. You will see some other stalwart davveners who like to take a little bit more time, and they and you are welcome to remain standing as long as you prefer. The *Amidah* can be for all of us a haven of complete silence, even from our articulated prayers.

The *Amidah* concludes with the private prayer of a Rabbi that became so popular it was incorporated into the *Siddur*. People often mention it to me as their favorite prayer in the entire *Siddur*—"O Lord, guard my tongue from evil and my lips from speaking guile." Knowing when to remain silent is part of gaining maturity. We often regret speaking, we rarely regret remaining silent.

Rabbi Bonnie Koppell

Silent Meditation

How can I love You, who are so far away?
How can I know You, whose face I have not seen?
How can I approach You, when I am laden with guilt?
I can love some of Your creatures, and so love something of You.
I can know some of Your world, and so know something of You.
I can approach You with repentance and prayer and righteous
    deeds,
But I can do none of these, my God, without Your help.
Help me to love You and know You and pray to You that this
    my existence may become a life,
A life that like a leaf in the afternoon sun
Reflects Your great and golden light.

From the Wilshire Boulevard Temple
High Holy Day prayer book

Why We Pray

Prayer is the voice we hear when we listen to what the universe is saying to us. This is what Martin Buber calls "God singing within us." God sings within us when we cease to think of ourselves and listen to what the universe is saying to us. This is the custom of one of the great Hasidic rabbis who would often delay reciting his morning prayers so that he could go out to a nearby pond and listen to the songs of the frogs. When he could hear their song within his own soul, he knew that he was ready to pray.

Sometimes we pray when we are looking for an answer. The prayer is our question. In order to hear the answer, we must stop praying and listen to the voice within. The technique of listening also involves opening ourselves up to the prayers of other people: *Shema*—"Listen! Take these words to heart." When we hear the voice that sings within the composer, we can understand what moved the hearts of our ancestors. Everything in the universe longs for higher rungs and deeper layers. That longing is prayer. The heavens pray, nature prays, the heart prays.

Prayer is a heart-to-heart conversation with the divine within. We pray at times of powerful pain and distress, pouring out our broken heart in search of comfort and healing. We empty the broken vessel of our heart before we can refill it with the healing light of God.

David S. Ariel

Tefilah: **Why We Praise God**

In a sermon that my grandfather, a rabbi in Poland, approached many years ago, he asked some questions that might have sounded like heresy and blasphemy. Why does God need so much praise from those who serve Him? Is The Almighty Unsure of His own powers?...

My grandfather gave short answers.... God does not need praise by men, but He knows that when men cease to praise Him, they begin to praise one another excessively....

I heard of the sermon when I was still a little boy, but only in later years did I grasp its profound truth. Those who deny God are bound to bestow all of His attributes on flesh and blood.... While the materialists of all epics have refuted God's wisdom, His mercy, His providence, they have ascribed all of His sublime qualities to Kings and dictators or to systems....

For all materialists and extreme rationalists, prayer was never anything but an act of religious fanaticism. Why pray to an entity that is nothing but a product of our imagination? I have seen more fanaticism among authoritative atheists than in any religious group of my time....

How different is prayer to God from worldly entreaties. Those who pray to God earnestly do so with the hope that their prayers will be answered. The very essence of prayer is an alleviation of the troubled soul. The faces of those who pray express a noble humility, an ardent belief that God's wisdom cannot exist side by side with cruelty.

Prayer to God is often man's only hope and refuge from the anguish of life. I have seen a look of prayer even in the eyes of the so-called mute animals in moments of great pain. Prayer is an instinct that no logic can uproot.

Isaac Bashevis Singer

With a Kiss

It is the little acts, positioned in the day,
    that make us:, the kissing of the fallen book
which doesn't feel;
not using the *Chumash*, the Talmud,
as a thing to lean on for other words; be they poetry books
    or tax forms (they take no precedence, watch where
you lean); not mistaking a *Pushka* for a paperweight;
    kissing (again) the Mezuzah as we pass through
or pass from (both passages ordained, be cognizant);
the covering of Challah till the time, wine blessed,
tasted, hands washed, is right; the kissing (again)
of *Tzitzit*; the kissing of the Torah scrolls when they
are marched by, the kissing (yet again), before closing,
of the *Siddur*.

From these, justice and *Menschlichkeit*.
Lifting the fallen book we may, just may some day,
lift the fallen neighbor, the stranger, who feels, with a kiss.

Danny Siegel

Tefilah: "Will You Say a Prayer for Me?"

"When I go forth to find You, I find You seeking me."
                                    YEHUDA HALEVI

"I'm not religious. I don't know the prayers. I'd feel hypocritical. I can't get into ritual. I'm not sure what I believe, so how can I pray?"

Would you say, "Since I'm not Einstein, I won't think," or "Since I'm not Michael Jordan, I won't move?

You are who you are, and whatever prayer may mean to you, it's real and important to you and it's probably the most honest thing you do.

In this rollercoaster life, people pray to connect with what is timeless. Awash in trivia, people pray to remind themselves that they are part of something important. We Jews, for example, have a blessing for everything—for sighting a rainbow or the ocean, for our food, for beginning and endings, even for lightning. Saying the blessings is a reminder: *Wait, look at this. Someone gave us this world. Stop a minute in wonder.*

Those blessings were written by people who did stop in wonder. And if you look for it, you may find that there is a voice for you among them. You may also find that somewhere in the prayer book are your fears and your dreams—and a way to express them.

Yes, there are risks is prayer. You can feel foolish, or hypocritical, or—worse—empty. This is a conversation in which there is no certainty of response.

But at the very least you put yourself in touch with who you are and what you could be. You are asking the oldest, best questions in the world: *Are You there? Do You care about me? What do You expect of me?*

The answers may be in the asking.

Start small. Bless one moment for what it brings you. Say one ancient prayer, link yourself with continuity and eternity. Fill one silence with your end of the conversation. No one can do this for you; it belongs to you.

**From a Jewish Theological Seminary
advertisment and mailing**

Benediction

Let me not pray to be sheltered from dangers
but to be fearless in facing them.
Let me not beg for the stilling of my pain
but for the heart to conquer it.
Let me not crave in anxious fear to be saved
but hope for the patience to win my freedom.

Rabindranath Tagore

The Song of God's Presence

> I've not seen the robin but I know he is there
>   because I heard him singing through my window from
>   the tree-top outside.
> I have not seen God. But I have looked at my child's eye,
>   and have been overwhelmed by the miracle of unfolding
>   life.
> I have watched the trees bedeck themselves with new garbs of
>   green in the spring,
>   and have been stirred by the miracle of continual rebirth.
> I have looked at the stars, and have been overcome by the
>   miracle of the grandeur
>   and majesty of the universe.
> I know that God exists, because I have heard the song of His
>   presence
>   from all the tree-tops of creation.

Rabbi Ben Zion Bokser

The Meaning of Mitzvah

I try to walk the road of Judaism. Embedded in that road there are many jewels. One is marked "Sabbath" and one "Civil Rights" and one *"Kashruth"* and one "Honor Your Parents" and one "Study of Torah" and one "You Shall be Holy." There are at least 613 of them and they are of different shapes and sizes and weights. Some are light and easy for me to pick up, and I pick them up. Some are too deeply embedded for me, so far at least, though I get a little stronger by trying to extricate the jewels as I walk the street. Some, perhaps, I shall never be able to pick up. I believe that God expects me to keep on walking Judaism Street and to carry away whatever I can of its commandments. I do not believe that God expects me to lift what I cannot, nor may I condemn my fellow Jew who may not be able to pick up even as much as I can.

Rabbi Arnold Jacob Wolf

Tefilah: Prayer Is Spiritual Ecstasy

Prayer is spiritual ecstasy. It is as if all our vital thoughts in fierce ardor would burst the mind to stream toward God. A keen single force draws our yearning for the utmost out of the seclusion of the soul. We try to see our visions in His light, to feel our life as His affair. We begin by letting the thought of Him engage our minds, by realizing His name and entering into a reverie which leads through beauty and stillness, from feeling to thought, and from understanding to devotion.

Rabbi Abraham Joshua Heschel

As We Begin Our Prayers Tonight

Prayer is not the words we recite from the prayer book but an experience of the soul. If the words of the prayer book, someone else's words, are not adequate, we can find our own words. Even if we sit or stand silent in the synagogue while everyone around us is reading, reciting, or chanting, the thing that truly matters is what we experience in our privacy. The only prayer that matters is the one that comes from our heart. If our heart is not touched by the written words of the prayer book, we can turn inward and listen to the inner voice. Then, we can turn that voice into a chant, a movement, a melody until it hums in our heart.

David S. Ariel

Sacred Blessing

What is more powerful than a blessing? It is the deep spiritual directive and wish of a soul. Judaism has blessings for special occasions, wonders, tragedies, joys, sights in nature, human exaltations and anomalies, for everything that has its source in God—in other words, everything that exists.

Our sages teach us that we can recite blessings spontaneously, in whatever language we understand. We are not confined by the blessings in the prayerbook; they are a springboard, not a straitjacket. A blessing first acknowledges God's presence: Blessed are YOU." The grammar is eloquent.

The second-person pronoun teaches that God is right there—we only use "you" in someone's presence. The effusion of gratitude which is a blessing has an object: we are indebted to the Source of all.

The Shulchan Aruch teaches that one should not do anything else while reciting a blessing. There is no multi-tasking a bracha. Before you bless, take a moment and a deep breath. Sanctity requires internal space and a focus on the moment. To do several things at once is to give oneself to nothing. Each blessing is an offering. Each offering of the human spirit is sacred.

Rabbi David J. Wolpe

Spontaneity in Prayer

Our forebears, of blessed memory, established for us the norm for prayers—how to praise God and how to pray before God. They did not, however, intend with their regulation to make the form of prayer fixed and unchangeable, to make it impossible to add or subtract.... Our Sages did not put in writing our prayers and blessings in book form. Contrariwise, they said: "They who write down Benedictions (prayers) commit as gross a sin as those who burn the Torah." They permitted each individual and each cantor to lengthen or shorten (the prayer) in accordance with his wisdom. Therefore they decreed that the Eighteen Benedictions [*Shmoneh Esray*] are to be recited silently so that the reader can organize his prayer in the meantime before he recites it aloud before the people (see Rosh Hashanah 34b). That is why R. Eliezer said (*Berakhot* 4:4), "One who recites a prayer in a mechanical manner, that prayer cannot be a supplication for God's grace."

Samuel David Luzzatto

A Paradox: Praying for Oneself or Praying for the *Shekhinah*?

Our sages have said, "Your fear be upon you," meaning that your prayer be not fixed by rote. One should not pray concerning one's own needs, but one must always pray for the blessed *Shekhinah*, that She be redeemed from Her exile. Thus all prayer must "be mercy and supplication," meaning that one must always supplicate the Lord for the sake of the *Shekhinah*, who is called "Space," *Makom*, as it is well known. Thus the Zohar calls those who pray for themselves, and not for the sake of the *Shekhinah*, by the name of "dogs with harsh souls." For they are ever screaming, "Give me, give me." And this is the intention of the sentence "One thing have I asked from the Lord, only this [Heb. *Otah*, literally, "Her"] do I seek." In other words, for the sake of the *Shekhinah* do I seek this and so I pray before You—to correct the injury that has been done through sin.

Rabbi Dov Baer of Mezritch

He answered: What is God? The totality of souls. Whatever exists in the whole can also be found in the part. So in any one soul, all souls are contained. If I turn, in *Teshuvah*, I contain in me the friend whom I wish to help, and he contains me in him. My *Teshuvah* makes the him-in-me better and the me-in-him better. This way it becomes so much easier for him-in-him to become better.

Pinchas of Koretz

Begin

O God, Creator of time and of the universe, Lord of all Being, as we gather in prayer to greet another new year, our hearts and souls tremble before the uncertainty of time and the mystery of life. On this evening, the symbolic anniversary of Your creation, we stand here humbly in Your presence, very much aware of our failings and our falseness, and of our attempts to escape Your challenges. In these moments, we are more sensitive to the ephemeral quality of our lives, and to our rationalizations and indifference.

Help us, O Lord, God of Love, to sense Your presence, to perceive Your voice amidst the din and tumult of daily life. Grant us the wisdom to distinguish between right and wrong, between good and better, and between that which creates and that which destroys, enabling us to achieve something of enduring value. During the forthcoming days of scrutiny and repentance, help us to concentrate, O God, on our tattered souls and our atomized personalities. Quicken our tired and insensitive hearts so that we may genuinely pray and thereby ennoble our being.

Our world is so complicated and confusing, so harsh and heartless, so filled with suffering, anguish, violence, and hatred, that many of us can no longer find sanctity, meaning, or beauty. Help us to believe in You, O God, and to live a life consonant with such belief and faith. Help us to break down the barriers of insensitivity and fear within us, allowing us to respond to life, creating and loving with the totality of our being.

May we hearken to those who yearn for liberty and freedom, seriously working to free the oppressed, feed the hungry, sustain the poor, clothe the naked, and bring hope to the depressed. Grant, O Lord, to Your people Israel scattered throughout the world the capacity to remain loyal to Your Torah and to bring Your message to a stumbling and bewildered humanity. Bless our brothers in the State of Israel so that this creation may be congruent with the sanctity and aspirations of the past. Grant, O God of history, that men everywhere be motivated to labor for peace and harmony, desisting from violence and suspicion so that human society may reflect Your love and Your glory.

Cause Your justice and Your wisdom to reign supreme in this world, O God, so that man can live and love and not be afraid. Amen.

Rabbi Marshall T. Meyer

Hamelekh: Prayer and Worship, *Keva* and *Kavanah*

Although we don't think about it very often, there's a difference between prayer and worship. Worship is more formal and institutional. It usually happens within the context of a community, and it often involves both tradition and conformity.

Prayer is altogether different. It emanates from the heart, and it's frequently spontaneous. We respond to a situation with words of prayer, or simply with silence. "Help me, God." "Thank God." "Dear God, just give me the strength to make it through this day," or "Why me, God?"

Of course there's no clear distinction between prayer and worship. Sometimes we turn to the community when we need to pray, and sometimes worship inspires us to utter a personal, heartfelt prayer. Still they are different from one another.

The sages of the Talmud speak about *keva* and *kavanah*, spontaneity and form, in the act of prayer. True worship, true prayer must have a measure of both. There is an element of discipline, formula, and history that shapes how and what we say. But there must also be another element of fire that comes from deep within our hearts, a quality that is unique to us, that connects us to God personally.

It's not enough to go through the words of the *Machzor,* to worship mindlessly. We must find a way to transform the words we recite into our personal prayer.

Abraham Joshua Heschel said, "To pray is to know how to stand still and dwell upon a word." As we worship together let us dwell upon the words we recite and transform them into words of prayer.

Rabbi Mark B. Greenspan

Individual Prayer

It is easier to connect with God when praying alone than when praying with others.

Therefore, when you are alone, be happy, for joy is necessary for achieving *deveikut* [closeness to God].

In truth, you should be just as close to the Creator throughout the day as you are in prayer.

The only difference is that during prayer, you are in a more expansive state than during the rest of the day.

Rabbi Dov Baer of Mezritch

Blessing God

Because the word *brakha* is usually translated "blessing," it can be valuable to begin our journey by investigating some of the questions this translation raises.

What does it mean to "bless"?

In common folk practice, when someone sneezes, we may say, "Bless you." The expression has its roots in the hope that the words will ward of evil. To bless someone is to wish the person good fortune or to pray that the Divine Providence will be favorable. But why, then, would someone offer a blessing to God? The notion seems absurd; God doesn't need blessing, and anyway, how could a human being bring God good fortune?

Blessing implies a transfer of intention, hopefulness, or awareness from a source to a recipient. If I bless you, I seek to move something of myself toward you. I want you to feel more confidence, more hopefulness, to become richer in some way. I am offering you something by blessing you. When we experience God as a Source of blessing, a Source of hope, confidence, and empowerment, we feel ourselves enriched. But the questions remain: Should we have to give hope and confidence to God? If not, what is it that I am moving toward God?

When we offer "blessing" to the Source of Blessing, we offer our gratitude not only for a particular gift but for the opportunity to experience our connection with the whole of life. Our brakha opens us to the sheaf of divine goodness moving through us, filling us and flowing back to God. We partake of the world and are invited to experience God within everything.

This practice conveys a radical teaching: Neither the food we eat nor anything we find in the world is as inert as it may seem! Becoming aware of this takes us almost by surprise, yet at the same time seems more like a recollection of something we have always known. Discovering God's aliveness in our world can feel as if a veil has been lifted and a joyous clarity returned. Ironically, our minds usually conceal this perception. We create mental constructs objectifying the world and obscuring its Godliness. On the path of blessing, we are reminded that the whole world is an expression of divine energy.

Rabbi Marcia Prager

Hitbodedut: Praying Separately

This world literally means "self-isolation" or separating oneself from the company of others. Historically, it has come to mean doing so in order to be alone with God.

The practice of *hitbodedut* is first described in this language by Rabbi Bahyah Ibn Pakudah, a philosopher and mystic of the eleventh century. He lived in a society where Sufi practice, including meditation, was popular among the Muslim majority. His Judaism reflects the great awe in which he held this practice, one he enthusiastically recommends for his readers.

But if the term is a later one, the practice of solitary prayer and silent standing in God's presence is biblical in origin. It is widely reflected in Psalms, in such tales as Abraham wanderings through the desert, and Moses and Elijah's forty days at Horeb, the mountain whose name means "desolation." Jeremiah and others among the prophets also felt the calling to a lonely life of dedication in order to seek God's word. The biblical practice was continued among later Jewish groups, especially communities such as that at Qumran, the "Dead Sea Scroll" community, where individual pursuit of God and communal life each had their place.

Practices of *hitbodedut* have varied over the centuries. The followers of Rabbi Abraham Abulafia, from the thirteenth century onwards, had techniques of visualized meditations that they developed with great skill. For them, *hitbodedut* came to mean "concentration" on the images before the inner eye. Some Hasidic leaders continued in this path, especially that of visualizing the letters of prayer.

Others see *hitbodedut* as a time for private, but not necessarily silent, prayer. The followers of Rabbi Nachman of Breslov, in fact, insist upon the spoken form. These regular practitioners of *hitbodedut* seek to pray in this way for one hour each day, pouring forth spontaneous personal prayer, in whatever language the heart knows best. The purpose of this prayer, they say, is to break the heart, for only in the wholeness of knowing our broken heart can we truly come into God's presence.

Meditation is being revived in our day as a part of Jewish spiritual life. Ancient Jewish techniques are being simplified and updated. Methods of concentration and mindfulness are also being brought into Judaism by those who have learned them elsewhere. All this is for the good, a part of our generation's effort to make the Judaism we hand on richer in this area than it has ever been.

Rabbi Arthur Green

WORDS OF FAITH: HEAR O ISRAEL!

The *shema,* or the proclamation "Hear O Israel, the Lord our God, the Lord is One," stands at the center of Jewish worship. The most essential declaration of Jewish faith is learned early in childhood. Pious Jews hope that it will be the last phrase they utter before they die. "His soul went out with the word 'One'" is often found in descriptions of martyrs' deaths.

The *shema* actually consists of three Biblical passages: Deuteronomy 6:4–9 and 11:13–21 and Numbers 15:37–41. The daily recitation of these passages is considered a Biblically ordained precept ("You shall speak of them ... when you lie down and when you rise up" [Deuteronomy 6:7]). Although surrounded by prayers, the *shema* itself is not a prayer. It is addressed to one's fellow Jews, and perhaps also to some broader notion of "Israel" *(yisra'el).* It proclaims God's Oneness, the obligation to love and serve God through the commandments, a warning that satiety due to too much worldly prosperity may lead one to turn away from God, and a faith that righteousness is ultimately rewarded. The *shema* concludes with an admonition to be holy and to remember that the Lord brought Israel forth from Egypt *(Mitsrayim)* in order to be our God.

RABBI ARTHUR GREEN, *THESE ARE THE WORDS*

Praise the Lord, O My Soul: Let Every Fiber of My Being Praise God

Towards the end of the beautiful Nishmat *prayer we say these words: "Praise the Lord, O my soul. Let every fiber of my being praise God." How is it possible for every single fiber, every nerve and muscle of our body, to praise God? A beautiful, poetic piece was written by an advocate of organ/tissue donations, which exemplifies in graphic terms how we can achieve such praise of God with every fiber of our being.*

To Remember Me

At a certain moment a doctor will determine that my brain has ceased to function and that, for all intents and purposes, my life has stopped.

When that happens, do not attempt to instill artificial life into my body by the use of a machine. And don't call this my "deathbed." Call it my "bed of life," and let my body be taken from it to help others lead fuller lives.

Give sight to a man who has never seen a sunrise, a baby's face or love in the eyes of a woman.

Give my heart to a person whose own heart has caused nothing but endless days of pain.

Give my blood to the teenager who has been pulled from the wreckage of his car, so that he might live to see his grandchildren play.

Give my kidneys to one who depends on a machine to exist from week to week.

Take my bones, every muscle, every fiber and nerve in my body and find a way to make a crippled child walk.

Explore every corner of my brain. Take my cells, if necessary, and let them grow so that someday a speechless boy will shout at the crack of a bat and a deaf girl will hear the sound of rain against her windows....

Give my soul to God. If, by chance, you wish to remember me, do it with a kind deed or word to someone who needs you. If you do all I have asked, I will live forever.

Robert N. Test

Ahavah Rabbah: Enlighten Our Eyes in Your Torah

There was a king who had two servants. He loved them with a complete love. He gave each of them a measure of wheat and a bundle of flax.

The wise servant, what did he do? He took the flax and wove it into cloth. He took the wheat and made it into flour. He sifted it, ground it, kneaded it and baked it. Then he arranged it on the table and spread the cloth over it. He left it until the king arrived. The foolish servant did nothing at all.

After some time, the king came to his palace and said, "My children, bring me what I gave to you." One brought out the bread on the table covered with the cloth. The other brought out the wheat in a box with the bundle of flax on top ...

When the Blessed Holy One gave the Torah to Israel, He gave it to them as wheat from which to produce bread, and as flax from which to produce cloth.

Seder Eliyahu Zuta

Enlighten Our Eyes in Your Torah: Torah as Unripe Fruit

Let us awaken to the mystery of Torah, musing on her day and night.... The written Torah is an unripe fruit of supernal wisdom....

But isn't the Torah the source of life? How can you say that she is unripe? What is unripe is inferior! Like fruit that falls prematurely from a tree and ripens on the ground: it isn't as good as fruit that ripens on the branch.

Look! The root of Torah is supernal wisdom—hidden and concealed, perceived only through its wondrous pathways. How wondrous are the offshoots! But since the root is wisdom, who can ever reach it? This is why Israel's sweet singer sang, "Open my eyes, so I can see wonders out of your Torah!"

Moses de Leon

Shema Yisrael: We Close Our Eyes for *Shema* because We're Blind

The more real a thing is the less you can see it. After you reach the level where you see all those things which are not to be seen, then you open your eyes and everything is clear to you, and it feels like you saw it all the time. To love someone is the deepest thing in the world, but you can't prove it. You can't put your finger on it, but it's the most real thing in the world.

God is the most, utmost real thing in the world, and you can't see Him, but after you don't see Him, you see Him. Then you can see Him everywhere, in every flower, in every cloud, in every little stone, in every candle. When we say the *Shema,* God is One, we close our eyes, because first we don't see God, we're blind. We just believe. But then we open our eyes, and it is so clear. He's always there.

Rabbi Shlomo Carlebach

Shema: Those Little Whispers

"I was taught by my mom and dad that in Judaism the most important prayer is the *Shema.* Hear O Israel, the Lord our God, the Lord is One. It was taught to me from childhood that the most important thing I could do as a Jew was to listen. It wasn't a way for my parents to say, 'I know more than you.' It wasn't that way at all. They meant listen to yourself. Listen to those little whispers that we tend to not want to hear because they're too soft and we tend to listen to the shout, not the whisper.

"So listening carefully is what I was taught all my life. When people don't listen, it's not that they don't learn, they just deny themselves tremendous opportunities and glorious choices."

Steven Spielberg

Shema: Awakening a Love of God

The Bible commands: "You shall love the Lord your God." Can feelings be legislated? The question of nature vs. nurture, heredity vs. environment, is old and perhaps insoluble. But one thing we are increasingly aware of is the extent to which environment actually affects genetics—nature via nurture, as one writer has it. Certain genetic tendencies can be realized or obstructed by the environment. A recent experiment kept mice in darkness for the first two years of their lives. When they emerged into the light, they could not see. The gene for sight existed, but it had to be switched on by the environment. Failing that, there was blindness.

"You shall love the Lord your God." The commentator S'fat Emet asks how the Torah can command something that is "dependent upon human nature." He replies that the answer is embedded in the question. It must be in our nature, he concludes, to love God, but that love is buried deep within us. The commandment is an exhortation to live a life that will awaken that love.

The command is to turn on the spiritual gene that lies dormant inside us. Through study, mitzvot, acts of goodness, we can awaken the capacity to love each other and to love God.

Rabbi David J. Wolpe

Shema: Teach Them to Your Children, in Four Languages

Most of us Jews teach our children three languages—at least. English, of course. And Hebrew, of course. We also teach them to read Aramaic, to recite or chant one form or another of the Kaddish, which is written in Aramaic. Our children also learn a fourth language at some point in their education—perhaps French, Spanish, or Latin.

But there is another language that we want to teach—both them, and ourselves. That is Yiddish. We want them to know such words as *mensch, nachas* (Yiddish for *nahat ruah*—spiritual satisfaction), and *kvell.*

When we teach our children the words of our Torah, we are teaching them to be and act like a *mensch*—an ethical, compassionate human being. We are also teaching them that they (and we) will receive and give *nachas* from studying and teaching Torah. And we will all *kvell* from our children's learning, and our learning from them, and in turn, teaching each other. Torah study multiplies exponentially, as we learn and teach to the next generation.

Rabbi Dov Peretz Elkins

Shema: With All Your Heart

*"You shall love the Lord your God with all your heart
and with all your soul and with all your might."*

DEUTERONOMY 6:5

1. But later (6:13) the Torah tells us "Revere/fear only the
   Lord your God...." There are those we respect and do
   their bidding only from fear, but to serve God is both to
   love and to revere/fear Him (and perhaps to maintain a
   balance between awe of what is beyond us, and love for the
   God Who is so near us (Based on *Sifrei 7, Yerushalmi
   Sotah* 25a).

2. This teaches that you should make God beloved by others,
   just as Abraham did, as we understand from Gen. 12:5:
   " ... and the persons that they had acquired/made in
   Haran ... " Because Abraham loved God and acted accordingly, he inspired others to love God so that others will.

3. It is to be understood in accord with what follows: "Take
   to heart these instructions ... " (6:6). By following these
   instructions, by performing the mitzvot, one comes to recognize God and cleave to Him. (Both of these texts are
   based on *Sifrei 7*.)

4. Abaye said: It means to cause the Name of Heaven to be
   beloved on your account, through learning and studying and
   serving the Sages, and by interacting with all people graciously, so that they will say of you: happy is the father and
   the teacher who taught him Torah (Talmud, *Yoma* 86a).

5. The quality of love involves more deeds than all of the
   other qualities. And when one uses the quality of love for
   evil, there is not a single quality so evil. But when a man
   uses the quality of his love for good, then that quality is
   higher than all others, as it is written: "And you shall love
   the Lord your God.... " And there is no greater virtue in
   the Service of the Creator than serving Him out of love....
   What is "proper love" for God? It is to love God with a
   great, mighty, and supreme love, until his very soul is
   bound up in it, and he is in the ecstasy of that love always

... as when a man is infatuated with a woman.... Even more than this must the love of the blessed God be in the hearts of those who love Him ... (*"Orchot Tzaddikim,"* "The Ways of the Righteous," ch. 5; Maimonides, *Mishnah Torah,* "Laws of *Teshuvah,"* ch. 10).

6. What does it mean to love God? Some suggest that it implies doing the mitzvot, learning Torah, being a kind person, and doing the kind of things which bring others to love God. Others regard it as an emotional attachment, a mystical ecstasy, or even an "infatuation" as Maimonides terms it.

How would you strive to fulfill the mitzvah of "loving God"?

Rabbi Danny Horwitz

Shema: **Listen**

Listen. Few of us reflect on how just six words from this week's Torah portion are supposed to change us, and are supposed to be reflected in our behavior, every day. The six words are the *Shema. Shema Yisrael, Adonai Elohaynu, Adonai Ehad.* Hear, Israel, Adonai is our God, Adonai is One.

Shema. Hear. Listen. When you listen, you're supposed to focus. You have to understand, and come to know deeply, what the sounds mean. When I drive, I listen to the radio or CD. But if you asked me what I heard, unless I focus, I may not have heard anything. Sometimes when I listen to the news, I miss entire stories; my mind is elsewhere. Perhaps the correct translation is "Pay attention."

Shema acknowledges that the hardest thing for many of us is to listen. So many of us have so much to say! Unfortunately, so often that which is so important for us to say is not necessarily worth listening to. *Shema* says "stop it." Be quiet. You don't know everything. Just listen, maybe you'll learn something new, maybe you'll hear something new. *Shema* says slow down, change your pattern of behavior, listen. As Rabbi Jonathan Omer-Man once told me, "Don't just do something, sit there!" Listen, *Shema.*

Yisrael. This sentence is directed at the people of Israel. It involves each of us, individually. *Yisrael,* in this sentence means take notice—

I'm talking directly to you, not to other groups of people. This sentence is configured exclusively for people who are a part of *Yisrael*. You, me, our hearts and our souls. Pay close attention. This means all of us. This means you.

Adonai. The name of God, written in Hebrew letters *yud hay/vav hay*, which can't be pronounced, because all the letters are vowels, and in Hebrew that just doesn't work. But it is the sound of breathing. According to Rabbi Larry Kushner, the holiest sound in the world is the sound of your own breathing. The letters in the name are all parts of the Hebrew verb for "to be." A good translation for it would be: "The One who Brings into Being all that is." In other words, God's name is the Name of Being.

In Genesis, we have two descriptions of the winds of God. In the first story of creation, *ruah*, the wind of God is blowing over the face of the depths before God created light. In the second creation story God breathes life into the nostrils of the first human being. Breath is life. In the First Book of Kings 19:11–12, we read "The Holy One passed by. There was a great and mighty wind; splitting mountains and shattering rocks by the power of God. But the Holy One was not in the wind. After the wind, there was an earthquake, but God was not in the earthquake. After the earthquake, fire; but the Holy One was not in the fire. And after the fire, the soft barely audible sound of almost breathing." There's a good reason we don't know how to pronounce the word spelled out by the letters *yud hay/vav hay*. How do you pronounce the sound of breath?

Shema Yisrael Adonai—listen, be quiet and hear the sound of your own breathing, the breath of God inside of you. You breathe 26,000 times a day. The Hebrew word for breath is *neshama*, the same word as "soul." We breathe our souls into ourselves, the breath of God, thousands of times a day, and yet we miss its importance. God is breathing your soul into your body. Listen, *Yisrael*, and you will hear the presence of God in your own body.

Elohaynu means our God. Not your God or my God or their God. Our God. Possessive. God is our God, and we are God's possession. We are affirming that our God is a shared God. We are all children of, and equally loved by, the same God. We all share in the blessings of God's spirit, *neshama*. Just as God and you are symbiotic, one, God is the same way with each and every person in this world. The spirit is what unifies us all in God's presence. Listen, Israel, to the sound of your individual God as that Presence is breathed into the people next to you. As you love yourself, love them, for the breath, the *neshama* of God is in them too.

Adonai. There's that name of God again, twice in six words. Three out of the six words are references to God, *Adonai Elohaynu, Adonai.* Can there be any doubt, if you are listening, as to where you can find your God? Find God in every breath you take, which you cannot see and you cannot touch, you can feel only with effort, or know when it's missing. Very few of us have doubts about our breathing: we believe we are alive and we breathe. Maybe we should learn the message in our breath. We know it's there. Breath is a symbol for God, Who put it there. As you have no doubt that you are breathing, have no doubt about God, Whose neshama you breathe. Want to know what God looks like? Look at yourself, look at everyone else. We are all reflections of the diverse ways in which that image is turned into a person.

Adonai ehad. Listen Israel, one. But what is one? Unique. Solo. Special. Holy. That one-ness can be hard for us. The Presence of God is referred to as the *shehinah,* which is a feminine form. God is seen as having justice, a male attribute, but also full of mercy, female. *Rahamim,* mercy comes from the root word *rehem,* which means "womb." God is one—male and female, Creator of all beings.

If there is one God, who is our God, shared by all, what does that imply about what we have to do? What is our relationship with the One? Listen, Israel, *Adonai* is Our God, *Adonai* is reflected in each of us, *Adonai* is unique. There is nothing else in the human imagination like God. Maybe if we begin to see how unique God is, we'll stop trying to be God, or to order God around, and attempt to really understand God. Maybe when we become humble enough to see the uniqueness of God we'll stop thinking we are so smart that we can judge God's motives, instead of the other way around. The Holy One is so unique we have to recognize that we will never understand much beyond that.

May it be Your will Holy One, our God, that we find ways to unify all humanity in our understanding of what it means to be human and to be blessed by a relationship with a unique and loving God who gives us something to listen to, if only we tune in. May we continue to search for the meanings of the messages You have given us, and may we always strive to grow to reflect Your Presence in each of us.

Rabbi H. Rafael Goldstein

Ga'al Yisrael: Redemption as Social Redemption

Ge'ulah, redemption, is the moment at which an unfinished world, in need of transformation through a covenantal partnership of the divine and the human, at last finds its decisive completion. Redemption, along with creation and revelation, forms one paradigmatic traditional Jewish theological and liturgical design. *Ge'ulah* achieves the meaning of creation which the Torah only reveals as possible. It takes possibilities inherent in creation and makes them real. In Judaism, redemption is primarily a social transformation, not the saving of individual souls. The redeemed world is one in which, as Jeremiah said, the entire world is full of the knowledge of G-d. For some this means a fundamental change in cosmic ground rules. Lions lie down with lambs. There is no war, no hunger, no sickness. For others, the minimalists, *ge'ulah* is no more than the freedom of the Jewish people from the limiting sovereignty of the gentile nations. For both, however, *ge'ulah* includes all nations. Redemption is a world-transforming event....

And where shall the Jewish people turn for redemption now, after forty-seven years of the State of Israel? For some, the *ge'ulah* has already begun. We are witnessing the dawn of our promised deliverance. For others, it is enough that the Jews are once again back in history, struggling as a people to heal an incomplete world and to bring its deepest holy possibilities into being. Even, or perhaps especially, when Jews speak of *ge'ulah,* there are more questions than answers.

Dr. Tsvi Blanchard

Jewish Courage to Hope for Redemption

Where does Israel get the strength—the chutzpah—to go on believing in redemption in a world that knows mass hunger and political exile and boat people? How can Jews testify to hope and human value when they have been continuously persecuted, hated, dispelled, destroyed? Out of the memories of the Exodus!

"So that you remember the day you went out of Egypt all the days of your life" (Deuteronomy 16:3). The Jewish tradition takes this biblical ideal literally. The exodus is the most influential historical event of all time because it did not happen once but recurs whenever people open up and enter into the event again.

                                        Rabbi Irving Greenberg

Footsteps of the Messiah

Despite the grave faults of which we are aware in our life in general, and in *Eretz Yisrael* in particular, we must feel that we are being reborn and that we are being created once again as at the beginning of time. Our entire spiritual heritage is presently being absorbed within its source and is reappearing in a new guise, much reduced in material extent but qualitatively very rich and luxuriant and full of vital force. We are called to a new world suffused with the highest light, to an epoch the glory of which will surpass that of all the great ages which have preceded. All of our people believe that we are in the first stage of the Final Redemption. This deep faith is the very secret of its existence; it is the Divine mystery implicit in its historical experience. This ancient tradition about the Redemption bears witness to the spiritual light by which the Jew understands himself and all the events of his history to the last generation, the one that is awaiting the Redemption that is near at hand.

                                    Rabbi Avraham Isaac Kook

STANDING BEFORE GOD: THE *SHACHARIT AMIDAH*

O ne of the best-known depictions of God in Jewish folk tradition is that of the Judge Who presides over the heavenly court. This imagery is especially connected to Rosh Hashanah, which is known as *yom ha-din* ("the day of judgment"). Judaism's strong sense of moral accountability calls forth this image. Each of us is responsible for our actions and we are all called before God to account for them.

RABBI ARTHUR GREEN, *THESE ARE THE WORDS*

Introduction to the *Amidah:* Praying with *Kavanah*

As we are about to begin the *Amidah,* the central prayer of the *Siddur* and the *Mahzor,* our sages tell us to concentrate with special attention on God's holiness and on the meaning of each paragraph—indeed on each word in this supremely important segment of our liturgy.

Our prayer during the *Amidah* takes on an aspect of deep thought and meditation. All religions have taught that serious concentration and focus is essential for effective prayer. According to the Sufis, "Meditation is the chief possession of the mystic." In Judaism, all are capable of the intensity necessary to open our hearts to God during the *Amidah.*

The famous Hassidic Rebbe, Rabbi Nahman, once said: "A person who does not meditate cannot have wisdom. He may occasionally be able to concentrate, but not for any length of time. His power of concentration remains weak and cannot be maintained."

Each time we increase our concentration and meditation during the *Amidah,* it makes it easier and more focused the next time.

Rabbi Dov Peretz Elkins

The *Amidah:* How Do We Find God?

Hasidic tale: A child wandered in the woods so often that her father became worried. The father asked: Why do you go into the woods so often? The child replied: To find God. The father reacted, out of his logical thought process: But God is the same everywhere, in the forest, and right here at home!

The little girl countered with a wise and theologically sophisticated idea: "But, father, I am not the same everywhere!"

Of course, God is in your homes, and at your place of work. But somehow we find it more comforting and more hospitable to pray to God here in the synagogue. For some it may make it easier for you to feel God's presence by focusing on the *Aron Kodesh,* the Holy Ark.

For others, you may want to imagine that you are in the midst of a beautiful, enchanted forest.

In either case, let the *Amidah* be a time in which we each find a special place where we can each find God in our own way.

Rabbi Dov Peretz Elkins

Amidah: Purify Our Hearts to Serve You in Truth

I asked the Confirmation class what they thought God was, and two of them very bravely stood up to me and announced that they didn't believe in God. Since tonight is the supreme symbol of faith in the Jewish year, I think it is only fitting for me to answer them, my way ... with a story.

It is said that once a pious Jew came to Rebbe Menahem Mendel of Kotzk and said, "Rebbe, I'm beginning to think that I no longer believe in God!" The Rebbe replied, "But Moishe, do you care?" "Rebbe? What do mean do I care?!" "Do you care about living a good life?" "Of course I care. I do everything that I can do to make sure I do right by everybody."

"Do you care what happens to your family?"

"Rebbe, you know that I care about my family, I would help them through anything."

"Do you care about your friends, your neighbors, people around you?"

"Yes, I care, I do what I can to be a good neighbor, a good friend. I do what I can. I give what I can."

"Well, Moishe, then it's simple, if you care then you believe!"

Rabbi Dannel I. Schwartz

Amidah: Saying Grace

In the *Amidah* you will find the word *Barukh* found many times. In our liturgy every blessing begins with the Hebrew word *Barukh*. This word is sometimes translated as "Thank you," or "Blessed [is God]," or "We acknowledge You [O God]." A traditional Jew recites the word *Barukh* at least one hundred times a day. There is a *brakhah* for everything—for bread, wine, for the Torah, for seeing a rainbow, for studying Torah, etc. etc.

G. K. Chesterton may have known of this Jewish custom when he wrote: "You say grace before meals. All right. But I say grace before the concert and the opera, and grace before the play and pantomime, and grace before I open a book, and grace before sketching, painting, and swimming, fencing, boxing, walking, playing, dancing, and grace before I dip the pen in ink."

As Jews, we too, say a *brakhah* for every divine experience, including the ones we mention in the *Amidah*.

D.P.E.

Amidah: Prayer Lifts Creation

Prayer is the ideal of all worlds. All of existence yearns for the source of its life. Every plant, every grass, every grain of sand, every clod of earth, everything with life force, revealed and hidden, the small and the large, every detail of everything, all yearn, strive, long for the completeness of their supreme, living, holy, pure and mighty Source. We constantly absorb all this yearning and are raised up by this holy longing. In prayer, these yearnings become revealed and go out in freedom and strength as a holy meditation to the wide God-expanses. We raise up the whole creation with our prayer, we become one with all existence, and raise everything to the source of blessing, the source of life.

Seder Tefilah (Order of Prayer) by Rabbi Avraham Yitzhak Hakohen Kook

> This may sound very deep and mystical, but what is involved is merely living fully in the present moment and experiencing everything in complete awareness. It is looking at what is happening without preconception and without illusion. As we look around and experience the world, we become aware of the life force contained in all things. In true prayer, the awareness of self fades, and with it, our deep connection to everything shines forth. We become one with creation and with the One Without End *(Ain Sof)*. This experience of being at one with the world and with the Holy One is the source of great joy and peace. Each small *tikkun* advances the process of *tikkun olam*.

Rabbi Aryeh Meir

Melekh Hafetz Ba-Hayyim: God Desires Life

Maya Angelou was interviewed by Oprah on her 70+ birthday. Oprah asked her what she thought of growing older. And, there on television, she said it was "exciting." Regarding body changes, she said there were many, occurring every day ... like her breasts. They seem to be in a race to see which will reach her waist first. The audience laughed so hard they cried. She is such a simple and honest woman, with so much wisdom in her words!

Maya Angelou said this: "I've learned that no matter what happens, or how bad it seems today, life does go on, and it will be better tomorrow." "I've learned that you can tell a lot about a person by the way he/she handles these three things: a rainy day, lost luggage, and tangled Christmas tree lights." "I've learned that regardless of your relationship with your parents, you'll miss them when they're gone from your life.

"I've learned that making a 'living' is not the same thing as 'making a life.' I've learned that life sometimes gives you a second chance.

"I've learned that you shouldn't go through life with a catcher's mitt on both hands; you need to be able to throw something back.

"I've learned that whenever I decide something with an open heart, I usually make the right decision. I've learned that even when I have pains, I don't have to be one. I've learned that every day you should reach out and touch someone. People love a warm hug, or just a friendly pat on the back.

"I've learned that I still have a lot to learn. I've learned that people will forget what you said, people will forget what you did, but people will never forget how you made them feel."

D.P.E.

Zokhrenu L'hayim

One phrase especially associated with the High Holiday period is inserted into the *Amidah*—*"Zokhrenu l'hayim"*—Remember us for life. You can find it in the *Shaharit Amidah*. We always begin the *Amidah* with reference to our ancestors, Abraham, Isaac and Jacob. We have recently begun to include the matriarchs as well, Sarah, Rivka, Rahel *v'*Leah, and there is even a movement afoot that we should also name Bilhah and Zilpah, Jacob's concubines, who were the mothers of some of the tribes of Israel.

We appeal to *"zekhut avot,"* the merit of our forebears, hoping that God will look favorably upon us if not for our own sake than for the sake of generations past. The phrase *"zokhrenu"* connects to the opening blessing, where we implore God to *"zokher hasdei avot,"* remember the lovingkindness of our ancestors.

You are undoubtedly familiar with the metaphor of the High Holidays, as we depict God with the Book of Life, determining our fate for the coming year. Presumably, the righteous are immediately sealed for a year of blessing, the irredeemably wicked for punishment, and the rest of us given a suspended sentence until Yom Kippur, allowing us ten days in which to prove ourselves. During this time we repeatedly implore God with this phrase, *"zokhrenu l'hayim,"* remember us for life.

The question has been raised as to why we should be allowed to offer such a request, when the time will come in each of our lives when, regardless of our merits, our life will end. Is this not an example of a *tefillat shav*, a prayer in vain, which is halakhically prohibited, like, for example, a prayer regarding the gender of a child who has already been conceived, or, a prayer, on seeing smoke coming from one's block, that the fire not be at one's home.

Life is such a supreme value in Judaism, that a prayer for life can never be regarded as vain, even when offered by a person who is dying. We boldly assert that it is in God's best interest to sustain us, as we read, *"l'ma-ankha,"* for Your sake, *"elohim khayim,"* God of life. So we ask for life not merely for its own sake, but life which will be dedicated to God's service in thought and action.

It is also noteworthy that we phrase the prayer in the plural. Acknowledging our own individual mortality, we still pray for the continued vitality of the Jewish people. As we davven the *Amidah*, we should focus special attention on this phrase, committing ourselves to a life which will truly be *"l'ma-ankha,"* a life directed towards God's service, as well as praying for the ongoing renewal of the Jewish people.

Rabbi Bonnie Koppell

Choose Life That You May Live

When all these things befall you—the blessing and the curse that I have set before you—and you take them to heart amidst the various nations to which Adonai your God has exiled you, and you return to Adonai your God, and you and your children listen to God's command with all your heart and soul, just as I enjoin upon you this day, then Adonai your God, with divine compassion, will restore your fortunes. God will bring you together again from all the peoples where Adonai your God has scattered you. Even if your outcasts are at the ends of the earth, from there Adonai your God will gather you, God will take you from there. And God will bring you to the land which your ancestors settled, and you will occupy it again; God will make you prosperous and more numerous than your ancestors.

Then, God will open up your heart and the hearts of your children to love Adonai your God with all your heart and soul, so that you may live.

Deuteronomy 30:1–6

Zokhrenu Le-Hayim: To Life!

What is the most important word in the entire *Mahzor*? I think everyone would agree that the word is *hayim*. As we recite in every *Amidah* prayer "*Zokhreinu L'hayim*.... Remember us *L'hayim*, for life, O Ruler who delights in life."

But I believe that we are asking for much more than life. We are praying: "God, *Zokhreinu L'hayim*, remember us in the year to come with many opportunities to say *L'hayim*—over a cup of wine at a bris, bar or bat mitzvah, a child's wedding, the birth of a grandchild, upon the completion of a tractate of the Talmud, or on the success of an important charitable endeavor.

May it be Your will, O God, to let us shout *L'hayim* at a joyous family *simchah*—may this year truly be a year of joy, of Jewish family celebration and continuity as we lift our voices and cups in Your praise.

Zokhreinu L'hayim—remember us in this year and grant us *L'hayim* at *simchas* of Jewish *nachas* in our families.

Rabbi Joseph L. Braver

L'El Orekh Din: God Searches All Hearts on the Day of Judgment

A person's soul testifies at night about whatever he or she does in the day.

ZOHAR I:92A

God searches our hearts in many ways: through dreams, through our conscience, through the repercussions of our acts. In one way or another, we can run from ourselves, but we cannot hide from God. The wisdom of the *Zohar* is consummate: our sleep, or lack of it, sometimes comes to haunt us because of what we did, or did not do, during that day.

D.P.E.

L'El Orekh Din: Justice Tempered with Mercy

L'El Orekh Din is the culmination of a series of *piyyutim* on God as sovereign and judge, and it teaches us a powerful lesson on the meaning of justice. Despite the repetition of *"din,"* of law, the overriding sense is of mercy. Note the verbs: *oseh hesed*—act graciously; *homel ma'asav*—is merciful to His creations; *kovesh ka'so*—overcomes His anger; *mohel avonot*—forgives sins; *rahem amo*—is compassionate to His people ... and on and on. Avraham asks God before the destruction of Sodom and Gomorrah: *"Hashofet kol ha-aretz lo ya-a-seh mishpat?"* Rabbi Levi tells us in a midrash that this is not really a question, it is a statement. God indeed will NOT do justice! If God did justice, we would all fail! Rather, divine justice must include mercy, and it is of this expectation that the *piyyut* reminds God.

But there is a lesson for us as well—can we expect mercy from *"shofet kol ha-aretz"* and not extend mercy ourselves? If we insist only on a justice that is black and white for those who have wronged us, what can we expect from God?

Rabbi Diane Cohen

The Righteous Will See and Be Glad, the Pious Will Rejoice in Song

There was a rabbi, a great scholar and sage, who filled his whole life with acts of piety. He knew that he would be justly rewarded in the world to come. So he prayed to God to let him see who would sit next to him in the next world, who would be his study partner. And God granted him his wish.

God took him to a little shop where a poor shoemaker slaved away. All day and far into the night the man made shoes, and yet he seemed to have little to show for it. The shop was poor. The man never took time to study. He badly needed to bathe and change his clothes. The rabbi was outraged. "O God, after all my acts of piety, this man is to be my neighbor and study partner! What kind of justice is this?" God answered, "Go talk to the shoemaker."

The rabbi introduced himself. The shoemaker answered, "I have heard of your great piety. I wish I had time to learn with you. But who has the time? All day I work hard to make shoes for the rich; they pay my living. And then, where there is leather left over, all night I work hard to make shoes for the poor. Nobody should be without shoes because they cannot afford them." The rabbi turned to God. *"Ribono Shel Olam,* Master of the World, I am not worthy to sit with him."

Retold by Rabbi Michael Gold

Kadosh Atah V'nora Sh'mekha: You Are Holy and Awesome

The reality of the holy can only be grasped from the standpoint of the mystery. Then one sees that the holy is not a segregated, isolated sphere of Being, but signifies the realm open to all spheres, in which they can alone find fulfillment. The face of the holy is not turned away from but towards the profane; it does not want to hover over the profane but to take it up into itself....

The contradictions between the spheres of the holy and the profane exist only in the subjectivity of humans who have not yet attained to spiritual unity and are unable, with their limited powers of understanding, to mediate between the two. In reality the main purpose of life is to raise everything that is profane to the level of the holy.

Martin Buber

Holiness and Righteousness

Ha-El HaKadosh Nikdash b'Tzedakah: *The Holy God is sanctified by righteousness.*

AMIDAH

Tzedek, Tzedek Tirdof: *Justice, Justice shall you pursue.*

DEUTERONOMY 16:20

Elie Wiesel tells the story of the one righteous man of Sodom who walked the street protesting against the injustice of his city. He was made fun of, derided. Then one day a young person asked him "Why do you continue your protest against evil; can't you see that nobody is paying attention to you?"

The righteous man answered "At first, I thought I would change the people and the city. Today, I know I cannot. By continuing my protest though, I'll keep them from changing me."

How important that we heed these words in today's society. It's far too easy to give up the fight for justice because it feels like one is hitting a brick wall. But if you are hitting a brick wall, that should tell you that the problem still persists. If you stop fighting, you'll easily become assimilated into the unjust culture you are protesting against. If you keep fighting, you may or may not make a change, but you will at least keep yourself from compromise of your own principles.

Adrian A. Durlester

Ve-ten Helkenu be-Toratekha: The Lesson of Nature

In all the writings of humanity's thinkers,
A design emerges—a design to give us insight for life.

An ark of light, the sparkling sun,
Guides our days, measures our lives,
So shall Torah shine in our lives.

Diamonds of light, the blinking stars,
Move regularly through heavenly paths,
So shall Torah move in our lives.

The winged beauties of the air, plumaged birds,
Rise on gusts of wind and dive among the trees,
So shall Torah free us to soar aloft.

The graceful swimmers, gliding fish,
In their watery element, move swift and sure,
So shall Torah give us security and purpose.

The myriads of living things, earth's animal beings,
Small and huge, bound by cycles of life,
So shall Torah help us in our human cycles.

In this grand design, it is Torah
Which teaches us, God's special creation,
How nature's design should be in our lives.

Rabbi Sylvan D. Kamens

Ve-Taher Leebenu: **Kindness**

The hardest part is people.
So Lord, help me face them
without rancor or disappointment.
Help me see the pain behind their actions
rather than the malice;
the suffering rather than the rage.

And in myself, as I struggle
with the vise of my own desire—
give me strength to quiet my heart,
to quicken my empathy, to act
in gratitude rather than need.

Remind me that the peace I find
in the slow track of seasons
or an uncurling fern frond,
is married to the despair I feel
in the face of nuclear war.

Remind me that each small bird shares atoms
with anthrax, with tetanus, with acid rain,
that each time I close my heart
to another, I add to the darkness;
Help me always follow kindness.

Let this be my prayer.

Karen Holden

Sim Shalom: **Thoughts on War and Peace**

Peace is an armistice in a war that is continuously going on.

—Thucydides, 400 B.C.E.

The tragedy is that we do not kill objects, numbers, abstract or inter-changeable instruments, but precisely, on both sides, irreplaceable individuals, essentially innocent, unique.

—Regis Debray

War is the unfolding of miscalculations.

—Barbara Tuchman

All wars are popular for the first thirty days.

—Arthur Schlesinger, Jr.

Either war is obsolete, or men are.

—Buckminster Fuller

The next dreadful thing to a battle lost is a battle won.

—Arthur Wellesley, Duke of Wellington

I think that people want peace so much that one of these days the government had better get out of their way and let them have it.

—Dwight D. Eisenhower

War will exist until that distant day when the conscientious objector enjoys the same reputation and prestige that the warrior does today.

—John F. Kennedy

Peace is not only better than war, but infinitely more arduous.

—George Bernard Shaw

Never think that war, no matter how necessary, nor how justified, is not a crime.

—Ernest Hemingway

D.P.E.

Sim Shalom: Grant Peace, Goodness, Kindness to All Your People

I read about a phenomenon in Marin County, California. Someone put up a sign on the Interstate: "Perform a random act of kindness today." Sure enough, reports came in, slowly at first, of people paying the toll for cars behind them ... people stopping to help stranded vehicles.... One man was caught in traffic. His cellular phone not working, he typed a sign on his laptop computer and printed it on his car fax: LATE FOR ANNIVERSARY DINNER. CALL MY WIFE AND TELL HER I LOVE HER (#). He came home an hour later to find that seventy people had called, one of them sent a bouquet of flowers, another sent a voucher for dinner for two at the local poshest resort. Over a four-month period, crime dropped 7 percent.

As we now pray for kindness in the prayer, *"Sim Shalom,"* may we be influenced by the beautiful words, ideas and actions, expressed in the prayer.

D.P.E.

Our Goal: Shalom

Peace, shalom
is not

the absence of difficulties
but
the handling of difficulties
without
loss of balance.
Shalom is not the absence of tension
but the acceptance of it as part of the Way.
Shalom is not the absence of war
but the careful waging of war
without losing one's balance.
Shalom, is not passive non-violence,
but active confrontation with truth.

Shalom is the ability to see the grain of life
and act in accord with it;
to discover that effortless effort,
action in tune with the Way of Universe,
is the secret of both peace and power.

Rabbi Rami Shapiro

Oseh Shalom Bim'romav

How is "peace" brought about?

According to a midrash taught by the late Rabbi Shlomo Carlebach, the root of the word *shalom* (peace) is spelled with the three Hebrew letters *shin, lamed,* and *mem.*

The *shin,* which looks somewhat like a capital "W," may symbolize that one way to achieve peace is to bring together two opposing sides, as does the letter's middle branch.

The *lamed,* which looks somewhat like a capital "L," is a particularly "tall" letter; it extends from the highest to the lowest point on the line. This may symbolize that, if you want to bring about peace, you have to be very "high" in the sense of extending yourself and "sticking out" your neck.

The *mem*, which looks somewhat like a large square, is a "closed" letter, one that is printed with no openings. This may symbolize that your commitment to *shalom* has to be complete; it can have no breaches. You can't say, "I am generally committed to pursuing peace, but I sometimes may need to depart from this commitment through violence or passivity, particularly if I'm facing a personal emergency." Rather, pursuing peace must be a whole-hearted commitment that, as the midrash suggests, requires using many facets of one's personality.

Rabbi Lori Forman

Sim Shalom: You Have Revealed to Us Your Life-Giving Torah

"You have revealed to us Your Life-giving Torah." Saadya Gaon has written that we are a people only by virtue of our Torah. Perhaps the most beautiful description of what study and practice of Torah can mean to a modern Jew was written several thousand years ago by the Psalmist in Psalm 119, verses 105–112. These verses will be the best exposition of that liturgical phrase that one can find:

Your word is a lamp to my feet,
  A light for my path.
  I have firmly sworn
  To keep Your just rules.
  …
  Adonai, preserve me in accord with Your word.
  Teach me, Adonai, Your rules.
  Even in danger I do not neglect Your teaching.
  Though facing peril I have not strayed from Your precepts.
  Your decrees are my eternal heritage,
  They are my heart's delight.
I am resolved to follow Your laws
To the utmost forever.

D.P.E.

AVINU MALKENU

The depiction of God as *melekh* or "King" was a key part of the legacy of symbols and images that ancient Israel received from the surrounding cultures. As human kings were revered as gods in the ancient Near East, so too were the gods depicted amid the trappings of royalty.

Post-Biblical Judaism continued to cherish the royal metaphor, perhaps more so than ever once historical circumstance denied the Jews earthly sovereignty. The idea that God is the only true King, and therefore that all flesh-and-blood rulers are more or less usurpers, was widely if quietly believed among Jews for a very long time. An emperor might dare call himself "king of kings," but God remained beyond him, since God was called *melekh malkhey hamelakhim*, "King over kings of kings"! The liturgy, and especially that of Rosh Hashanah and Yom Kippur, is especially enamored of royal imagery.

RABBI ARTHUR GREEN, *THESE ARE THE WORDS*

Avinu Malkenu: Become a Ruler over Yourself

The image of God as Ruler is a predominant theme throughout the High Holiday liturgy. From the shape of the round, crown-like *hallot* to the many prayers in which the word *"Melekh"* is substituted for other names of God, the High Holidays are filled with references to this time of the creation of the world and the coronation of its Sovereign.

Avinu Malkenu is, of course, a primary example of this ubiquitous mention of the sovereignty theme, along with *Alenu* and other prayers.

The late Lubavitcher Rebbe, Menachem Mendel Schneerson, was apparently asked by many women to help them choose a Hebrew name. He often suggested to them to choose *Malkah*—Queen.

His reason: he wanted them to become a ruler over themselves. He would say to them, as he could say to a male who wants a Hebrew name such as *"Melekh"*:

"You are the master over the animal within, not the slave. Just because it burns inside like a furnace doesn't mean you must obey."

As we refer to God as Sovereign, it helps to remember that God's reign over the universe supports our own ability to rule over our own passions and desires.

D.P.E.

Avinu Malkeynu—Our Father, Our King

The *Avinu Malkeynu* prayer includes the plea *"Shema Koleynu"*—Hear our voice.

As we contemplate our lives and the year ahead, we don't always have the proper words to articulate our hopes and dreams.

But if our voices convey sincere intention, even that can be enough.

God heard the voices of Ishmael and the Children of Israel crying wordlessly in the desert. God granted Hannah's petition when she wept her prayers in the Temple. She moved her lips, but only her soul poured out; no words were discernible.

Shema Koleynu. May the Holy One hear our voices, too.

And may God bless us with Solomon's gift—*lev shomeah*—a listening and discerning heart, so that we may hear God in reply.

Avinu Malkeynu, Shema Koleynu.

Rabbi Debra Orenstein

Aseh Imanu Tzedakah Va-Chesed: Deal with Us Charitably and Lovingly

The summer I was eight, my parents and I visited a well-off family at their Adirondack camp. The family's three daughters—the eldest of whom was my age—had a stuffy, dictatorial governess. Not only were the girls awed by Miss Miller, but so was my own governess—a dreary person who agreed with Miss Miller on the importance of what I considered unimportant details, such as whether we folded our napkins at the end of each meal even though no napkin would be used again.

Miss Miller was learning to dive. So was I. The only place to practice was from the end of the boat dock. Miss Miller took an endless amount of time walking there, projecting her toes over the edge and bending over, with her arms over her head. Finally, finally, she would drop head-first into the water.

I would follow almost immediately, but even though I often climbed back out of the water first, my governess made me wait for Miss Miller to dive ahead of me. One day I could stand it no longer and as Miss Miller stood at the end of the dock, I gave her a push.

Right after she had belly-flopped into the lake, I followed with a dive—but there was no way I could hide out in the water forever. When at last I emerged, my governess marched me, dripping and shivering, to the cabin where my father usually worked before lunch.

He looked up from his desk to see a wet small daughter and an outraged governess. She told him what I had done. I knew it was wrong and dreaded the punishment.

Oh help, I thought, as I saw his face working. This must be even worse than I realized. My shivering increased.

"June pushed *Miss Miller* in the lake?" He was incredulous.

"Yes! She is a wicked girl."

It was then I realized his facial twitching was the result of the effort not to laugh. I edged over to him. Wet though I was, he put his arm around me. "You *are* a wicked girl," he said, shaking with laughter. "But I can't entirely blame you."

My governess quit—who could entirely blame her? Yet for my whole life, the memory of my agnostic father's forgiveness has spurred me to forgive other people more readily and more wholeheartedly than I ever could have otherwise.

June Bingham

Avinu Malkenu, Judge Us according to Our Actions

If the wicked turns from all the sins that he or she has committed, and keeps all My statutes, and does that which is lawful and right, he or she shall surely live, you shall not die. None of the sins that were committed will be remembered against him or her; for by the righteousness that he or she has done shall live you. Have I any pleasure at all that the wicked should die? Says God; and not rather that he or she should return from their ways, and live? ...

Therefore I will judge you, house of Israel, every one according to their ways, says Adonai God. Return, and turn yourselves from all your transgressions; so shall they not be a stumbling block of iniquity unto you. Cast away from you all of your transgressions, wherein you have sins, and make you a new heart and a new spirit; for why will you die, house of Israel? For I have no pleasure in the death, says God; wherefore turn yourselves, and live.

Ezekiel 18:21–23, 30–32

Avinu Malkeinu, Graciously Answer Us, Even Though We Are Without Merit....

After chanting a litany of requests for God's assistance and forgiveness we end with the verse *"Avinu Malkeinu, honeinu v'aneinu, ki ein banu ma'asim. Aseh imanu tzedakah v'hesed v'hoshiyanu."* This is translated in our *Mahzor* as "Our Creator, Our Sovereign be gracious with us and respond to us, for we have no deeds to justify us; deal with us in righteousness and love, and save us now." Of course, all translation is commentary, but this modern, egalitarian, politically correct translation is similar to most of the traditional translations in intent. The Silverman *Mahzor*, with which many of us from Conservative backgrounds grew up, translates this as "Our Father, Our King, be Thou gracious unto us and answer us; for lo! We are unworthy; deal Thou with us in

charity and loving-kindness and save us." It is this translation that troubled me from the moment when I first thought that I understood what
it was saying. "God, please be good to us and answer our prayers even
though we are worthless and undeserving. But please treat us with
charity and kindness regardless of that fact and save us anyway." This
was not a sentiment that I wanted to associate with my Judaism. I
didn't want to accept the idea that Judaism believed that human beings
are basically worthless. First of all, that contradicts the teaching that we
are each created in God's image. Secondly, if we are basically worthless then why bother doing *Teshuvah*, since inevitably we're just going
to mess up again.

In struggling with this verse I realized that the translation can also
simply read "Our Parent, Our Sovereign, be gracious to us and answer
us for there are no deeds within us." While struggling to find a new
interpretation within me that could help me to understand and accept
the underlying meaning of this prayer I came across Alan Lew's discussion of this verse in his book *[This Is Real and You Are Completely
Unprepared]*. Basically, what Lew (who is a long time practitioner of
Zen Buddhism as well as a rabbi) says is that the verse means that no
matter what deeds we have done, no matter how much preparation
we have done for *Teshuvah*, when the moment arrives to face God, ourselves and those whom we have harmed we are utterly unprepared. It is
as if we are completely empty. We have nothing in us. We are a spiritual
tabula rasa. As the title of his book says "this is real, and you are completely unprepared." The act of *Teshuvah* is about as real as it gets,
and no pre-planning or prior deeds can help us. It all goes out the
window. The only thing that matters at that moment is that moment
itself and what we do with it. Our house has been laid waste. The constructs and facades on which we all build and rebuild our lives each
and every day are gone. The ground beneath us has either disappeared
or is constantly shifting. We only have ourselves and now we must do
what we must do. This is also as frightening as it gets. But remember,
the prayer is stated in the plural and must be chanted in community. So
even though *Teshuvah* is ultimately an individual act, the fact that we
are doing it in a communal context can give us strength.

Rabbi Steven Nathan

Avinu Malkeinu: Graciously Answer Us, Even Though We Are Without Merits

The Talmud tells us that Alexander the Great, in one of his travels to conquer other lands, once came to a river. When he drank the water, he felt like a new man; after bathing in the river, he felt totally refreshed. Alexander decided to find the source of the river. He followed it until he came to a gate. He knocked on the gate and asked to enter.

A voice answered: "This is the gate of *Gan Eden* (Paradise). Only the righteous may enter." Alexander asked to be given something from there. He was given a human eye. When he arrived back, he asked the Jewish sages for an explanation.

"Put the eye on one side of a scale and gold on the other side," they told him. When Alexander did this, the eye tipped the scale. He added more and more gold on the other side, yet the eye still weighed more. "Can anything outweigh the eye?" Alexander asked. "Take off the gold and put some earth on the scale," the sages told him. As soon as he did this, the earth tipped the scale.

"What's the meaning of this?" asked Alexander. The sages answered: "As long as one is alive, the eye is never satisfied. As much as it sees, it always wants more. Yet a little earth (death) takes away all its desires." This was meant as a lesson to Alexander who was never satisfied, and desired to conquer the entire world.

For how many of us is our only merit our yearning to achieve power and to conquer wealth? Perhaps that is the meaning of the last line of *Avinu Malkenu—"kee ayn banu maasim."*

D.P.E.

Avinu Malkenu: With Compassion and with Favor

Avinu Malkenu.... Accept our prayer with compassion and favor. Ordinarily a father is associated with the quality of compassion, as Scripture says: "As a father has compassion on his children" (Psalms 103:13).

On the other hand, "favor" is connected to a King, since it is the will of the sovereign to decide whether a petition will be granted.

Thus we pray, *"Avinu Malkenu"*—we ask God in both roles, as Father and as King, to accepted our prayer: As a father, "with compassion," and as a King, "with favor."

Hafetz Hayyim

Avinu Malkenu

Avinu Malkenu is perhaps the best known and loved prayer of the High Holiday liturgy, certainly one of the most evocative melodies of the season. The simple phrase *"avinu, malkenu"* describes the complexity of our relationship with God.

We relate to God, first of all, as *Avinu,* as our Parent. Just as our parents want the best for us, offering us unconditional love and forgiveness, so, too, do we experience God as being on our side and constantly rooting for us. Paralleling our relationship with God, we may question our parents' decisions, but we do cede to them ultimate authority. It is part of Judaism's uniqueness and greatness that the attempt to understand God's will has been raised to the level of a spiritual value, as our holy books recall the generations of teachers who have struggled to interpret God's word. Even when our response is less than enthusiastic, we firmly believe that God will hear our pleas for atonement and reconciliation.

However, at the High Holiday season, we see God more in the aspect of sovereign, as our Ruler, *Malkenu.* As a Ruler, God has the right to demand unquestioning obedience to the Divine will. It was Rabbi Akiva who first employed this phrase while officiating at a special service to intercede for rain during a period of drought. He was so successful in his mission, that the people locked on to the formula *"Avinu, Malkenu"* as especially efficacious.

The rest, as they say, is history. In typical Jewish fashion, the prayer has taken on a life of its own. While Rabbi Akiva's version contained only five lines, the prayer has been expanded by numerous *hazzanim* articulating the particular needs of their own communities. The Sefardic version has 29 lines, the Ashkenazi 38, and a Polish rite contains 44. The great nineteenth-century liturgist Seligman Isaac Baer testifies to having seen as many as 53 variants in the texts he reviewed.

We include *Avinu Malkenu* in the prayer service following the *Amidah* on Rosh Hashanah and Yom Kippur, and at the morning and evening services throughout the *Aseret Y'mei Teshuva,* the Ten Days of Repentance. Some scholars have suggested that we do not include it on Shabbat because of its correspondence to the weekday *Amidah,* while others suggest that it is excluded because of its petitionary nature. On Shabbat we feel especially close to God, secure in the knowledge that God is well aware of our needs without our having to articulate a "laundry list."

Indeed, we do ask for many things in this prayer. We pray for God's help as we seek repentance, we ask for a good year in general, for healing for all who are ill, for physical sustenance and for redemption, and we ask these things while acknowledging in the concluding verse that *"eyn banu ma-asim,"* we have an insufficient quantity of good deeds to override the verdict against us, therefore we rely on God's grace and lovingkindness to save us.

Rabbi Bonnie Koppell

Avinu Malkenu: God, Help Us Raise the Level of Your People's Jewish/Spiritual Consciousness

The *Rebbetzin* predeceased Rabbi Sholom, and he was inconsolable. In the eulogy he referred to her with all the endearing terms found in the Song of Songs: "My dove, my perfect mate, my sister, my partner in building the holy synagogue." When the *tzaddik* of Sanz came to see Rabbi Sholom after the thirty days of mourning were over, he found, him weeping as though it were the first day of the shivah. The *tzaddik* asked, "My teacher, is it permissible to continue to mourn so bitterly?"

"I am weeping for the greater spirituality I could have achieved if she had lived on. We were one soul, and together we absorbed the spirit of *chassidus.* Together we built the holy Sanctuary."

Rabbi Sholom paused to catch his breath, then continued. "When I cry for the wife of my youth, I say to God, 'If only I had the capability to restore her to life, nothing would stand in my way. But I am a frail human being, so powerless and helpless. But You, O God, are all powerful. We are Your chosen people, we are the wife of Your youth. We have been buried by repeated persecutions, and it is well within Your ability to restore us to life, to the glory of our youth. You can resurrect us, with the Redemption of *Mashiach*. Why do You not do so?'

"And God said to me, 'If My people were as totally devoted to Me as your wife was to you, I would indeed bring about their redemption promptly.'" And with this, Rabbi Sholom wept even more, but this time not for the loss of his beloved wife, but for the downtrodden state of his people, whose elevation to glory lies in their hands, and they fail to take advantage of it.

Rabbi Abraham J. Twerski, M.D.

When God Answers Yes

"But the Lord was wrathful with me on your account
and would not listen to me. The Lord said to me,
Enough, never speak to Me of this matter again."

DEUTERONOMY 3:26

I know a man who will never set foot in synagogue. He is willing to send his child to religious school, but claims that he has no use for religion. When each of his parents was sick, he prayed for their full recovery. And each time his prayers went unanswered. Both parents passed away. The man told me that if God is going to answer "no," then he has no use for such a God. So this man decided to boycott God.

He is not the first to be answered by a "no" by God. Long ago Moses prayed to God, and actually begged God to let him into the Promised Land. God's answer was a clear "no." "Never speak to Me of this matter again." If God answered our greatest prophet with a clear, uncompromising "no," why should we feel that we always deserve a "yes?" As a pundit once remarked, "God always answers our prayers. But sometimes God answers no."

Too many of us have a mistaken view about prayer. We believe that God is like a giant vending machine; put in the right change and you get the right result. Say the right prayers and God will respond in the appropriate way. That is one reason people request me to pray for them. They believe that as a rabbi, I know the right words to elicit the right response from God. Prayer is a kind of magic, a way that we can control the universe. So many of us believe that by saying the right words, we can control God.

Perhaps it is time to explore the real meaning of prayer. The Hebrew word for prayer, *tefilah*, comes from the root, *lehitpalel*, literally "to judge yourself." Prayer is not something we do to God, but something we do to ourselves. Prayer connects us to the spiritual dimension of life. And through that spiritual connection, we can change ourselves. In other words, prayer is a way to change us. And when we change for the better, it is as if God answered "yes."

When we are going through a difficult time and we pray to God for the serenity to cope with adversity, then God answers "yes."

When we are coping with difficult people in our lives and we pray for understanding and patience, then God answers "yes."

When we face a challenge in our lives and pray for courage to confront whatever we may face, then God answers "yes."

When we must make a difficult decision and pray for wisdom to make the correct choice, then God answers "yes."

When we face temptation and pray for the self-discipline to say no to ourselves, then God answers "yes."

When we must make an ethical choice and pray for the strength of character to do the right thing, then God answers "yes."

When we have a God-given talent and we pray for the ability to develop that talent, then God answers "yes."

When life has been good to us and we pray for a sense of gratitude and appreciation, then God answers "yes."

When life has been difficult and we pray for the inner strength to keep going, then God answers "yes."

When sadness envelops us, and we pray for the ability to walk calmly through the valley of the shadow of death, then God answers "yes."

God does answer yes. But we need to know how to pray, and what prayer really is supposed to accomplish. If we pray to try to change God, then there is a good chance that God will answer "no." If we pray to change ourselves, then there is a good chance that God will answer "yes." We humans have the unique ability to touch the spiritual dimension of existence and walk away transformed. Prayer is a means to renew ourselves.

Rabbi Michael Gold

Cleansed with Tears

Reb Elimelech and Reb Zusya had a third brother—a village tavern-keeper. Now would it not be interesting to find out what manner of man this was? Surely he was no common fellow! Fired by curiosity, the disciples of Reb Elimelech decided one day to make the journey to his village, in order to find out for themselves. There, sure enough, they found him—standing foursquare behind the counter of his tavern, selling vodka to the surly yokels of the province. There was certainly no hint here of any spiritual flights to the lofty Worlds Above. All they noticed was that from time to time he took out his little notebook and wrote a few words in it.

The bar was closed at nightfall, and they asked to sleep in the inn. Then, late at night, when the household was fast asleep, they listened in from the room adjoining his, and heard him turning pages and reading to himself, from time to time striking himself on the chest, and weeping bitterly all the while.

Overcome by inquisitiveness, they walked right into his room and asked: "How is it that a man should strike himself?"

Their host answered them simply that this was his regular custom. Every day, whenever it seemed to him that he had sinned in some way, or that an unholy thought had crossed his mind, he noted this in his little notebook. Then, when night came, he would never go to sleep until he had repented with a *teshuvah* that came from the bottom of his heart. And he even had a sign by which he could know whether his repentance had been found acceptable in the eyes of Heaven. For when he saw that the ink in his notebook was blotted out by his tears, then he knew that in Heaven too his sins had been erased.

Rabbi S. Y. Zevin

ROOTS AND THEMES FROM THE TORAH

Judaism's openness to continuing religious creativity turns on the notion of the rabbis' authority to interpret the text. Since that authority itself comes from Sinai, it cannot be questioned. But the process of interpretation opens the text to multiple readings: Aggadic *(aggadah)*, halakhic *(halakhah)*, grammatical, philosophic, and mystical currents of thought have all been applied to Torah throughout the ages. These add constant new levels of richness and subtlety to our understanding of it. In this way Judaism remains a highly faithful text-based tradition without becoming fundamentalist, since each text is always open to a multitude of interpretations. "The Torah has seventy faces" is a well-known saying, meaning that there are a great many legitimate ways to understand the same verse. Literalism is generally not privileged over other ways of reading.

RABBI ARTHUR GREEN, *THESE ARE THE WORDS*

A Sacred Occasion

God spoke to Moses, saying: Speak the following to the children of
Israel: In the seventh month, on the first day of the month, you will
observe complete rest, a sacred occasion commemorated with loud
blasts. You will not work at your occupations; and you will bring an
offering by fire to Adonai.

Leviticus 23:23–25

In the seventh month, on the first day of the month, you will observe
a sacred occasion: you should not work at your occupations. Observe it
as a day when the shofar is sounded. Present a burnt offering of pleasing odor to God: one bull of the herd, one ram, and seven yearling
lambs, without blemish. The meal offering with them will be choice
flour with oil mixed in: three-tenths of a measure for a bull, two-tenths
for a ram, and one-tenth for each of the seven lambs. And there shall be
one goat for a sin offering, to make expiation on your behalf, along
with the burnt offering of the new moon with its meal offering and
the regular burnt offering with its meal offering, each with its libation
as prescribed, offerings by fire of pleasing odor to God.

Numbers 29:1–6

Sarah's Song

Why did I keep silent? Why did I not speak
When I saw the smoke and fire in your father's eyes?
I stood in anguished silence waiting for some word,
A word I heard from angels' mouths who mocked me in old
 . age.
  Steal him away you prowler in the night,
  Fly away; flee before my silence breaks.
  I lied for greater glory in a great king's camp.
  I offered up my body against the enemy's sword.
Once I was a woman praised in her generation,
Who thought all things possible were my right.
I voiced the arrogance of heart;
The danger of abject contempt.
  No child for me in vibrant youth

When arms were strong to carry him in joy.
In old age my sealed womb parted
And swelled my breasts to bursting.
Now I have my son—my only son—
Child of my laughter, child of my dreams.
How dare they take you from me across the desert sands?
To a place of smoke and fire, to Moriah's ancient spire?
Who will draw the first drop and who will weep the
most?
And who will take her vengeance on the father of the
child?
And who dares the Father of a promised nation born?
I stand on my Moriah and challenge You, Creator,
To shed Your immortal immunity;
To discard Your awesome power.
I faced my husband's darkling fear,
Defying angels who listened to me laugh.
Now rise up women of silence, sing a new song.
With voices echoing over time, make known
How, with strength of heart we mastered God and men;
With strength of love we forged a covenant of hope.

Michael Halperin

Memory and New Beginnings

Why do we read Genesis 21, the poignant paired stories of Isaac's birth
to Sarah and Abraham and the exile of Hagar and Ishmael, on the first
day of Rosh Hashanah? Why, on a festival celebrating God's creation of
the world, do Jews beseech God for favorable judgment by reminding
ourselves of a narrative in which the privilege of divine destiny exacts
such a painful price?

The Rosh Hashanah liturgy, constructed around *Malkhuyot,
Zikhronot* and *Shofarot,* God's sovereignty, remembrance, and the
sounding of the shofar, provides a template for supplicants to contemplate relationship with God. However, we can only enter the covenantal space by first squaring our relationships with our fellow human
beings. *Teshuva,* the process of repentance and return, resembles psychotherapy in its demand that individuals reconstruct an emotional and
historical accounting of personal experience.

The narrative in which God remembers and fulfills God's promise that Abraham will be the father of a great nation opens by naming Sarah three times. Abraham can only become the patriarch through his relationship with Sarah. Miraculously, the aged couple conceives Isaac. Immediately after describing Isaac's weaning feast, the text turns ominous as Sarah demands that Hagar and Ishmael be banished. Abraham's joy vanishes as he sends his concubine and their son into the wilderness.

Just as Abraham must for the rest of his life bear the responsibility for sending away his eldest son, so too must we recall and examine our own actions. Reconstruction of personal narrative does not alone suffice, rather it is a necessary prelude to restitution and hopefully even reconciliation. Only after acknowledging the complexities of our hearts and shouldering the responsibility to make amends for thoughts, speech and actions that cause hurt to others, can we truly stand in the heavenly court and hear the triumphant cry of the shofar.

Michelle Friedman, MD

Opening Our Eyes

The text says not that a well suddenly appeared, but that Hagar's eyes were opened so that she could now see it. The miracle is spiritual rather than physical or supernatural. The well had always been there, but Hagar, paralyzed by fear, despair, and her own sense of powerlessness, was blinded to the possibility of salvation. In calling out to God, she finds the strength to discover what she needs to do. Only then does Hagar see the well.

Hagar's example can serve as a comfort and an inspiration when the pain and difficulty of our own lives seem too overwhelming, when taking the next step seems impossible. We are reminded that there are always unseen possibilities. As we call out in prayer during the *Yamim Nora'im*, we, too, can reorient our vision, see new possibilities in our lives and adjust our attitudes and actions.

Rabbi Rami Shapiro

The Importance of Children

One aspect of the service on Rosh Hashanah never ceases to fill me with wonder. Rosh Hashanah is the anniversary of creation. *Hayom harat olam,* we say in our prayers: "Today the world was born." What then would we expect to find as the biblical readings for the day? From the Torah, the opening of *Bereishit.* "In the beginning G-d created ..." And for the haftorah? What better than the last two chapters of Isaiah, "Behold I will create new heavens and a new earth"?

Opening the *machzor* we find that this answer is logical but wrong. Instead, on the first day, we read the story of the birth of Isaac, and in the haftorah, about the birth of Samuel. Two stories of great women— Sarah and Hannah—who longed to have children, but could not, and were then blessed by G-d.

Why these two stories? Beautiful, certainly. But what is their connection with Rosh Hashanah? The answer tells us much about the humane, counter-intuitive vision at the heart of Jewish life.

The famous Mishnah in *Sanhedrin* states (Steven Spielberg used it in his film *Schindler's List*) that a single life is like a universe. "One who destroys a life is as if he destroyed a universe. One who saves a life is as if he saved a universe." The birth of a human life is like the birth of the universe. Rosh Hashanah is the festival of creation, and if you want to understand the ethical implications of creation, don't study astro-physics. Think of the birth of a child.

Throughout the centuries, Judaism has been the great child-centered civilization. Only once does the Torah tell us why Abraham was chosen: "So that he will instruct his children and his household after him to keep the way of the Lord." Abraham was chosen for the sake of his children.

On the brink of the exodus, Moses gathers the people and addresses them (Exodus 12–13). He speaks about none of the things we would expect—freedom, the journey, the land of milk and honey. Instead he speaks three times about children: "And you shall tell your child on that day ... "

Children have been the casualties of our age. In the West they have suffered from the breakdown of marriage and the exploitations of a consumer culture. In Ossetia a year ago they were the victims of terror. They have even been trained in the Middle East to become terrorists, suicide bombers, themselves. The voices of protest, sadly, have been too few.

There are cultures that live in the present. Eventually, inevitably, they lose their way. There are cultures that live in the past. Nursing grievances, they seek revenge. Judaism is a supreme example of a culture that, while celebrating the present and honoring the past, lives for the future—for its children.

If I were to choose one Jewish message for the world in these tense times, I would say: forget power, pride, violence, revenge, wealth, prestige, honor, acclaim—and instead ask, Will our next act make the world a little better for our children?

That is the message of Rosh Hashanah—the day on which, to understand the universe, we think about the birth of a child.

                                                    Rabbi Jonathan Sacks

Are You an Abraham or a Hannah?

On Rosh Hashanah we juxtapose the stories of Abraham and Hannah. Both stories are about being granted, and then sacrificing, a much yearned for child. But the tone and style of the two stories are in sharp contrast.

When God bluntly commands Abraham to sacrifice his son, so miraculously born to old age, Abraham immediately springs into action, bringing Isaac to the site, tying him to the altar, and raising the knife for the slaughter. There is no indication of what Abraham thinks or feels about this terrifying command.

In contrast, the story of Hannah resonates with sorrow and despair. The only thing Hannah does is weep and pray, her lips barely moving. There is no action, only a pain and longing that reverberate through the text. The culmination of her prayer is a vow to God that if granted a son she will give him up after weaning. Unlike Abraham, the impulse to sacrifice her child does not come from the outside, but from an intense, internal process.

What is more precious than a child born after years of yearning? Both Hannah and Abraham experience this miraculous gift, and both arrive at the same spiritual insight—that even that which is most precious, is but a fleeting gift of God. It is an insight we all strive for—to revel in the gift of the moment precisely because it is so ephemeral, can be reclaimed at any time. But Abraham and Hannah arrive at this insight through different paths. Abraham's is the path of external action; Hannah's is the path of internal focus. The stories are caricatures of contrasting spiritual styles.

Most of us lean more heavily towards one of these paths. Some of us, when we think of *teshuvah*, decide to take on more mitzvot; others yearn to pray with greater *kavanah*.

But perhaps the *teshuvah* we most need to do involves shifting the internal/external balance of our spiritual lives. I tend to be a Hannah, loath to engage in action unless I have internally processed its value. And yet, I know that taking on an action without thinking it through can have enormous unforeseen benefits. Sometimes I need to be an Abraham and spring thoughtlessly into action. I know this to be true, yet it is a surprisingly hard lesson to take in, because my spiritual style is so strongly to be a Hannah.

This Rosh Hashanah, if you are an Abraham, think about becoming a little more of a Hannah. If you are someone who already lights candles Friday night, instead of deciding to also do *kiddush*, think about adding five minutes of silent intention before you light the candles. On the other hand, if you are a Hannah, think about becoming a little more of an Abraham. Instead of deciding to add more time for meditation or prayer, think about adding a practice to your life that you don't really understand, and see where that journey takes you.

There is a poem by Judy Chicago which looks toward messianic times and says, " ... and then both men and women will be gentle, and then both women and men will be strong." In our spiritual lives as well, we need a balance of the male and the female, the internal and the external, the Abraham and the Hannah. The broader our range of options, the deeper our spiritual lives can be.

Rabbi Rena Blumenthal

Allowing the Hand of God to Work through Us

On the first day of Rosh Hashanah, we read in scripture the story of Sarah giving birth to Isaac. The figure of Sarah is central to the meaning of Rosh Hashanah—she is an old barren woman married to an old man who hears three mysterious men outside her tent predict that she will become pregnant. She laughs at the absurdity, even though she believes in God and divine prophecy. When she does become pregnant, she names her son Isaac, which means "laughter."

New beginnings are always unexpected. They occur at a threshold where the old is passing away and we don't yet know what is going to happen. In fact we may think that life is coming to an end, like Sarah, who believing that before her was only death, was stunned to learn that she was with child. There is little we can do to prepare for the unexpected, except to honor and celebrate the ebb and flow of life through our bodies, hearts and spirits. This is perhaps the deeper meaning of Rosh Hashanah—one of opening, and allowing the hand of God to do its works through us.

Sara Shendelman and Rabbi Avram Davis

And God Remembered Sarah: Prayers and Rituals for an Infertile Couple on Rosh Hashanah

Rosh Hashanah is the birthday of the world, a time when the air is touched with the scent of creation, a time when everything is filled with newness, hope, and possibility. It was on Rosh Hashanah, the rabbis say, that God remembered the longings of Sarah, Rachel, and Hannah (Rosh Hashanah 11a), and they conceived not long thereafter. Such an association turns Rosh Hashanah into a propitious and proper time to place our prayers for a child before God.

A Prayer for the Woman to Say on the First Night of Rosh Hashanah When She Lights the Candles

Creator of the World, You answered the prayers of our matriarchs Sarah, Rachel, and Hannah during this month of Tishrei. You listened to their pleas and opened their wombs, helped them conceive and brought them to a healthy birth. So may You answer me, too. On this, the day that celebrates the birth of the world, remember me. My God and God of my ancestors, be gracious unto me. Let me conceive this year with my beloved, and let the child who comes from this union be endowed with a soul of gentleness and holiness. Let no harm come to me all the months of my pregnancy. Let me give birth at a good time, a proper time. May my beloved and I merit the pleasure of raising our child in health and happiness, together. So may it be Your will.

A Prayer for the Couple to Say on the Second Night of Rosh Hashanah

It is a well-known Rosh Hashanah custom to take a bit of apple, dip it in honey, and ask God for a good and sweet new year. This is a remnant of an age-old tradition in which we once ate many ritual foods on Rosh Hashanah, representative of the dreams we hoped would come true in the coming year. Sometimes the connection between the food and the desire was linguistic, playing on the closeness of sounds between the name of the one and the words describing the other (as if upon eating a turnip one would say: may blessings turn up wherever I go). Sometimes the connection was found in the property of the food, like the sweetness of honey; or in the food's symbolism, as with fish and fertility, or round foods and the renewal of life. The modern couple seeking to be blessed with a child may reclaim this tradition by eating a pomegranate, a fruit storied with tales of love and fertility, and already associated with Rosh Hashanah. In many families, the pomegranate serves as the new food it is customary to eat on the second night of the New Year, enabling us to recite again the *shehecheyanu,* the blessing of appreciation, of being grateful for this moment that we are able to enjoy together.

At dinner, the husband and wife open the pomegranate and each selects a choice seed from the fruit. Before eating, the woman says: "God, as I chose a seed from this round, luscious fruit, so You too choose a seed from me. Plant it deep in my body, and give it time to grow. When it is ripe, let it spill forth from me, whole and healthy and full of life. So may it be Your will." The man says:

"God, as I chose a seed from this round, red fruit, may You choose to join my seed with my wife's. Let the joy of our love mingle and bring forth fruit of its own. This year, may we be blessed with a child. So may it be Your will."

Barukh ata adonai eloheinu melekh ha'olam, borei pri ha'eitz.

Blessed are You, God of all creation, who creates the fruit of the tree.

Barukh ata adonai eloheinu melekh ha olam, shehecheyanu, v'kiyimanu, v'higiyanu laz'man hazeh.

Blessed are You, God of all creation, who has sustained us, cared for us, and brought us to this moment.

New Year's Compote—Second Night

Pink grapefruits, navel oranges, and pomegranates combine to make a Rosh Hashanah version of a classic Ashkenazi dessert: compote. The fruit of the New Year blends with comfortable memories of our grandmothers' kitchens, serving up helpings of hope and connection. Cut citrus fruit into bite-size pieces. Roll the pomegranate between your hands to soften. Open it and add the seeds to the fruit slices. In a saucepan, combine white wine and sherry with brown sugar and honey to desired sweetness. Heat mixture until the sugar is dissolved. Scoop the fruit into a bowl and cover with the syrup. Serve cold.

Rabbi Nina Beth Cardin

Hearing the Silent Scream: And God Heard the Voice of the Boy

I open the still crisp pages of the *Mahzor*
and look at the *parsha* selected for Day One of Rosh Hashannah
the first day of the New Year,
the Day the World comes into Being again.
And the conversation begins.
It is Ishmael's story that we read—
first born, beloved of our ancestor Avraham,
cast out due to familial conflict,
along with his mother Hagar
to die in the wilderness, too young to form any words

"And God heard the voice of the child where he was."
The text does not mention that Ishmael cried out,
only that his mother Hagar did.
Yet God does not respond to her,
but the "voice of the child."

According to Rebbe Menachem Mendel of Vurkah
the text hints to us that although Ishmael did not cry out
    openly,
his heart screamed inside him with a silent scream
that only the Holy One could distinguish.
On this day—what voices do we listen to
that have no form,

that are beyond words,
speechless shouts,
silent screams,
the stilled small voice.
Who will discern the pulse of the hidden heart
that has lodged in our throats?
As we struggle to cry out,
to allow the broken heart to be
without rushing in to mend it too quickly,
let us find You as the Source of our outrage and compassion,
bewilderment, shock and sorrow, and let us not be consumed.

Ishmael, it is your story we read today,
this first day of a New Year.
Are you here to remind us that even if you were sent away,
seen as Avraham's first born,
but not the inheritor of our lineage,
that you are our teacher too?
Do you come to us as the Torah of the day
to defy all inhumane action?
Left to die under a tree,
God heard you in your silence.

Perhaps the questions can suffice for now
as we move through these next ten days of *teshuvah*
    consciousness.
As we look to each other,
we may become the eyes, ears and hearts
of the Source of Life coursing through us—
we may be able to hear the silent screams
beneath the functional exterior and the "getting-on-with-it."
Then we ourselves can become
like the angel was for Ishmael
showing his mother a well of water
springing up beside her.
We can become a hand to direct someone
to a fountain of support,
a comforting glance or embrace,
a knowing wordless look
that speaks volumes of tenderness.

We are the blessings waiting
to be shared with each other in these days to come.
Life's fragility
has perhaps never been more apparent
than in this moment.
Hear the silent cry we all hold—
and may the Source
that is Life itself,
be witnessed in our listening.

Rabbi Shawn Israel Zevit

Sacred Questions

As the sanctuary fills with people, look around. Each person who enters carries the sacred story of his or her life. We all enter with the promising and uplifting pieces as well as the scary and scarring parts of our complex narratives. If you are experiencing or have ever suffered emotional, verbal, physical, or sexual abuse, you know that you are not alone. Statistically, someone else entering this sanctuary has a similar story. If you have never confronted this violence through your own history or a friend's, you will meet someone who has faced this cruelty. This Rosh Hashanah you will meet Hagar, who we will bring into the sanctuary through the reading of the Torah. She faced abuse including her attempted murder.

Abuse existed in our tradition even before we were a Jewish people. Hagar repeatedly was a victim. The rabbis in *Genesis Rabbah,* a fifth-century text, believe that Sarai controlled Hagar sexually, abused her physically, and/or forced her to do strenuous work as the text states:

> R. Abba said: She restrained her from cohabitation. R. Berekiah said she slapped her face with a slipper. R. Berekiah said in R. Abba's name: She bade her carry her water buckets and bath towels to the baths.

She tries to leave this abusive situation, but the divine messenger, after some inquiry, sends her back.

On Rosh Hashanah we meet Hagar at the height of her oppression. She is a woman cast out into the desert with only a little bread and a skin of water. Could she be a person in our congregation? What is our responsibility to her? Is our synagogue leadership able to hear her story and direct her to resources when she cries for help? When she goes to the bathroom will she find phone numbers that could help save and improve her life and the life of her child/ren? Is there someone who can help her if she is no longer in an abusive situation but has flashbacks from previous unholy holy days? When the Jewish values of "forgiveness" and *"teshuvah"* are presented, are they delivered in the complex and sensitive nature they deserve so they do not alienate congregants who have/are suffered/ing?

I have just asked a lot of questions. Do we learn to question in our congregations? Are our questions valued? As the New Year begins, we need to encourage questions and help students of all ages learn to develop all sorts of questions and learn that they are valued. This questioning needs to occur, not just at Passover and not just regarding text and theology, but about the way we live our lives. If people have the ability to question and know that their questions are worthwhile perhaps they can use these skills to help identify difficult situations that otherwise might seem normal, and then use the same strategy of questions to help themselves seek help. Through a question, answer, and action process we can also ensure that our sanctuaries are safe places for our congregants and places where they can effectively seek help. Persevere in questioning. If you do not find the answer, help, or response you need in one source, keep looking. Go door to door. Hagar left two times. The first time she was told to go back—the second time, after incredible suffering, she and her son were free.

God, this year may we find the courage to seek the help we need. May we speak up against abuse and violence in our community. May we not be afraid to question and get involved. This year will be a year of change. Praised are you God, who hears our prayers.

Rachel Schwartz

Who Is Holding Whom?

When Avraham sends Hagar and her son Yishmael out into the desert, at the behest of jealous Sarah, Hagar cannot bear to watch the pain of her son.

An angel appears and advises her: "Fear not, for God has heard the cry of the lad.... " *"Hahaziki et yadaykh bo"*—"Come, lift up the boy and hold him by the hand."

Rabbi Harold Kushner translates the Hebrew words literally and sees an important lesson about life in this verse. Here is how he translates the words, *"Hahaziki et yadaykh bo"*—"Give yourself strength through him!" *"Hahaziki et yadaykh"*— "strengthen your own hand," *"bo"*—by helping him.

Explains Rabbi Kushner, famous author of *When Bad Things Happen to Good People* and many other popular books, that when you feel bad things coming your way, the most healthy response is to focus your attention on those who are also in need of help. By helping others, you turn away from self-pity and give yourself a purpose to carry on. Hagar can find the strength to survive the ordeal of the desert and of her son's trauma, by doing something constructive for Yishmael—and thus, for herself!

D.P.E.

God Accepts Our Newer Selves: Genesis 21:1

It is not surprising that Genesis 21 is read on Rosh Hashanah. This chapter begins with the powerful, though profoundly simply words, *"And God remembered Sarah ... as God had promised to do so"* (Genesis 21:1). Remembering is the major motif on Rosh Hashanah. We pray that God will also remember us, even as we remember how we have treated others.

These stories remind us that our tradition believes in the efficaciousness of prayer, i.e., prayer can be answered. But what about those people who find it hard to believe that a supernatural entity listens to us and stands ready to answer our prayers? The solution to that dilemma is found in Rambam's interpretation of the *Teshuvah* repentance process. Rambam teaches us that our prayers, reflections on the year past, apologies to those we have harmed, and acts of *Tzedakah,* do not effect a change in God. They effect a change in us. Think of prayer and *Teshuvah* as ontological experiences, something which changes our entire state of being.

One cannot ignore the troubling story of the expulsion of Hagar and Ishmael. The account of Hagar's travail was written to elicit our sympathy. It suggests that God has a game plan and that things are not as arbitrary as they might seem. We are reminded that the younger brother has been chosen over the older one. This happens repeatedly in the biblical narratives. Rather than birth order, a son's character determines his worthiness to inherit the blessing promised to his father.

Despite the fact that both Hagar and Ishmael tormented Sarah and Isaac, God hears Hagar's prayer. She is told, "Fear not Hagar for God has heard the cry of the child from where he is" (Genesis 21:17). The last three words seem superfluous. From where else could God hear that voice? It had come from where Ishmael was. The Midrash believes those three words are a hint to us. The angels argued that Ishmael should be allowed to die because his progeny would kill countless Jews. But according to the Midrash, at this moment Ishmael had repented and was worthy of being saved. God responded that every individual is judged on the basis of where they are now, not on the basis of what they or their progeny will do. Therein is the lesson to us; we need not have a perfect past or future as we approach God in prayer. If we are sincere God will hear us based on where we are *now*, not where we will be in the future.

When God rescues Hagar the text says that *God opened Hagar's eyes.* So too may our eyes be opened so that we can see what we must do to make our lives a blessing for ourselves and others.

Dr. Deborah E. Lipstadt

Genesis 21 and 22: Two Versions of the Same Story

The Torah reading for the first day of Rosh HaShanah is chapter 21 of Genesis. I have always wondered why we read this chapter on Rosh HaShanah. The fact that it precedes the *Akedah* in chapter 22, read on the second day of Rosh HaShanah, has never been a satisfying answer for me. There must be something about chapter 21 that makes it especially appropriate for Rosh HaShanah in the same way that the *Akedah* reflects the challenges and angst of the Day of Judgment.

Perhaps they are not two different chapters but rather different versions of the same story. In both chapters Abraham is asked to sacrifice his son. In both chapters he rises up early in the morning in order to fulfill his task (21:14; 22:3). And finally, in both chapters the son is saved by an angel of God calling forth out of heaven (21:17; 22:11, 15). The angel is sent, in both cases, by a merciful God agreeing to lessen the severity of the original decree which Abraham set out to fulfill.

In one case Abraham is asked to ritually slaughter his son, while in the other case he sets him off on his way with his mother. Abraham gives Hagar and Ishmael "bread and water" which does not last long in the desert. The narration gives the impression that had not the angel intervened, Ishmael would have died. Setting a child off with rations for but a day was a form of ancient "passive" infanticide. Sometimes the unwanted mother and child were each set on "their way" where it was assumed they would meet their end. A colorful example of this is the Greek myth of Telaphos, which is illustrated as a magnificent frieze that surrounded the inner courtyard of the Pergamon altar. This temple from Asia Minor (Turkey) can be seen magnificently reconstructed in the newly re-opened Pergamon Museum in Berlin. Telaphos, a minor character in Greek mythology, serves as the "patron-saint"—to borrow another culture's terminology—of the Hellenistic city of Pergamon, and so the temple freeze tells the myth. I bring this to light because the myth begins with a king learning from an oracle that his wife will give birth to a son who will do harm to the father, which is parallel to the beginning of the Oedipus myth. To protect himself, the father sends mother and son off into the wilderness so that they might perish, although they are saved by divine intervention. The image of mother and child sent into the wilderness was a loaded image for the ancient reader, no less so than ritual slaughter. We must not lose sight of that implication.

If we read the two chapters as variant versions of child sacrifice, we should also note the acute differences. In chapter 21 Abraham is troubled (21:11) whereas in chapter 22 we are given no hint of Abraham's emotions. In chapter 21 the separation of father and son is explained as an unfortunate outcome of family strife, whereas in chapter 22 there is no family beyond the two principals. In chapter 21 God must mediate between failed relationships, whereas in chapter 22 there is no struggle, no joy and no regret—only obedience.

While Islamic tradition identifies Ishmael as the child of the *Akedah* and Isaac as the rejected son, our tradition, at least in this ancient form, preserves both as tales of Abraham's requirement to give up his son in order so that the son may go on to receive God's legacy. Both accounts end with the son's survival and eventual marriage (21:21; 22:23, which relates the birth of Rebekkah). Thus, in both cases the father must give up patronage of the son so that the son can achieve his destiny as determined by God.... I suggest that we can understand both stories as a complex meditation on the nature of divine justice. All Abraham would have liked would have been to grow old with a son by his side. Yet twice he must give up a son to die. Abraham understands that it is God's decision whether or not to grant him his "reward." Both sons are saved miraculously, although in both cases the pain of Abraham's action could not have easily been forgotten. And they are saved for the sake of God's plan, not their own or their father's happiness.

On the Day of Judgment we are asked to stand as Abraham. We must recognize that we may at any time be "asked" to give up what is dear. We are challenged with the realization that nothing really belongs to us, and that we are given another year of life only by divine pardon. We pray that we may merit that pardon and find our own place in God's world.

Rabbi David J. Fine

The *Akedah:* Giving Freely

The *Akedah,* the binding of Isaac, is a story fundamental to our tradition. It is found in our daily liturgy, we read it on Rosh Hashanah, and then again in the yearly Torah reading. It's a story we stumble over again and again, an endlessly provocative story. A story that's been disturbing me my whole life, it only bothers me more since I've become a mother. Why would God command the sacrifice of a child? I may temporarily achieve a flash of understanding using one commentary or another, but still I don't ever fully grasp it. This is a story whose mystery is not to be exhausted.

Nevertheless, I will try again to understand the story using a *midrash* from *Genesis Rabbah,* one that Rashi picks up on, to wrestle with its meaning yet again.

Consider this comment on Genesis 22:12 using a midrash from *Genesis Rabbah:*

Look God, I will explain to you my gripe [Abraham said], Yesterday you said to me "in Isaac you will have offspring named for you" then you came back and said, "take please my son" and now you say "do not do anything to the boy"!

The Holy One Blessed Be He said: "I will not desecrate my covenant, and what emerged from my lips I will not change" (Ps. 89:35). When I said, "go take him," "what emerged from my lips I will not change." I didn't say to you "go slaughter him," rather "take him up." Now that you've taken him up, put him down!

The *midrash* turns the story completely around. God emphatically reassures Abraham that God has been consistent all along. Abraham has misunderstood God. And, moreover, the reader has misunderstood the story. It's as if someone would say, "Go jump in the lake" and when confronted concerning their rudeness their response would be "Well, I only suggested you to go for a nice refreshing swim." It's the phenomenon sometimes referred to in film as *gas lighting*—being told that the reality you know doesn't exist by a person you trust and love. It's crazy making. The more you trust the person, the crazier you become.

For the sake, it seems, of God's consistency, we are not to believe the plain meaning of what we just read. Are we, then, to believe that this story is all about miscommunication—this story of ultimate sacrifice whose mystery is at the heart of our tradition?

I can think of a number of ways we might understand this *midrash*. The Rabbis, post the failed *Bar Cochba* rebellion, were frightened by the kind of religious zeal that would lead one to sacrifice one's son. Thus, with the powerfully transformative tool of exegesis they radically tame the story. They take the edge off, and the knife out. Rather than a story about being willing to kill for God it becomes a story about being willing to serve God peacefully.

Alternatively, reading the *Akedah* according to this midrash, I ask if Abraham has misheard God's command, what was in the way of his listening accurately? Why would he hear a command to slaughter in a simple command to raise up his son?

Perhaps Abraham was making a mistake, a common mistake made in the course of our most important relationships. We often misunderstand the voices of those we are most intimate with, hearing echoes of a harsher voice from the past, voices that drown out the reality of the present. Instead of hearing the gentle voice of our beloved or a trusted colleague, we hear a critical demanding voice belonging to another time and place. And we act on that misunderstanding in a way that can reinforce our mistaken belief. Instead of a modulated measured request we might hear in the voice of the other the unconditional demand "Give me everything. Do the impossible. Destroy your life for my sake, I will take nothing less." We then resist, or perhaps we withhold, pretending to give what we believe is required, but, after all, giving nothing in response. Or, maybe, in a misguided act of protest, we set out to destroy ourselves as we believe has been commanded.

If, then, the *Akedah* developed in a cultural context of human sacrifice, as some scholars claim, perhaps Abraham hears the divine voices that guided him *before* the God of the Israelites revealed himself to Abraham (I use "him" because the God of the Bible is a male character). He is hearing the divine voices from an earlier period in his life that drown out the strange, unfamiliar voice of Abraham's new God. While the voice of God is not tentative, Abraham's hearing might be— a hearing, that is, weakened by what he is used to and by the sheer fear of the unknown God. What he hears then is the unspoken command to sacrifice his son echoing from a distant time and place.

But, as it turns out, Abraham was utterly wrong about who his new God was. He was confusing this God with the gods of the past. When God told him to take up his son, he heard "kill your son." But that wasn't it at all. This God is not a God who demands the lives of our children.

If I were to end this *drash* here I would say it was about love. And I would cite Rashi again. Abraham saddles his own donkey in order to embark on his journey to sacrifice his son. Rashi is troubled by this and cites the rabbinic idea of *Ahavah mikalkel et hashurah*, Love upsets the natural order of things. Perhaps it is love that allows us to emerge from the past, which might appear like the "natural order of things" into the radical newness of what is real and present.

And I will, after all, end this *drash* here. And I will say that what this *midrash* teaches us, after all, is this: If we truly heard the gentle and loving voice of a divine or human other reminding us that giving does not have to be annihilating, we might then give more freely. Only in trusting the other not to destroy or require destruction, would the possibilities of gifts freely offered multiply.

Were we to listen to this lesson the command, the demand in our own psyches might be transformed. Instead of hearing the internal destructive voices we might hear these words instead:

"Take please your son, your only son, the one you love, and go, raise him up, hold him high up and show him to me, for he is beautiful. Raising him up is all the thanks offering I need. And put that knife down!"

Rabbi Dianne Cohler-Esses

God Tested Abraham: Our Moral Senses Are Tested Again and Again

God tested Abraham by requesting the sacrifice of his son Isaac. If this test is understood as a test of devotion, Abraham passed. But on another level, if this was a test of Abraham's moral sense, whether he would question the justice of sacrificing his son, Abraham failed. Abraham had previously demonstrated this moral sense by arguing with God about the possible burning of the innocents with the guilty in Sodom. Why did he not argue with God about the planned burning of his son Isaac?

Abraham may have been incensed that God would test his moral fiber yet again in such a dire way. He may have decided to turn the tables, to test God's fiber, cynically returning the onus to God to save the day. Abraham failed this test by tiring of the moral challenge. He refused to engage God once again in a moral discussion.

Our moral senses are tested again and again. We must continue to respond with genuine concern. After this test, God did not speak to Abraham again. The lesson of the *Akedah* may be that to keep in contact with God, what is necessary is not blind obedience, but an inner sense of justice and constancy, and overcoming the anger, fear and cynicism that impedes the continued expression of that justice.

Ed Levin

Yitzhak—He Laughed

The name *Isaac* is connected in this and in other biblical passages with the Hebrew root *tzahak*, meaning "to laugh." In this context this has the connotation of "mocking laughter." To their contemporaries, even to themselves, there was something absurd about the birth of a child to Abraham and Sarah, this man and woman of advanced years. Jewish teachers have read into the account an anticipation of the fate of Isaac's descendants, the people of Israel. The very birth of this people was a miracle. Who but a Moses, under divine aid, could have succeeded in welding a rabble of slaves into a great nation? In subsequent Jewish history it seemed on more than one occasion that the Jews were doomed to extinction. The mocking laughter which attended the birth of Isaac re-echoed at the destruction of the first and second Temples, at the expulsion from Spain, and, in our own day, in Nazi-dominated Europe. But always the laughter was silenced to wonder as bruised Israel survived to rebuild its life in new surroundings.

Rabbi Louis Jacobs

Generations

Rabbinic authorities disagree over how old Isaac was at the time of the *Akedah*. The story evokes an adolescent: strong enough to carry the wood, yet young enough to want to please his father. Others have suggested Isaac was much older. A full-grown man, thirty-seven years old, on the other side of a midlife crisis, who knew all along what was going on and how to play his part in the drama. According to one midrash:

> While Abraham was building the altar, Isaac kept handing him the wood and the stones. Abraham was like a man who builds the wedding house for his son, and Isaac was like a man getting ready for the wedding feast, which he does with joy.

One curious feature of the *Akedah* is a frequently noted omission. In a tale that obviously has been crafted with great precision, how odd that, on two separate occasions, on their way to the mountain, we are told that Abraham and Isaac "went along, both of them together," yet after whatever it was that really happened up there, we read only "and Abraham returned to his servants." What happened to Isaac? What did the father and the son talk about as they went along, both of them together? "Tell me about grandpa Terah again, Dad, and how you used to work in his shop when you were a kid. Did you really smash all his statues?"

Often sacred legends can be decoded by broadening our defini-tion of participating characters. Perhaps it is time to reconsider the ram as a more important player in the drama. Perhaps it was more than a surrogate sacrifice. As Dr. Nahum Sarna observes, "The depiction of a god in the form of a bull was widespread throughout the entire ancient Near East. That animal was a symbol of lordship, strength, vital energy, and fertility, and was either deified and made an object of wor-ship or, on account of these sovereign attributes, was employed in rep-resentation of deity." We remember also that the Baal idol the Hebrew prophets railed against was a bull. Furthermore the sin of the North-ern Kingdom of Israel was the worship of a cow. Indeed, the paradig-matic idol in Jewish tradition is a golden calf. Perhaps it was no accident that a ram was slaughtered.

Perhaps it was not Abraham who killed the ram after all. Perhaps Isaac did the slaughtering because he realized that after all those years even Abraham's new unitary god had begun to harden into a graven and predictable image. No longer the unrepresentable fire of Being but now the culturally convenient image of a ram. "This is my God, O Isaac, who brought me out of Ur of the Chaldeans...." Who can say? Only the two of them were up there together. And Isaac did not return.

From another midrash comes what may be the missing piece. Apparently, Abraham's father did not die of a broken heart, never to be heard from again. We read that "for many years Terah continued to be a witness to his son's glory, God accepted his repentance and when he died he was admitted into paradise. Indeed, one tradition teaches that he did not die until Isaac was thirty-five years old." Which, as we have already noted, may have been about the same time that Abraham and Isaac went up on Mount Moriah. The old man was waiting for his son, Abraham, when he came down the mountain alone. He looked into Abraham's eyes freshly washed with tears and saw that they were now clear and bright.

"Dad? Is that you? What are you doing here? I thought you were dead. How did you get here? Isaac, my son is gone. I'm so confused. Is Mom still alive? God told me to take Isaac up there and kill him on an altar. Isaac even carried the wood himself. Then I don't know what happened. I tried to show Isaac how this ram we found was a beauti-ful way to imagine God, but he only said I was blind. He said that my god had stopped moving years ago. He called me a moron. We fought. There was screaming and blood, then Isaac hacked off the ram's head. Look, I have one of its horns. Then I remembered what I had done to you. But when I turned around, Isaac was gone. Dad, I'm sorry. I didn't mean to destroy your idols. Did you really believe in them? Were they covered by the insurance? I mean, I didn't mean to hurt you; I just wanted to show you what I couldn't seem to tell you. Then I ran away and I was too ashamed to go back. All these years. And now my Isaac is gone. I don't know where he is. I swear I didn't kill him. See, I have this horn of the ram he killed instead. Oh Daddy, I love you. Forgive me.... Now I understand."

Terah was silent. He reached out his arms and held Abraham, his little boy. "And they went along, both of them together."

Rabbi Lawrence Kushner

The Binding of Sarah

A midrash on the familiar story of the binding of Isaac demonstrates several of these generalizations and conveys the flavor of midrash as a whole:

At that same hour [when an angel stayed Abraham's hand from killing Isaac], Satan went to Sarah and appeared to her with the visage of Isaac. She said to him, "My son, what has your father done to you?" He said to her, "My father ... took me up mountains and down valleys, and brought me up to the summit of [Mt. Moriah], and built an altar and ... arranged the firewood and set me up on the altar and bound me and took the knife to slay me. And if the Holy One blessed be God had not said to him, 'Do not send your hand against the child,' I would already be slaughtered." Satan did not even finish speaking these words before her soul went out of her. Thus, scripture says (immediately following the story of the binding of Isaac): "And Abraham came to lament for Sarah and cry for her" (Gen. 23:2). From whence did he come? From Mt. Moriah (*Tanhuma Vayera* 30 on Gen. 22, 23:2).

This midrash is especially elegant because it responds to so many issues at once. On the most superficial level, it addresses the curious, and therefore problematic, locution "and Abraham came to lament for Sarah." It also implicitly deals with the ambiguous time-lag between the end of the story of the binding of Isaac and the news of Sarah's death that follows. Midrash—which loves to discover hidden relationships among proximate texts—posits a causal connection. The biblical text itself prompts readers to imagine what Abraham and Isaac are thinking. It is not a far cry from there to wondering what Sarah knew. In addition, the appearance of Satan fits with another traditional midrash. Satan is said to have proposed a challenge: Even a person of great faith would not continue to love and obey God when stripped of rewards and incentives. This raises a key moral question: How and why would God command a parent to kill his child? Answer: It all originated with Satan. Second, more subtle answer: The moral objection must stand. After all, it originated with Satan—and what Satan spawns must be evil. Regardless of who set this trial in motion, our midrash makes it clear that Sarah found it literally insupportable. Thus, another moral question: How could Abraham comply? Isaac's innocence, the father-son bond in this biblical episode, and the contrast with Abraham's earlier plea to God to save the people of Sodom and Gomorrah (18:23–33) all raise doubts about the "greatness" of this father's faith.

The *Tanhuma*'s single tale about Sarah and Satan simultaneously makes use of two important gaps in the biblical story. First, Isaac is never recorded as returning from Mt. Moriah (22:19). Satan can therefore impersonate him. Elsewhere in Rabbinic literature, Isaac's disappearance is resolved by imagining that he actually died. Over the centuries, Jews who suffered persecution wrote midrashim comparing their martyrdom to that of Isaac. Our midrash portrays Sarah as a kind of martyr. It thus fills in the second major gap: her absence from the story. Abraham's obedience seems paltry in contrast to Sarah's heroic death.

Rabbi Debra Orenstein

Akedah

Ever since I was a child, I've struggled with a fundamental question about Abraham's personality.... When God comes to Abraham to inform him that the city of Sodom is to be destroyed for its wickedness, Abraham responds aggressively by shaming God into agreeing to spare the city if fifty righteous can be found within it, saying, "Far be it from

You! Shall not the Judge of all the earth deal justly?" (Genesis 18:25).
Then, with a bargaining style that would be the envy of any used-car
buyer, teenager or trial lawyer, he lowers the number to forty-five, to
thirty, to twenty, to ten.

In contrast, when God comes to Abraham and commands him,
"Take your son, your only son, whom you love, Isaac, and offer him
as a burnt offering" (Genesis 22:2), Abraham does not respond and
heads off to do God's will. How could Abraham care so deeply for
strangers, and not fight for the life of his own son?

I stand further in awe of the zeal and single-mindedness that Abraham brings to his assignment. Rather than prolonging goodbyes, he
does not delay—arising and setting out first thing in the morning, and
attending to many details himself. When God summons Abraham to
offer up his son (Genesis 22:1), God calls his name once, and Abraham responds, *Hineni*—here I am. In contrast, when God's messenger
calls upon Abraham to stop, at the last moment (22:11), it is with a
twofold repetition "Abraham, Abraham"—Abraham must be asked
only once to raise the knife, but twice before he will stay it.

I think the sages were trying to soften that perception when they
re-imagined each phrase of God's command to Abraham as one side of
a conversation, with Abraham taking the other side *(Sanhedrin* 89b):

"Take your son"

"But I have two sons!"

"Your only son"—

"This one is the only child of his mother, and this is the only child
of his mother."

"Whom you love"—

"I love both of my sons."

"Isaac."

And Abraham is unable to respond further.

The tone of this conversation sharpens the question in a different
way, because it puts these events into the context of Abraham's treatment of his older son. When Sarah demands that Ishmael be sent away
after Isaac is born, Abraham is deeply distressed. It is only after God
reassures him that all will be well with his eldest son that Abraham
sends him off to risk death in the dangerous desert.

There are many approaches to the resolution of this paradox. For
instance, many Jewish sources (e.g., *Pirkei Avot* 5:3) understand that

the banishment of Ishmael and the binding of Isaac were the culmination of God's ten "tests" of Abraham's faith. Some would argue that seen in this context, the changing responses show a progression of deepening faith. At first Abraham had challenged God's wisdom aloud (in the case of Sodom) or required reassurance, even though his doubts were unspoken (in the case of Ishmael). Abraham's willingness to give up his own son could then be seen as an example of having reached the most profound level of faith, a deep appreciation that indeed everything belongs to God. There are those who find this explanation comforting, but for me it rings false when viewed in light of the actions of Moses and later prophets—men and women of faith. In the words of my teacher, biblical scholar Yochanan Muffs, they "stood in the breach" to ask God to overturn the divine decree and defend the innocent.

Abraham's behavior makes sense in light of his cultural milieu. Archaeologists may debate the actual prevalence of the custom of child sacrifice in the ancient Near East, but the Biblical text portrays it as a norm of religious expression that was a temptation for Israelites even long after Abraham's day. Abraham's relatively advanced moral sense might have enabled him to perceive that collective punishment of innocents was wrong. However, if the false, powerless idols received human sacrifice, why should Abraham give any less to the one true God, a God who had already given, and demanded, so much? Some modern thinkers have suggested that the true test was not whether Abraham would indeed offer up his son, but whether he would not.

One could also see Abraham's behavior as reflecting a certain purity of purpose. Abraham was a man of such humility that he would challenge the creator of the universe on behalf of others, but would recuse himself from the divine court when the matter was one of personal interest. Of course Abraham's care for the people of Sodom need not be seen as purely disinterested; his estranged nephew Lot lived among them, and he had already acted once (in the battle of the five kings against the four kings) to rescue its people from disaster.

Recently, I've come to appreciate the paradox in light of what it means to balance responsibilities as a parent with responsibilities to the larger community. I have a renewed respect for my own parents, who somehow managed to make family their first priority despite their devoted involvement in the life of our local community and the larger

Jewish world. Even though many struggle with the question of how to balance family time with work and professional life, the challenges are particularly vexing when one is involved in the work of communal leadership, or in one of the "caring" professions, responsible for the physical and/or spiritual well-being of others. I am certain that my own experience, and that of colleagues in the rabbinate, resonates with that of educators, lay leaders, political leaders, physicians and others. The urgent demands of the larger communal family threaten to overtake those of one's own, and many fail to find a point of balance. Abraham was perhaps the first, but by no means the only, Jewish leader to nearly sacrifice his children in the process of promoting the Jewish tradition.

Given the terseness of the Biblical text, it is difficult to make an argument from silence, but I am struck by the fact that the Biblical text records Abraham's many conversations with God and with foreign leaders, but only one with Isaac. That single conversation comes while they are on their way up the mountain, knife and wood in hand. Perhaps Isaac was willing to walk toward oblivion, with the ram mysteriously absent, so long as it provided an opportunity for father and son to "walk together."

One could read the text as proof that Abraham did not love his son. Before the *Akedah*, God refers to Isaac as "your son, your only son, whom you love" (Genesis 22:2). Afterward, God twice refers to Isaac as "your son, your only son" (Genesis 22:12, 16), omitting the phrase "whom you love" I believe that the opposite is true—I have always perceived great tenderness and love in the way Abraham carried the dangerous objects himself, and the way he responded to his son with the same *"Hineni"* ("Here I am")—the same "presence"—that he offered to God.

Rather, it took the threat of the knife for Abraham to appreciate the relative importance of the single, unique soul that he and Sarah had made together, as opposed to the many souls/followers that they had "made" in Haran and brought with them to Canaan (Genesis 12:5). It took an unfathomable divine decree, for Abraham to be truly present with his son. All of us face the test of Abraham. Will it take a moment of crisis before we walk together with those we love?

Rabbi Joshua Heller

Hineni: Here I am!

"Hineni" means, simply, here I am. But there are so many ways to hear that word. We can hear it as Abraham must have said it when God called him. Abraham, old and tired, had just sent off Hagar and his first son Ishmael. When God calls him to require the offering of Isaac, *"Hineni"* must have sounded exceedingly weary and resigned. The subtext must have been "What does God want of me now?"

Or we might hear it eagerly, as Isaiah spoke it when God asked, "Whom shall I send? Who will go for us?" How many prophets have been so ready as to reply *"Hineni, sh'laheyni*—here I am—send me."* Or, we may hear it as we are about to hear it, with complete humility and awe at the task set before the speaker.

Weariness at yet another task to be completed at the command of the Creator; the sense of inadequacy that Moses expressed at the Burning Bush; or eagerness to do God's will. Each of us will hear God's voice in our lives. Each of us will respond *Hineni,* for there is nowhere to hide when God calls. The question is, how will we respond? What will God hear?

Rabbi Diane Cohen

After These Things

"And so it was, after these things, God tested Abraham" (Genesis 22:1). With these words, the Torah urges us to look for the reasons for the binding of Isaac—the test of Abraham—in the things that came before.

More than that. The rabbis read the word *ahar* (after) with intimations of the word *hirhur* (misgivings). So they believed that God had misgivings about what came before and about the person chosen to be the first of us. The first misgiving happened at "the spring of the God of seeing" (Genesis 16:1–6). God saw there a pregnant Hagar become arrogant towards her mistress and a Sarai turned vengeful. And Sarai said to Abram, "The wrong done me is your fault! I myself put my maid in your bosom; now that she sees she is pregnant I am lowered in her eyes. The Lord decide between you and me!"

But Abram did not put the matter before God. Instead, he gave Sarai power over her rival. And God saw Sarai torture Hagar so much that Hagar fled into the desert. There, an angel told her to return and bear the indignities, for her child would be the ancestor of a nation "too many to count." Hagar called the God she met in the desert *El Ba'i* "the God of seeing."

God did see. He saw Abram willing to judge instead of God. He saw that Abram could not see that it is wrong to put any person in the hands of one so full of hate that he or she is blind to what is just. And God saw that Abram had no vision for the things God wanted him to see. Abram would have to be tested. When Abram argued for the fate of Sodom and Gomorrah, God knew Abram had to learn that his love of justice within his own family ought to be as strong as his love of justice for two foreign cities.

The second misgiving was over what happened at Be'er Sheva (Genesis 21:1–12). There, God saw Sarah urge her husband to cast out Hagar and Ishmael, "for the son of that slave shall not share in the inheritance with my son Isaac." And God saw Abraham's ambivalence. Instead of telling Sarah that such a demand was itself a sin, a call to murder his wife and son, instead of telling Sarah that he loved them all, he vacillated. So God interrupted Abraham's vacillation. "Do not let this matter of the boy and your maidservant be evil in your eyes. Whatever Sarah tells you, listen to her voice. For through Isaac your seed shall be named, and I will also transform the son of the slave woman into a nation, for he is also your seed."

God's irony drips from every word. "Do not let this matter be evil in your eyes": It should be evil in your eyes! This is a request to murder your wife and son. "The boy and the maidservant": That is how you have treated them, not as members of your family. "Whatever Sarah tells you, listen": As if listening to this jealous woman and her venom should replace listening to the word of God. If you do not listen to God, you cannot see what God wants you to see, what God needs you to see.

Then God set the terms of his test of Abraham. He gave Abraham two linked promises: His line will be through Isaac, and Ishmael will be made into a great nation. One makes no sense without the other.

Now we understand the language of the Torah in describing how Sarah saw Ishmael at play, *metzachek*. The word is from the same root used to make the name Yitzchak, Isaac. Yitzchak and the *metzachek* are linked: They are like one person and are heirs to the same promise.

But until Abraham can treat them with the same love, they are at risk from his moral lassitude.

These are not separate stories; they are part of the same test, linked word by word, step by step. That is why Abraham was commanded to sacrifice Isaac in so torturous a manner: "Take your son, your only son, whom you love, Isaac" (22:2). Each phrase cuts Abraham with the irony of a test that did not have to be, save for his lack of moral vision.

"Take your son." Because Abraham now has two sons, he understood the words to mean, "Take the one whom you treated as a son." "Your only son, whom you love." More appropriately, "the only one left, he whom you loved more," for that is how the words were heard by Abraham. "Isaac." Finally, Abraham understood. He was commanded to kill Isaac because he was willing to kill Ishmael. The only way for God to know that Abraham expelled Hagar and Ishmael because he trusted God to care for them was to see if he trusted God to care for Isaac at the binding place. The only way to know if Abraham trusted the promise regarding Ishmael was to see if he trusted the promise regarding Isaac.

Abraham understood at last that the willingness to sacrifice the least loved leads inevitably to the sacrifice of the best loved. The Binding of Isaac was the only possible test to know the heart of Abraham. And God needed to know Abraham's heart. God saw and Abraham saw. And Abraham named the place *adonai yireh:* "For as it is said unto this day, 'On the mountain of the Lord there is vision'" (22:14).

"After these things," Abraham could be the father of two nations for he had learned at last what it meant to be the father of two sons.

"After these things," Abraham was free.

Rabbi Marc Gellman

And the Two of Them Walked Together: A Parent's Advice to a Child

If
If you can keep your head when all about you
Are losing theirs and blaming it on you;
If you can trust yourself when all men doubt you,
But make allowance for their doubting too;
If you can wait and not be tired by waiting,
Or, being lied about, don't deal in lies,

Or, being hated, don't give way to hating,
And yet don't look too good, nor talk too wise;

If you can dream—and not make dreams your master;
If you can think—and not make thoughts your aim;
If you can meet with triumph and disaster
And treat those two impostors just the same;
If you can bear to hear the truth you've spoken
Twisted by knaves to make a trap for fools,
Or watch the things you gave your life to broken,
And stoop and build 'em up with wornout tools;

If you can make one heap of all your winnings
And risk it on one turn of pitch-and-toss,
And lose, and start again at your beginnings
And never breathe a word about your loss;
If you can force your heart and nerve and sinew
To serve your turn long after they are gone,
And so hold on when there is nothing in you
Except the Will which says to them: "Hold on";

If you can talk with crowds and keep your virtue,
Or walk with kings—nor lose the common touch;
If neither foes nor loving friends can hurt you;
If all men count with you, but none too much;
If you can fill the unforgiving minute
With sixty seconds' worth of distance run—
Yours is the Earth and everything that's in it,
And—which is more—you'll be a Man, my son!

Rudyard Kipling

Akedah: **The Two of Them Went Together**

On Rosh Hashanah the opening prayers include the following: What
are we? What is our attainment and our power? What can we say, our
God and God of our ancestors?

One answer can be found in the story of an elderly Jewish lady, a
widow, a great-grandmother, who sat in shul on Rosh Hashanah and
talked with God. This particular lady had long been on intimate terms
with God, seeking help and encouragement during times of sickness,

health, poverty and prosperity. Being a good Jewish mother, she began to wonder what she could do for God. After all, her life was full and fulfilled, and she had little by way of unfinished business. She had all she needed and could look exclusively to the needs of others.

"*Nu, Tatenyu, Gottenyu,*" she said, "What should I wish for you, riches? You have no need of money or material things. Power? You are already Creator of the Universe, and Ruler of all Creation. So what can I wish for You—the one thing You don't always have and can't create in the year ahead I wish you should have *naches fun die kinder*—spiritual pleasure from all your children."

Perhaps this is the ultimate prayer for Rosh Hashanah.

Rabbi Bernard Solomon Raskas

Teaching Children Jewish Ethics

A wonderful story is told of Ralph Waldo Emerson coming upon a group of rural people in the midst of constructing a building. As their product looked a bit odd, he asked to see the architect. "There isn't any architect," the man replied. "We're just building the building. Next week a man is coming up from Boston to put some architecture into it."

It seems to me that we have gone too long building children without a clear set of moral blueprints. The fruits of our labor are evident. Our responsibility is to create whole children and that begins at home. Whether it is reading to our children or exposing them to great literature, let us be up to the challenge of helping to complete our children's character, giving them the best of everything, including our ethical tradition.

Rabbi Michael S. Siegel

The *Akedah:* A Test within a Test

The *Akedah*, the story of the binding of Isaac, is at once a daily staple and a Rosh Hashanah highlight. It is a daily staple, since it is part of the regular daily prayer liturgy. And it is a Rosh Hashanah highlight, as it is the Torah reading for the second day of Rosh Hashanah.

We tend to consider the *Akedah* as a test of Avraham's faith. Would Avraham agree to a request from God that went against logic and reason and seemed to contradict basic human and theological principles?

But there may be another, and primary, dimension to the test—
the adequacy of Avraham's parenting. The real challenge to Avraham
was not whether he would offer his beloved son as a sacrifice but
whether he could convince Yitzhak to agree with him.

God approached Avraham, and gave him a possible escape hatch.
Avraham could have returned to God with the information that
Yitzhak refused to cooperate and thus the Lord's wish could not be fulfilled. The test therefore was two-fold: Firstly, did Avraham's faith
allow him to do God's will? And second, would Yitzhak agree to be the
sacrificial lamb?

For Yitzhak to be willing to go along, two basic ingredients were
required: Avraham's eagerness and insistence, and a solid parent-child
relationship between Avraham and Yitzhak.

With regard to Avraham's eagerness, it is self-evident that if Avraham would have approached the situation half-heartedly, he could not
have inspired Yitzhak to agree. With regard to the parent-child relationship, only if Avraham and Yitzhak had developed a mutual trust
over the course of the years would Yitzhak be likely to say yes. Yitzhak's
attitude would reflect Avraham's success as a parent. Was Avraham an
indulging parent who catered to every whim of his child, or was he able
to elicit from his child the faith and transcending commitment that
knew no bounds?

Twice in the *Akedah* story we are told that both of them, Avraham
and Yitzhak, walked together (Genesis 22:6, 8). One can understand
from this language that a sense of togetherness prevailed between father
and son. As the classic commentator on the *Humash*, Rashi, added:
"b'lev shaveh," "with the same heart." The trust of the son in the father
was so strong that even when Avraham came to Yitzhak with what must
have seemed an outlandish request, Yitzhak did not say no.

The *Akedah* narrative is a daily staple because it addresses not only the
notion of faith, but also the essentiality of parent-child trust. This confidence only develops through daily interaction and mutual love, forbear-
ance, and responsiveness. At the same time, the story is a Rosh Hashanah
highlight, because how the parent raises the child and how the child
behaves towards the parent determine whether the transgenerational ties
that guarantee the continuity of Judaism have been properly cemented.

Some time ago, I read of a famous football coach, Jackie Sherrill,
who was well known for his recruiting strategy, so important in

building a strong football team. This college coach once traveled three hundred miles to interview a much heralded prospect. However, about five minutes into the interview, which Sherrill, as was his habit, conducted in the player's home, the prospect said to his mother, "Shut up." Sherrill instantly got up and left. For Sherrill, a person who did not properly honor parents was not promising material for a football team. What applies to football applies even more significantly in life. The *Akedah* stands out as that experience in which the respect of child for parent gained ultimate expression.

Rabbi Reuven Bulka

The *Akedah:* Coming Down the Mountain

Rabbi Menahem Mendle of Kotzk once put this question to his students: What was the hardest part of the *Akedah* for Abraham? Was it the initial call, the long walk to Moriah, or the binding? His answer: the hardest part was coming down the mountain.

In peak moments of our lives, the immediacy, the rush of adrenaline, often carries us through. What happens afterward is the true test of sincerity, for afterward we must live with the consequences of our actions. Are we faithful to those peak moments? Do we forget them, or disregard them?

The hardest part of Yom Kippur is not the fasting. The hardest part is two months later, when we are supposed to live by the promises we made. There is great drama in falling in love. But the test of a love is not in the falling; it is in the staying. The test of life is not in moments of passion that can stir the blood and push even the sluggard to new swiftness and resolve. The test of life is after the crisis has passed. Our worthiness is measured not in the pinnacle, but in the persistence.

In teaching, there are times when we are kindled by the task at hand. Such experiences are wonderful, but ultimately it is in the daily work, when we come down the mountain, that our achievement will be measured. In our teaching we should recall that education is not a parade of peaks, but a long, loving walk together through valleys and level plains. We should treasure the summit of inspiration, but not live by it. Here below, once we have come down the mountain, our task awaits.

Rabbi David J. Wolpe

The *Akedah* from Isaac's Point of View

While there are any number of midrashim in which Isaac is seen as a willing and enthusiastic participant in the *Akedah,* I am especially intrigued by some *midrashim* that express Isaac's hesitation or even terror and anger:

1. There is a Sephardic *piyyut* for Rosh Hashanah called *"Et sha'arei ratzon le-hipate-ah"* about the *Akedah,* which includes two entire stanzas written from Isaac's point of view. When I read it, I hear Isaac expressing anger at his father, something that is not usually found in *midrashim* on the *Akedah.* It can be found in any Sephardic/*mizrahi mahzor,* and David de Sola Pool's Sephardic *mahzor* includes a good English translation.

2. *Tanhuma* 23: Isaac warns Abraham: when you go back and tell Sarah about how you killed me, make sure she is not on the roof or at the edge of a pit, or else she may jump off and die and then you will have killed both of us!!

3. *Sefer Hayashar* 46b and *Yalkut Shim'oni* 247:101: Isaac asks Abraham to bring Sarah some of his ashes, so she will know what happened to him.

4. *Ner Haskalim,* a Yemenite midrashic collection: Isaac asks his father: *"Chazek hakesher, shema ev'ot b'cha ve'evtol mikvodekha."*

"Tighten the knot, lest I kick you and diminish your honor." I understand Isaac as implying that he is so angry that he does not know what he might do to Abraham if he were not bound tightly. (A more "pareve" form of this midrash is brought in *Breishit Rabbah* 56:5, *Tanhuma* 23, and *Sefer Hayashar* 46b: Tie me tightly or else I may flinch and the sacrifice may be invalidated.)

Rabbi Robert Scheinberg

Consequences of *Akedah*

To read the *Akedah,* the story of the binding of Isaac, means to be gripped by the pathos of this incredible trial that was visited upon Abraham.

So many questions are thrown up: principally, why God needed to test Abraham at all. Was not his piety and faith and devotion to God beyond any shadow of a doubt? And secondly, why the episode opens with the statement, And God Tested Abraham. Surely the one who was truly tested was Isaac, who must have suspected what his father was up to, especially when he received no satisfactory answer to the loaded question: "I see the fire and fuel and the knife: but where is the sacrificial lamb?" (Gen. 22:7).

Isaac was no fool. His father's evasive answer, "God will provide the lamb for the sacrifice, my son," must have left him very troubled and confused. They were traveling to a far-off place, some three-days' journey away. Lambs do not roam wild. They are bred in flocks. How could his father Abraham be so sure that the place he was journeying to would have flocks, and that they would have an unblemished lamb suitable for sacrifice, available for sale? If one is going on the Lord's mission, as a pilgrimage to a far-off place, surely one leaves nothing to chance. The first thing to be loaded is the sacrificial lamb, the must important item of the ritual.

After Isaac's question, the dialogue suddenly goes silent. A brooding and telling silence. It is inconceivable that Abraham's solemn mood would not have betrayed his foreboding and inner torment. And it is inconceivable that his son, Isaac, his daily companion from birth, would not have been able to read the signs of all that anguish, and its implications, written all over his father's face.

Isaac is saved in the nick of time, but at what expense to his mental equilibrium. He turns inward. He cannot subsequently give of himself to others. He can no longer build relationships. Certainly the bond with his father had been snapped. Understandably the Torah does not record a single word exchanged between them subsequent to the *Akedah*.

Rabbi Jeffrey M. Cohen

Abraham the Fundamentalist?

One of the most dramatic stories in the Torah is *Akedat Yitzhak,* the Binding of Isaac. The Rabbis call the *Akedah* the last and perhaps most difficult of the tests of Abraham. We know that Abraham was not a simple listener and blindly obedient servant, like Noah. When God told Noah of His intent to bring the flood to destroy life on earth, Noah said nothing. On the other hand, when God tells Abraham of his plan to annihilate Sodom and Gomorrah, Abraham challenges God (18:25): "Shall not the judge of all the earth do justly?" So we know that Abraham is an active partner in the story, which makes his silence and eager participation in the *Akedah* that much more enigmatic.

The command which opens the story is clear: "And God tested Abraham and said: 'Take your son, whom you love, Isaac ... and offer him there as a burnt offering....'" The story is familiar. Abraham rises at the crack of dawn to fulfill the terrible command, and he and Isaac go off with the young servants. Twice the Torah tells us, "And they went both of them together," once on leaving the servants and again after Isaac asks his father the seemingly innocent but frightening question "where is the lamb for an offering?" Rashi explains those words in the latter case "with the same ready heart." Even after he realized what was at stake Isaac remained as committed as Abraham to fulfilling God's command.

Yet the story gets more complex on the mountain. Abraham prepares the altar, binds Isaac, takes the knife and is ready to act, when a very strange thing happens: "And the angel of the Lord called unto him: 'Abraham, Abraham ... Lay not your hand on the lad nor do anything to him.'"

First of all, the original command came from "God" and the new one from "the angel of the Lord." What does a loyal soldier do when he gets contradictory orders from different authorities?

Secondly why does the angel of the Lord call him twice? Rashi says it is a "sign of affection" but others see a different significance. The Natziv of Volozhin says that Abraham was so wound up in a frenzy of the act that he did not hear until the angel repeated the call, "in an angry voice."

Rashi's comment to the double demand "lay not your hand ... nor do anything," supports this. He says Abraham was almost disappointed. "At least let me draw some blood," Abraham said, to which the angel responded "do nothing to him." The rest is an anti-climax. In verse 13, where Abraham sees the ram in the thicket and sacrifices it, there is no mention of God or of the angel.

Isaac is spared, but the story does not have a happy ending. Abraham returns to the young servants but without Isaac. He and his father do not appear together again. And the Midrash attributes Sarah's death, in the next chapter, to the shock of the story of her son's close brush with death at his father's hand on Mount Moriah.

The *Akedah* is not only a difficult story theologically; it was clearly a trauma for those who went through it. The Jewish people have known too many *Akedot,* even in recent times—the Holocaust, the wars of Israel, acts of terror, the murder of a prime minister. The challenge is if somehow today, we, *Am Yisrael,* can succeed where, perhaps, Abraham and Isaac failed—to be able to come away from these *Akedot* united and reinforced, so that future generations will say about our generation, despite all the disagreements and disputes—"and they went together."

Rabbi Daniel C. Goldfarb

And Abraham Grew Big—Like God

The probable etymology of the term "fan" (as in "Baltimore Orioles fan") is a shortened form of "fanatic." The expression is somewhat of an endearment, an innocent word, for folks who have a healthy or even mildly obsessive (or even downright obnoxious!) enthusiasm for a given team or sport. Seldom, however, is a devotee of a sport a true fanatic, even if they may become somewhat single-minded, and boorish. Tennis players may have colorful language, but they seldom take hostages.

What is a religious fanatic? An apt question for a rabbi and a proper subject for religious study. After all, if "sweet religion" is a good thing, can anybody conceivably get too much of it? And does the Torah tradition, which teaches us about scholars ready to go up in flames for their beliefs, ever tell us when to "lighten up"?

And can Judaism have any lasting value if we Jews are merely "fans" who, vicariously, watch a cantor and rabbi perform Friday-night religion like it was Monday-night football? The couch potato gets little exercise. The pew potato gets little in the way of religious ecstasy.

Can Judaism survive, indeed, should it survive, if it is something between a religion and a hobby, something meant to entertain us and "uplift" us and "edify" us like another segment of *Masterpiece Theater*?

In our *sidrah,* Abraham is a fanatic. And God teaches him how not to be. God tells Abraham to sacrifice his son, his "only" son Isaac. (Isaac, in effect, was now his only son; one can hardly blame Isaac's older brother Ishmael for keeping clear of the old man, when, in the previous chapter, Abraham willingly sent the boy and his mother Hagar into the desert to die, only to be saved by Divine intervention.) Abraham, founder of this new monotheism, was a fanatic. God said "do it" and Abraham was ready to "do it," no questions asked. He was prepared to haggle with God a bit to save strangers at Sodom, but with regard to his own son, Scripture tells us "And Abraham got up in the morning" bright and early without a hint of protest.

I am not suggesting that Abraham was without human feeling or compassion. On the contrary. He became overwhelmed by a sense of duty and, as a result, became somewhat of an automaton. When he had bound Isaac on the altar and was about to sacrifice the lad, God calls out to him "Abraham! Abraham!" But why does God need to call out twice? Had Abraham ever hesitated to perform God's will enthusiastically? Did God doubt that Abraham—who had always been so obedient—would listen this time?

It is as if Abraham had been in a stupor. It is as if Abraham had been in a trance. How could God order the Patriarch to do such a terrible thing? It must have been like a terrible dream. Abraham is under a religious anesthesia which removes him from his normal self. No longer is Abraham a father or a husband, but an unquestioning extension of the Divine will. So God wakes him up and calls Abraham back to his human self.

God wants Abraham to be human. God wants us to be human. God does not want Abraham to forget his personal feelings. God wants the heart.

When religion causes us to forget that other people are created in the Divine image, we become fanatics. When we are prepared to sacrifice others on the altar of our beliefs, we become fanatics. When we use religion to make God small like ourselves, rather than trying to become big like God, we are fanatics. "Spirituality" is not something separate from our lives as husbands, as wives, and as parents. If you want to embrace God, embrace the child. If you want to cleave to God, hold your spouse. God is telling us, as God told Abraham: Wake up! Be human. That is what I created you to be.

And so Abraham grew. Big, like God. May the children of Abraham learn well the words of Isaiah (11:9): "They shall not hurt nor destroy in all my holy mountain; for the earth shall be full of the knowledge of the Lord, as the waters cover the sea."

Rabbi Kenneth L. Cohen

Hineni: Send Me

Someone once cried to God: Adonai, the world is in such a mess—
everything seems wrong. Why don't you send someone to help and
change the world?

The voice of Adonai replied: I did send someone. I sent you!

We pray for life—we ask God for a year of health and happiness. We
cannot merely ask. Tell the Almighty—tell the world—tell yourself:
Send Me! *Hineni, sh'laheni!* Here I am, Send me!

Rabbi Gerald I. Wolpe

Akedah

The story of the binding of Isaac which we read on the second day of
Rosh Hashanah is a powerful precedent for sustaining our dual commitment, for recognizing the dangers of reality while still insisting that
we shall overcome.

Examine the biblical story and you will see that paradoxes abound:
in God commanding Abraham to sacrifice his son, yet promising that
the covenant would continue through that same son, in the willingness
of both Abraham and Isaac to carry out God's shocking command,
despite Abraham's vocal protest of God's intended destruction of
Sodom and Gomorrah, in the complete absence of Sarah from the story
despite her centrality in previous moments in Abraham's career.

Perhaps most puzzling of all is the very idea of God testing a chosen friend: Some time afterward, God put Abraham to the test (22:1).
But what, precisely, was the test about? Was the test whether or not
Abraham would engage in child sacrifice? We know that human sacrifice was universal in antiquity. Cemeteries with the remains of sacrificed
children, and even an example of a pagan king who sacrificed his son
within the Tanakh itself, testify to the far-too-frequent perception that
the gods require human offerings. If that is so, then Abraham would
not have been surprised that his God, like everybody else's, wanted a
child sacrifice. Noting that his God was more like other deities than
he had previously surmised, Abraham would have simply recognized
this demand as being typical of what Supreme Beings generally require.

So if human sacrifice is not the test, if the suspension of the ethical
is not unusual, then what was it that Abraham was being tested on?

Abraham's test, I would suggest, was his ability to live with paradox, to be able to take the tension inherent in human existence and utilize that tension to generate growth, insight, and depth. Tension can be fruitful, its resolution can lead to a higher plateau. The paradox that faced Abraham challenges us as well today. In the face of an ominous and threatening reality, how can we affirm our trust in God's promise to our People? In other words, how can we act with sufficient confidence and commitment to ensure that Judaism and the Jews survive and grow? How can we contribute to a reality which adheres more closely to our highest ideals?

If we look back in the Torah, we see that just one chapter earlier, God had assured Abraham, It is through Isaac that offspring shall be continued for you (21:12). God promises Abraham that the brit, the covenant made between Abraham and God, a covenant that extends to the entire Jewish People throughout time, will be transmitted through Isaac. And, then, one short chapter later, God orders Abraham to sacrifice that same son, thereby threatening to terminate the promise of a Jewish future.

Abraham's test, in short, is to affirm the possibilities inherent in paradox, to hold on to the polar opposites of the world as it is and the world as it might be, refusing to abandon either one in the process of repairing them both. Abraham's test was to accept God's command to go through the motions of offering up Isaac, fully confident that Isaac would indeed be the vehicle through which the covenant with the Jews would begin.

Indeed, we see hints of that insight throughout the story. Whereas Abraham always spoke out against injustice in the past, in this moment—most crucial of all!—Abraham is silent. How to explain his silence except to recognize the boundless depth of his faith that the crisis was only apparent, that his God would not abandon his covenant with the Jews.

Or, again, the silence is broken only once, in a conversation between father and son that marks their only recorded conversation in the entire Torah! Isaac asks his father: Here are the firestone and the wood; but where is the sheep for the burnt offering? (22:7) Abraham's response provides the essential information necessary to make sense out of our story. His reply is traditionally translated as, God will see to the sheep for His burnt offering, my son (22:8). Yet I must tell you that the punctuation of the biblical text is medieval, and might be more profitably read in a different way. Following Rabbi Sheldon Zimmerman, we can also hear Abraham as saying: God will see. He has the lamb for the offering, my son.

In that second reading, Abraham reveals to his pliable son that the lamb for the offering will be on the top of the mountain when they get there. Abraham's faith is that strong. And, in fact, Abraham proves to be right. Once Isaac is strapped to the altar, they do find a ram trapped in the branches of a nearby tree. As Abraham knew all along, God did provide a lamb for the offering.

The second half of Abraham's answer was correct—God did provide the offering on the mountain top. But what of the first part of Abraham's response, where he claims that God will see. These two words are pivotal, so significant that when Abraham names the altar where his son was to be sacrificed, he calls it "God will see."

What is it that Abraham knew God would see? And what is it that God will see in our lifetimes? What God saw on that mountain top was that Abraham and Isaac were there, body, mind, and soul. When God called them, no matter how paradoxical was the call, those two responded actively, totally. To God's summons, they both said, *Hineni*, Here I am. Abraham did not deny the terror of his situation. He did not ignore the pain and the uncertainty of what he was ordered to do. But he refused to surrender to the pain and the fear. He refused to allow the situation, any situation, to dictate the content of his identity as a Jew.

Abraham's test was whether, in trying times, he would still insist on his Jewish identity, would still retain confidence that God's promised covenant would survive. By refusing to abandon hope in the face of a bleak reality, by refusing to wish away a challenging reality in favor of simplistic beliefs and wishful stories, Abraham remained true to the brit, the covenant.

We too face that same test. In the luxurious abundance of America, in the threatened trenches of Israel, in the poorly supplied and still-risky gatherings of Soviet Jews, our people are called to recognize the reality of the threats facing us, to admit the statistical improbability of Jewish survival, and then to do the hard work necessary to transcend those statistics. Threatened by assimilation and anti-Semitism, by Jewish indifference or disinterest, we, like Abraham, are tested. For we, too, are the heirs to the promise, and the transmitters of that promise.

God needs us to supply the hands to do the work, the hearts to bear the love, the mouths to give speech to the ancient primal utterance.

Netzakh Yisrael lo Yishaker, the Eternal One of Israel does not lie, and the eternity of the Jewish People is no lie. Here, today, if we resolve to survive, then we will. Here, today, if we determine to take our Judaism just a little more seriously than we did last year, if we undertake to grow in knowledge, in practice, and in participation—to take the next step—then we can remain the agents for God's Torah and for our People's Heritage.

Like Abraham and Isaac before us, we too can say *Hineni,* we are here.

With faith in the merit and permanence of Judaism, recognizing that the reality of our lives and our community require special effort on our part, we too can pass the test.

Hineni.

Rabbi Bradley Shavit Artson

Akedah: Sinai or Moriah?

In *Surfing the Himalayas,* the protagonist in the story has an interesting line. As he is snowboarding down the mountain he happens to collide with a Buddhist monk. After which he declares: "interesting stuff happens at mountains." Well, interesting stuff does happen at mountains—and then some.

There is a rabbinic tradition authored by Rabbi Tanhum who suggests that four things were created on the first day of creation: and one of them was "mountains" (*B'reisheet Rabah* 3:8). There is something majestic and magnificent about mountains. Our tradition suggests that when one looks at the heavens, as I did the other night witnessing the lunar eclipse, one ought to be filled with wonder and awe. So too, when one looks at a mountain or is on a mountain the feeling of G-d's majesty is magnified and one's "creature feeling" (to steal from Rudolf Otto) is heightened. Mountains should evoke feelings of the *mysterium tremendum.*

The Chassidic master, Rabbi Hayim of Sanz makes a fascinating observation. There are two prominent mountains in our tradition where monumental things happened. There is the mountain of Sinai and the mountain called Moriah. At Sinai, G-d descended and gave

Torah to the Jewish people. At Moriah, according to this week's parashah, Abraham ascended together with his son Isaac to "bring him up" on the altar (*V'ha'leyhu*—related to the word *aliyah*—to go up). The latter is referred to as the *Akedah*, the binding of Isaac.

These two mountains are sites over which major Jewish dramas play out. I would think that priority should be given to Sinai—after all, without the Torah, we would not be a Jewish people. And yet. When the Temple is built, it would be on Mt. Moriah and not Mt. Sinai.

There is something magical and powerful about this mountain called Moriah. It is the spot that defies all logic and legal definition. Remember the proposal to give the "top" of this mountain control to the Muslim wakf and "below" the mountain control to the Jews? A distinction and division, by the way, with which even international law is unfamiliar.

It is a powerful place, this Mt. Moriah. How else can you explain the hypnotic feeling one has when standing at the bottom of this place next to the *Kotel*—which is the Western retaining wall of the Temple on Mt. Moriah?

Not only that. But there is an interesting Jewish law twist in this drama. Halakha—Jewish law—allows one to climb up Sinai. I myself did it at 3:00 A.M.—once upon a time. Jewish law does not allow one to freely traipse and traverse the Temple mount. It is accorded the highest degree of sanctity.

Why so? Rabbi Hayim of Sanz answers simply and elegantly. At Sinai, we, the Jewish people were "receivers." At Moriah, we became "givers." Of course, in Abraham's example, it was the ultimate giving—the giving of one's soul, at least, potentially.

At Sinai, G-d came down. At Moriah, man went up. At Sinai, the voice of G-d was dominant. At Moriah, the response of man was dominant. At Sinai, G-d was the principal actor. At Moriah, man was.

The Jewish call is more a Moriah response than a Sinai response. Spirituality is achieved when one gives. Even Hebrew admits of this tremendous principle. The word "love" *(oheiv)* really means, "I will give." The Jewish notion is—by giving to others one forms an intimate bond—a relationship is created. Indeed, this is the cardinal principle of marriage.

Mt. Moriah is the priority mountain. At Sinai, yes, G-d descends—but it remains a mountain. At Moriah, we ascend—and it becomes holy.

Rabbi David Gutterman

The *Akedah*

Abraham's challenge to God regarding the destruction of Sodom and Gomorrah and Abraham's submission to God's command to sacrifice Isaac provide a profound insight into the nature of the covenant. In the first story, Abraham questions, argues and convinces God to back down from an extreme position. The radical assumption underlying Abraham's protest is that God must follow a standard of justice comprehensible to Abraham. This suggests that human judgment over and against God is valid and that the human partner plays an active role in determining what is right and wrong.

Yet the same bold, challenging Abraham demonstrates absolute submission before God's terrifying command to sacrifice his son, though this surely violates his sense of justice. Only after Abraham has proven he will obey this command is a ram provided in Isaac's place. This story suggests that there is no alternative to the acceptance of God's will and that the human role in the covenant is submission.

The Torah's inclusion of both stories teaches that the Jewish way cannot be reduced to either perspective. By itself, the deeply autonomous thrust of the Sodom and Gomorrah story would lead to a Judaism in which the human conscience would eliminate anything that offended it. God, Torah, the tradition would become synonymous with whatever human beings want. Every person would decide what is right and wrong. But reducing the Jewish way to the deeply submissive thrust of the *Akedah* would lead to a fanaticism in which no act, no matter how repugnant, could be ruled out—a mindless obedience enslaving the human being and destroying his/her dignity.

The genius of the covenantal way is that these two powerful principles, autonomy and heteronomy, are yoked together and held in creative tension. Both challenging and submitting to God and the tradition are authentic covenantal responses to the dilemmas of Jewish life. The covenantal question addressed to each generation and even each person is when to act in which way.

Rabbi Irwin Kula

INSPIRATION FROM THE PROPHETS

The haftarah is a reading from the prophetic books of the Bible *(tanakh)* that follows the Torah reading in the synagogue on Sabbaths *(Shabbat)* and festivals. There is usually some relationship between the Torah and *haftarah* passages, though the connection is sometimes obscure and hence the subject of many a sermon by rabbis or *bnai mitzvah (bar/bat mitzvah)*.

The term *haftarah* means "dismissal" or "completion," since it was the passage that came at the end of the longer Torah reading and lesson. *Haftarot* were in use by the 3rd or 4th century c.e., as witnessed by early *Midrash* that connects Torah readings to various prophetic passages. The choice of specific prophetic texts to be used as *haftarot* for each occasion is, however, a matter of custom rather than entirely fixed law. This is witnessed by the many variations between Ashkenazic and Sephardic tradition in this realm, and even by varying customs of individual communities.

RABBI ARTHUR GREEN, *THESE ARE THE WORDS*

Prayer from the Heart Is Better than Prayer from the Lips

"Hannah prayed in her heart; only her lips moved, her voice could not be heard."

1 SAMUEL 1:13

The art of prayer is illustrated by Hannah, mother of the prophet Samuel: Dejected, this barren woman, "bitter in emotion" and "heavy in mood," prayed for a child at the Shiloh temple. She was "speaking to her heart; only her lips were moving, yet her voice could not be heard" (1 Samuel 1:13). The biblical idiom "speaking to her heart" means that she was praying silently *(be-lahash)*.

Describing how news of the reunion between Joseph and his brothers reached the royal court, Torah says: "The voice was heard in Pharaoh's palace" (Genesis 45:16). The Hebrew for voice *(kol)* sounds like "slight" (*kal,* faint). According to Kabbalah (Zohar 102a), this teaches us that the "silent voice" *("kol kal")* can be better heard and more forcefully penetrating than the spoken voice. So it is in worship: The quiet and unassuming expression is heard more than any noisy shouting. Prayer, in its quintessential sense and pristine form, is *avodah sheba-lev*—labor of the heart, not of the mouth. Hannah is the model of the silent yet effective voice of devotion.

Rabbi Zvi Yehuda

A Story of Consolation (1 Samuel 1:1–2:10)

More than the birthday of the world, Rosh Hashanah celebrates the birthday of humanity. In most cultures, the sense of time harks back to the pivotal event of their past. So Christianity counts time from the birth of its savior, whereas Islam counts time from the success of its prophet. Judaism is distinguished by the fact that for over a millennia it has counted time from the creation of all. This universalist posture is well reflected in the annual practice of commemorating the birth of humanity. Typically, we do not celebrate the birth of humanity just in general, but through the birth of individuals such as Isaac in the Torah reading and Samuel in the Haftarah reading.

In commemorating the birth of Isaac and Samuel, we also celebrate the motherhood of Sarah and Hannah. Sarah and Hannah were each the favorite, albeit barren wife. Sarah was wedded to the first biblically mentioned prophet, Abraham, and Hannah gave birth to the prophet Samuel. Through the birth of Sarah's son, Isaac, the covenant was sustained; through the birth of Hannah's son, Samuel, the monarchy and the messianic line were consecrated.

Although Sarah was the first matriarch, it was Hannah who became the paragon of prayer. She set the standard for heartfelt prayer. More rules of liturgy and devotion are derived from her prayerful experience than from any other biblical personage. God's reply to her prayers sets the tone for our pleas on Rosh Hashanah.

The various links between birth and motherhood along with that of divine solicitude are summed up superbly in Isaiah's simile of consolation: "As a mother comforts her child, so will I comfort you, says the Lord."

Rabbi Reuven Kimelman

Hannah's Tears

"Then Hannah opened herself up in prayer and said:
My heart exults in the Holy One, my self-esteem has
been raised up through Yah, my mouth is wide open in
the face of those who oppose me for I have rejoiced in
being stretched by You!"

1 SAMUEL 2:1–10, TRANSLATION OF THE AUTHOR

I invite you to take a moment, to close your eyes and take a breath.... and to recall the last time you cried. Recall, if you can, what or who moved those tears to rise in you, how it felt to release them, and how you felt afterward.

I want to speak with you today of Hannah, the first person in Scripture to entreat God in prayer. I want to speak with you about the resonance of silence, of words, half-formed, inchoate, whispered from the depths of a soul struggling to open to its own pain. I want to speak with you about voice, the full-throated voice, ebullient in song, that bursts from the belly of a being touched by God. And I want to speak

with you about the power of tears—tears that trickle and tears that
burn; tears that seep from the hidden, sore spots of the soul and tears
that simply overflow when the heart is full; cleansing tears, purifying
tears, tears as salty as the oceans that birthed life, tears that melt and
soften, tears that transform. All these are Hannah's legacy to us, her
torah, and it's no accident that the sages chose to include her story
among the texts that guide us through this season in which we seek
to rectify our relationships with ourselves, our fellow beings and
with God.

At a recent Jewish Renewal *Kallah,* one rabbi shared an amazing
teaching that wove together many of the texts chosen by our sages
for inclusion in the *machzor,* the "script" for the drama of our Rosh
Ha-Shanah experience. The theme that unites all these texts is not
judgment—for Rosh Ha-Shanah is never referred to in written Torah
as *Yom Ha-Din,* the Day of Judgment—but tears. Long before the
current psychological trend represented by Daniel Goleman's book
Emotional Intelligence, the Pietzetzner Rebbe, chief rabbi of Poland
who died in the Warsaw Ghetto during World War II, taught the
primacy of emotion in our spiritual lives. The *tzaddik,* the righteous
person, he wrote, is one who owns her heart, and a person who owns
her heart is one who can access her tears.

So on Rosh Ha-Shanah we read of Hagar's tears of resignation as
she abandons her son Ishmael under a bush, unwilling to watch him
die of thirst in the wilderness. And we hear the implied crying of the lad
"ba-asher hu sham," from where he has been left, to which God
responds by revealing the saving spring of water to his mother. We note
the tears of Abraham, conspicuous by their very absence, as he prepares
his beloved son Isaac for sacrifice. Isaac's tears, also absent, are
replaced, in midrash, by the tears of angels, which fall into Isaac's eyes
as he lies bound upon the altar and cloud his vision forever after.
Today's haftarah from Jeremiah vibrates with the sound of Rachel's
"bitter weeping" for her exiled children, tears of radical empathy that
shame God into the promise of redemption. Even the crying of a figure as minor as the nameless mother of Sisera, the wicked general
whose death at the hands of Yael is chronicled in the ancient Song of
Deborah, is evoked by the sages of the Talmud, who prescribe that
the very manner of blowing the shofar should recall the quality of her
wailing when she realizes her son will not return from battle. It was

suggested at the *Kallah* that all these different flavors of tears—shed or unshed—teach us something about the nuances of our participation in the drama of these holy days, about what is being asked of us here and in the year to come—and in our lives.

He did not, however, speak about Hannah's tears. What, I asked myself, is their taste and how do they nourish us? Like so many of the matriarchal figures in scripture, Hannah is childless. She is presented as a painfully unfulfilled woman, whose ability to feel loved by her adoring husband is blocked because she has been denied her heart's deepest desire, a son. Doctors and psychologists are coming to understand how prolonged or extreme pain, whether physical, mental or emotional, leads to a numbing of our senses, a kind of inner paralysis that dulls our very participation in life. Our organisms cut off feeling in order to survive. I have noticed that even minor disappointments, piling up over time, lead to an attitude of subtle cynicism, a closing of the heart that keeps us protected—both from pain and from joyous participation in life.

Hannah, sunk in her own sorrow, verbally abused by her husband Elkanah's other wife, the fertile Peninah, and unable to receive his offerings of love, somehow finds it within herself to break the cycle of numbness and despair and to respond in a radically different way. Surrendering her pain to God, she circumcises her heart, spilling her soul tears and whispered words upon the altar of the Holy One at the Shiloh temple.

What inspires an action so unusual that it causes the aging priest Eli to chastise her for what seems to him to be drunkenness? The text tells us only: "*v'hi marat nefesh* [and she was bitter of soul] *va-titpallel al YHVH* [and she prayed to YHVH], *u-vakhoh tivkeh* [all the while crying her heart out]" (1 Samuel 1:10). *Marat,* bitterness, speaks literally of bitter water, specifically the undrinkable waters found by the thirsty Israelites who, after crossing the Sea of Reeds, had spent three frightening, waterless days in the wilderness. Hannah's soul is filled with these bitter waters, her heart a brackish pool in the barren wilderness of her body. Yet somehow she is impelled, despite the custom of her world, where an orderly and correct relationship with awesome Divinity is maintained through the priests' prescribed ministrations and the sacrifice of animals, to approach God directly, to offer up her tears and the silent movements of her lips.

The Hebrew root *l'hitpallel,* which we translate as "pray," and which can be rendered more precisely as "intercede" or "interpose," comes from an Arabic root meaning "to cut oneself in worship." A wise *rebbe* recently reminded me that the word "tears" can also be pronounced "tears" (tares). In the depth of her pain, Hannah tears herself open with implicit trust that the Holy One will witness her suffering. If God will open her womb, she vows, she will dedicate its fruit, the son she will bear, to God's service: *v'Hannah, hi midaberet al libah* ... and Hannah was speaking upon her heart. In the act of weeping out her longing and passion to God, Hannah speaks also into her own heart, opening at last to the depths of her own desire, silently mouthing words of yearning too ardent, too intimate to be spoken aloud. In one breath, she surrenders all—her pain, her longing, even her unborn son—to God, and in this moment begins to find inner peace.

Diane Elliot

Prayer for an Expecting Couple during the Days of Awe

Prayers to Be Said between Rosh Hashanah and Yom Kippur

The nine months of pregnancy find resonance in this holiday season. There are nine days from Rosh Hashanah to Yom Kippur, and nine occurrences of God's name in Hannah's prayer of thanksgiving that we read as the haftarah on Rosh Hashanah. The Hebrew letter for nine, *tet,* written in script looks like a profile of a pregnant belly. In the following ritual, every day of these nine days of renewal and repentance the couple recites a line from the tradition that recalls the mystery and the joy of childbirth. The recitation of these verses can be accompanied by the giving of *tzedakah* (a dollar amount equal to the day count), or they may be recited when the couple settles into bed.

Day 1 (first night of Rosh Hashanah)

There are three keys that the Holy One entrusts to no one else but are kept always in the divine hand. They are: the key of rain, the key of eternal life, and the key of the womb. Please God, on this anniversary of the birth of the world, remember the key, open Your hand, and give us a child.

Day 2 (second night of Rosh Hashanah)

We do not know the way the spirit of life enters the one that lies within the womb of a woman. And we cannot understand the deeds of God, the One who is the author of all (Eccles. 11:5). But please, God, visit this miracle upon us and give us a child.

Day 3

My dove, in the cranny of the rocks, hidden by the cliff, let me see your face, let me hear your voice, for your voice is sweet and your face is sweet (Song of Songs 2:14). We await the voice of our own little one. Please, God, give us a child.

Day 4

Sing, barren one ... for the time has come to expand the length of your tent. Let the drapes of your dwelling billow out (Isa. 54:1–2). Please, God, make this call come true for us. Remember us and give us a child.

Day 5

Unless the Lord builds the house, it is built in vain (Ps. 127:1) for it takes three to build a household: a man, a woman and the Holy One. Please, God, remember us and give us a child.

Day 6

And God remembered Rachel, heard her cries, and opened her womb (Gen. 30:22). Hear us too, God, and give us a child.

Day 7

The God of your father will help you. Shaddai will bless you. Blessing will flow from above, and blessings will flow from below. Blessings of the breast and blessings of the womb (Gen. 49:25). We await our blessings, God. Give us a child.

Day 8

They shall not labor and produce nothing. They shall not give birth in vain, for their children shall be the blessed ones of God, and their children shall always be with them (Isa. 65:23). We long to be among the blessed ones, God. Please, give us a child.

Day 9

The soul is Yours, the body Your creation; have compassion on Your creation. We will care tenderly for the one entrusted to us. Please, God, give us a child.

Rabbi Nina Beth Cardin

Debtors Are We All

The Haftarah reading on Rosh Hashanah is a familiar story from the book of Samuel. Childless Hannah visits the Temple and vows that if God blesses her with a son, she will dedicate the child to the service of the Lord. God answers her prayer. Hannah bears a son and calls him Samuel, because "I have borrowed him from the Lord." In that terse phrase, "I have borrowed him from the Lord," is implied a much needed philosophy of life. Our attitudes and values, indeed our entire mode of living, would undergo a complete and blessed metamorphosis if we but consider that not only our children, as Hannah asserted, but all of our possessions—health, comforts, talents, wealth, time, and opportunity, even life itself—are borrowed from God and entrusted to us for useful purposes and consecrated living.

Nowadays, the papers are full of stories of corporations who cannot repay their financial debts and of men and women who go bankrupt because they borrowed over their heads. Few people seem to realize that they have other debts that should be repaid, but because these obligations cannot be translated into dollars and cents, they are constantly overlooked. Even before we were born, each one of us borrowed from our mother some of her vitality, marrow from her bones, and calcium from her teeth. And after birth, do we not borrow food from Mother Earth, light from the sun, beauty from the skies, and fragrance from the flowers? We also borrow from one another. Merchant and purchaser, teacher and pupil, musician and audience, rabbi and congregation—all are indebted to each other.

Not only individuals, but peoples borrow from one another. America owes its arithmetic to the Arabs, the alphabet to the Phoenicians, law to the Romans, art to the Greeks, opera to the Italians and the French, and religion to the Jews.

As borrowers from life and from one another, we must repay our debts, just as Hannah did. Borrowed love must be repaid with thoughtfulness; borrowed labor with adequate wages; borrowed beauty with appreciation; and borrowed leadership with fidelity. Children borrow from parents and they discharge their obligations by offering understanding and reverence; parents borrow from children and they owe them companionship, guidance, and noble example. The whole structure of society rests upon mutual exchange. We must give as well as take.

But the greatest paradox of life is not that men and women are loath to pay once they borrow, but that they are unwilling to borrow. We are poor payers, but we are even more wretched borrowers. Life offers us all its precious goods, but what do we select? Not the riches of thought, faith, beauty, and love, but the cheap shiny glass beads. Only the few know how to borrow wisely, and, by and large, they are the most apt to repay.

Why do we treat our financial debts with more consideration than our human debts? Perhaps the story of the solicitor for the local Jewish Federation who came to see a well-to-do prospect supplies the answer. After the solicitor explained the costs of Jewish education, family services, and aid for Israel, he asked for a pledge. The prospect refused, claiming that he borrowed heavily to expand his business and needed all the money he could muster to make the required payments. "But," said the solicitor, "think of your beautiful wife, lovely children, fine home, all the pleasures of life that are yours! Don't you think that you owe something to God who made all this possible?" "I sure do," answered the prospect, "but you see God doesn't dun me like my other creditors."

The greatness of Hannah was that she sought something valuable and repaid without being dunned. Let us learn from her example. Let us borrow the riches of beauty and truth, of love and friendship, of charity and forgiveness. And let us repay our debts willingly, generously, and nobly, thus making our lives on earth worthwhile and leaving the world richer because of our presence.

Rabbi Hillel E. Silverman

God Is Merciful

> Go, and announce these words toward the north, and say:
> Return, oh backsliding Israel, says God
> I will not frown on you;
> For I am merciful, says God, I will not bear a grudge forever.
> Only acknowledge your sin that you have transgressed against
>   Adonai your God
> And have scattered your ways to the strangers under every
>   leafy tree,
> And you have not hearkened to My voice, says God.
> Return, my backsliding children, says God; for I am a ruler
>   for you, and I will take you one of a city, and two of a fam-
>   ily, and I will bring you to Zion.

Jeremiah 3:12–14

Thy Children Shall Return to Their Own Border

In these modern times when Israel is returning land to its neighbors in exchange for full peace, perhaps today's Haftarah was truly prophetic, when it said: "Thy children shall return to their own border." The midrash was also prophetic, in terms of predicting the return of our People to its Homeland. In *Eikhah Rabba* we read these words:

> Our mother Rachel came forward before the Holy One,
>   blessed be he, and said:
> Master of the universe, it is clearly known to you
> how your servant Jacob loved me with an exceeding love,
> and worked seven years for my father for me,
> and when he had completed those seven years,
> and the time came for my marriage to my husband,
> my father took counsel, and gave my sister to my husband in
>   my stead.
> And it was a very hard thing for me to bear,
> yet I had compassion on my sister,
> lest she go forth to shame,
> and I acted with charity toward her,
> and was not jealous of her.
> And if I, who am flesh and blood, dust and ashes,

was not jealous of my rival,
and did not send her forth to shame and disgrace,
You, O King, living, enduring, and compassionate,
why are you jealous of idols which are nothing real,
and have exiled my children,
so that they were killed by the sword,
and the foe did with them as they wished?
At once the compassion of the Holy One, blessed be he, was
    aroused, and he said: For your sake, Rachel, I shall return
    Israel to their place.

Therefore it is written:
Thus saith the Lord:
A voice is heard in Ramah, lamentation, and bitter weeping,
Rachel weeping for her children;
"she refuseth to be comforted for her children, because they
    are not" (Jer.31:15). And it is written:
"Thus saith the Lord:
Refrain thy voice from weeping, and thine eyes from tear; for
    thy work shall be rewarded" (ibid., v.16).
And it is written:
"And there is hope for thy future
and thy children shall return to their own border" (ibid. 4.17).

Lamentations Rabbah 24

Prayer for the Gift and Raising of Children

Dear God, I thank You for the gift of this child to raise, this life to
share, this mind to help mold, this body to nurture, and this spirit to
enrich. Let me never betray this child's trust, dampen this child's hope,
or discourage this child's dreams. Help me, dear God, to help this precious child become all You mean him to be. Let Your grace and love
fall on him like gentle breezes and give him inner strength and peace
and patience for the journey ahead.

Marian Wright Edelman

We Are Dear Children to God

The Biblical tradition teaches us that Israel, the northern kingdom, suffered from recalcitrance, moral corruption and disloyalty to God. This chapter from the prophet Jeremiah forms part of a message of reconciliation between God and Israel. This idea marks the profound significance of the last three verses of the haftarah for the second day of Rosh Hashanah, in particular:

> I [God] can hear Ephraim [another name for the northern kingdom] lamenting: You [God] have chastised me, and I am chastised; like a calf that has not been broken. Receive me back, let me return, for You, O lord, are my God. Now that I have turned back, I am filled with remorse; now that I am made aware, I strike my thigh [in self-reproach]. I am ashamed and humiliated for I bear the disgrace of my youth. Truly, Ephraim is a dear son to Me [God], a child who is dandled! Whenever I have turned against him, My thoughts would dwell on him still. That is why My heart yearns for him; I will receive him back in love, declares the Lord. (Jeremiah 32:17–19)

The description of "sinful" Israel as "a dear son to Me—*haben yakir lee Ephraim*" seems anomalous. Where is there room for endearment when the northern kingdom's relationship to God is characterized by disloyalty? Rabbi Joseph Kara, the twelfth-century French exegete, explains

> There was not a single tribe which sinned or caused others to sin like the tribe of Ephraim. Jereboam [who was from the tribe of Ephraim and served as the first king of the northern kingdom] sinned and caused others to sin by setting up worship places for the golden calf in Dan and in Bet El. But because the northern kingdom showed remorse and repented their wickedness, God yearned for them and showed love for them.

This idea underlies the reason that the verse "a dear son to Me" is mentioned in the Shofar service of the *Musaf Amidah* for Rosh Hashanah. This verse reminds us that in our encounter with God, there is always room for repair and return to God. Rabbi Eliahu Dessler, the twentieth-century philosopher of the Lithuanian yeshivot expressed it this way:

"Any slight movement in the direction of *teshuvah* and immediately we are 'a dear son to Me [God].'"

Rabbi Mordechai Silverstein

There Is Hope for Your Future, Declares God (Jeremiah 31:17)

The buoyant optimism of Judaism in teaching that a new beginning can always be made feels strange in our day and age. The fashionable philosophies of our time speak of anxiety and frustration, of failure and despair, of our "creaturely" helplessness and "existential" tragedy, of the knell of doom in the distance, sounding dark and implacable. But we must remember that the message of Judaism always sounds strange to human ears. Even in the ages of faith, when people walked about with long pious faces, mortifying their flesh in penitence and contorting their minds to fit rigid dogmas, the healthy optimism of our faith sounded strange and unbelievable. For Judaism is healthy minded and open-eyed. It does not close its eyes to evil in nature or to sin in human nature, but it asserts with tireless persistence that God is "King" over nature and that we are capable of triumphing over the evil in our makeup. "It is at the door that sin lurks, lusting for you, but you may rule over it" (Genesis 4:7).

Adapted from Rabbi Jacob Agus

The Metaphor of Parenthood

Several years ago there was a movie entitled *Parenthood* starring Steve Martin. At one point in the movie a teen comments to his friend how ill prepared most people seem to be for parenthood. "I don't get it," he says. "We live in a world where you have to earn a license for almost everything—to drive, to go fishing, to hunt. But any dope can have a child, without any preparation or experience. There ought to be a license for bearing children...."

If there's a common theme to the Torah and Haftarah readings of Rosh Hashanah it is the complexities of "parenthood." I'd like to comment on why these chapters were chosen by the sages as the readings for Rosh Hashanah.

At first glance these chapters don't appear to have a direct connection to this holiday. They deal with Jewish families, not the creation of the world or the theme of judgment. On closer study, however, I would suggest that the connection can be found on a metaphorical rather than a literal level.

We read about the prolonged period of childlessness that afflicted both Sarah and Hannah. The birth of a child was viewed as a miracle and a gift from God. And on the second day of Rosh Hashanah we read about the binding of Isaac. Though the Haftarah for the second day of Rosh Hashanah does not deal with families per se, the prophet Jeremiah speaks of mother Rachel crying for her exiled children. The prophet also describes the relation of Israel to God as that of a favored child, *"Haben yakir lee Efraim, im yeled sha'ashu'im."* "Is not Ephraim my precious son, my darling child?"

So why these chapters? What connection do they have for the themes of these holy days? The Sages offer many different answers to these questions. Some explain that both Isaac and Samuel were born on Rosh Hashanah. Others claim that the connection is to be found in the opening words of Genesis 22: *Va'Adonai pakad et Sarah*—and the Lord remembered Sarah—Rosh Hashanah is *Yom Hazikaron*, the day of remembrance. It seems to me that there's a simpler answer to the question of why these chapters were chosen.

The answer, I believe, is to be found in the metaphor of parenthood. God is our parent. So if we want to understand our relationship to God we must begin at home. At this time of year, more than any other, we're asked to think of our relationship to God as that of a child to a parent. Sure, God is *Malkaynu*, "our Sovereign"; but God is also *Aveenu*, "our Parent."

At times our relationship to our parents can be just as complex and ambivalent as our relationship to God. We love our parents but we're constantly striving to free ourselves of them. We're caught between obedience and autonomy, between loyalty and rebellion. The same can be said about our relationship to God. The Torah portions of Rosh Hashanah challenge us to think about our relationship to our parents and to our children—and then to take it one step farther and ask, "What can this teach me about my relationship to God?"

The Zohar says, "Honor you father and mother, even as you honor God; for all three were partners in you creation." For the sages, then, it's not such a far jump from "Abraham, Sarah and Isaac" or "Hannah and Samuel" to *"Aveenu, Malkaynu."* It's nice to think in grand universal terms, but if a person can't respect his parents, what does it all really mean. Today's Torah portion begins at the foundation of all civilization—at home.

Rabbi Mark B. Greenspan

God Is a Source of Comfort

On Rosh Hashanah, as we seek to do *teshuvah*, repentance, we want to know that God is a source of comfort. Comfort is not an answer for the way the world is, but is a relationship of caring. Caring is greatly needed. In the haftorah for the Second Day, we read a promise of redemption. The prophet Jeremiah describes a scene of joy: the Jewish people, scattered by exile and war, will return in triumph to their land. God will bring back everyone, even those who are weak or ill, turning their grief into cheer. "They shall come weeping and with compassion I will guide them. I will lead them to streams of water … for I am ever a Parent to Israel."

And yet, the scene is mixed with sadness. God hears a voice crying, the matriarch Rachel weeping for her children who have been exiled. She refuses to be comforted, because they are gone. They were exiled because of their sins, and despite divine promises, she does not believe that God will ever bring them back. The next voice is that of Ephraim, who has been chastised by God for those sins and who is now asking to return: he has truly repented and is filled with remorse for what he has done. One gets the impression that he does not really expect God to accept his *teshuvah*. And yet, God does: *ki midei dabri bo zakhor ezkerenu od al ken hamu mei'ai lo rahem arakhamenu ne'um adonai.*" God says, "Whenever I have turned against him, my thoughts would dwell on him still. That is why my heart yearns for him. I will receive him back in love." God cannot just be the ruler who judges, but must also be the protector who comforts. God cannot forget those God has been in relationship with. God hears the desire to return, to do *teshuvah*, and must truly listen.

The message of the end of the haftorah, which is incorporated into the *zichronot* section is particularly welcome during the season of *teshuvah*. When we open ourselves up to ask for forgiveness, we feel vulnerable, and the potential exists for us to become estranged from God. The haftorah teaches us that there is hope. I think these are some of the more beautiful expressions of God's relationship to us. In never abandoning Ephraim, God understands the fact that we are imperfect and need the opportunity to change. No divine decision is final. Usually in the prayer, it is we who express our own imperfection. But here we have an explanation of honesty from God. God knows we are imperfect, and God still trusts.

Rachel Kahn-Troster

The Divinity inside You

"Return, O Israel, unto Adonai your God"

HOSEA 14:2

With a creative spin on the Hebrew words of the verse from Hosea, read as the Haftarah of *Shabbat Shuvah,* between Rosh Hashanah and Yom Kippur, Rabbi Yisrael, the Maggid of Kuzhnitz, explained this verse as follows: Return, O Israel, until Adonai becomes your God— that is, bring back the godliness that is actually part of you. Returning to God is a vague concept. Returning to the point that you actually internalize God's presence into the very fiber of your being is of a different degree and level. Rabbi Yisrael advises his listeners to truly return, to God, and to their own internal divinity.

D.P.E.

TIKU VA-CHODESH SHOFAR: THE BLOWING OF THE SHOFAR

The sounding of the *shofar* is considered an act of great mystery. The wordless but wailing *shofar* sounds are taken to be a "higher" or deeper expression of Israel's outcry than words can express. While the liturgy of Rosh Hashanah is perhaps the most eloquent and poetic of the year, the raw emotion of the season ("Thank You for bringing us alive to this time! Give us another year of life!") is so elemental and primitive that it is better expressed by these unrefined cries of the horn than by words of great poets.

The mystics attributed great significance to the order of the *shofar* blasts. One such *kavvanah,* attributed to Rabbi Isaiah Horowitz (who lived in Prague and Jerusalem in the seventeenth century), notes that each group of sounds begins with a *teki'ah,* a whole note, proceeds to *shevarim,* a "broken" note, divided into three parts, or even to *teru'ah,* an entirely fragmented sound, at least seven very brief sounds. But each broken note is followed by a whole note, another *teki'ah.* This, he says, is the message of Rosh Hashanah: "I started off whole, I became broken, even splintered into fragments, but I shall become whole again! I shall become whole again!"

RABBI ARTHUR GREEN, *THESE ARE THE WORDS*

The Lesson of Abraham

"And Abraham lifted up his eyes, and looked, and behold behind him a ram caught in the thicket by its horns (Genesis 22.13)." This teaches us that the Holy One, blessed be God, showed our ancestor Abraham the ram tearing itself free from one set of bushes and getting entangled in another. The Holy One, blessed be God, said to Abraham: "Similarly, your children and descendants are destined to be caught by iniquities and entangled in sin but ultimately they will be redeemed through the horns of the ram." Therefore it is written, "Adonai your God will blow the shofar" (Zechariah 9:14).

R. Huna son of R. Isaac said: "It teaches that the Holy One, blessed be God, showed Abraham the ram tearing itself free from one set of bushes and getting entangled in another. The Holy One, blessed be God, said to Abraham: 'In a similar way, your children and descendants are destined to be caught by the nations and entangled in troubles, being dragged from empire to empire, from Babylon to Media, from Media to Greece, and from Greece to Edom [Rome], but they will ultimately be redeemed through the horns of the ram.' Therefore it is written, Adonai shall be seen over them, and God's arrow will go forth as lightning; and God will blow the shofar" (ibid.).

Leviticus Rabbah 29.10

Sound the Shofar!

Sound the shofar at the new moon,
At the full moon for our day of feasting.
For it is a statute for Israel,
A law of the God of Jacob.

Psalms 81:4–5

A Prayer for Blowing Shofar

This prayer is based on the notion that blowing shofar is related to the Hebrew midwives Shifra and Puah who birthed the Jewish women in Exodus. The word Shifra *is related to* shofar *and Puah means "to blow."*

At this awesome season
pregnant
with all possibility we pray today:

By our choices and deeds,
with Divine Intervention,
Supernal Midwife of Israel
and of All Creation,
attend,
assist us
to birth as yet unknown wonders,
miracles of Life.

With an awesome fear of God,
I place this shofar to my lips.

May the breath
You breathe inside me,
now return to You
to be renewed and return again
to this world for Life, for Peace

May the birthcries of my shofar blasts
be pleasing to You,
as the words and deeds of Shifra
with fear of You, she
lovingly births Your People:
Freedom
to do Your Will.

Like Puah,
be *hutzpadik* (nervy)
in Your advocacy
Encourage us toward Life
even when we ourselves may feel discouraged,
distressed in the midst
of life's hard pangs.

Breathe life into us anew!
While others take us for dead.
Lest we face despair of lost hope,

even we,
may abandon ourselves.

In the name of Shifra, Puah,
Sara *Emainu* (our mother)
Hana,
in the name of Rahel *Emainu,*
let her tears for her children,
be of gladness and joy.

In the name of God that is Birth,
let the joy of becoming, of hearing
sounds from this birthing shofar
overcome and become us all.

God, cleanse us of our sins
like the midwife
who cleanses the newborn infant.

Wrap us in the beautiful garments
of the Soul.
Bathe us in Your Light
so our Divine nature may shine
even as we walk joyously in Your Light—
B'or paneha yehalayhun! (may we walk by the light of your
   presence)

May the breath of my being
blown into this shofar
hearken us
back to the shofar
that is Shifra
and the breath
that is Puah.

Deliver us from the narrows
of, God Forbid, an evil decree,
into the breadth of sound.

Signal in us an expansion.
Together God
may we birth this coming year!

God,
Supernal Midwife,
send me no angel, no seraph, not even
Hayot Hakodesh! (Holy midwives!)

Be Thou my Midwife!
Be Thou my angel!
Be Thou My Self!
Birth me yet again anew,
renewed for this coming year.

• Janet Zimmern

The Trumpets of Rosh Hashanah

The blowing of the shofar ... has become such a major part of the Rosh Hashanah service for almost two millennia that we tend to forget that in Temple times, it was only one of the two types of trumpets used. The Torah, in Numbers 10:1–10, specifically instructs the Israelites to: "Make thee two trumpets of silver; of beaten work shall thou make them ... and in your appointed seasons, and in your new moons, you shall blow with your trumpet over your burnt offerings, and over the sacrifices of you; peace offerings; and they shall be to you for a memorial before your God."

These large, sacred, silver trumpets, known as *chatzotzrot* in Hebrew, were blown by the priests as part of the ... *musaf* sacrificial service on every Sabbath and on Passover, Shavuot, Succot, Yom Kippur and Rosh Hashanah. The silver trumpets were distinctly different instruments from the shofar, although the notes blown were similar.

The trumpets were initially used during the period of wandering of the Israelites in the desert as a means of assembling the people. A blast on one trumpet was a signal for the assembly of only the princes of the tribes. Blasts on both of the trumpets signaled the assembly of the entire congregation. The blast of the *truah*, a series of sharp, separate notes on the trumpets, was the signal for the camps of the Israelites to begin their journeys.

According to the Mishnah, on Rosh Hashanah in the Temple a straight shofar, fashioned from the horn of an ibex or wild goat and fitted with a golden mouthpiece, was blown between the pair of silver trumpets. Since the shofar was the prime instrument of the day, its sound was long and maintained, while the sound of the trumpets was cut short. On fast days, two curved ram shofars with silver mouthpieces were used, and the two silver trumpets were placed between them. Since the trumpet was the prime instrument for the call to assembly on fast days, this time its tone was prolonged and the shofar's notes cut short.

With the destruction of the Temple and the cessation of the sacrificial service the blowing of the silver trumpets as part of Jewish ritual ceased. Even during Temple times, however, the shofar, without accompaniment of trumpets, had been blown in the synagogues in Israel on Rosh Hashanah. This custom has continued as one of the central themes of the holiday.

Herb Geduld

The Torah Was Given with the Sound of the Shofar

The shofar was created for the sake of the welfare of Israel. The Torah was given to Israel with the sound of the shofar, as it is written: "When the sound of the shofar grew louder and louder" (Exodus 19:19). Israel conquered its enemies in the battle of Jericho with the blast of the shofar: "When the people heard the sound of the shofar that the people shouted with a great shout, and the wall fell down flat" (Joshua 6:20). Israel will be told of the coming of the messiah with the sound of the shofar: "And the Lord God will blow the shofar" (Zechariah 9:14). And the Holy One, blessed be God will sound the shofar at the time of the ingathering of the exiles of Israel to their place: "And it shall come to pass in that day, that a great shofar shall be blown; and they shall come that were lost in the land of Assyria, and they that were dispersed in the land of Egypt; and they shall worship God in the holy mountain at Jerusalem" (Isaiah 27:13).

Eliyahu Zuta 2

How Can I Sound the Shofar?

I've been asked again to sound shofar. Do they understand what is being asked? I believe, sincerely, that the person who sounds shofar should be a good person. On Rosh Hashanah, as I sit in my sanctuary seat before the time, the apprehension churns in me. It has been in me for a month, all during Elul. I have acted on stage and this apprehension is deeper in me than the nervousness that precedes an acting performance. When it is almost time for the sounding, when I go into the space behind the *bimah* to prepare, my apprehension grows, stirs my insides even more strongly.

I put on my white kittle that sets me apart from the congregation. I wrap myself again in my prayer shawl, the prayer shawl I expect to wear in my grave. I take up the soft shofar bag sewn by my wife, and I feel the shofar, the mystical instrument inside the bag.

What will happen?

What will happen when I force my wind into the horn? (To deflate the ego of shofar "performers," it is written that the *baal tekiah* is just a bag of wind.) In all the previous years when I sounded shofar, during all the previous month of Elul when I lifted the shofar to my lips, I was not certain.

There always is the concern, the wonder, the worry. What sounds will emerge? Will it be strong or a dry rush of air? Will it be right?

The primitive, earthly instrument connects me, personally, through the thousands of years, with all the Jews of everywhere and forever, who have sounded and heard the sounds of the shofar. Within its animal horn is the mysterious message that attempts to motivate mankind to improve, to behave better than animals.

Can I find that message? Can I bring it out for all the congregation to hear? Will anyone hear it and try to better themselves, ethically, try to behave better with each other in the coming year? Or will they look on me as a performer?

Am I worthy?

Who am I to presume to be the bearer of this message? Am I worthy? Have I tried to improve my own behavior in the past year? I can do better to control myself, my passions, my appetites and my awareness of others.

Have I tried to make peace with myself and with others, friends and opponents alike? Am I worthy? I must listen, myself, to the sound of the shofar. I begin to tremble, literally tremble with humility. Tears of trepidation well up, threatening to overflow from just beneath my surface.

The congregation waits. The shofar blower should be a good person, a person all others can admire, an example for them and their children. Am I worthy?

Author Unknown

Why the Shofar?

The following twenty-four formulations of the meaning of *teki'at ha-shofar* may be used—one each day—on the twenty-four weekdays in *Elul* when the shofar is sounded. They may also be used on *Rosh-ha-Shanah* or after *Ne'ilah,* either recited (one or more at a time) by the Rabbi (or some other person) or read (after rearrangement) as a responsive reading.

May the sound of the *shofar*

1. Shatter our complacency—revealing the corruption of our situation, and summoning us, with God's help, to correct it.

2. Penetrate into our inmost being and cause us to turn back to our Father in Heaven.

3. Renew our trust in the promise of the *mashiah*—and inspire us to work toward hastening (and not, God forbid, delaying) the day of his coming.

4. Alert us to the danger of the enemy, and remind us who the enemy really is.

5. Renew our loyalty to the true King, and strengthen us to withhold obedience from all usurpers.

6. Break the hold of our evil temptation, and free us to bend our will to the service of the Holy One.

7. Summon us to sacrificial service, and stir us to respond, in love and in obedience, with Abraham's response: "Here I am."

8. Reveal to us the brokenness of our existence, and open us to the mending power of God's love.

9. Awaken us to the enormity of our sin, and to the vastness of God's mercy for those who truly repent.

10. Recall to us the moment at Sinai, and enable us again to pledge that "all that God has spoken we will do and obey."

11. Summon us to dethrone all false gods, and restore us to the true worship of Heaven.

12. Renew our hope for the ingathering of our exiles, when Israel will be restored and all humankind redeemed.

13. Remind us that we stand in judgment before the one true Judge, who is mindful of our deeds—and of our needs.

14. Make us tremble at the right moment, for the right reason, in the right spirit, before the right one; the righteous Judge.

15. Herald the triumph of right over wrong, of good over evil, of peace over war, of love over hate, of blessing over curse, of life over death.

16. Teach us what to remember and what to forget, how to work and how to wait.

17. Herald the fall of all citadels of evil and the conversion of enemies into friends.

18. Shatter the shackles of all human bondage and summon all slaves to go free.

19. Teach us when to be afraid and when not to be afraid.

20. Awaken us from our lethargy and arouse us to do what must be done.

21. Renew our trust in God's promise to resurrect the dead; for judgment and chastisement, for cleansing and refining, and for life eternal.

22. Alert us to the shortness of the day, the magnitude of the task, and the abundance of resources that God makes available to us for the performance of His will.

23. Strengthen us to make our will accord with God's own will, no matter what the cost.

24. Become our jubilant shout of joy and gratitude for the promised redemption.

Rabbi Hershel Matt

The Call to Battle

"Blessed Is the People Who Know the Sound of Teruah."

PSALMS 89:16

The Baal Shem Tov, founder of Hasidism, interpreted this verse to mean: How wonderful it is when the entire people knows the call of battle, to defend themselves, and stand in the Gate to face the enemy, and thus need not always rely on their leaders.

The Besht wanted to empower the people to act on its own, to be in a state of readiness to perform its national spiritual duties, without even being called by its leaders to do so. A people is only as strong as its followers, not its leaders.

D.P.E.

Shofar: The Clarion Call of Hope

Just a little over five hundred years ago the Spanish Inquisition was raging. Torquemada, the grand inquisitor was rounding up hundreds of Jews and burning their bodies in order to save their souls. Many Jews continued their Jewish practices in secret, in closed rooms, and in damp cellars. Though they longed to be in the synagogue to hear the blasts of the Shofar; they knew that it would be impossible because the agents of the hated Torquemada were everywhere, and any display of Jewish custom or ritual could betray family and friends. The Jews of 1492 Spain knew that they could not fulfill the sacred commandment to hear the Shofar.

But then a rumor began to spread in the street: "Shhh, keep it to yourself." It was in the city of Barcelona that word began to spread of a special concert to be given to Spanish royalty and church officials. Jews bristled at the thought of spending Rosh Hashanah eve, one of the most sacred days of the year, in the Royal Concert Hall, but it was also an opportunity to show their tormentors that no ties remained to the despised religion, Judaism.

An undercurrent, a whisper, "Just go, you won't be sorry." The hall was filled to capacity, with huge crowds outside. Spanish royalty believed the full house to be due to the prominence of the composer Don Fernando Aguilar. Don Fernando, himself a secret Jew, had announced that on Rosh Hashanah eve he would present a concert featuring instrumental music of various peoples.

By now you may have anticipated the end of this remarkable tale. The compositions were many and the instruments unusual. At the crescendo of one very moving piece came Shofar sounds in full keeping with Jewish tradition.

All this was done without any of the dignitaries aware of its significance to their Jewish compatriots, all the royalty and the leading figures of the Inquisition were present—they all heard, and saw, but knew nothing. They could not sense the hidden emotion that electrified the air all around them. Do you wonder why these Jews imperiled their lives to hear this call that we can listen to in this land of freedom?

There have been other times in Jewish history when Jews risked death to hear the sound of the Shofar. Among the many things that it has come to signify, it is a reminder of the indomitable spirit that struggles to survive all attempts at subjugation and repression. But there is more than just a reminder of the will to survive in a hostile world.

To the sounds of the Shofar, I have listened and I have heard the echoes of our lives. The Shofar has spoken to Jews across the span of time and the bridge of years. In it I have heard the voice of childhood, the dialogue of youth, the wisdom of adulthood and the sagacity of old age. It is a call to life; it sounds the clarion call of hope.

Rabbi Stephen S. Pearce

Shofar: Awaken Our Slumbering Hearts

Oh God of the spirit of all humanity, as we rise to listen to the sharp and penetrating sound of the shofar, may our hearts hearken to your call so that we may be able to arise from our spiritual and moral lethargy. Help us to cast off that paralyzing insensitivity which makes of our lives a series of tiny, meaningless moments, and which converts us into small people, with small hearts, living small lives, with small dreams. May the sharp and trembling blasts of the shofar awaken our slumbering hearts, making them beat faster and pumping into our veins the life-giving blood of multi-dimensional awareness and creativity. Help us, O God, to understand the call of the shofar. Help us to sensitize our hearts and souls so as to achieve in the coming year a life more dedicated to noble goals. May the sound of the shofar reach into the hearts of all your children wherever they may be so that we may walk together toward an era of peace and harmony. Amen.

O people Israel! Hearken to the broken notes of the *Shevarim*. Let us mend our tattered souls and broken lives so that we may serve God and the creation with the fullness of our being. May the weeping of the ram's horn invoke in us the willingness to sacrifice and labor for the dawn of a new world in which men and women of all creeds, colors, and races may live in justice and equality. Amen.

Humankind! Hearken to the call of the shofar. Let us awaken from our apathy and egotism. Let us realize our capacities as beings created in the image of God with the power to create, to love, and to build.

Let us cast away our fears and anxieties, our suspicions, our aggressions, our hostility and violence. May these shofar blasts strengthen our decisions to lead more significant lives dedicated to the search for Your love and Your eternal truth. May we dedicate ourselves to the sanctification of all life. Amen.

Rabbi Marshall T. Meyer

Guided Imagery Meditation on the Blowing of the Shofar

Sit back, relax, take a few deep breaths, and imagine yourself sitting in synagogue on the morning of Rosh Hashanah, and the *Hazzan* is repeating the *Musaf Amidah*. Excitement builds as you approach the blowing of the shofar....

In your mind's eye take yourself back to other times at Rosh Hashanah services when the shofar was blown. Recall many different people who have blown the shofar in years gone by. Out of the forest of your memory recall the person who blew the shofar in the synagogue you attended as a child.... Bring back the sight, sounds, smells and other senses of that early shofar blowing experience. What was it like? ...

Now hear the blasts of the shofar one more time.... Another year has passed. The crisp air outside as you entered the synagogue reminds you that Fall has come again. Summer is over, vacation time has gone, and the new school year, the organizational program year, and the Jewish calendar year, are about to resume.... Notice the twinge of sadness about losing the summer that has zipped by so quickly.... Nevertheless you are excited about what things are in store for you in the coming year....

Just before the *Baal Tekiah* raises the shofar to his lips, the rabbi explains some of the meanings that Jewish history has given to the blowing of the shofar. Listen carefully....

Listen as the rabbi retells the famous story of Abraham's sacrifice of Isaac, when a ram in the thicket took the place of Isaac on the altar. The ram's horn reminds us, says the rabbi, of the readiness of Abraham to obey God's will even at the cost of the greatest sacrifice anyone can make. Think to yourself: Was Abraham really being tested during the *Akedah*? Or maybe it was God who was being tested! Was God actually going to go through with this cruel act? In our story, explains the rabbi, both God and Abraham passed the test.... There was to be no more human sacrifice. It was now forbidden for all time.

Think to yourself, Am I being tested too? ... Have I been tested during this past year? In what ways? ... Were the trials and tribulations which faced me in the past twelve months part of God's testing of my faith, my courage? Did I pass these tests? ... In what other ways does God test us? ... How do we test God? ...

If there is a Covenant, a mutual contract between God and us, can we not also demand that God fulfill the divine part of the agreement? Does God ask too much of me and others? ... (Pause) The blowing of the shofar is about to begin. The congregation rises.... The rabbi pronounces the blessing. *Baruch atta ... ve-tzeevanu lishmo-a kol shofar.* "Blessed be God Who has commanded us to hear the blowing of the shofar."

Something inside you is deeply moved. More than all the words and prayers, the sermon and the Torah reading, the blowing of the shofar stirs you, awakens you, shakes you.... It takes you all the way back to Abraham, Sarah and Isaac, the Founders of our People. They had the courage they showed to follow an unknown and invisible God. They thought of things which were never thought of before.... A new religion was founded four thousand years ago, and you are one of those who still upholds it, and transmits it to those who come after you!

The shofar blasts resound throughout your heart and soul. Will you be worthy to be inscribed in the Book of Life for the coming year? Will the shofar succeed in awakening you from your lethargy to become a better person, a more faithful servant of God?

Take some time to think about these questions.... (Pause).

The sounds of the shofar fade into the distance. The worship services continue. The questions remain inside you.... They haunt you, and yet they inspire you.... They prod you to be a better person, a better Jew, a more loyal child of your Divine Parent....

It is time to return. This is the holiday of Return. Now we will return to this room, and the questions will continue to stir within you.... At the count of three you will be completely awake and refreshed, ready to greet another New Year....

Rabbi Dov Peretz Elkins

Shofar Ceremony

Today we sound the shofar to awaken our hearts to the diverse expressions of Jewish life. May each blast of the shofar remind us of the precious contribution of every Jew to the wholeness of our people. May we be stirred from a place of judgment and moved to a place of compassion. May the sound of the shofar shatter the walls which divide us and raise the call of joy for the essential contributions of our partners in covenant.

For Conservative Jews, who preserve the balance between tradition and today, and strive for deeper understanding of our covenant with God. For the Jewish Theological Seminary, source of scholarship and inspiration and consistent vision ... *Tekiah!*

For Reform Jews, whose devotion to social justice keeps alive the prophetic call, and who are unafraid to explore new ways to reach to God and each other ... *Tekiah!*

For modern Orthodox Jews, who live a life of commitment to Torah and halakhah in contemporary society, showing us a path of possibilities ... *Tekiah!*

For Chassidim, who preserve an intensity of spirit and certainty, denying themselves material gain in pursuit of the goal of a world under God's sovereignty ... *Tekiah!*

For Haredi Jews, filled with a sense of mission to bring redemption by building a fence around the Torah and lifting up its message of God's dominion over all ... *Tekiah!*

For Israeli Jews, gathered from the four corners of the earth and led upright to our homeland, who maintain a place of belonging for us all ... *Tekiah!*

For Zionists of every land, whose devotion to our people for 100 years has brought into existence a miracle our ancestors only imagined ... *Tekiah!*

For cultural Jews who, by their commitments, preserve the joys of Yiddish, the romance of Ladino, the literature of Hebrew, the music and poetry and humor and art of a thousand Jewish communities ... *Tekiah!*

For gastronomic Jews, help us feed our bodies as well as our souls with chicken soup and kasha, falafel and shawarma, kugel and baklava, balaweh and bunuelos ... *Tekiah!*

For philanthropic Jews who nurture the world with their generosity and fund day schools and universities, synagogues and hospitals, free loan societies, cultural arts ... *Tekiah!*

For members of Jewish organizations who gather to socialize or to learn or to promote the interests of our people and our nation ... *Tekiah!*

For the Jews who are "*mishugah ladavar,*" devoted beyond measure to the causes we must consider—disabilities, renewal, inclusiveness, environment, hunger and housing, civil rights, Jewish defense ... *Tekiah!*

For Jews who marry Jews and create a Jewish home, a link across generations and a link to others who preserve our tradition ... *Tekiah!*

For Jews who marry non-Jews and struggle to define a sense of Jewishness which honors both their heritage and their love ... *Tekiah!*

For every one of us, single or married, old or young, religious or secular, enthusiastic or ambivalent, Jewish by birth, by choice, by soul or by sympathy, for the essential contribution we each bring which makes our people whole and which testifies to the many reflections of God's image in which we were created ... *Tekiah gedolah!*

Rabbi Jack Moline

Tik'u Va-Chodesh Shofar: Linking Our Lives Below with the Unknowable Above

"Tik'u bahodesh shofar bakeseh l'yom hageinu." This verse, which is read in the synagogue on Thursday morning as part of the psalm of the day, and which is familiar as well from our Rosh Hashanah liturgy, is generally translated as "sound the shofar at the new moon, at the full moon for our festive day." However, the word *tik'u,* the verbal form of *tekiah,* the shofar blast, has the meaning as well of connecting, of inserting. In modern Hebrew, a *teka* is a plug which goes into a *sheka,*

a socket. The S'fat Emet, the famous Chasidic commentator, takes our verse and retranslates it, *"tiku bahodesh,"* means connect everything new, *"lakeseh,"* to the hidden world above. On this day of Rosh Hashanah, when we hear the sound of the Shofar, we try to make connections, we try to understand, we try to link our lives below with the unknowable, with that which is hidden above. We seek to find God and understand who God is, and create a connection with our Creator.

Rabbi Edward M. Friedman

My Father's Shofar

For several years after my father's death, his shofar languished on my shelf. Just glancing at the simple rough-hewn horn unleashed memories of my father's preparations for the Holy Days. His gleaming white kittel was starched and ready weeks before. In the month of Elul, his shofar blasts woke us up for school. My parents owned a small kosher hotel in central New Jersey and every Rosh Hashanah our guests were my father's *landsman*, fellow survivors from the small Carpathian town which had been Czechoslovakia for most of his life. Leading those services was a duty he approached with solemnity and pride.

When the egalitarian *minyan* where I davened needed someone to sound the shofar, I picked up the neglected instrument, put my lips to the mouthpiece, and blew. A sound, more closely resembling a squeak than the magnificent blasts my father elicited, came out. But the tremulous mousy noise empowered me. I enthusiastically volunteered. Services were a month a way—plenty of time to master the calls. I am woman; hear me roar. The long powerful *Tekiah* blast was not a problem. The three shorter *Shvarim*—the plaintive mournful broken cries— were a bit more challenging. But the *Teruah* calls, a rapid series of nine or more very short notes, were impossible.

Sounding and hearing the shofar are very important Rosh Hashanah commandments. The primitive unearthly sounds break through to God's heart. And here was my pushing-the-ritual-envelope congregation, certainly in need of leniency, with a shofar-blower who couldn't. I prayed for my father's heavenly intervention.

As my despair grape-vined through the community friends called to reassure me. But one friend called to tell me that his shofar was incredibly easy to use.

I didn't believe him but he insisted on bringing it over. He was right. The instrument was truly amazing. The shofar was magic. So that year and the next, always with my friend's shofar, I helped guide our congregation's prayers to the right place. I think my father would have been proud of me but maybe he just didn't want me to use his shofar.

Helen Weiss Pincus

The Original Shofar

The Midrash tells us that the ram created on the sixth day of Creation was used for many important purposes, including the shofar which will be blown in the Messianic Age.

Rabbi Chaninah ben Dosa said: From that ram, which was created at the twilight (after the sixth day of CREATION), nothing came forth which was useless. The ashes of the ram were the base which was upon the top of the inner altar. The sinews of the ram were the strings of the harp whereon David played. The ram's skin was the girdle around the loins of Elijah ... (2 Kings 1:8). The horn of the ram of the left side was the one which God blew upon Mount Sinai, as it is said ... (Joshua 6:5) (REVELATION). (The horn) of the right side, which is the larger, is destined in the future to be sounded in the world that is to come, as it is said, "And it shall come to pass in that day, that a great trumpet shall be blown" (Isaiah 27:18); and it is said, "And the Lord shall be Ruler over all the earth" (Zechariah 14:9) (REDEMPTION).

Pirke de R. Eliezer, chapter 31

Meaning of the Blasts: One, Three, Nine, Longest

In ancient cities and villages of the Land of Israel, in the days of Kings and Prophets, the Holy Day of Rosh Hashanah was welcome with the sounds of a trumpet, or a Shofar. Each different blast brought its unique message to the Israelite People gathered in prayer.

As our ancestors before us, we listen to the sounds of the Shofar. First we hear a voice, calling by name, each of the blasts. Then we hear the sound of the Shofar trumpeting towards us with its special message.

Tekiah—The single blast of *Tekiah* commands us to care about others and to reach out to them.

Shevarim—The three blasts of *Shevarim* command us to keep the many promises we make on this Rosh Hashanah, when a new year begins.

Teruah—The nine blasts of *Teruah* command us to respond to the many needs of the Jewish people wherever they live, in the hope that many will choose to return home to Eretz Yisrael.

Tekiah Gedolah—The final blast, the Great *Tekiah*, commands us today to begin our work to make this year a better year for all people. As the ancient sage Hillel said (Pirke Avot), "If not now, when?"

**Adapted from *High Holy Day Family Service* of
Stephen S. Wise Temple, Los Angeles**

Shofar: Cleaning the Earth for Those Who Come after Us

We cannot achieve everything we want in life. Sometimes it seems that there are more things we cannot do than the ones we can. Our part in the short time we have here on earth is so minuscule. Yet, as Rabbi Tarfon said, "We are not at liberty to desist from the work."

Perhaps the famous author J.R.R. Tolkien defined best the true meaning of the shofar call when he wrote:

> It is not our part to master all the tides of the world, but to do what is in us for the succor of those years wherein we are set, uprooting the evil in the fields that we know, so that those who live after us may have clean earth to till. What weather they shall have is not ours to rule.

If we can do this, clean up the physical and moral earth on which we live, then the meaning of the blast of the shofar, awakening us to our moral obligations to society, will have achieved its purpose.

D.P.E.

Blowing God's Breath into the Shofar

On Rosh Hashanah we have an extraordinary opportunity. On the New Year, the anniversary of the day on which humankind was created, we blow the shofar which mirrors the cry of the soul. The Bible tells us that on this day God breathed the soul of life into the first person.

Every Rosh Hashanah we blow our breath, the breath that God breathed into us, through a ram's horn, in order to hear the sound of our soul reverberate. Through the cry of the shofar we renew our connection to our essential being, to our soul, and carry that strength into the year ahead.

But why a ram's horn? The sheep or ram is known to be the most gentle and innocent of creatures, void of the aggressive nature of other animals. The ram reminds us that our soul is that part of ourselves that is gentle and innocent, untainted by the aggressive manipulative world we inhabit. Our soul is not seasoned by experience, nor is it the result of our connections, accumulated wealth, social status or ability to dominate others. The voice of our soul comes from the most subtle innocence within.

We cannot use something human-made to express this voice, because the human being is affected by his circumstances, his experiences and his ego. We therefore take something outside of ourselves— the ram's horn, the simplest instrument—that produces the haunting, piercing cry most closely approximating the pure sound of the soul.

Rabbi Simon Jacobson

The Shofar Is Not Magic

The *Magid* of Dubnov had a special talent of bringing out a point through parables. When he saw that many people came to synagogue to listen to the Shofar yet neglected to pay attention to the rest of the holiday prayers, he related the following parable:

Years ago, when a fire broke out in the village, all the people would drop everything they were doing and band together to carry water from the well to put out the blaze.

Once, when one of the villagers came to the big city, he suddenly heard bells ringing and horns blowing. "What is this noise?" he asked. "Whenever there is a fire, we ring the bells and blow the horns to put out the fire," came the reply. When he returned to the village he told the elders about his great discovery. "From now on," they said, "whenever there is a fire, we too will blow horns and ring bells, like in the big city and this way put out the fire!"

The next time there was a fire, the town elders started blowing their horns and ringing their bells. But the fire only got worse. Before long, half the village was gone.

When the villager returned to the big city and asked the people, "How come when we rang the bells, the fire didn't go out?"

They replied, "Do you really think that the bells and horns put out the blaze? They only alert the people that there is a fire. It is up to every one of us to extinguish it!"

"It is the same," says the *Magid* of Dubnov, "with the sounding of the Shofar. The sound of the Shofar is an awakening call to alert us to repent and better our ways. Now it is up to us to pray sincerely and make the proper New Year resolutions that will bring us closer to God."

Author Unknown

Shofarot

We believe in tomorrow. We believe that we have the power to make tomorrow different from today. We believe that poverty need not be permanent and that people need not learn war anymore.

We believe that there can yet be a time of peace and a time of justice, a time of tranquility for all who live on earth.

We believe that we can have a share in bringing that day closer by the way in which we live in the New Year.

The world may smile at our dreams—but no matter, we still believe. We, as Jews, persist in our belief that the human being was created not for evil, but for good, not a curse, but a precious blessing.

Author Unknown

Kol ha-Shofar: The Voice of the Shofar

The ancient voice calls:
Awake—and know fear!
Choose! Decide!
Which road will you travel this year?
But today—Shabbat—
the shofar's voice is not heard.

In this silence, in this stillness,
Where is God?
Is silence God's absence?
Or is it a call to respond?

Sh'ma Yisrael—Hear now, O Israel—
The sound of silence—
The sound that pierces the strongest armor.

The voice of the shofar
Helped bring down Jericho's walls,
But silence can shatter
The strongest walls—
The walls we build around ourselves.

Sh'ma Yisrael—Hear now, O Israel—
The sound of silence—
The crushing, deafening sound of silence—
And choose life.

                              Rabbi Stephan O. Parnes

Shofar: The Primal Scream

How do I demonstrate that there is a language without words? Well, we can do that with the shofar. With the blowing of that horn, there is the real sense of a cry. The Rabbis say that the *shevarim* and *teruah* sounds of the shofar are "whimpering" sounds. Psychologists used to talk about the "primal scream." They would say that unless you get to the place that evokes the "primal scream," you haven't gotten to the true source of the broken heart. In other words, ego will not let us reach our "primal scream," and so the shofar tries to get us to that place. Sometimes when Rosh HaShanah falls on Shabbos, and I don't want to blow the shofar, I ask people to scream, which gets beyond words, and in that scream we can share with people across generations, cultures, and languages.

                           Rabbi Zalman Schachter-Shalomi

The Wailing of the Shofar: Feeling the Other's Pain

Abaye expounded: The disagreement regarding how to sound the *teruah* revolves around the following: The Biblical verse in Numbers 29 instructs "It should be a day of sounding the *teruah*," and the Aramaic translation for "*teruah*" is "*yevavah,*" "trembling sound."

Now regarding the mother of Sisera, the Bible remarks that when she heard of her son's death, "the mother of Sisera stood at the window *'vativav.'*" One opinion is that the meaning is that she sighed and sighed—and therefore the *teruah* should sound like *shevarim*—a gasping sound, and one opinion is that she cried and cried and therefore the sound of the *teruah* should be constantly broken like uncontrollable crying (B.T. Rosh Hashanah 33b).

It is an extraordinary midrashic interpretation, for the Rabbis contend that what we are to hear in this sound of the shofar is the cry of the mother of Sisera. In the Book of Judges, Sisera was a Canaanite general who oppressed Israel. Deborah, the prophetess, gathers an army to oppose him; he is defeated, runs away and is killed by a woman, Yael, as he seeks refuge. The Bible celebrates this moment in the wonderful Song of Deborah. One of the verses of that song describes Sisera's mother watching from the window, waiting for her son's return, crying as she realizes that he has not come back.

The Rabbis argue that what we should hear in the trembling sound of the shofar is the crying of the mother of Sisera. Some say that it should be sounded like the *shevarim*—like gasping. Some say that it should be a wailing, a constantly broken cry. But all agree that what we are to hear is the pain and suffering of the mother of Sisera.

Make no mistake—the Rabbis are proud of Deborah's victory, she acted to save Israel and did what was required in that hour. And yet, on Rosh Hashanah we are to feel not only the pride of victory but the pain that was caused the mother of our enemy even when we fought in a righteous cause.

If the sounding of the shofar on Rosh Hashanah is to signal the final redemption, if we hear in it a taste of messianic longing, we should realize that the moment of redemption can only arrive when we are able to incorporate the pain of our enemy within our own longing. In the final victory, in the ultimately redemptive moment, we are asked to be able to see both sides of the story—our own need, and the humanity of the "other" who may even be our enemy.

The road not only to our own redemption but to the redemption of the "other" may lie in each side experiencing the pain of the other. If each could understand the other's suffering, if Palestinians could cry over the death of Jewish teenagers killed by a suicide bomber while they danced in a discotheque, and if Jews could feel the pain of the parents of an eight-year-old child killed by a scared Israeli soldier firing wildly at a checkpoint, then perhaps the redemption would be at hand—or at least, then, a peaceful alternative would seem possible.

Rabbi Edward Feld

The Meaning of the Shofar

One the greatest of Jewish philosophers, Saadia Gaon, once listed ten reasons for the sounding of the shofar on Rosh Hashanah. One reason he gives is that the shofar reminds us that Rosh Hashanah is the anniversary of creation by recalling that it is God who is the true sovereign of the universe not human beings. Often we live our lives as if God does not exist. This is not only a theological problem, but an ethical and moral one as well. If the world only centers around our self (and let's face it, we spend most of our time in that kind of mindset), then we also forget how we are connected to the environment and all the other kinds of life that help sustain us. Putting God back at the center is a humbling experience, which forces us out of ourselves.

The Shofar is one of the most ancient musical instruments known to humankind. It is human made, but out of the rough horn of a ram. This combination of natural material and human artifice reminds us not only of our humble origins as a people but also how indebted we are to the rest of creation for all that we have, eat, wear, and celebrate with. The music it makes is loud and not subtle. It is as if the voice of the Creator is sounding out the beginning of time. It is a call back to our origins and to the better future that we must bring about. God is calling us to restore ourselves as we restore creation.

Rabbi Lawrence Troster

Shofar: Because It's Imperfect

The sounds of the shofar are odd, squawky, uneven. They are echoes of an ancient world.

We've made technological advances to improve virtually every area of human life. Yet we still use *shofarot* made as they always have been, from sheep or goat horns, minimally cleaned up, hollowed out, with a roughly cut mouthpiece.

Why hasn't someone made a better shofar? One that would *tekiah* with a pure and clear blast like a trumpet. That would *shevarim* to break your heart like a blues saxophone. That would *teruah*, vibrating like, well, like a vibraphone. Why not a better shofar? We could do it.

The bleating, blasting, burping shofar gives a most haunting sound. It's not pretty, no. But it stirs us, perhaps because it is imperfect, as are we.

Rabbi Laura Metzger

YOM HA'ZIKARON: THE DAY OF REMEMBRANCE

Shalom or "peace" is Judaism's highest aspiration for the world in which we live. It is a value that is placed above all others. Rabbinic teaching describes it as the only "vessel" through which God's blessing can flow into this world.

Shalom is a value within the individual person as well. In our complex world we are too torn between conflicting goals, values, dreams, and aspirations. *Shalom* is related to *shelemut,* meaning "wholeness." We need to set our course and live it wholly. *Shalom* with oneself and with God are impossible without one another.

RABBI ARTHUR GREEN, *THESE ARE THE WORDS*

Yom Hazikaron: **This Day of the Year**

At this turning of the year,
Let my heart be open
To every broken spirit,
To those who try my patience,
To those I have wronged and hurt,
To those groping and lonely in the shadows.

Let my senses be open
To bearers of wisdom and new light,
Awakening me to behold anew
This green, flowering world,
That I may grasp the secret
Of blossoming into blessing,
Turning frustration into forgiveness,
And forgiveness into love
Without expectation of reward.

Essence of my life,
Urge me to honesty,
Judge me in mercy,
Bend me into giving,
Guide me in this turning of the year.

**From the Wilshire Boulevard Temple
High Holy Day prayer book**

Memory

[Remembering] is the telling and retelling each year of stories of the past. The history of the Jews is kept live in its religious forms, the exodus from Egypt, the stay in Babylon, the giving of the commandments at Sinai, the destruction of the Temples. Jewish religious schools all teach Jewish history and in doing so create Jewish nationhood. Jewish children know the story of the Spanish Inquisition, and the condition of the Jews in modern Russia. Jewish schools tell the tale of the sufferings of the Wandering Jew, who, according to Christian myth, is wandering because he mocked Christ and, according to the historical fact, because Christians have not truly accepted the teachings of their Christ....

This makes Jews continually the witnesses of their own past and gives the odd flavor to their reasonings—as if history were happening in both the vertical and the horizontal time line—as if things moved forward and stayed still at the same time.

Anne Roiphe

God Remembers Everything You Forget

When I jog, I love to run through cemeteries, and sometimes I stop to read the headstones. I saw one on Cape Cod recently at the grave of a man who died at twenty-eight—so young! The message read, "His life taught us how to live; his death, how to die." That's what ought to be on every headstone—I'd say this boy accomplished whatever he needed to accomplish in twenty-eight years. Now, other people had on their headstones that they went to Yale or Harvard, that they were lawyers or manufacturers. But I don't think God cares where we were graduated or what we did for a living. God wants to know who we are. Discovering this is the work of the soul—it is our true life's work.

As a matter of fact, over God's desk [is a] plaque that says, "God forgets everything you remember and God remembers everything you forget."

Bernie Siegel, M.D.

The Kindness of Your Youth

In the *Musaf* prayer we quote verses from the Torah, Prophets and Writings which speak about God's Kingship; Remembrance and Shofar.

The following words which God said to the prophet Jeremiah are quoted in the *Musaf* service: " ... Go and call in the ears of Jerusalem saying, thus said the L-rd, I remember to you the kindness of your youth, the love of your bridal state; how you went after me in the wilderness.... I will remember My covenant with you in the days of your youth...."

What is the significance of mentioning "the kindness of your youth" and "the days of your youth"?

A woman once came to Rabbi Israel, *Magid* of Koshnitz, complaining that her husband wished to divorce her because she wasn't attractive.

"It is not fair," she cried. "When I was young, I was very beautiful and my husband found me very attractive. Now when I have grown old and lost my beauty should my husband be allowed to abandon me?"

"You are 100 percent right," said Rabbi Israel to the woman.

Rabbi Israel then began weeping. He lifted his eyes to Heaven and said, "Ruler of the Universe, aren't we, the people of Israel, in the same situation? In our youth, when you took us out of Egypt and accepted your Torah, You supplied all our needs, You sent us the manna from heaven and showed us Your great love. Now that we have grown old and may have lost the beauty of our youth, is it just of You to abandon us?"

Thus, on Rosh Hashanah we quote God's words to the prophets, " ... thus said the Lord, I remember for you the kindness of your youth. ... I will remember My covenant with you in the days of your youth...." As in the above story, we ask God to invoke Divine love on this Day of Judgment as in the days of our youth—at the Exodus and the Giving of the Torah.

Author Unknown

The Day of Remembering: The Family Reunion

The family reunion is an event that punctuates and dramatizes
the flow of our lives.
Children are born, they grow up,
Our own parents pass on, friends die
It is growing late, it is years since we began,
And we hardly remember growing older!
At the family reunion we look from the oldest member;
Who may not be present next time,
To the youngest, who was not here last time.
We suddenly glimpse our lives
As a trajectory in time
Beginning at one point and ending at another.
To a higher network of interconnecting arcs.
Life is not only a series of experiences;
It is a whole—real, objective, and unique.
Life is a process of tracing on sand.
With some patterns deeper; larger and more beautiful.

Yet the wind and water ultimately wash over all.
By the same process, time constantly erases its own surface
While forming a deeper structure we never see.
For beneath the sand there is rock
Constantly being shaped by our lives—by our tracings in sand.
At the family reunion the great chain of generations
Threads its way to the present moment,
Linking the old to the young, the dead to the unborn.
It contains—and is contained—by our own life.
As human beings, we are born into a family.
We live without and within it; we color it and shape it,
We bring to the family our gifts, our acts, our children,
Shaping it with all the days of our lives—
And even with our inevitable passage into eternal life.

Rabbi Arnold M. Goodman

Naming the Day

"God does not predetermine whether a person shall be
righteous or wicked, that God leaves to us."

MIDRASH TANCHUMA, PEKUDEI 3

Like the many facets of our lives that we put under the looking glass
at this time of year, so this day has many names it has associated with it.
In the names themselves, the beauty of our meaning-laden Hebrew
language reveals to us a road map for the journey we might undertake
in these Days of Awe. What of that overarching term—the Days of
Awe? We have the opportunity to feel these days like never before:
The liturgy can speak to us in a way it has never spoken to us, for we
have the potential to be so open and unguarded. We will encounter
words, which will take on new meaning and relevance. Some will move
us to tears, some will anger us and some will move us to joy, and some
will evoke fear and awe.

Ultimately we do not have to be defined by any single act as we
reflect on the year, rather our actions in the face of the places we have
missed the mark are what Rosh Hashannah and Yom Kippur call us to
examine. First we need to feel, to self reflect and evaluate. We each have
our own individual challenges that existed prior to today and will con-

tinue. Yet the work that is called for is the work of the High Holy Days, which of course is the work of every day: It is the sacred work of *teshuvah, tefillah,* and *tzedakah*—self-repair, honest connection, and loving acts that restore justice. The work starts right here, starts right now, with us, with me, with …

Rosh Hashanah is also *Yom Harat Olam*—the metaphorical birthday of the world when new possibilities are born into opportunity, and hope for what can be and not only what is permeates our hearts and the liturgy. We blow the shofar and declare, "Happy creation day Universe! That we are here, that we have each other, that we can think and feel and not be numb and despairing in the face of harsh reality, is God in action working through us. It is the way we bring in the Jewish New Year—not be losing ourselves through partying, but regaining ourselves through self-examination. Each of us is a world unto itself our Sages would offer. So the world that is us and the world that is beyond us, all are born into the possibility of the new and different and more conscious and aware. This is not nostalgia and museum piece liturgy—this is us now in this room. Tomorrow will begin to tell us if today was a return or just a rehearsal for a far-off opening night.

The call of the shofar informs another name of this day—*Yom Teruah*—a day for blasts. We wait, childlike next to our children in anticipation of the sound that transports us in time and also asks us to be fully present to take it in. Can you find the stillness and clear space inside today to fulfill the mitzvah? To not only hear the shofar, but also really listen to its echoes in your own being?

What places will the shofar resonate with?

What doors will it unlock?

What wounds will it sooth or stir?

What memories will it evoke?

What possibilities will it call on?

What illusions will it shatter?

Past, present and future are all called into the moment by the shofar. This day, this *Yom Teruah,* is also training for living life unencumbered, and yet respectful of the past, anticipating the future, undistracted and open to the flow of the present.

This Rosh Hashanah also has another name. *Yom Hazikaron.* The Day of Memory, of remembering. We remember the dreams we yearned for, comforting the broken hopes that lie aching on the ground of a lifetime. We remember the dreams we buried, that with some watering are lying, waiting for nurturance to blossom into heaven in our lifetime. We remember those who share our lives that we have forgotten under the weight of making ends meet or habitual ways of relating, or taking for granted. We remember that "I'm sorry" is not a defeat, but freedom from our own prison of closed-heartedness. We remember the world outside our little narratives, a world that longs for us to accompany it in discovery, compassion and healing.

So this Rosh Hashanah, this day of many names, begins a journey of the ten days of repentance, culminating in Yom Kippur. The journey of today asks us to explore what can be born anew, what physical, emotional, intellectual and spiritual barriers need to be broken down by the blast of the shofar, what needs to be remembered so we do not forget our roots or repeat the same errors again unconsciously. My heartfelt prayer for all of us is that the journey we are taking together will help us lay the foundation for a year in which we become more of who we can, engage the world as emissaries for social change and social justice, heal the hurts in ourselves and those we have contributed to in others, and find in this loving community God's presence in our lives and in the world around us.

Rabbi Shawn Israel Zevit

The First Day of the Year

It was taught in the name of R. Eliezer: "The world was created on the twenty-fifth of Elul." The view of Rav agrees with the teaching of R. Eliezer. We learned in the prayer for the shofar which Rav composed: "This day, on which the work was begun was, is, a commemoration of the first day, for it is a statute for Israel, a law of the God of Jacob. On that day, sentence is pronounced upon the countries of the world: which of them is destined to the sword and which to peace, which to famine and which to plenty; and each separate being is visited then, and recorded for life or for death." Thus you are left to conclude that on New Year's Day, in the first hour the idea of creating humankind entered God's mind, in the second God took counsel with the ministering angels, in the third God assembled Adam's dust, in the fourth God kneaded it, in the fifth God shaped the human, in the sixth God made the human into a lifeless body, in the seventh God breathed a soul into the body, in the eighth God brought the person into the Garden of Eden, in the ninth Adam and Eve were commanded against eating the fruit of the tree of knowledge, in the tenth they transgressed, in the eleventh they were judged, in the twelfth they were pardoned. "This," said the Holy One, blessed be God, to Adam and Eve, "will be a sign to your children. As you stood in judgment before Me this day and came out forgiven, so will your children in the future stand in judgment before Me on this day and will come out from My presence forgiven." When will that be? In the seventh month, in the first day of the month (Leviticus 23:24).

Midrash Leviticus Rabbah 29:1

Not Just Today, but Every Day

Rabbi Eliezer said: "Repent one day before your death." His disciples asked: Does anyone know on what day he will die?" "All the more reason to repent today," answered the Rabbi, "in case you die tomorrow. Thus a person's whole life should be spent in repentance."

Babylonian Talmud, Shabbat 153a

Zakhor

Jewish liturgical and sacred texts are replete with the injunction to remember, *zakhor*. Indeed, from the very beginning of Jewish history, the importance of collective memory is clear. "I am the eternal, Your God, who brought you out of the land of Egypt, out of the house of bondage" *(Exodus 20:2),* God tells the Israelites. In other words, I am not a deity whom you have never before met, but one who has already acted on your behalf. I am the same deity whose relationship with your ancestors is connected and continuous with my relationship with you. Standing at Sinai with their families and friends, the Israelites similarly acknowledge both the communal nature of the covenant and the obligation to remember. Yet, as Yosef Yerushalmi has astutely noted, the nature of Jewish memory has never been dispassionate recollection but rather evocation, identification, and re-actualization. In remembering the binding of Isaac, Jacob's wrestling with the angel, Rachel's longing for a child, slavery in Egypt, the journey to Sinai, and the moment of God's revelation, we hear cries of pain and terror, feel confusion, fear, and a sense of hope, and taste the bitterness of slavery and the sweetness of freedom—in short, we experience all that our ancestors experienced as if we, too, had been there.

The obligation to remember cannot be separated from the obligation to observe. A rabbinic explanation of why the fourth commandment is alternatively recounted as "Remember the Sabbath" (Exodus 20:8) and "Observe the Sabbath" (Deuteronomy 5:12) is that both versions were miraculously pronounced together by God and thus heard as if they were a single word. We remember relatives who have died by lighting *yahrzeit* candles and saying Kaddish; we remember God's word by affixing them to our doorposts in *mezuzot;* we remember the journey in the desert by dwelling in *sukkot* and the miracle of Chanukah by lighting the Chanukah menorah. Similarly, we remember God's completing the work of creation by observing the Sabbath as a day of rest. Jewish identity is enriched, strengthened, and preserved through memory, for retelling and re-experiencing the past intellectually and emotionally connect us to rich and valuable resources of both comprehension and meaning.

Dr. Ellen M. Umansky

The New Year for Years

On the first of Tishri is New Year for years. R. Nahman ben Yitzhak explained the Mishnah as referring to the Divine judgment, as it is written: "From the beginning of the year to the end of the year (Deuteronomy 11.12)," which means, "From the beginning of the year, sentence is passed as to what will happen up to the end of it." How do we know that this takes place in Tishri? Because it is written: "Blow the horn at the new moon, at the covered time for our festival (Psalms 81.4)." Which is the feast on which the moon is covered over (i.e., it is the beginning of a new month)? You must say that this is New Year, that this is Rosh Hashanah; and it is written in this connecting verse: For it is a statute for Israel, an ordinance for the God of Jacob (ibid., 5).

Our Rabbis taught: "For it is a statute for Israel, an ordinance for the God of Jacob." teaches that the heavenly court does not assemble for judgment of people until the court on earth has sanctified that the new month has begun.

Rosh Hashanah 8a–b

Remember

"Remember" is a pivotal biblical verb. But review the list of its appearances and you will discover an interesting phenomenon: God is described as remembering far more often than are humans. Memory is, primarily, a divine quality, representing God's ability to overcome the limitations of a particular time, to see the part as one segment of a far greater whole. When humans remember, therefore, we are imitating God, overcoming our own limits and, in God-like fashion, identifying with the breadth of history.

God is also subject to the "command" of remembering. In Psalms and elsewhere, Israel addresses God and asks God to "remember Your mercy," "remember Your servants, Abraham, Isaac and Jacob," "remember the Edomites." True, the contextual purpose of these "remembers" is to appeal to God, but the form of the verb is command. So, as we recognize God's divine qualities, we appeal to God to remember. Likewise, when God recognizes our divine qualities, God commands us to remember.

Remembering is essential, because memory is divine. It is part of what makes us images of God. Fundamentally, our memory is who we are.

David Kraemer

Remembrance: The Key to Redemption

According to the Baal Shem Tov, the eighteenth-century founder of Hasidism, remembrance is the key to redemption. Remembrance is a central them of the Bible because the Hebrew word *Zakhor,* which means "to remember," appears 169 times in the Bible. Money may be lost, health may fail, but memories of good deeds and kindnesses are the greatest blessing.

Immortality is attained through the memory of the survivors. Damon Runyon is immortalized not only by his writings, but by the Cancer Fund raised in his name. Mary MacArthur, the daughter of a famous actress, died of polio at the age of nineteen. Hundreds of children will live because of the Memorial Fund established in her memory, whereby iron lungs and nursing care is being provided for countless polio victims.

California's (former) Governor, Leland Stanford, had an only child who died of a rare disease. The parents decided to immortalize their son by endowing a university in his name. Since that day, tens of thousands of students at the Leland Stanford University have had an opportunity to acquire a higher education through the memory of a nine-year-old boy.

Rabbi Saul Teplitz

Yom Hazikaron

From the diaries of Rabbi Mordecai M. Kaplan, Sunday, September 21, 1952:
The sermon today on "The Quest for Universal Peace" ... I pointed out that of all the holidays in our calendar Rosh Hashanah is the only that is not designated in the liturgy by the same name as in common parlance. In the liturgy it is called [*Yom Hazikaron*] as it is in the Torah where the term Rosh Hashanah is not to be found.

Originally the [*Yom Hazikaron*] was celebrated not as marking the beginning of a new year but as the beginning of the seventh month. Seven seemed to connote for our ancestors completion or fulfillment. The fulfillment in question was that of God's power in the world. The term [*Zikaron*] is therefore not to be understood as "memorial" or "remembrance" but as "proclamation." God is to be proclaimed king by means of the shofar. The [*Yom Hazikaron*] is thus the equivalent of "I am an American day." It means "I am a world-citizen day," "I am a subject of God's Kingdom" day.

Rabbi Mordecai M. Kaplan

The Day of Remembrance

Rosh Hashanah is *Yom Hazikaron*, day of remembrance. That concept may be understood in many ways. One of these was illustrated by Simon Wiesenthal, as indicated in the last paragraph of his obituary in the *New York Times* (9/21/05):

He was often asked why he had become a searcher of Nazi criminals instead of resuming a profitable career in architecture. He gave one questioner this response: "You're a religious man. You believe in God and life after death. I also believe. When we come to the other world and meet the millions of Jews who died in the camps and they ask us, 'What have you done?' there will be many answers. You will say, 'I became a jeweler.' Another will say, 'I smuggled coffee and American cigarettes.' Still another will say, 'I built houses,' but I will say, 'I didn't forget you.'"

D.P.E.

The Past Lives in Me

Ours is a long and rich history. In fact, one of the reasons that motivated the eminent non-Jewish historian of Judaism, Paul Johnson, to write his *History of the Jews* is the incredible longevity of Jewish history. In his words, he found "excitement ... in the sheer span of Jewish history. From the time of Abraham up to the present covers the best part of four millennia. That is more than three-quarters of the entire history of civilized humanity."

And yet the Bible—twenty-four books that record much of Jewish history and is the linguistic basis of the Hebrew language—and the rabbinic literature which spans thousands of years of Jewish history does not have a word for "history." Do you know how to say "history" in modern Hebrew? The word is, "historia" clearly an adopted and adapted word. Jews don't have a word for history—but we have another word—a more powerful word: and that word is *Zachor*—memory.

To paraphrase a brilliant insight by Dr. Jonathan Sacks: history is "his" story—memory is "my" story. History can often be a conglomeration of facts, dates, events, and happenings. Memory is different. It molds, shapes, and guides ones identity. History happened to someone else—once upon a time; "memory is the past as present, as it lives on in me."

I recall a retort that Elie Wiesel offered an interviewer: "Professor Wiesel, you seem to live in the past," was the comment. To which Elie Wiesel—or should I say, Reb Eliezer Wiesel—grandson of a pious Chasidic Jew, Dodye Feig from the shtetl of Sighet, Transylvania, responded: "I don't live in the past. But what can I do—the past lives in me." That's not a statement about history—that's a statement about identity.

Rabbi David Gutterman

Fragments of Memory

Memory is perhaps one of the most powerful elements in the formation of a person—a certain kind of memory, in which not facts, but rather, intangibles such as sensations, impressions, and scraps of images are the primary resources that shape the way we see the world.

Memory: the convergence of unrelated fragments. The bringing together of pieces of the world in such a way that they tell a story. The linking of thoughts and pictures until they make sense. Memory is the narrative we tell the world and ourselves and that forms the present reality.

The Jewish New Year has many names, among them the Day of Remembrance and the Day of Judgment. The Day of Remembrance asks us to turn around and look into the past for its lessons, its mistakes, its greatness. The Day of Judgment asks us to look ahead, realizing that all our deeds have ramifications and consequences.

Two names for this holy day, which commemorates the creation of the world. To recreate our lives in the New Year, it seems that we are to use the materials of the past to form a vision for the future. This takes great care. Memory can serve as a crutch if we believe that we are somehow crippled, or memory can serve as a foundation for growth; it can make the difference between living in the past and building on the past.

It seems that history is intertwined with destiny; we simply cannot anticipate what lies ahead without remembering what came before. We climb a ladder toward redemption, each rung in the past and yet advancing us to greater heights. We are born to be great storytellers of fantastic tales. All those moments weaving their way through our lives have become the raw material for the plot, the senses, and the images that create our conclusions about what is true and what is not, what is good and what is not, what is likely to happen and what is not.

As we retell the story of our lives, one question is most helpful. What have we learned? Every moment, event, person, is an opportunity for learning and is ultimately the foundation for growth. In fact, that may be the difference between being someone who lives in the present and someone who is frozen in the past. Have you learned the lessons of the moment? Until you do, you will not move on.

Rabbi Karyn D. Kedar

REPENTANCE

One of the most important and original terms of Jewish moral thought, *teshuvah* is quite inadequately rendered by the usual translation "repentance." To repent is to turn away from sin and seek forgiveness. *Teshuvah* is a broader concept, one that goes to the very root of human existence. It is no wonder that the *Talmud* lists the power of *teshuvah* as one of those seven things that existed before God created this world. Human life is inconceivable without *teshuvah*.

The first person to undertake *teshuvah* was the very first human. Adam realized the magnitude of his sin in the Garden, according to the *Midrash,* and sought to be reconciled with God. *Teshuvah* in this case would mean re-establishing the intimacy and trust that existed between God and God's beloved creatures before the expulsion from Eden. *Teshuvah,* in this key story, could not mean the re-creation of innocence. That childlike aspect of Eden was gone forever. But a new relationship, one more mature since it had faced and overcome the moment of doubt and betrayal, was Adam's goal. It is this deeper faith, one that emerges from struggle with the self, that is the goal of *teshuvah*.

RABBI ARTHUR GREEN, *THESE ARE THE WORDS*

Teshuvah: Forgiveness and Exoneration Require Acknowledging Our Wrongdoing

If we, as a society, are going to be so determined in pronouncing people wrongdoers, we should at least have given half a moment's thought to what we expected of them in the first place and require of them now to expunge the offense. We leave people who have not done all that much wrong in permanent limbo. We lustily welcome back others who are much worse and have declined even to acknowledge their wrongdoing. Such an acknowledgement should surely be the basis of public forgiveness. But almost none of the people who have deservedly fallen from public grace in recent times has taken this step, let alone shown anything that could conceivably be called remorse, as distinct from regret and resentment at being caught. Maybe that's because they have seen they don't have to, that the thing will come around again if they just wait.

Meg Greenfield

Teshuvah: Making a U-turn

While bicycling on the first day of summer, I passed a church bulletin board. It carried the message: "If you are headed in the wrong direction, God allows U-turns." That is a perfectly good translation of our term *"teshuvah,"* which literally means "turning around."

You might remember the story of the passenger plane caught in a storm, when the pilot announced, "I have some good news and some bad news. The bad news is that our radio compass is inoperative. The good news is that we are making excellent time." Of course, whatever speed we may be traveling, it doesn't matter if we aren't heading in the right direction. And if we're headed wrong, the smartest thing we can do is turn around.

That's why, in the *U'netaneh Tokef*, when we pray about a good life, the first thing we mention is *teshuvah*, the ability to recognize when we've gone off course, and the courage to make a U-turn, and head in the right direction again. Perhaps in English-speaking congregations, we should mispronounce the prayer *"U-Netaneh Tokef."*

Let's take time, during the *U'netaneh Tokef*, to think about where we are going, and what parts of our lives need to make a U-turn, so that we can look forward to lives of blessing in this new year.

Rabbi Shamai Kanter

Forgiveness: A Bag of Nails

Her mother gave her a bag of nails and told her that every time she lost her temper or insulted somebody she must hammer a nail into the back of their fence.

The first day the girl hit fourteen nails into the fence. Over the next few weeks, as she learned to control her anger, the number of nails hammered daily gradually dwindled. She discovered it was easier to hold her temper than to drive those nails into the fence.

Finally the day came when the girl didn't lose her temper at all. She told her mother about it, and the mother suggested that the girl now pull out one nail for each day that she was able to hold her temper. The days passed. Finally, she told her mother that all the nails were gone.

The mother took her daughter by the hand and led her to the fence. She said, "You have done well, my daughter, but look at all the holes in the fence. The fence will never be the same. When you say things in anger, they leave a scar just like these."

"How can I repair the fence?" asked the girl. "Will it have to remain damaged forever?"

"Yes and no," said the mother. "Our Rabbis say that if the fence is alive and responds to the way you have changed, it too can change and heal itself. If the fence is dead to the possibility of your repentance it will carry its scars onward. The fence will never be as it was before, but it doesn't have to become like new to be a good fence. If you do your part and change, and the fence does its part in response, God will do something wonderful. God will promote a healing that will make you and the fence better. This process is called atonement. It means that the changes that come about from repentance and forgiveness lead people to higher levels of relationship than was the case before."

"What happens if the fence doesn't respond?" asked the girl. "Can I ever make it whole?"

"You should try on three different occasions," said the mother, "but if the fence remains dead even after you have changed, you can't force it to become whole. In that case you should fix another fence somewhere else. There are always lots of fences that need fixing, and whenever you fix a fence, God will make something wonderful happen. That is the miracle of atonement. God always responds to our attempts to change by helping us change, and always responds to our change by giving us new and wonderful opportunities for atonement. This is why we have a Day of Atonement at the beginning of every new year; so the new year will be a better one than the last one."

Rabbi Allen S. Maller

Teshuvah: "I Am Still Growing"

A true story. Sir Edmund Hillary was the first man to conquer Mt. Everest though he failed his first attempt. Speaking to the Science Academy in England after his first unsuccessful climb, Hillary stopped in the middle, paused a pregnant pause, turned toward the large mural of Everest which was on the wall and declared: "Next time I will succeed—for I am still growing and you have stopped growing."

Rabbi David Gutterman

Joining in the Great Return

Teshuvah is the ever-present possibility, urge and gesture of returning to our Source, the Holy One of All Being. Through *teshuvah* all life is returned to its source. As Rav Kook teaches, it flows unnoticed throughout creation. *Teshuvah* is not simply apologizing or making right the damage we have done, though these are prerequisites. It is only this: the Return.

Teshuvah is the hardest thing in the world, for to fully make it would bring the Messiah. But it is also the easiest thing, since the process of *teshuvah* begins with the simple thought of wanting to begin.

More than just an individual gesture, *teshuvah* is a great world-yearning that flows through and animates all creation. Through attempting to repair and heal what we have done in the past, we set it within a larger context of meaning and effectively rewrite the past. What was once only some thoughtless or even wicked act, now—when viewed from the perspective of our present *teshuvah*—becomes only the embarrassing commencement of this greater healing now realized.

We stubbornly and despite all the evidence look forward to a time when all creation with join in the Great Return—a unity of all the world reflecting the Unitary Source of all Creation.

Rabbi Lawrence Kushner

Change Begins with Me

I believe deeply that true change is possible only when it begins inside the person who is advocating it. Mahatma Gandhi said it well: "We must be the change we wish to see in the world." And a story about Gandhi provides a good illustration of how hard it is to "be the change."

Gandhi, we are told, was approached one day by a woman who was deeply concerned that her son ate too much sugar. "I am worried about his health," she said. "He respects you very much. Would you be willing to tell him about its harmful effects and suggest he stop eating it?" After reflecting on the request, Gandhi told the woman that he would do as she requested, but asked that she bring her son back in two weeks, no sooner. In two weeks, when the boy and his mother returned, Gandhi spoke with him and suggested that he stop eating sugar. When the boy complied with Gandhi's suggestion, his mother thanked Gandhi extravagantly but asked him why he had insisted on the two-week interval. "Because," he replied, "I needed the two weeks to stop eating sugar myself."

Al Gore

Confession

> Almighty God, God of our ancestors,
> Abraham, Isaac, and Jacob,
> And all of their righteous descendants:
> You who have made the heaven and the earth with all their
>   system;
> Who have controlled the sea with Your word of command;
> Who have captured the great deep, and sealed it with Your
>   glorious name;

Before whom all things shudder, and tremble before Your power,

For the majesty of Your glory is unbearable, and Your anger against sinners is unendurable, immeasurable and unknowable is the mercy You promise,

For You are God Most High, tender-hearted, long-suffering, and most merciful, and regretful of the wickedness of people.

You therefore, God of upright people, have not ordained repentance for the upright,

For Abraham, Isaac, and Jacob, who did not sin against you; You have ordained repentance for a sinner like me.

For my sins are more numerous than the sands of the sea, my sins are multiplied, God, they are multiplied! I am unworthy to look up and see the heights of heaven, for the multitude of my transgressions.

I am weighed down with many an iron chain, so that I bend beneath my sins and I have no relief, because I have provoked Your anger, and done what is wrong in Your eyes, setting up abominations and doing many offenses.

So, now, I bend the knee of my heart, begging You for kindness. I have sinned, God, I have sinned, and I know what I have done. 1 earnestly beseech You, forgive me, God, forgive me. Do not bring me down in the midst of my transgressions. Do not be angry with me forever and give me an evil fate, or condemn me to Gehenom.

For you are the God of those who repent and you will act kindly towards me.

For as much as I am unworthy, You will save me with your abundant mercy.

I will praise You always as long as I live, for all of heaven sings your praise and Yours is the glory forever. Amen.

The Prayer of Manasseh

Teshuvah: Lessons from a Fish

In a recent article in the *New York Times* it was reported that scientists discovered a fish that changes shape when it detects the presence of hungry predators. It transforms itself from something that is easily swallowed into something difficult to swallow. What an amazing feat!

The researchers commented on their discovery: "Plasticity is the only way for an organism to adapt to a rapidly changing environment within its life span…. This opens up the door for more careful examination of plasticity in vertebrates. People are going to have to stop thinking that there's not going to be this kind of change during an individual's lifetime."

This particular fish changes in order to survive. We humans need to learn that in order to survive we too need to learn the trick of changing our shape, our attitude, our values, our actions, in order to survive. In order to survive as moral, value-oriented creatures, we often need to make large and small changes in our personalities, our souls, our selves.

Change, in short, or *teshuvah*, as our ancestors called it, is the key to survival, in an ever increasingly changing world.

D.P.E.

When *Teshuvah* Doesn't Work

In the story in Numbers *(Shelah Lekha)* about the twelve spies who were sent by Moshe to find out what kind of place the Land of Canaan was, and whether they would have a difficult time conquering it, we recall that the majority report, by ten of the spies, was that the land was formidable, the people were giants, the country was fortified. They returned to the Israelite camp to demoralize the people. Their punishment was that this whole generation was not to be permitted into the Promised Land. Only their children would have that privilege.

One of the commentators ask the question why the punishment was so harsh, since the people admitted their sin (Numbers 14:40—*hatanu)*, and repented. He answers by saying that certain kinds of sin cannot be undone even by *Teshuvah*. Namely, a sin against the Jewish People.

Sins against God can be forgiven. Sins against our fellow human beings can be forgiven if we apologize and ask forgiveness. But sins against our people are so grievous and so fraught with dangerous consequences for our future, that even authentic *Teshuvah* cannot effect a wiping away of the punishment. Thus, the generation of the wilderness was not permitted to enter the Land of Israel.

This comment places a very high premium on loyalty and commitment to our People and its welfare. Many are the failures committed by us Jews today against our people—our failures to support the State of Israel financially and morally; our failures to visit Israel; our failures in not teaching our children the values of our heritage, and the importance of preserving our people through endogenous marriage. The consequences of these acts are so long-range and detrimental to our people's welfare, that their effects may never be undone.

Rabbi Dov Peretz Elkins

Four Results of Sin

What happens to the sinner according to Jewish Tradition? Since Judaism never has just one answer to a question, the Midrash supplies four possibilities, according to which biblical book one consults. Four different verses are quoted in one Midrash, each with its own theological approach. The biblical books in this Midrash are personified. I quote the Midrash:

1. Wisdom was asked: The sinner, what is his destiny? She said to those who asked: "Evil pursueth sinners" (Prov. 13:21).

2. *Prophecy* was asked: The sinner, what is his destiny? She said to those who asked: "The soul that sinneth, it shall die" (Ezek. 18:4).

3. The *Torah* was asked: The sinner, what is his destiny? She said to those who asked: "Let him bring a guilt-offering, and atone for him" (Lev. 1:4).

4. The Holy One, blessed be he, was asked: The sinner, what is his destiny? God said to those who asked: Let him turn in repentance, and atonement shall be made for him; as it is written: "Good and upright is the Lord; therefore does God instruct sinners in the way" (Ps. 25:8).

Pesikta De-Rav Kahana 158A

The Power of Our Most Banal Acts

Not only do we fail to prepare for these days [of Awe] but we have far too limited an understanding of their potential. Our traditional conception of *teshuvah* is saying sorry to those we have wronged. We make our relationships with them whole again. We return a certain equilibrium to our community. But *teshuvah* can also be a transformational experience which makes us realize the impact of our most banal actions. Maimonides, Rambam, describes the mental state we should adopt in approaching this process. We should think of ourselves and the world as perfectly balanced: exactly half guilty and half innocent. If we commit one sin we press down the scale or guilt against ourselves and the entire world and cause its destruction. And if we perform one good deed we press down the scale of merit and bring salvation to the entire world. Our simplest acts become infused with profound meaning.

Dr. Deborah E. Lipstadt

Teshuvah: Taking Care of Others

Rabbi Yisrael Salanter's student asked him a question: "How do you take care of your spiritual needs?" He answered: "By taking care of the physical needs of others."

Setting out on a path of doing *Teshuvah* is easy from the perspective of Jewish tradition. A Hasidic master once asked his students: How far is it from east to west? He answered: Easy—just one turn. Turn around in the opposite direction. The most important act of *Teshuvah* begins by turning around, taking one small step.

D.P.E.

It Is Not Enough to Repent

There was a husband and wife who fought for years over one of his habits that she found so annoying. He would never remember to put the top back on the toothpaste. This went on for fifty years. Finally, he decided one day that he was going to change. After all, this was a small habit to unlearn and she was so good to him that he ought to do it. Besides, the High Holy Days were coming near and this is a time when people are supposed to repent and change their bad habits.

So he began putting the top back on the tube. He did it for a day, two days, three, a week and she never said a word. Finally, she said to him: "Dear, why have you stopped brushing your teeth?"

It is not enough to repent. We also need to SAY that we are repenting, we need to tell the one whom we have hurt that we are sorry and that we are changing. Changing is half the job; saying so is the other half.

Author Unknown

Teshuvah as Ending Self-Exile

There are three types of exile and they are of increasing severity. The first is when Jews are in exile among other nations.

The second is when Jews are in exile among other Jews.

The third and most severe is when a Jew is alien to him/herself, for then s/he is both captor and captive, in exile within him/herself.

Rabbi Sholom ben Elazar Rokeah of Belz

To Be Human Is to Be Capable of Change

A memory retold from the Torah: Jacob, a father of the Jewish people, must run for his life. He has stolen his brother's birthright and deceived his blind, invalid father. He flees into the desert of the Judean hills. Night falls. Jacob, the son of rich and blessed parents, places a rock under his head and lies down on the hard, dusty ground. Tomorrow, he will cross over into another land, a new family and a world that knows nothing of a covenant with God. Jacob has reached the borders of his life with no assurance that the blessings of power, wealth and progeny he received from his father, Isaac, will ever be fulfilled. Jacob dreams of a ladder to heaven with angels ascending and descending. He envisions God at his side, renewing the covenant made with his father, Isaac, and grandfather, Abraham:

> The ground upon which you lie I will give to you and your descendants. Your progeny shall be as the dust of the earth, spreading out to the west and the east, to the north and south.

All the families of the earth will bless themselves through you and your descendants (Genesis 28:14).

Jacob awakens from his sleep and says: "Surely there is God in this place and I *(Anokhi)* did not know."

What is it that he did not know? Two Hassidic masters provide contrary yet harmonic insight for us. Each responds to Jacob's confusion over God's presence. One explains that the place where God was found was in the *Anokhi*—the self of Jacob. Consumed with fear and deceit, Jacob suddenly becomes aware that he is more than the sum of his angers. He locates the latent divinity within himself, the infinite potential, as the place where God can reside. He can become a covenantal human being because he found, along with all the negative traits, a sense of the divine within himself, the *Anokhi* he discovered in his nighttime vision. He now knows he has self-worth.

The second Hassidic master, Tiferet Shlomo, intuits another facet of Jacob's insights. At the very moment that Jacob becomes aware of God's presence, he exclaims: It is *Anohi* (the self) "that I do not know." Only when one is not filled with the self, when a person empties herself or himself of the ego and self-serving explanations which encrust, can that person truly experience God's presence. All the excuses in the world, from insensitive parents or unsupportive teachers to selfish bosses or funny-looking teeth, cannot justify one's failure to improve. In this understanding, the preoccupation with oneself blocks God's presence, diminishing the potential for change and improvement.

The two faces of the story revealed by the Hasidic rebbes create the foundation of *teshuvah*. One must find the *Anokhi*, the awareness of self, that lets a person know that he or she is worthy as a human being filled with infinite potential. Yet one also must not be so filled with a limited and inadequate self to block the divinity within and the need and capacity for change. Both interpretations suggest how ever-present God can be and how easy it is to proffer the excuse, "But I did not know." *Teshuvah* gives people the right to both be unhappy with themselves as they are and still believe that they are worthy of perfection, of personal *Tikkun* (repair). To support this, the rabbis said:

A person should always carry two pieces of paper, one in each pocket. On one is written, "I am but dust and ashes." On the other, "because of me the world was created."

The art of living is knowing when to pull out the piece of paper and from which pocket. Our focus on *teshuvah* helps us to develop this art so that we can each become the person we seek to be.

David Elcott

To Be Forgiven, Learn How to Forgive

To be forgiven one must first learn how to forgive. Many of us waste years waiting to be forgiven. But since we have never offered forgiveness ourselves, we do not know how to recognize when it is extended to us.

To "forgive" means not only to excuse someone for having committed an offense, but also to renounce the anger and claims of resentment. Forgiving someone therefore means you are willing to endure the risk that he will hurt you in exactly the same way again, but that you trust him not to.

Rabbi Lawrence Kushner

Teshuvah: Is My Life Tuned to My Own Note?

Integrity is an ongoing process, a dynamic happening over time that requires our ongoing attention. A medical colleague describing his own experience of staying true to himself told me that he thinks of his life as an orchestra. Reclaiming his integrity reminds him of that moment before the concert when the concertmaster asks the oboist to sound an A. "At first there is chaos and noise as all the parts of the orchestra try to align themselves with that note. But as each instrument moves closer and closer to it, the noise diminishes and when they all finally sound it together, there is a moment of rest, of homecoming.

"That is how it feels to me," he told me. "I am always tuning my orchestra. Somewhere deep inside there is a sound that is mine alone, and I struggle daily to hear it and tune my life to it. Sometimes there are people and situations that help me to hear my note more clearly; other times, people and situations make it harder for me to hear. A lot depends on my commitment to listening and my intention to stay coherent with this note. It is only when my life is tuned to my note that I can play life's mysterious and holy music without tainting it with my own discordance, my own bitterness, resentment, agendas, and fears."

Deep inside, our integrity sings to us whether we are listening or not. It is a note that only we can hear. Eventually, when life makes us ready to listen, it will help us to find our way home.

Rachel Naomi Remen, M.D.

Teshuvah: Why Should I Go Elsewhere?

There is a story told about Reb Zussya, who was sitting and studying the Talmud. Reb Zussya's students once looked over his shoulders and saw him studying a certain page of the Gemara. The next day they saw their Rabbi was studying the identical page. The following week they saw him on the same page still! It bothered them and they finally questioned him. "How come you are still on the same page?!" To which Reb Zussya responded, "It feels so good here, why should I go elsewhere?" Interestingly, rabbinic legend ascribes great erudition to Reb Zussya. But like many of us, he reached a point in his life where it was easier to study the same page over and over and not move on to new challenges and opportunities. For some of us, it may mean doing something as innocent as always eating at the same restaurant. We know the menu so well—what's good, what's not so good—and we fear that a different restaurant might leave us unsatisfied or bewildered. And so back we go, time after time, to the same place, not because the food is so sensational but because "it feels so good, why go elsewhere."

But many of us are stuck on the same page concerning matters of far greater importance: Maybe we're in a job that gives us little satisfaction and perhaps inadequate compensation, but we stay where we are because we're afraid to take chances and venture out. Maybe our lives are in a rut—we find ourselves doing the same things over and over, week in and week out—and we're afraid to try something new or go some place different. Maybe our relationship with God and the Jewish community has been stagnant, and we'd like to develop a deeper and richer spiritual life but we're afraid of what others might think or say.

Yes, it's often easiest to stay on the same page where "it feels so good, why go elsewhere." The High Holy Days are approaching. We may come for *Kol Nidre,* but powerful as that prayer may be, we won't stay on that same page for long, but move forward. And so doing, we will experience a wealth of emotions and insights that will challenge and inspire us from one page to the next. May this holiday season push us to move forward in life, to bring our realities closer to our dreams, and enable this new year to be one of both sweetness and fulfillment and growth.

Rabbi David Rosen

Teshuvah

One day a father of a very wealthy family took his son on a trip to the country with the firm purpose of showing his son how poor people can be. They spent a couple of days on the farm of what would be considered a very poor family. On their return from their trip, the father asked the son, "How was the trip?" "It was great, Dad." "Did you see how poor people can be?" the father asked. "Oh yeah," said the son. "So what did you learn from the trip?" asked the father.

The son answered, "I saw that we have one dog and they had four. We have a pool that reaches to the middle of our garden and they have a creek that has no end. We have imported Japanese lanterns in our garden and they have stars at night. We have a small piece of land to live on and they have fields that go beyond our sight. We have servants who serve us, but they serve others. We have walls around our property to protect us, they have friends to protect them." After hearing all this, the father was speechless. Then his son added, "Thanks, Dad, for showing me how poor we are."

Likewise, all too often we don't realize how emotionally and spiritually poor our lives have become—we don't recognize the need to make a U-turn. All too often we are like racehorses—charging full force to finish but wearing blinders so as not to notice or be distracted by the world around us.

The High Holidays call out to us—take off your spiritual blinders—take notice of the world around you. Do what *teshuvah* demands—TURN AROUND, make a corrective U-Turn in your life.

Rabbi Mark Mallach

Forgiveness

There is a beautiful tale found in the Zohar, that central text of Jewish mysticism. We read there of a Rabbi Abba who once sat at the gateway of the Town of Lud, which is now home to Ben Gurion Airport. He saw a traveler sit down on a pile of rocks at the edge of a mountain overlooking a cliff. The man was exhausted from his journey and immediately fell asleep. Rabbi Abba watched this innocuous scene for a bit until to his dismay he saw a deadly snake slither out of the rocks making its way towards the sleeping man. A giant lizard suddenly jumped out between the rocks and killed the serpent. Then the man awoke and stood up, perplexed to see a beheaded snake lying in front of him. He quickly gathered his possessions and rose to continue his journey. As he did so, the pile of rocks he was sitting on collapsed and fell into the ravine below.

Rabbi Abba ran after the man and recounted everything he had witnessed. He asked, "My friend, to what do you attribute all these miracles that just transpired?" The traveler responded as follows:

"Throughout my life it has happened that someone harmed me and I did not pacify him. Never have I gone to sleep without forgiving someone for hurting me in any way. If anyone ever hurt me, I always endeavored, with all my heart, to resolve whatever animosity was between us. And lastly, I would turn the hateful situation into an opportunity to do acts of kindness for the person involved in the misunderstanding."

When R. Abba heard this he burst into tears. This person's actions were greater than Joseph's. For Joseph had to deal with his brothers; of course he was going to forgive his brothers. But this man forgives anyone and everyone who has harmed him. It was no surprise that God performed miracles on a daily basis for this blessed man.

This man received God's blessings because of his ability to forgive. If we refuse to forgive others, how can we ask God to forgive us, to bless us in the coming year? For surely we are not so arrogant as to say to God we are righteous and have not sinned. Verily, we have sinned. That is why one of the most important questions you can ask yourself on this Yom Kippur, is, who do you have to forgive in order to be at peace in your life?

Author Unknown

Crime and Punishment

Sometimes we can understand a tradition by its punishments. For those guilty of heinous sins, almost every religion has some form of excommunication. Although this practice virtually disappeared over the centuries, *herem* was once an important factor in Jewish civil and criminal law.

As Rabbi Harold Kushner pointed out years ago, excommunication in Roman Catholicism prevents one from receiving communion, cutting one off from receiving communion, cutting one off from God. In Judaism, excommunication cuts one off from other people.

This remarkable fact has two equally important implications. First, it shows how transgression prevents us from maintaining a relationship with others in our community. Sin cuts one off from other people. Repairing the relationship with others, if possible, is imperative. We have severed the ties with those whose lives and destinies we ought to share. To recover is to join the community.

Second, it teaches that in Judaism no one can ultimately cut another off from God. One can feel estranged from God, it is true. Jews from the Bible forward have at times felt distant. Some of the psalms give eloquent expression to the pain of the psalmist when he feels far from God. Many rabbis and Jewish theologians have written about God's hiding, or absence.

That, however, is the individual's status, not the community's decision. Moreover, there is always return. We are never barred from prayer or repentance. As the prophet declares in God's name: "In love I will take you back" (Hosea 14).

Rabbi David J. Wolpe

Teshuvah: Tilt the World to the Side of Good

"If [walking] along the road, you chance upon a bird's nest ... and the mother is sitting over the fledglings or on the eggs, do not take the mother together with her young. Let the mother go and take only the young, in order that you may fare well and have a long life" (Deuteronomy 22:6).

The Talmud labels this mitzvah the "lightest" (the most insubstantial) of all the commandments, probably because it takes little effort to perform. Sending away the mother might well involve merely making a loud noise. Indeed, just walking close (or advancing menacingly) might induce the mother to fly away.

Commentators in every generation have wondered why there is so extravagant a reward (a good, long life) for so "trivial" an act! Indeed, one Talmudic commentator points out that the same reward is specified in the Torah for honoring parents. Yet fulfilling that commandment takes a lifetime and often involves money, emotion and effort without limit. He concludes that the equality of reward is the point. The "lightest" of commandments rewarded as much as the "weightiest" to teach us to treasure and observe all commandments equally—for the reward of any mitzvah is incalculable.

Through this commandment, the Torah teaches that every act is of immense significance. Therefore, no act is inherently trivial. When you eat, you can choose food and prepare it to express reverence for life or commitment to being a Jew *(kashrut)*. When you speak, you can say a word of encouragement, truth or love or you can say a word of malicious gossip, falsehood or degradation.

Maimonides writes in his laws of repentance that every person should consider himself or herself as perfectly balanced between good and bad and the world as perfectly balanced between good and evil. The next action you do—however trivial—can tilt you and the whole world toward the side of good and life or to the side of evil and death. Choose life!

Rabbi Irving Greenberg

Forgiving Yourself: A Guided Imagery Meditation

Lie down in your bed. Enjoy the horizontal position of rest and the surrender of tension you can sense in your body. Take a moment to feel good about yourself for finishing a day to the best of your ability.

As you gaze around your sukkah of peace, a warm breeze gently blows open one of the curtains and reveals a magnificent garden glowing in the moonlight. Imagine that you rise and walk out into the garden, discovering that it is lit with fireflies. It is as if angels surround you with lanterns of God's light. As you look around the garden, you see that the flowers are lit from underneath, and their colors are vibrant against the blue-black of the night. As you walk, you step on a shimmering stone pathway that leads you to the center of the garden.

All is well. The sounds of night awaken your ears. You hear crickets and the sound of the breeze. Notice the sound of your own breath, your own heartbeat, and your footsteps. With each step, the breeze sweeps your body gently, cleansing away any remnants of the day that just ended. You feel the breeze clean your scalp and your mind ... your throat, heart, arms, hands, and fingertips ... your solar plexus, your belly, your pelvis, your groin ... your legs, your feet. A warm breeze blows down through your whole spine, cleansing each vertebra from top to bottom.

You now come to the center of the garden, where there is a place for you to sit next to a reflecting pool. As you sit down, peer into the pool and see your image. Do not judge what you see there. Know that it may be just a vague outline or shadow. Seeing yourself is not easy. Ask God to reveal to you the image that God sees. Try to be gentle and non-critical. This is essential for your healing. Notice how you feel, and how you have been treating yourself. Gently ask: How have I harmed myself? Have I harmed my body? My possessions? My honor or self-esteem? Have I hurt myself through relationships with family or friends? Have I done it accidentally or willfully?

What do you feel guilty or angry about in the deepest core of your being? You must try to focus on only one small aspect of yourself that you want to forgive—one place of disappointment or anger, pity, doubt, or guilt. This is your hardest task because self-criticism can stop the healing process. Use your most loving self to focus on the place that is hurting the most right now.

Try to name the feeling that you feel toward yourself. For example, "I feel angry at myself for working at a job that never let me grow." "I feel guilty that I wasn't a more involved parent." "I feel disappointed in myself about my smoking habit (or your eating or drinking habits, etc.)." "I feel frustrated that I continually doubt myself." Now that you have named it, ask God to help you stop hurting yourself. Know that you are not bad, that you are only human, and that mistakes are how we learn.

Look again into the pool before you. See your reflection being washed with a shower of light that comes from the moon. The light falls on the surface of the pool like a mist, then melts into a healing salve. Dip your hand into the salve and coat those areas of your body where you feel the pain.

Let the warmth of healing dissolve into your body. Notice that downy soft wings now surround you, holding and comforting you as you say, "*Ribbono shel olam,* Master of the universe, I forgive myself to you. Help me accept myself and learn from my mistakes. Show me my lesson. Help me hold myself in my own wings of acceptance and inner love."

Breathe. Sit silently for a moment. Look into the reflecting pool now and see your image shining back at you with joy and light. Your image thanks you, and you respond by thanking God for helping you find the courage to do this work. Slowly you stand and walk back from the garden on the moonlit path. Your sukkah of peace opens again, and you slip into your warm bed. Now you can rest. Say the forgiveness prayer for yourself:

Ribbono shel olam, I hereby forgive myself for what I have done that blemished my Divine image, whether my body, my mind, my self-esteem, whether accidentally or willfully, in this incarnation or another. May it be Your will, Adonai my God and God of my ancestors, that I may sin no more. Whatever my error before You, may it be blotted out in Your abundant mercies, but not through suffering or severe illness. May the words of my mouth and the thoughts of my heart be pleasing to You, Adonai, my Rock and my Redeemer.

Master of the universe, I hereby forgive myself.

Tamar Frankiel and Judy Greenfeld

U'NETANEH TOKEF: REPENTENCE, PRAYER, AND JUSTICE CAN ANNUL THE DECREE

What does it mean that a person's fate is "sealed" for the year? Is God not free to accept *teshuvah* at any time? And is the loving God not merciful to sinners even on these Days of Awe? Is the whole picture not too anthropomorphic and too paternalistic to allow for a mature religiosity? Might this not be a tale for children, inappropriately imposed upon the adult worshipper as well? Even for children, one might add, today's educators would question whether the threat of judgment is a proper motivator for moral growth.

For these and other reasons, various interpreters tend to internalize this imagery. The God of judgment stands for conscience; Rosh Hashanah becomes a time for self-examination and commitment to growth and change of habits. The essential statement of faith is that we *are* capable of change. God calls upon us, symbolically through this season but actually at all times, to be the best human beings, morally and spiritually, that we can be. This demands of us a constant openness to change and growth.

RABBI ARTHUR GREEN, *THESE ARE THE WORDS*

U'netaneh Tokef

On Rosh Hashanah it is written, and on Yom Kippur it is sealed. How many will die and how many will be born? Who at a ripe old age and who before their time? Who by fire and who by water? Who by sword and who by beast?

It hurts so much to live in the face of death that even on Yom Kippur, even when we rehearse our own death by fasting and wearing shrouds and non-leather shoes, we want *u-netaneh tokef* to be a metaphor. We want the inevitable question of who was here last year that isn't here now and who is here this year that won't be here next year to be a poem, or a parable. It's not. It's a wake-up call, it's a shofar blast of warning. No one knows when the gates will close forever so while we are inside them we had better love passionately, fight passionately, learn passionately, live passionately. "*U-netaneh tokef kedushat hayom, ki hu norah v'ayom:* Let us declare the holiness of this day, because it contains an awful truth."

Awe-full. I'm filled with awe every day now. Every sunrise, every sunset. I say *shehecheyanu* a lot now: who has kept us alive, and sustained us, and helped us to reach this day. This day. *U-netaneh tokef kedushat hayom,* let us declare the holiness of this day, because it is the only day we have for sure. I love with urgency now. I fight with urgency now. I live with urgency now. I'm not waiting to have that anniversary party, I'm taking the kids to Disneyland when they are too young, I'm going to that family Bar Mitzvah in New York, I'm eating another chocolate.

Rabbi Elyse Goldstein

You Record and Seal, Count and Measure

In the famous interview that Carl Stern of NBC had with the late Rabbi Abraham Joshua Heschel, three weeks before Heschel's untimely death in 1972, Stern asked the famous rabbi: "What message have you for young people?"

Rabbi Heschel replied: "Let them remember that there is a meaning beyond absurdity. Let them be sure that every deed counts, that every word has power, and that we all can do our share to redeem the world in spite of all absurdities and all frustrations and all disappointments…. And above all, let them remember … to build a life as if it were a work of art."

A beautiful challenge as we begin to chant *Unetaneh Tokef,* which reminds us that God "records and seals, counts and measures" all of our deeds.

D.P.E.

Are "Politics" and Prophetic Social Justice the Same?

What is the proper relationship between "the life of the spirit" and the life of "politics"? The life of the spirit needs the time to breathe and reflect, to love and to laugh, to learn and to teach. "Politics" is—

Who gets fed, and who starves?

Who gets beaten, tortured, or killed by the police, and who is treated with dignity?

Who wanders the streets, who owns a pretty house with trees and flowers, and who owns a dozen mansions on three continents?

Who gets a cushy job for toadying to the boss, who gets fired for pointing out that the health-insurance plan is almost useless, and whose union is so strong he can demand his employer fix the dangerous walkway?

Who gets to meditate in quiet comfort for a week, and who must hold three jobs in order to feed her children?

Who get to sing their sacred songs in public, and who must hold their tongue?

Who drinks pure water from a local well, and who coughs in clouds of chemical smoke and dies young of asthma or of cancer?

Who slaves to build the store-houses of *Mitzrayyim,* that Tight & Narrow land, and who sits upon the throne?

There are some who say that politics is a minefield, where few can walk a spiritual path. Stay off it.

Yes, it is a minefield—but no more than the passion, strife, and turmoil inside one human being, which we strive to calm and focus through davvening, chant, and meditation. The strife we strive to calm—and often fail. And strive again. A private minefield. No more a minefield than the effort to make mentshlich face-to-face community when majorities scoff at consensus, minorities chafe against the stifling of their truth, individuals demand they be allowed to go their own way, and some cry out for a rebbe who will light up the way for everyone.

No more a minefield than the struggle to understand the Torah, to distinguish its deepest values from its ephemeral minutiae, to see how a letter can—or mustn't—shape a thousand years of history, to know when we are swimming in the sacred flow and when we have carved out a frozen idol.

No more a minefield than the effort the cells and organs of our bodies make to stay in balance.

More important, "politics" is not a minefield that any serious spiritual leader can refuse to walk—because it is one of the most important worlds in which human beings live. And any so-called "spiritual leader" who cannot walk that minefield with compassion should call forth as much concern about his/her leadership as if s/he were abusing children or spreading malicious gossip.

Which is to say: *Teshuvah* from these serious mis-steps is always possible, but first one must know that they really are mis-steps, not to be shrugged off because the path is strewn with mines and walking the holy walk is difficult. Of course it is.

Rabbi Arthur Waskow

V'kol D'mama Dakah Yishama: God's Presence in the Silence

The ABC movie critic Joel Siegel defined the difference between an actor and a star in this way:

At the Academy Awards, the crowd standing outside cheers everyone who walks into the building, even the film critics and reporters get loud cheers. But when Sean Connery appears, the crowd quiets to a hush, and they point and whisper to each other, "Sean Connery!"

That awe is the reaction to a real star.

The Talmud tells a story about Rav Sheshet who was blind, and turned up among the crowd at a parade. One of the bystanders scoffed, and remarked that his presence was a waste, since, being blind, he wouldn't be able to tell when the emperor passed by. The rabbi insisted he would be able to tell exactly when.

As every legion approached, the crowds cheered but he said, "That isn't the emperor." At last there was a pervasive hush, and Rav Sheshet said, "Now the emperor is approaching. You can tell his presence from the silence" [*Berakhot* 58a].

V'kol demama dakah yishama ... we recognize God's presence in the sound of silence.

Rabbi Shamai Kanter

We Pass by God, One by One, Like a Flock of Sheep

The *U'netaneh Tokef* prayer recalls a passage in the Mishnah (Rosh Hashanah 1:2) that on Rosh Hashanah "all who come into the world pass before the Creator like sheep, to be judged, one by one."

The commentator known as the Maharsha (Morenu HaRav Shmuel Eliezer Edels, sixteenth- to seventeenth-century Poland) asks the logical question: Surely God is capable of judging us simultaneously. Why must we pass one by one? Like all good commentators, he answers his own question. God separates us one by one so that we can see ourselves better.

The Maharsha is trying to tell us that at least as important as the judgment which God makes on our lives is the judgment we make on ourselves! All true knowledge begins with self-knowledge. Unless we know ourselves, the good and the bad, we cannot change and become the people we really long to be.

D.P.E.

Who Will Live and Will Die....

The same God that made Moses made me, made you, and he made us for a brief time. So let us not depend upon others to do the work in this world. Let us not give our lives away. It is a profound tradition that begins the new year by reminding us of death. But it is only by acknowledging death that we understand the inestimable, the incalculable value of our own lives.

Only that is precious which passes away. Only that is priceless which will not last forever, and we will not last forever. By facing death we are spurred to life. The year to come will bring death. That is the inescapable certainty that haunts us each Rosh Hashanah and Yom

Kippur. Some whom many of us knew who were with us last year are no longer with us. We can be certain that next year too will bring in tragedies. The next year will bring the gradual ebbing of our powers, and the sudden, unfair catastrophe of death. The question which each of us must answer in the hidden chambers of our souls and our hearts is simply this: knowing that next year will bring death, will we fill our days with the force, the promise, and power of life?

Rabbi David J. Wolpe

Our Lives Are in the Balance: Who Shall Live and Who Shall Die?

It was the first pulpit Rabbi Cynthia Culpeper ever had—Montgomery, Alabama's Agudath Israel Synagogue, where she began her rabbinic service in the summer of 1995. She had been a Registered Nurse at San Francisco General Hospital, and decided to return to rabbinical school. Her excitement knew no bounds when she was ordained and then called to serve as spiritual leader in her own congregation in Alabama.

Shortly before Rosh Hashanah she went to have a sore throat checked. The day after Rosh Hashanah she was told that she was HIV-positive, and two weeks after that she was diagnosed with AIDS. She immediately informed her congregation. In January 1994 she received an "occupational exposure" at the hospital where she served, and was tested twice within the year following, both times negative. Now, shortly after the High Holy Days, she was given a death sentence. In her letter to her congregation she wrote: "You can well imagine how intense Yom Kippur was for me this year, my first as a rabbi at that. Its unending primary liturgical message of how our lives are in the balance took on a whole new meaning for me."

Rabbi Culpepper died in the summer of 2005.

In so many ways the *U'netaneh Tokef* prayer still resonates for each of us as we stare fate in the eye and wonder what the future will bring for us. There is no clear answer in the prayer, but only the hope that through *Teshuvah*, *Tefilah* and *Tzedakah*—through Repentance, Prayer and Acts of Kindness—we can make our lives meaningful, whether we have one year or eight years left on this earth.

D.P.E.

Prayer Must Be Backed by Deeds

The three-fold prescription for healing and wholeness in the *U'netaneh Tokef* is *Teshuvah*, *Tefillah* and *Tzedakah*.

One message in this three-fold formula is that repentance and prayer are prerequisites, but in Judaism it is in the last analysis the DEED which cleanses us. We make the world whole, we bring *Tikkun Olam,* we right the wrongs in ourselves, our family, our society and the universe, through righteous action. When we do *Teshuvah*, when we pray and contemplate and meditate, it is always toward some ultimate action that we must take in order to complete the cycle.

Our broken world is desperately in need of redemption. But redemption comes, in the theology of Jewish tradition, through the actions and deeds, the kindness and compassion, which are the fruit of both our heart and our hands.

Rabbi Dov Peretz Elkins

Changing Your Fate for the Coming Year

Our tradition teaches that we can have a direct and active role in changing our fate for the coming year. While our desire to change our lives is particularly strong during the days between Rosh Hashanah and Yom Kippur, we can make important changes all year long: Turning, prayer, and deeds can change our fates.

Meditation
Help me to take a good look at my life and give me the courage to make changes I want to make. Guide me on my journey as I strive to make good changes, in myself and in the world in which I live.

Ritual
Jewish tradition teaches that you can change your fate in several ways:

Tzedakah: Changing the world.

Use your resources and talents to create more justice in the world. Decide: what can you do this day … this week … this month … to make an immediate difference?

Tze'akah: Crying out.

You can cry out about all that's unfair in the world, but you can choose other equally effective actions, such as letters, petitions, social action, prayers of words, and prayers of tears. Strategize: How can you increase the possibility that your most pressing outcry is heard?

Shinui ha'shem: Changing your identity.

You can alter some aspect of your identity, expanding beyond the way others define you in your relationships and in your work. Ask yourself: How could a small adjustment in the way you see yourself allow you to recognize your own personal dreams and aspirations?

Shinui ma'aseh:

You can break some old, familiar patterns of behavior, such as the way you relate to family, friends, or colleagues. Decide: If you were to commit yourself to establishing a new pattern of behavior at home, at work, or in the community, how could you increase the possibility it becomes habit?

Blessing

(as you meditate upon the change you will make)

May we all be remembered and recorded in the Book of Life, blessing, sustenance, and peace (High Holidays liturgy).

Teaching

Rabbi Isaac said: "Four things change a person's fate, namely *tzedakah,* crying out, changing one's name, and changing one's conduct ... and some say changing one's place" (Babylonian Talmud: Rosh Hashanah 16b).

Will you hear our regrets? Will you release us from being prisoners of habit? Will you accept our prayers ... and tune in to our heart's intent? (Adapted from the *Kol Nidrei* service)

Accordingly, throughout the entire year, one should always took at oneself as equally balanced between merit and sin, and the world as equally balanced between merit and sin. If one performs even one sin, one tips one's balance and that of the entire world to the side of guilt and brings destruction upon oneself. [On the other hand,] if one performs even one mitzvah, one tips one's balance and that of the entire world to the side of merit and brings deliverance and salvation to oneself and others. This is implied by [Proverbs 10:25]: "A righteous person is the foundation of the world"; that is, one who acted righteously tipped the balance of the entire world to merit and saved it (Maimonides, *Hilkhot Teshuvah* 3).

Because the world is a different place each moment I am alive, there is unlimited potential for change (Kerry M. Olitzky and Rachel Sabath, *Preparing Your Heart for the High Holy Days*).

Rabbi Irwin Kula and Vanessa L. Ochs

You and Your Neighbor

If you have done your neighbor a little wrong, let it be a great wrong in your eyes, and go and rectify it.

If you have done your neighbor much good, let it be little in your eyes.

If your neighbor has done you a little good, let it be great in your eyes.

If your neighbor has done you a great wrong, let it be little in your eyes.

Avot d'Rabbi Natan

U'Teshuvah: Changing Ourselves

Why is it so easy to give others advice, but difficult to take it ourselves? Changing others is so much easier than changing ourselves.

A story about Levi Yitzchak of Berditchev relates that he started out his rabbinic career wanting to change the world. After several years, he realized that was too hard, so he decided to try to change his community. Several years later, that goal was abandoned as too difficult, and Levi Yitzchak chose just to concentrate on changing his own family. He finally concluded that the only one he could really change was himself! That's the only person we can truly change anyway. If we decide not to help ourselves, we are totally lost.

Traditional

U'Teshuvah: Teshuvah Affects Our Relationships, but Even More So, Ourselves

According to Jewish tradition, sin is an act which is wrong, not just because of its consequences, but because of what it does to our own sense of being. Not just the act is sinful, but what it does to us is sinful. That is what Sadya HaGaon seems to have meant when he wrote: "Every sin is inscribed in the soul."

Sin is not just what is done to someone else, whether that someone else be another person or God—it is what *I do to myself* that makes it a negative act.

Herein lies the most profound aspect of *teshuvah*. It results in far more than just a new harmonious society in which interpersonal anger has been greatly reduced. A sociological act, an act between two people that is designed to bring back harmony to the society in which it has taken place ultimately becomes an individual act. We generally consider an apology to be something done to make wronged people feel soothed, to assuage their pain. An act of *teshuvah* does more than just soothe the hurt person: it changes the person who has performed *teshuvah*. Tshuvah has the ability to cleanse the soul. It is a revolutionary act that we perform on ourselves.

Dr. Deborah E. Lipstadt

U'teshuvah: How Do People Change—Through Honey or Vinegar?

Reb Zusha asked the holy Seer of Lublin: "How would you make a person repent?" The Lubliner answered, "I'd show him, in the *Shulhan Arukh,* what he did wrong."

Reb Zusha answered, "I don't think that would work. Do you think that would make the person feel good? On the contrary, it would make him feel bad. And if he feels bad, he would run away from you."

The Lubliner asked Reb Zusha, "Rebbe, how do you do it?" To which Reb Zusha replied, "I would shine light into him, into his heart, the great light the love of *Hashem* has for every human being."

I need so much light in my life. Everyone does. So hopefully whatever small light anyone has, they will just share it and make the night a little brighter.

Yehoshua Rubin

U'Teshuvah: **An Environmental Confession**

Rosh Hashanah and Yom Kippur are traditionally called the Ten Days of Repentance. Part of the Jewish concept of repentance is the act of confession. In the High Holiday liturgy are numerous public confessions that are couched in general terms for a whole series of sins.

We confess publicly rather than privately, and in general terms rather than in specifics, because it allows everyone to confession with shame or embarrassment. It also binds the sins of one person to those of the whole community so that all take responsibility. In all our acts of repentance, we are supposed to try and undo the damage we have caused.

While the old list of sins is fairly comprehensive, the time has come to add a new one: the careless destruction of Creation. At a conference, I once heard an environmental educator say that we can become more environmentally aware and responsive by publicly confessing our environmental sins. He then proceeded to do so. Everyone there laughed a nervous laugh of embarrassment, because we all realized, without saying a word, that we all have such sins to confess.

Here is one of my environmental sins about which I have rarely spoken. While it would be more fitting to confess over a river in Northern Ontario (you will soon see why), because this is the season of repentance, I do it now.

When I was sixteen, as part of my summer camp program, I went on a canoe trip in Northern Ontario and I participated in a frog massacre. Five of us and a "tripper" (a counselor who specialized in taking out canoe trips) set out in two canoes from the middle of Algonquin Park for a six-day trip that would take us to North Bay.

It was a wonderful trip and we had many adventures. Somewhere along a river about a day east of North Bay, we came across an area that was filled with frogs of many different kinds. One of us hit a frog with a paddle, and then we all went out of control. We began killing the frogs as we went, and I can't even tell you how many we destroyed.

Afterwards, I remember feeling a little ashamed, but we said nothing about it to each other. It was one of those mindless adolescent acts of cruelty that seemed to be a part of growing up.

Every once in a while, I have thought of this thing that I did. I have learned in the past few years that the frog population of the world is in sharp decline, probably from environmental factors. This has worried scientists because they don't quite know why it is happening, and the frog may be a kind of environmental canary in the mine, warning us of the overall decline in the earth's ecosystems.

My part in the frog's decline has been in the back of my mind for some time. Since I believe, that on some level, we must treat all life with the same kind of ethical concern with which we treat each other, I felt that I must confess. To do the frogs justice, according to Maimonides' rules, I should go back to that river and make confession there. Maybe someday I will. In the meantime, I must do so now: I have sinned. I confess that I broke the commandment against the wanton destruction of creation. I confess that I was on the side of death and not life. I confess that I broke the command of the Torah to choose life and not death. I am sorry. Slowly, I have tried to change the way I live to lessen the impact that I have on the earth. Perhaps one of the reasons for my involvement in environmentalism has been an attempt to bring about some kind of restoration for what I had done.

Maimonides said that the true measure of one's repentance is found when you are faced with the same situation and you do not repeat your sin. This is a very high standard when it comes to sins against creation, since so many of the things that we do every day can be considered environmental destruction. Nonetheless, this should not stop us from trying to undo the damage we have caused to God's creation.

Maybe we can begin by confession.

Rabbi Lawrence Troster

Maimonides' Five Steps to True *Teshuvah*

The great medieval giant of Jewish Philosophy and Law, the Rambam, or Maimonides, who lived in twelfth-century Egypt in a suburb of Cairo, describes the process of *Teshuvah* in five separate, equally important stages.

First is *Hakarat Ha-Het*—recognition that one has done something wrong.

Second is *Haratah*—an inner sense of regret for having done the misdeed.

Third is *Vidui*—one must articulate in words, in a form of confession, that one recognizes the misdeed, and regrets doing it.

Fourth is *Kabbalah Le-atid*, the acceptance on oneself not to repeat the same action.

Fifth, an occasion when the opportunity to repeat the misdeed occurs, and one in fact behaves differently, and does not repeat the sin.

These five complicated steps are far more complicated than the surface notion of just "being sorry." *Teshuvah* is one of Judaism's most significant and all-encompassing moral demands on any human being. It is for that reason that this season of the Jewish calendar of the High Holy Days is called in Hebrew *Aseret Yemai Teshuvah*, the Ten Days of *Teshuvah*.

D.P.E.

U'Teshuvah: Much More than Repentance

Every major author, from the medieval sage Maimonides, to modern philosophers and theologians, attests to the fact that *teshuvah* is not just "repentance."

The Rambam, in his classic work, the *Mishneh Torah*, urges his readers to reach out to people who were harmed, and that the power of confession is enormous in healing old wounds. The modem saint, and some say Maimonides' twentieth-century counterpart, Adin Steinsaltz, in his book *Teshuvah*, takes the position that *teshuvah* is a spiritual awakening, a desire to strengthen the bond between us and the holy in all Being.

Rabbi Pinchas Peli, in his book outlining Rav Soloveitchik's ideas on *teshuvah*, explains that it connotes not just remorse, but a complete break from the old environment and the old self—the veritable creation of a new personality.

Clearly, the idea of *teshuvah* is one of the most cogent theological concepts ever created by any tradition, ancient or modem, in empowering human beings to make new beginnings and to re-create their own lives.

D.P.E.

Nightly *Teshuvah*

Be among those people who take stock of themselves each night before
    going to sleep.
Give a nightly account of your sins and repent for them.
Know that even a thought of repentance will suffice.
For *teshuvah* was one of the seven things that preceded the creation of
    the world.
It is beyond time.
Therefore a single thought of *teshuvah* can "sweeten" all of your mis-
    deeds.

Rabbi Menahem Nahum of Chernobyl

Teshuvah: Coming Home

The world endures because of the ever-present yearning and gesture
of returning home to our Source. Through this return, all life is
reunited with the Holy One of All Being. In the words of the Talmud,
"Returning home is the hardest things in the world, for truly to return
home would mean to bring the Messiah. Returning home is also the
easiest thing to do, for it has only to occur to you to return home, and
you have already begun."

This going back to our Source is a great longing that flows through
and animates all creation. Through apology, repair, and attempting to
heal damage done, we effectively re-write the past. What was once
some thoughtless or even wicked act, when set within the present context of meaning, becomes the commencement of a greater healing.

Kavanah

In the family album or in one of those little frames that stands upright
on an end table in your mother's apartment is a photograph of you
when you were a child. You have come a long way since those days in
many beautiful ways and in a few shameful ones. If you were given a
time machine, what would you tell the child in the photo who was
once you? Just looking at who you were seems to awaken the possibility that you could go back to that time and, if not relive your life, at
least begin again. Just this is the beginning of the return.

Rabbi Lawrence Kushner

U'Tefilah

What is your reaction when you are talking with a friend and your conversation is suddenly interrupted by the piercing wail of an ambulance siren? Is it pure sympathy for the person inside—or about to be picked up by the ambulance, or do you feel some measure of annoyance? Similarly, how do you react when you are awakened from a deep sleep by a series of clanging fire trucks or the wail of a police car?

I am embarrassed to admit that, along with many others, my initial reaction to such noises is often impatience and annoyance rather than empathy. My friend Rabbi Zalman Schachter-Shalomi, known throughout the Jewish world as "Reb Zalman," suggests that whenever we hear the sound of a passing ambulance we offer a prayer that the ambulance arrive in time. Similarly, whenever our sense of calm is interrupted by fire trucks, we should pray to God that the trucks arrive in time to save the endangered people and home. We should also pray that no firefighter be injured. And when we hear police sirens, we should implore God that the police respond in time to the emergency.

Reb Zalman's suggestion is profound. By accustoming ourselves to uttering a prayer at the very moment we feel unjustly annoyed, we become better, more loving people. The very act of praying motivates us to empathize with those who are suffering and in need of our prayers. Furthermore, imagine how encouraging it would be for those being rushed to a hospital to know that hundreds of people who hear the ambulance sirens are praying for their recovery.

Speaking to a Jewish group once in Baltimore, I shared Reb Zalman's suggestion. After my talk, several people commented on how moved they were by this idea, but one woman seemed particularly emotional when she spoke of this suggestion. When she was ten, she told me, she had been awakened from a deep sleep by passing fire trucks. It was almost one in the morning, and now, twenty-five years later, she still remembered her first response: it was so unfair that her sleep had been ruined.

The next morning she had learned that her closest friend, a girl who lived only a few blocks away, had died in the fire. Ever since, she told me, whenever she hears fire trucks go by, she prays that they arrive at their destination in time.

Loving one's neighbor is usually carried out through tangible acts, by giving money or food to those in need, by stepping in and offering assistance to a neighbor who is ill, or by bringing guests into one's home. But sometimes loving is expressed through a prayer that connects us to our neighbor, even when we have no way of knowing just who our neighbor is.

Rabbi Joseph Telushkin

U'Tefilah: The Prayer of an Anonymous Confederate Soldier

I asked God for strength, that I might achieve;
I was made weak, that I might learn to serve.

I asked for health, that I might do great things;
I was given infirmity, that I might do better things.

I asked for wealth, that I might be happy;
I was given poverty, that I might be wise.

I asked for power, that I might earn the praise of others;
I was given weakness, that I might feel the need of God.

I asked for all things, that I might enjoy life;
I was given life, that I might enjoy all things.

I got nothing I asked for, but all I hoped for.
Despite myself, my unspoken prayers were answered,
And I am, among all people, most richly blessed.

Author Unknown

U'Tefilah: Thanking God for God's World

One of the important goals of prayer, it seems to me, is to heighten our awareness of the beauty and majesty of nature and God's world.

The *Amidah,* which we recite three times daily, including Shabbat and every major festival, understands the question that children ask all the time. When I meet with young students in the Religious School, they always ask about how did the Sea of Reeds split, and how did the sun stop for Joshua, and similar questions. But the *Amidah* makes it clear that the greatest miracles are those that occur every day—the rising and setting of the sun, the growth of flowers, the changing of the leaves, the birth of a child—things which we too often take for granted.

Walt Whitman (1819–1892) captured this idea beautifully when he wrote:

> To me, every cubic inch of space is a miracle ...
> Welcome is every organ and attitude of me ...
> Not an inch, nor a particle of an inch is vile ...

What the *Amidah* is telling us in the words *Al nisekha she-be-khol yom imanu* is that "every cubic inch of space is a miracle."

D.P.E.

U'Tefilah: Like Baseball, Prayer Needs Practice

It would not be realistic or fair to expect a home run each time one is at bat in prayer any more than it would be in baseball. Those who pray very little often make that mistake. A home run in prayer, like one in baseball, requires much practice, many trials and errors, and, ultimately, consummate skill. Even that is not enough. One needs some luck, too. The conditions have to be just right, and one's body, mind, and emotions have to be perfectly attuned to one another and to the task at hand. This does not happen very often.

Moreover, one should not pray only in hopes of having such an experience any more than one plays baseball only for the times one hits a home run. In fact, some of us will play baseball all our lives and never hit a home run. Indeed, if our praying or baseball playing were to succeed on every level each time we tried, we would be very different individuals and societies from what we know, and prayer—and baseball—would have to be restructured to speak to our needs. The fact that prayer (or anything else) cannot remake us into ideal human beings does not negate its value, however, for prayer can remind us what to strive for and motivate us to try. Although it cannot move us in all its dimensions every time, it can affect us on some level on many occasions. It thus can be a valuable practice even if it is not always or totally successful.

Rabbi Elliot N. Dorff

Tefilah

Prayer only sounds as if you're talking to God. In truth, prayer is reciting the words of a script evolved and evolving over the centuries that gives form to the inchoate yearnings of your inner-most being. There is nothing new to say in prayer. Surely God "has heard it all before." What you need to do in order to pray is surrender your own expressions of gratitude and petition to the syntax of tradition. Only one who can allow the annulment of his or her self is capable of being transformed through the words of prayer, the lines of the script. As long as you cling to your discreet selfhood, you will be unable to transcend yourself and your prayers will go "unanswered." For this reason, the keys to unlocking our most important songs is the script recorded in the prayer book.

Of course, like any good actor, occasional ad libs, inflationary modifications, and even forgetting one's lines at times are part of the business. Even the sensation of improvisation has a place, as long as you remember that your "new creation" has already been recited by the Heavenly retinue since before the creation of the world. The script, in other words, is present whether or not the "play" is performed in a human prayer hall.

Rabbi Lawrence Kushner

Tzedakah: The Root of Life

Tzedakah is the root of life
When you give to others, you raise the sparks from their broken state
And you elevate your own soul.

The word *Tzedakah* [charity] contains within it the word *tzedek* [righteousness].

In acting as a *tzaddik* [righteous person], you become a spark of the Cosmic *Tzaddik*, and you help elevate *Tzedek* from poverty and exile.

Enough said.

Here is the idea: by carrying out a holy deed or an act of life-sustaining charity, you redeem a spark from the evil forces and thus increase your own holiness....

Rabbi Menahem Nahum of Chernobyl

Who Gains Most from *Tzedakah?*

Rabbi Yehoshua taught: More than the housewife does for the poor, the poor do for the housewife *(Vayikra Rabba* [medieval collection of *midrashim* on the Book of Leviticus] 34:8).

An important Jewish teaching is that the person who gives *tzedakah* benefits as much, or more than, the recipient of his or her help. While the poor person obtains material assistance, the donor derives the merit of sharing in the Almighty's work of responding compassionately to the poor.

The Baal Haturim (great Bible commentator, 1269–1343) makes this point in a beautiful commentary on the word *v'natnu* ("and they will give"), a palindrome in Hebrew, that appears in Exodus 30:12. He notes that the fact that *v'natnu* is the same when written backwards as forwards teaches us that whatever a person gives to *tzedakah* will return to him or her. Thus, that individual will experience no "lack" (shortage) because of his or her generosity.

Rabbi Lori Forman

U'Tzedakah: Kindness and Compassion

It is Rosh Hashanah, the first day of the Jewish year 5759, and I am thinking about a message I keep spotting on bumper stickers and T-shirts: "Practice random kindness and senseless acts of beauty."

At first glance, it seems a warm, uplifting sentiment. In a world filled with random cruelty, what could be more welcome than some unexpected kindness? With all the senseless violence human beings inflict on each other, we can all use a little more beauty in our lives. Who wouldn't welcome anything that can inspire us to deeds of kindness and beauty—even if only an expression on a bumper sticker?

Yet the more I see this expression, the more it bothers me. The words are sweet. But taken literally, they convey a troubling message.

For what our society needs more of is not random kindness, but sustained and dependable kindness; not senseless acts of beauty, but beautiful behavior that is deliberately cultivated. Of course a random kindness is better than no kindness at all. But it is the ethical equivalent of sitting down at the piano to bang out "Chopsticks": quick, easy, and not very serious.

The meaning that lurks in the interstices of "Practice random kindness" is that treating others with compassion and decency is something to be done as a lark. That is not a philosophy that promotes kindness as an essential element of good character. It is a philosophy that promotes kindness as a fun activity for a slow weekend. This attitude suffuses the recent spate of "kindness" books. "Guerrilla Kindness," for example, recommends burying nickels in sandboxes for children to find when they play. "Random Acts of Kindness" suggests buying coffee for strangers in a diner or secretly washing a neighbor's car. Something called The Kindness Society offers this on its Web site:

"Random acts of kindness are those sweet or lovely things we do for no reason except that, momentarily, the best of our humanity has sprung into full bloom. When you spontaneously give an old woman the bouquet of red carnations you had meant to take home to your own dinner table, when you give your lunch to the guitar-playing homeless person who makes music at the corner ... when you anonymously put coins in someone else's parking meter ... you are doing not what life requires of you, but what the best of your human soul invites you to do."

I am all for spontaneously giving bouquets to old women. Any good deed is to be encouraged, even if it is only done on a whim. But if kindness is merely spur-of-the-moment gestures, if it is "not what life requires of you," why bother? Because it feels good? Then what happens when it doesn't feel good? What happens when it takes a real effort of will—or a financial sacrifice—or a significant commitment of time—to treat someone with kindness and charity?

How different is the understanding of kindness conveyed by the Rosh Hashana liturgy.

Today and tomorrow, Jews will revisit the story of Abraham, the father of the Jewish nation. Each of the three Biblical patriarchs is regarded as the exemplar of a particular trait, and Abraham is remembered above all for his acts of loving-kindness. (Isaac's trait is self-sacrifice; Jacob is the paradigm of scholarliness.)

The Bible portrays Abraham as a man intensely concerned with the comfort and well-being of others. He leaves his sickbed when he sees strangers in the distance, ignoring his pain in order to show them hospitality. He pleads with God to spare the cruel sinners of Sodom and Gomorrah. So thoroughly does he inculcate the habit of kindness in the members of his household that when his servant Eliezer journeys to find a wife for Isaac, the litmus test he applies is one of compassion: He looks for a girl who is willing not only to offer him a drink of water, but to draw water for his camels as well—a backbreaking chore.

This is kindness of a far higher order than dropping nickels in a playground or handing out carnations in the street.

"Jews are the compassionate children of compassionate parents," the Talmud teaches. "One who is merciless toward his fellow creatures is no descendant of our father Abraham." Jewish tradition teaches that kindness is what life requires of you—and even that it is required for life. On Rosh Hashanah, God sits in judgment, deciding who will live and who will die, whose days will be peaceful, whose tormented. But His decisions are not unalterable. At the climactic moment of the service, in the famous prayer of Rabbi Amnon, Jews remind themselves that "repentance, prayer, and acts of charity can dissolve a bitter decree."

The sages taught that God Himself is the original model of kindness: He clothed Adam and Eve when they were naked, visited Abraham when he was sick, comforted Isaac in his grief, buried Moses after he died. We, who are commanded to follow in God's ways (Deuteronomy 13:5), must likewise clothe the naked, visit the sick, comfort the bereaved, bury the dead. We pray on Rosh Hashana for God to treat us with charity and kindness—*asei imanu tzedaka va'hesed*—not randomly but daily, not on a whim but constantly. He wants the same from us. "For I desire kindness, not sacrifices," said the prophet Hosea 2,700 years ago.

My resolution for the coming year is to practice consistent kindness and thoughtful acts of beauty.

Jeff Jacoby

Adam Yesodo Me-Afar: Our Origin Is Dust and Our End Is Dust

The Hebrew novelist and Nobel laureate, Shmuel Yosef Agnon, was told that he had just been awarded the Nobel Prize in literature. His friends and neighbors rushed to his simple home in the Talpiot section of Jerusalem to bring him greetings of Mazal Tov. Soon the small home was filled also with scores of journalists and photographers. He was asked by a photographer to have a seat at his writing desk, and pretend that he was in the process of composing one of his famous short stories. Agnon complied, sat down at his writing desk, and scribbled a few words on a piece of paper, while the cameras flashed away.

After the crowds left, a friend casually walked over to his desk to see what he had written. It turned out to be a quote from the High Holiday *Mahzor*, part of the prayer which follows the *U'netaneh Tokef: Adam Yesodo me-afar, ve-sofo le-afar.* "Our origin is dust and our end is dust."

The famous novelist felt instinctively that he needed to be reminded at this crucial and vulnerable moment in his life of these important words from the *Mahzor.*

D.P.E.

Like a Fading Flower, a Passing Shadow, a Fugitive Cloud and a Vanishing Dream

David Gelernter teaches computer science at Yale. He is an observant Conservative Jew, who has written for the popular magazine *Conservative Judaism.*

Do you remember his name? He was one of the victims of the Unabomber. Several years ago he got a package in the mail. He opened it up, and by doing so, he set off a bomb. It blew up in his face, and he lost an arm ... for no reason ... with no notice, sent to him by a man whom he had never met. In one split second ... his whole life changed.

When the Unabomber was caught a couple of years ago, Prof. Gelernter was interviewed. He spoke about what he had learned from his recovery.

> Mostly, I didn't learn anything new, but I had the satisfaction of having my hunches confirmed. I emerged, knowing that, as I had always suspected, the time that I spend with my wife and my children is all that really matters in the end. I emerged as a practicing Jew. (Admittedly, I had always been one).
>
> By inclination, I am a writer and a painter. I got into computer science because of the Talmudic injunction that a person should learn a useful trade in order to support his family. Shoemaking was what the Rabbis had in mind ... but I have never shown any aptitude for shoes, so I don't regret my choice. The

explosion smashed my right hand, and for several months, I was under the impression that I would never paint again. I bitterly regretted the work that I had never put down on canvas. But then I learned how to paint with my left hand, and I will never again neglect my duties as a painter.

By the same token, I had been planning a book about the 1939 World's Fair. It was to be such an abnormal book—part history, part novel—that I figured it would be years before I worked up enough courage to write the thing. But when I got home from the hospital, it was clear that I ought to just sit down and do it. To my surprise, it was a success. A number of people even bought copies.

Here was a man who came to an unexpected divide in the road and was able to move on.

Rabbi Jonathan Waxman

V'KHOL MA'AMINIM: THAT WHICH WE ALL BELIEVE

God's seal of truth commands us to be honest and to live with integrity. This has to do with every aspect of our lives, from our business dealings to the way we express our faith in God. What we do and say should be out in the open, accessible to all who want to see it, and capable of passing common human tests of truth.

In the Bible *emet* refers to a deeply held and unshakable belief; it is closely related to the word *emunah* or "faith." The truth of one's position is shown by how firmly it is held. Ultimately that which we are willing to live for and die for becomes our personal truth. It is in this spirit that our liturgy adds the word *emet* to the conclusion of the *shema,* affirming our personal witness to God's truth.

RABBI ARTHUR GREEN, *THESE ARE THE WORDS*

Ve-khol Ma-aminim: Permanent Trust or Permanent Mistrust

In the prayer *Ve-khol Ma-aminim* we speak of trust in God—that we all are believers, *ve-khol ma-aminim.*

My colleague Rabbi Gerald Zelizer tells the story of three tortoises who stopped for a cup of coffee at a local restaurant. When it started to rain, the eldest asked the youngest to please go home and bring back his umbrella. The youngest agreed, with one condition—namely, that the eldest would not drink his coffee. The agreement was made, and the youngest went to retrieve the umbrella. The other two waited, and time passed, more and more time. Finally, after two years, the old tortoise said: "Well, I guess he's not coming back, I might as well drink his coffee." At that point a tiny voice was heard from behind the door: "If you drink it, I won't go."

Some of us are never capable of trusting anyone—ourselves, our friends, or God. For others, trust is a permanent part of their make-up—*ve-khol ma-aminim.* They are among the permanent believers, not the permanent mistrusters.

On the *Yamim Nora-im* we are all asked to deepen our trust, so that *kol ma-aminim*—so that all of us with have faith!

D.P.E.

Faith Comes Slowly, Gradually

The prayer *Ve-Khol Ma-ameenim* talks about belief and faith. "We all believe," is the refrain. It limns the prisms of our faith in great detail.

Faith is not something that comes immediately or easily. In fact it is won hard, over a lifetime. This is how it came to Anne Lamott, in a beautiful metaphor that comes from her book, *Traveling Mercies: Some Thoughts on Faith:*

> My coming to faith did not start with a leap but rather a series of staggers from what seemed one safe place to another. Like lily pads, round and green, these places summoned and then held me up while I grew. Each prepared me for the next leaf on which I could land, and in this way I moved across the swamp of doubt and fear. When I look back at some of these early resting places ... I can see how flimsy and indirect a path they made. Yet each

brought me closer to the verdant pad of faith on which I somehow stay afloat today.

As we recite *Ve-khol Ma-ameenim*, let's think of the next round green lily pad to which we must jump to deepen our faith.

D.P.E.

Can Faith Be Justified?

Can we ever really know whether faith is justified? Do we, citizens of modernity and post-modernity, not take for granted what Hume, Kant and Nietzsche labored to establish, that the existence of God cannot be proved? And do we not as Jews—always inclined to rationality, and now chastened and chilled by the Holocaust—have more reason to doubt than most? Yet I have to admit, even as a professionally trained philosopher, that I am unmoved by this whole trend of thought, rendered trivial by its own circularity. Of course it is possible to live a life without God, just as it is possible to live a life without humor, or music, or love; and one can no more prove that God exists than one can prove these other things exist to those who lack a sense of humor, or to whom Schubert is mere noise, or love a figment of the romantic imagination. The late Sir Isaiah Berlin used to say to me, in his sonorous voice and with a mischievous smile, "Chief Rabbi, don't talk to me about faith. When it comes to God, I'm tone-deaf." I never argued the point with him: at the age of eighty, I felt he was entitled to his agnosticism. But on reflection I see I should have done so. He had striven to appreciate music and poetry, Russian literature and the history of ideas. He knew that one can live a life without these things, but it will be a smaller, more circumscribed and impoverished life. How much more so in the case of faith.

Rabbi Jonathan Sacks

Trying to Believe

When the great psychoanalyst Carl Gustav Jung was asked: "Do you believe in God?" he replied, "I know. I don't need to believe. I know." How can anyone reply with such certainty and conviction? How can anyone be so sure?

Perhaps the answer lies in the way we understand what faith really means. There is something beautiful about the origin of the Hebrew word for faith, *Emunah*. Most of us are familiar with a slightly different form of it—the response, Amen. Both of these words come from the root a-m-n, which is related to the concept of "nursemaid" or "nurturer." Hidden within that root is the word for "mother" *(em)*.

When we seek faith, we are actually searching for an inner mother, someone or something to nurture us, particularly during the hard times.

Often before a young couple marries, one of them gets cold feet. Some actually cancel or postpone their weddings. Some just need reassurance from a dear friend or parent. "Get me my Mama," one bride-to-be cried out to those around her an hour before her wedding. "I need to talk to Mama now."

Similarly, at the end of life, many people seek the same sort of comfort. Dying patients, even when they are surrounded by other loved ones and friends, cry out one word more than any other: "Mama."

Regardless of your actual relationship with your mother, the word "Mama" symbolizes the person who gave birth to you and nurtured you. So as you reach your final moments, you may once again call out, "Mama," as you give birth to a new part of yourself.

Rabbi Levi S. Meier

Gratitude

Gratitude is a pure expression of faith. We recognize that we have been blessed with all abundance of good things in our lives. So we take a moment to say "thank you." It shifts our focus from getting, and away from thinking about the things we don't have.

Gratitude does not come easily to most of us. We enjoy complaining and usually have no trouble finding something to complain about. Maybe we should just be grateful to have something to complain about! It has been suggested that we keep a gratitude list of all the things in life to be appreciated—to be used as a little "pick me up" on those "Poor, Poor, Pitiful me" days when the calendar beckons us to return.

There is never any shortage of things to be grateful for in our lives. We just don't always see it that way. *Berakhot,* blessings, help us to see the world through thankful eyes.

For growth and renewal: To reach the level of thanksgiving where we call utter, as the rabbis suggest, one hundred each day may seem a difficult goal. It all begins by being grateful for one thing: life itself. Today, at the beginning of the year, find something to be grateful for. Then say a prayer of thanks.

Rabbi Kerry M. Olitzky

V'khol Ma'aminim: We Believe, We Hope

The medieval work of Jewish mysticism, the Zohar, explains that when Israel went into exile, the Divine Presence also was exiled. God's name in the Book of Exodus is *EHYEH*, "I shall be." But the name of God was broken, and the first letter, the *alef*, remained in Heaven, while the other three letters, *heh vov heh* attached themselves to Israel.

However, taking away the *alef* meant taking away the indicator of the future tense. In other words, because God's name was broken into two parts—*alef* and *heh yod heh*—all the people of Israel had left was the past—*hayah*, the memory of past glory, the historic connection of closeness with God.

Thus, explains the Zohar, the exile of the people became dreadful because it forced the people of Israel to lose hope. Without hope, without *HaTikvah,* our people is lost. In the prayer *Ve-khol Ma-aminim* we assert our faith and hope in God and in our future, in the redemption of *Am Yisrael.*

D.P.E., adapted from Rabbi Arthur Green,
Restoring the Aleph

Ve-khol Ma-minim She-hu Tamim Po-olo: God is Wholehearted, So Must We Be

Moshe tells the people of Israel: "You shall be whole-hearted, *tamim,* with the Lord your God" (Deuteronomy 18:9–13). What does it mean to be *tamim,* "whole-hearted"?

Some commentators say it means we shouldn't think one thing and do another. We shouldn't say one thing and do another. We should be dependable. We should be genuine and be sincere.

Some commentators say it means that when we are behind closed doors and no one is there watching us, and we are "with the Lord your God" alone and no one else, then, too, we must be wholehearted as if we were in the presence of others. We are to do the right thing even when no one is looking—even when we know we're not going to get caught.

But probably the simplest understanding of *tamim* comes from the context of the verse. The Torah there describes all the other nations engaged in pagan practices. "But, you, you are to be *tamim*, wholehearted with God." In other words, we are to refrain from engaging in such practices. We are to be different. We are to listen to the voice of God and not the culture around us.

Some people argue that the most difficult environment in which to be a Jew is one that restricts religious freedom. That makes sense. We need to think only of the Soviet Union during the period of the Refuseniks. Being a Jew was difficult. There was anti-Semitism. It was uncomfortable. There was no religious freedom. Jews had no opportunity to get a Jewish education.

Others would argue just the opposite. The most difficult land to survive as a Jew is a land of freedom—like America. Here there is no enemy reminding us to be Jewish. Anti-Semitism is rare. Here if we are going to remain Jews, it's not going to be because someone else defines us as Jews, but because we define ourselves as Jews.

This was the dilemma that Jews faced during the period of the French Revolution—the late 1700s. The motto of the French Revolution was "liberty, fraternity, and equality." All around the world countries were giving their citizens rights. And the question Jews asked was whether or not they should support the French Revolution. Should the Jews fight for political and religious freedom? And most Jews did.

But one Rabbi in Russia was asked whether the Jews should support the Czar or support Napoleon. And he answered, "the Czar may take your body, but Napoleon will take your soul."

That's the cost of freedom. We have the freedom to embrace our religion. But we also have the freedom to leave it behind.

A Gallup poll reported that one American adult in four has changed faiths or denominations at least once. About one American adult in three, according to another study, has changed ethnic identity at least once. In America we are Jews by consent, not descent. We choose. No one forces us to be or remain Jews.

The greatest challenge we face as Jews is to be *tamim* ... whole-hearted with God—to be sincere in our relationships with others, to do the right thing even when no one else is present, and to follow a path in life on which God walks too.

Rabbi Lee Buckman

Ve-khol Ma-aminim: What Is True Faith?

In the prayer *Ve-khol Ma-aminim*, the author speaks of the many ways in which the Jew has faith in God—our Creator, our Judge, our Redeemer, etc.

The famous Danish philosopher Kierkegaard gave an illustration of the true meaning of faith, which is not too different from the author of this medieval poem. Kierkegaard explains what faith is NOT. Faith is NOT: when the sea is calm, the sun is shining, the captain is sober, and you believe that the ship will reach the shore. Most likely it will. Faith, explains Kierkegaard, is when the seas are raging, the ship is floundering, the captain is drunk, but with it all, you have faith that the ship will reach its destination.

That is true faith. Is it the kind of faith that you and I have? It's a question we might well ponder as we recite *Ve-khol Ma-aminim*.

D.P.E.

A Weak Faith, a Strong Faith

Just as a small fire is extinguished by the storm whereas a large fire is enhanced by it—likewise a weak faith is weakened by predicament and catastrophes whereas a strong faith is strengthened by them.

Viktor E. Frankl

V'khol Ma'aminim: Seeing the Invisible

The notion that all of our talk of God is composed of metaphors created by human beings leads inevitably to the charge that human beings "invent" God. The only appropriate response to this charge is that no, human beings discover God and then invent metaphors to characterize the God they experience. Sometimes the metaphors come first; they make it possible for us to feel God's presence in our lives in certain distinctive ways. However, these metaphors also originate in an act of discovery, a genuine experience of a reality that infinitely transcends us.

How do we know that these experiences are genuine? How do we respond to the charge that these experiences of a God who is "out there" are simply wishes, projections, or illusions? This question touches upon the central issue in the philosophy of religion, an issue that has agitated philosophers for centuries and that is clearly beyond the scope of this inquiry. It must be addressed here in a preliminary way, however.

One way of addressing it is to show that religion is not the only instance in which we speak at great length about realities that are not clearly visible, and that we do so in ways that remain quite indispensable and meaningful. For example, suppose I am sitting next to a clinical psychologist who is observing the behavior of a child through a one-way mirror. Suddenly the psychologist turns to me and exclaims, "Neil, look at this child's ego!"

I look. What do I literally see? A child playing with dolls, blocks, and a tricycle. The psychologist sees all this but also something more—the child's ego, which he clearly admires. Yet, where is this ego? …

Believers in God are like psychologists: they too want to explain what they do explicitly see—in this case the ultimate canvas, the entire complex of nature, history, and human experience viewed as one integrated whole. To explain all this, believers have to posit that beyond what they do see, there is an invisible world that must be there if what they see is to make sense. Part of this invisible world includes a reality they call God.

There is no way of proving objectively and conclusively that God exists. For centuries philosophers have tried to devise such proofs, but with little success…. This God may not be directly seen, but it can be "seen" as the ego is seen by the psychologist. Like the ego, God is not all object but more like a pattern that suffuses all things. Just as the ego is elusive, so is God; that's precisely why we need the range of metaphors to bring this God sharply into our consciousness, just as we use metaphors to bring the ego to life.

Finally, like the psychologist, the believer must have a certain refinement, some education or training, a knowledge of what to look for. Without this training, all the looking in the world would not help. The entire task of religious education can be summed up this way: it is the attempt to train people to see the world as suffused with the presence of God, just as the psychologist is trained to see the ego in the behavior of a child. Believers, like psychologists, are members of a community that sees the world in a certain way. The community of believers has endured infinitely longer than that of psychologists, and—to use an admittedly pragmatic criterion—their way of seeing the world has worked remarkably well to help people in widely different ages and cultures make sense of the world and of their human experience. That conclusion may not be objectively true, but it is true enough to dispel any notion that God is a total human fabrication. That may be as much "proof" as we can ever attain in this matter.

To answer the question "Who is God?" is to study the twists and turns of the complex metaphorical system that Jews have used to try to make sense of the world and their lives, as this system winds its way through the generations.

Rabbi Neil Gillman

VARIOUS ASPECTS OF THE *MUSAF AMIDAH*

Cantorial tradition over the centuries has favored the *mussaf* service and embellished it with especially rich musical expression. In some synagogues the cantor typically leads only the Torah and *mussaf* services on *Shabbat*. In Reform and some other liberal congregations, however, *mussaf* has recently been eliminated, abbreviated, or changed due to contemporary discomfort with reciting the details of animal sacrifices.

On *Rosh Hashanah* and *Yom Kippur*, the chief liturgical focus is on this part of the prayer service. On *Rosh Hashanah*, the three sections of Biblical verses declaring God's kingship (*malkhuyot*), memory or providence (*zikhronot*), and power as proclaimed by the *shofar* blast (*shofarot*) are added to the *mussaf 'amidah*.

RABBI ARTHUR GREEN, *THESE ARE THE WORDS*

Introduction to the Silent *Amidah*

No one is as remote as You, Lord our God,
yet no one is closer to us, Fatherly Ruler.

You are beyond the confines of all creation,
yet forever present in every moment.

Our deepest thought cannot grasp Your infinity
nor understand the shadow of Your glory's reflection.

But the whispered prayer,
rising from the depths of despair,
the unvoiced cry of mute needs,
the soft sigh, draining the broken heart of its sorrow,
the silent supplication of a thin, stilled voice—

All these are like great shofar blasts,
tearing the fabric of Your sphere's peace,
touching Your endlessness wherever You are.

Suddenly You, whom the utmost heavens cannot contain,
deign to dwell in each single searching heart.

May the words of my mouth and the meditations of my heart
find favor in Your eyes. Amen.

Rabbi Immanuel Lubliner

Ve-yay-asu Kulam Agudah Ehat ... The Need for Community

Back in the fifteenth century, in a tiny village near Nuremberg, lived a family with eighteen children. Eighteen! In order merely to keep food on the table for this mob, the father and head of the household, a goldsmith by profession, worked almost eighteen hours a day at his trade and any other paying chore he could find in the neighborhood.

Despite their seemingly hopeless condition, two of Albrecht Dürer the Elder's children had a dream. They both wanted to pursue their talent for art, but they knew full well that their father would never be financially able to send either of them to Nuremberg to study at the Academy.

After many long discussions at night in their crowded bed, the two boys finally worked out a pact. They would toss a coin. The loser would go down into the nearby mines and, with his earnings, support his brother while he attended the academy. Then, when that brother who won the toss completed his studies, in four years, he would support the other brother at the academy, either with sales of his artwork or, if necessary, also by laboring in the mines.

They tossed a coin on a Sunday morning after church. Albrecht Dürer won the toss and went off to Nuremberg.

Albert went down into the dangerous mines and, for the next four years, financed his brother, whose work at the academy was almost an immediate sensation. Albrecht's etchings, his woodcuts, and his oils were far better than those of most of his professors, and by the time he graduated, he was beginning to earn considerable fees for his commissioned works.

When the young artist returned to his village, the Dürer family held a festive dinner on their lawn to celebrate Albrecht's triumphant homecoming. After a long and memorable meal, punctuated with music and laughter, Albrecht rose from his honored position at the head of the table to drink a toast to his beloved brother for the years of sacrifice that had enabled Albrecht to fulfill his ambition. His closing words were, "And now, Albert, blessed brother of mine, now it is your turn. Now you can go to Nuremberg to pursue your dream, and I will take care of you."

All heads turned in eager expectation to the far end of the table where Albert sat, tears streaming down his pale face, shaking his lowered head from side to side while he sobbed and repeated, over and over, "No ... no ... no ... no."

Finally, Albert rose and wiped the tears from his cheeks. He glanced down the long table at the faces he loved, and then, holding his hands close to his right cheek, he said softly, "No, brother. I cannot go to Nuremberg. It is too late for me. Look ... look what four years in the mines have done to my hands! The bones in every finger have been smashed at least once, and lately I have been suffering from arthritis so badly in my right hand that I cannot even hold a glass to return your toast, much less make delicate lines on parchment or canvas with a pen or a brush. No, brother ... for me it is too late."

More than 450 years have passed. By now, Albrecht Dürer's hundreds of masterful portraits, pen and silver-point sketches, watercolors, charcoals, woodcuts, and copper engravings hang in every great museum in the world, but the odds are great that you, like most people, are familiar with only one of Albrecht Dürer's works. More than merely being familiar with it, you very well may have a reproduction hanging in your home or office.

One day, to pay homage to Albert for all that he had sacrificed, Albrecht Dürer painstakingly drew his brother's abused hands with palms together and thin fingers stretched skyward. He called his powerful drawing simply *Hands,* but the entire world almost immediately opened their hearts to his great masterpiece and renamed his tribute of love *The Praying Hands.*

The next time you see a copy of that touching creation, take a second look. Let it be your reminder, if you still need one, that no one—no one—ever makes it alone!

Remember to sincerely thank those who have helped you to get where you are!

Author Unknown

The Power of Groundless Hate

In the *Musaf* service on the days of awe we say, "Because of our sins were we exiled from our land."

In the Talmud (*Yoma* 9b) we read: Why was the first Sanctuary reduced to ruins? Because of three practices that were current then: idol-worship, conjugal immorality, and bloodshed…. In the time of the second Temple, however, they busied themselves with Torah study, mitzvot, and acts of kindness; then why was that destroyed? On account of the hatred for nothing, without cause, that prevailed then. So this teaches you that hatred without cause is equal in its effect to those three enormous kinds of sin: idol worship, conjugal immorality, and bloodshed….

We go ahead and implore the Almighty in our prayers and supplications, especially in the *Musaf* service on the holy days, to have the holy Temple rebuilt. We hope and yearn for it every day, to see it standing once more on its sacred site. Yet we do not consider or reflect on the máin deterrent, the main factor that keeps the Sanctuary from being rebuilt: If the dire sin of hatred without cause was powerful enough in its effect to bring the destruction of our Sanctuary, although the people spent time on Torah study, mitzvot and acts of kindness, how much more thoroughly certain it is that this vile sin is strong enough to prevent the rebuilding of the Temple in our own day!...

If we will not reflect and give thought to repair the spiritual damage we have done ... we shall be taken to task for the disgrace of the honor of Heaven that we have caused during our bitter exile.

The Hafetz Hayyim (Rabbi Yisrael Meir HaKohen Kagan)

Al Neesekha She-be-khol Yom Imanu

Toward the end of the *Musaf* service we say five words which are repeated three times daily towards the end of every *Amidah*: *Al neesekha she-be-khol yom imanu*—We thank you, God, for Your miracles which are with us every day!

The *Amidah* defines a miracle not as the splitting of the sea, or the sun standing still, but as the daily natural occurrences which we mostly take for granted. A miracle is the sun rising and setting; the oxygen we breathe nourishing our brains and our blood; the food which grows out of the ground which sustains us. Part of what religion does for us is to make us aware of the repetitive nature of the miracles in our world which surround us at every moment, at every turn.

Albert Einstein said it beautifully in these words: "There are only two ways to live your life. One is as though nothing is a miracle. The other is as though everything is a miracle."

D.P.E.

Rosh Hashanah on Shabbat: *Retzay Bimenuhatenu* ... Accept Our Rest

The Sabbath is more than an escape from the week of toil and entanglement; a refuge from his exertions; therapy for his weariness. It is the fulfillment toward which all his labor reaches out. The Sabbath brings detachment from the immediacies of life that man may achieve attachment to the great purposes of life. Neither the state nor business or success are the farthermost limits of man's loyalty or the loftiest goals of his striving. To serve God, which in human terms means the realization of his own most characteristic potentialities, is man's final and most authentic purpose. Any government, social system, or doctrine that intervenes and stays man from pursuing that goal is destructive and dehumanizing. The Sabbath upholds with a constancy and emphasis, equaled by no other institution, the right, indeed the obligation, of man to make the fulfillment of his humanity under God the greatest goal and ultimate purpose of his endeavors, to discover for himself the meaning of re-creation.

Sabbath dramatizes the fact that every human being is invested with a creative potential. There is something of the artist in each of us, even if we have never painted on canvas, sculpted, or joined words together in poetic harmony. Getting and spending we lay waste our creative powers. We often nip our most human capacities in the bud. We doom to sterility fruitful possibilities. Tenderness, love, vision, appreciation are stifled amid the hurry and tumult of our habitual lives.

Blessed is he who opens his life to it and frees himself of the encrustments of routine, the dictatorship of the contingent, the authority of the impulsive, and the enthronement of the trivial. Both man and Sabbath are the climax of creation. Man fully becomes man when he has the Sabbath in his life.

Rabbi Morris Adler

Sanctify Us through Your Mitzvot

In the early part of the *Musaf* service, after *Kedushah,* we recite in the *Uve-khen* paragraphs this phrase: *Kad-shenu be-Mitzvotekha*—Sanctify us, God, through your mitzvot, your commandments.

Rabbi Arthur Green, in *Seek My Face, Speak My Name,* reminds us that mitzvot bring us near to God in many ways.

Among Hasidic teachers, the Hebrew "mitzvah" is related to Aramaic *tsavta*—or "togetherness." The mitzvot bring us together with, or join us, to God. The mitzvot do this through raising our spiritual awareness and deepening our level of devotion to God. Some mitzvot sanctify the divine name because they are performed in concert with the entire community—*be-tzavta*. Jews have always placed a high premium on mitzvot carried out in public.

Still other mitzvot bring about God's presence in the world because "they enhance the lives of needy humans and lessen their suffering." Mitzvot make us better individuals, a better community, and bring about a better world. By doing so they enhance divinity through improving God's world.

D.P.E.

Think before You Speak

"God, open my lips that my mouth may declare your glory."

PSALM 51:17

I love teaching at late-morning brunches. The women who attend them take a couple of hours to pause for matters of the spirit. For one of these brunches on a Tuesday morning late into Chicago's winter, I had prepared a lesson on the meaning of the above verse in Psalm 51. I sat silently watching the women chatter and get into their cups of coffee. My eyes scanned the room looking for a direction, for a place to begin. The women here were loosely connected by temple affiliation, and most did not know each other. They were different ages and at different stages of life. I saw women who were curious about what I would say; I saw troubled women who came to find answers; I saw women who came in silence and would leave in silence. Just before beginning to teach, my attention turned to one of the women. Slight with hollow, deep-set eyes, she was one of the silent ones. Her face was tight, angry, sad. I began to teach:

"This is a little verse that is traditionally said before the major part of the prayer service: God, open up my lips that my mouth may declare your glory. What if every time we went to speak, we said that phrase first? If before I answered my spouse, I asked if what I am about to say reflects my spiritual aspirations? If before I went to share a story about another person's life, I asked whether it would reflect the holiness in the world? If before I engaged in idle conversation, I said, "God, when I speak, may it declare your glory?" If you paused before you spoke, would your conversation be different? Would it force you to elevate your thoughts towards glory?"

When I was done, a few women shared their comments. The more private ones shared their sighs.

Several months later, we had another brunch. The woman with the deep-set eyes spoke up before I had a chance to begin. "You know that verse you taught us, about thinking before you speak? Well, I tried it, and I never realized how many negative thoughts I had. When my words couldn't reflect God's glory, I kept silent. I was very quiet these last months."

Some in the group laughed, for they thought she was joking. But she was very serious. Having said what she needed to say, she fell silent. A few months after that morning, I heard that she left an abusive relationship.

May God guide her thoughts and words as she ventures towards living a life worthy of glory.

Rabbi Karyn D. Kedar

MALKHUYOT, ZIKHRONOT, SHOFAROT: GOD RULES, GOD REMEMBERS, GOD LISTENS

Tikkun 'olam, which means "mending the world," is an ancient Hebrew phrase that has taken on new life in the past few decades. Its verbal form is found in the 'alenu prayer, which concludes every service in the traditional synagogue. There le-takken 'olam means "to establish the world in the kingdom of the Almighty (shaddai)," or to bring about God's rule on earth. In contemporary usage it refers to the betterment of the world, including the relief of human suffering, the achievement of peace and mutual respect among peoples, and the protection of the planet itself from destruction.

RABBI ARTHUR GREEN, *THESE ARE THE WORDS*

Malkhuyot, Zikhronot, Shofarot

Much has been written about the sounds of the shofar. We may hear a call to battle when the shofar is sounded, or we may hear the plaintive wail of a Jew who stands in fear before her Creator. We may hear the joy of a Jew who has once again reached Rosh Hashanah, or the laughter of Jewish children as they prepare to enjoy their apples and honey.

But I would like us to focus on three distinct time frames, the past, the present and the future. I would like us to link the three sections of the *Musaf* service to these three time frames, and then I would like us to listen very carefully to hear what the shofar is telling us.

Malkhuyot: In this section of liturgy, we praise God who rules the world. As Jews, we acknowledge God's sovereignty. Listen to the voice of God speaking through the sounds of the shofar. What do you hear?

Zikhronot: In this section, we remind God of God's promise to preserve our people. We remember God's commitment and our own declaration at Sinai—*na'aseh v'nishma*—we will do and we will obey. What memories are evoked for you by the sound of the shofar? Do you remember Sinai? Do you remember the trumpets that sounded as God spoke? Listen.

Shofarot: This section focuses on the future, and God's promise of future redemption. But in truth, who will bring redemption? Rabbi Jules Harlow tells us: both God and people. We make the world worthy of redemption; God redeems the world and history. If we believe that we alone can bring redemption, we fall into the error of false messianism. If we believe that God alone will bring it, we fall into the error of despair and inaction. What actions are being required of you when you hear the blasts of the shofar? How is God describing a perfect world?

Rabbi Diane Cohen

Naming Our Relationship with God

What we call God has meaning. Sometimes, some of us for whom our relationship with God is complex wish it could be simple. We struggle to pray something meaningful with the image of God as all powerful king in mind. Our sense of unease is somewhere in our gut, something we can't define but which makes us look for more from God, something that cannot be found in a God who exists in nature or a God who is the good in the world. In this moment, on this day when the world was born, we need a personal relationship with God. And we don't know what it looks like.

But we have a guide. Our guide is the liturgy of the *musaf* service. The *musaf* has three parts, each of them rooted in an image of God found in the *Tanakh*. And it is by viewing them as parts of a whole that we get a different sense of a caring God with whom we can engage in prayer, who relates to us and whom we praise.

God protects. The first part is called *malkhuyot*, traditionally translated as kingship. The verses that we read proclaim God as ruler of the universe. We read the *Aleinu* prayer, declaring God's oneness. This image of God is not a monarch who is judge, but a ruler with whom we are in constant relationship, now and for eternity. By recognizing the presence of God in our world, God in return keeps that world safe. God alone protects. And in protecting us, we have the safe space to ask for forgiveness. We have the calm in our lives necessary to begin anew.

God remembers. In the *zikhronot,* the remembrance section of *musaf,* we acknowledge that nothing is forgotten by God. This remembrance is so that our good deeds are never forgotten. They get noticed. Moreover, God does not forget those who have been abandoned by other people. Some of the key verses in this section are taken from the story of the flood, when God remembers those who are left when the world has come undone, and from the story of the Israelites as slaves in Egypt, when God hears their cries. God remembers us even when we think that we are disgraced or abandoned. Knowing this means that we can trust that our prayers—or our struggle to find meaningful prayers—have not gone unnoticed. The fact that God is the source of remembrance is God's part of the covenant, God's obligation to hear our cries, to witness our moments of despair, and to take note when we do good.

Likewise, we have an obligation not to forget God. "Blessed is the one who forgets You not, who draws courage from You." As we acknowledge God's presence, we are reminded of the ways in which we can have the strength to create a better world. We can imitate God by remembering others for good and fulfill our destiny as human beings by recognizing God's *kedushah,* God's holiness in this world.

God hears. The final section is called *shofarot.* We blow the shofar in the month of Elul, in the weeks before Rosh Hashana and Yom

Kippur to wake ourselves up. We remember that it is time to repent, to heal the relationships with others that have broken, to take an accounting of our lives. The verses for *Shofarot* tell of awesome encounters with the divine: when the Torah was given at Sinai, the shofar sounded amidst the lightning and the thunder. The shofar announced the arrival of God in our midst, is the trumpet that proclaims God's arrival. But shofar is not just a call to us. "At Sinai, the blare of the shofar grew louder and louder. As Moses spoke, God answered him in thunder."

The shofar, then, is an invitation to God for conversation with us. God does not speak first at Sinai, but responds. The shofar calls out to God that we are ready to engage. And then, God listens. God is not revealed first through demands, but through listening to the words of humanity. On the High Holidays, we need to know that God is hearing us, not just words but emotions. Indeed, the *brakhah* for the *Shofarot* praises God who hears the sound of the shofar with compassion. We do not enthrone God as a distant king with the shofar. Rather, we open God up to the possibility of conversation, and allow God to listen to what is in our hearts.

Rachel Kahn-Troster

On That Day, God Will Be One and God's Name Will Be One

In the most influential book of Jewish mysticism, the thirteenth-century Zohar ... and in the sixteenth-century mysticism of Rabbi Isaac Luria, the notion of the dual faces of God was taken to radical extremes.

[The two sides of God:] *Ein-Sof* and *Shekhinah* are viewed as split apart, or, to use the actual language of the mystics, the *Shekhinah* is "in exile." This exile is not simply a historical fact but a profound symbol for the state of disharmony that exists throughout creation, even up to and including God Himself since creation is pervaded by God.

Not only Israel, but the world and even God Himself is in exile. This cosmic exile will end with the coming of the Messiah. At that point, Israel will return to its land, the *Ein-Sof* and the *Shekhinah* will be reunited, and the harmony that existed at the moment of Creation will be restored.

Rabbi Neil Gillman

Tikkun Olam

The concept of *tikkun olam* (literally, repairing the world) is connected
to the passage in the second section of the *Aleinu* prayer, *litaken olam
bimalkhut Shaddai*—to perfect the world through [the establishment
of) God's kingdom. God's kingdom is the messianic age when the
world is finally made whole. What will be the actual state of the world
when *tikkun olam* is attained? Life will triumph over all its enemies,
including death itself. "Death will be swallowed up in eternity, and
the Lord God will wipe away the tears from all faces" (Isaiah 25:8).
The earth will be filled with life ("it was not brought into being to be
void, it was created to be settled [filled with life]" Isaiah 45:8)—especially life in the image of God, that is, human beings. Then, God's
blessing to humanity, "be fertile and increase and fill the earth" (Genesis 1:27), will be fulfilled.

In the messianic era, poverty and hunger will be overcome. One
can project a permanent sabbatical year in which God truly owns the
earth and the exclusive privileges of private property are renounced. All
people will sit under their own vines and fig trees in contentment and
plenty, without fear (Micah 4:4). Wise and fair rulers will assure justice to everyone: the poor and the meek, as well as the rich and powerful. Violence will stop and peace will reign between nations: "They
shall beat their swords into ploughshares ... They shall not learn war
anymore" (Isaiah 2:4). People will pursue spiritual ideals and self-fulfillment. According to Maimonides, "They will have none to exploit or
distract them ... there will be no hunger nor war, no jealousy and rivalry
... so the population will be occupied only with the effort to know
God" *(Mishneh Torah, Hilkhot Melakhim* 12:4–5).

Tikkun olam can also be defined as the process by which the world
will be brought to this stage of final perfection. This understanding
draws on Lurianic Kabbalah which interprets the imperfect state of
the universe as the outcome of a cosmic catastrophe. Humans are commanded to participate in the process of *tikkun,* which restores the cos-
mic/divine wholeness to a shattered world. As Rabbi Joseph B.
Soloveitchik writes, "It is as if the Creator impaired reality so that mor-
tal man will repair its flaws and perfect" (*Halachic Man,* pp. 101, 105).
In Rabbi Soloveitchik's vision, both physical nature and spiritual-his-
torical existence suffer from chaos and destructive forces; their fates

are parallel also. In the messianic age, the ideal halachah will be actualized in the real world and the flaws in nature also will be overcome. This is the vision of the end of days, the fulfillment of all the hopes in the world of Judaism (*Halachic Man*, pp. 107, 99).

Rabbi Irving Greenberg

Le-taken Olam B'malkhut Shaddai

Daily we should take account and ask:
What have I done today to alleviate the anguish, to mitigate
the evil, to prevent humiliation?
Let there be a grain of prophet in every human being!
Our concern must be expressed not symbolically, but literally;
not only publicly, but also privately;
not only occasionally, but regularly.
What we need is the involvement of every one of us as
individuals.
What we need is restlessness,
a constant awareness of the monstrosity of injustice.

Rabbi Abraham Joshua Heschel

Mending the World

Tikkun olam, which means "mending the world," is an ancient Hebrew phrase that has taken on new life in the past few decades. Its verbal form is found in the *Alenu* prayer, which concludes every service in the traditional synagogue. There *le-takken 'olam* means "to establish the world in the kingdom of the Almighty *(shaddai),*" or to bring about God's rule on earth. In contemporary usage it refers to the betterment of the world, including the relief of human suffering, the achievement of peace and mutual respect among peoples, and the protection of the planet itself from destruction.

While associating these ideals with *tikkun olam* may be a recent innovation, the values themselves are deeply rooted in Jewish tradition. Spreading our most basic moral message—that every person is the divine image *(tselem Elohim)*—requires that Jews be concerned with the welfare, including the feeding, housing, and health, of all. The Torah's call that we "pursue Justice, only justice" (Deuteronomy

16:20) demands that we work toward closing the terrible gaps, especially in learning and opportunity, that exist within our society and undermine our moral right to the relative wealth and comfort most of us enjoy. The very placing of humans on earth "to work and guard" (Genesis 2:15) God's garden, as well as the Halakhah forbidding wanton destruction of resources, tell us that protecting the natural order is also a part of that justice.

Rabbi Arthur Green

Alenu: Is Judaism then Asserting Itself as the One "True" Religion?

Judaism asserts that there is one true God. There is also a Divine standard, but it is always mediated by human beings. That the people will inevitably get it wrong sometimes is told in the biblical narrative itself. All religions are interpretations of God's word. While they may be able to capture some of God's will and essence, they are flawed and incomplete. Indeed, it would be idolatrous to assert any human creation is the "one true religion." Judaism simply insists on faithfulness.

A parable: A man who has to believe that his wife is the most beautiful woman in the world has no wife, for he is constantly looking at other women to be sure that none may be more beautiful. He thereby surrenders responsibility for faith in his own marriage, for sacred relationship with his life partner. You can never know whose wife (or religion) is fairest of them all, anyway, since such knowledge requires the intimacy of a life lived together (or the journey of a religious life). The purpose of religion is not to learn what is good, but to learn to do what is good, not to disclose secrets but to achieve persons. This is the discipline of living in faithfulness.

Rabbi Zalman Schachter-Shalomi

God Is King

> All length, height, depth;
> Every light, rejuvenation, fertility process;
> Every impulse in poetry
> And every spark of reason;
> Lights which flame eternally

And lights which burn for a moment only;
All this sublime reality is in truth;
Nothing but refractions of God's being, sparks of Divinity
Genuine science teaches us the unity of the world,
Of body and soul, of imagination and reason,
Of the lowly and the exalted ...
Yet, this truth far transcends the limited findings
Of the scholarly disciplines which man has designed to
Illuminate and clarify the world.
We cannot make any absolute distinction
Between various levels of being;
Their differences are merely ones of degree.
The world unites and reconciles all contradictions;
All souls and all spirits,
All events and all things,
All desires, drives and enthusiasms:
Everything is part of a larger order and kingdom.
God is King.

Rabbi Avraham Isaac Kook

Alenu: Le-takken Olam: "To Bring Healing Perspective"

The well-known journalist, commentator and social critic, I. F. Stone, defined his task in *Who's Who in America,* in the following words, which capture beautifully the essence of what the *Alenu* prayer means by the phrase *le-takken olam be-malkhut Shaddai,* to repair the world in the Rule of the Almighty:

> To write the truth as I see it; to defend the weak against the strong; to fight for justice; and to seek, as best I can, to bring healing perspective to bear on the terrible hates and fears of mankind, in the hopes of some day bringing about one world, in which men will enjoy the differences of the human garden instead of killing each other over them.

The *Alenu* ends with the prayer that the world will be one, when God's name will be one. If we can carry out the vision of Mr. Stone, we will help to do our share in repairing our broken world.

D.P.E.

Aleinu: The Particular and the Universal

The two paragraphs of the *Aleinu* prayer complement each other. In the first paragraph we read of a God who did not make us like the other nations of the earth. In the first paragraph we are a special, unique and different people.

In the second paragraph, we are part of all of humanity, and look forward to the time when "all flesh shall prostrate themselves before You, O God," to repair our world, *le-taken olam be-malkhut Shadai.*

Sometimes our enemies and sometimes we ourselves are uncomfortable with the passages in our Heritage which set us apart, and make us less like the rest of God's children. The *Aleinu* expresses the wonderful idea that both messages are important, that we are indeed part of all humanity, and we are also a people with its own ideas, its own history, its own place under the sun.

Rudyard Kipling explained it very clearly when he wrote in his poem *Sussex:*

> God gave all men all earth to love
> but since our hearts are small
> Ordained for each one spot should prove
> beloved over all.

We are part of God's children everywhere, but we have our Tradition, our own language, and our own Land. These are our "one spot" that is uniquely and only ours.

D.P.E.

Mending the Soul, Mending the World

Each time we do something that raises consciousness, we lift sparks of holiness to new levels. This is called *tikkun ha-nefesh,* mending the soul, and *tikkun olam,* mending the world, bringing it closer to its source. Although initially the ideas of mending the soul and mending the world seem different, in reality they cannot be separated; we cannot raise sparks in ourselves without raising those in the world, and vice versa. Even more important, according to Kabbalah, the process of expanding awareness in ourselves and the world is the fundamental reason for our existence. In fact, when we make no effort to raise our own consciousness and that of the world, we abdicate our humanness.

Rabbi David A. Cooper

Alenu: Perfecting Society through Reduced Consumption

The second paragraph of the *Alenu* contains the famous phrase which is often quoted when we think about improving the world: *le-takken olam be-malkhut Shaddai,* "to perfect the world in the Reign of the Almighty."

One of the major problems we face as we enter the twenty-first century is over-consumption and materialism. We earn more and more income, spend more and more of our energy, time and human resources in continually raising our standard of living. Yet our tradition teaches that the more possessions we have, the more trouble and aggravation we have: *"Marbeh n'khasim, marbeh d'agah,"* i.e, the more possessions, the more worry.

While many of us would not consider ourselves to be extravagant consumers, the fact is that we in North America, on average, consume ten times as much of the earth's resources as people living in China, India and other developing countries. And yet, our material abundance has not brought us the true spiritual fulfillment of which the *Alenu* prayer speaks: the perfection of society under God's sovereignty.

A modern social thinker has put this cogent idea into these well-written words (Michael Argyle, *The Psychology of Happiness*):

> The upper classes in any society are more satisfied with their lives than the lower classes are, but they are no more satisfied than the upper classes of much poorer societies nor than the upper classes were in the less affluent past. Consumption is thus a treadmill, with everyone judging their status by who is ahead and who is behind.

The ideal of *tikkun olam,* perfection of society, begins with considering a serious change, during these Ten Days of Repentance, in our standards of conspicuous consumption.

D.P.E.

Passing before God

According to the custom of the world, when two charioteers race in the hippodrome, which one of them receives a wreath? The victor. Thus on Rosh Hashanah all the people of the world come forward like contestants on parade and pass before God, and the children of Israel are among all the people of the world and also pass before God. Then the guardian angels of the nations of the world declare: "We were victorious, and in the judgment we will be found righteous." But actually no one knows who was victorious, whether it was the children of Israel or the nations of the world. After New Year's Day is gone, all the children of Israel come forth on Yom Kippur and fast on that day, clothed in white and humble garments. But even after the Day of Atonement is gone, still no one knows who was victorious, the children of Israel, or the nations of the world. When the first day of Sukkot comes, however, all the children of Israel, grownups and children, take up their festive wreaths *(lulavs)* in their right hands and their citrons *(etrogs)* in their left, and then all people of the world know that in the judgment the children of Israel were proclaimed victorious.

Midrash on Psalms 17:5

Zikhronot Meditation

> You remember the fathomless depths of space, the formless
>   beginnings of creation.
> Nothing is hidden from You. Remind us that we are Yours.
> You remember Your covenant with our people. Instruct us in
>   its wisdom that we may remove all shallowness from our
>   lives and fulfill Your sacred purposes.
> Nothing is hidden from You. Remind us that we are Yours.
> You remember the fate of nations, the anguish of our people
>   tormented and tortured by cruelty, their bravery in defying
>   dark despair with bright visions of justice, mercy and peace.
> Nothing is hidden from You. Remind us that we are Yours.
> You remember each of us. Our acts, our schemes, our
>   thoughts and desires, our failure and merits come before
>   You this day,
> Nothing is hidden from You. Every noble act is a sign of Your
>   goodness. Remind us that we are Yours.

Be praised, O God, who remembers the covenant made with
our people. Let the sounds of the Shofar remind us that we
are Yours.

From the Wilshire Boulevard Temple
High Holy Day prayer book

Zikhronot: Memory Transfigures

The famous British author C. S. Lewis made a fascinating comment
on the power of memory *(Letters to Malcolm: Chiefly on Prayer)*:

The dullest of us knows how memory can transfigure; how often
some momentary glimpse of beauty in boyhood is a whisper which
memory will warehouse as a shout.... Don't talk to me of the
"illusions" of memory. Why should what we see at the moment be
more "real" than what we see from ten years' distance?

The memories of the youth of the Jewish People, in the biblical period,
have had such a powerful impact on our historical memory and on our
entire destiny, they can in no way be considered "illusions," but rather
"reality." It is the "reality" of our historical memory which is the theme
of the *Zikhronot* prayers, as well as the memory of God who remembers
our individual and corporate deeds.

D.P.E.

How to Remember Yourself

Our Rabbis taught: "A person should always regard him- or herself as
though he or she were half guilty and half meritorious. If he or she performs one good deed, one is happy for adding weight to the scale of
merit. If he or she commits one transgression, woe to the one for being
weighed down in the scale of guilt, for it is said, 'but one sinner
destroys much good' (Ecclesiastes 9:8); on account of a single sin
which a person commits much good is lost to him or her."

R. Eleazar son of R. Simeon said: "Because the world is judged by
its majority, and an individual too is judged by his or her majority of
deeds, good or bad, if he or she performs one good deed, there is much
happiness for turning the scale both for the person and for the whole
world on the side of merit. If the person commits one transgression,

woe to him or her for weighting that individual and the world on the scale of guilt, for it is said, 'but one sinner ... ' On account of the single sin which this person commits he or she and the whole world lose much good."

R. Simeon b. Yohai said: "Even if he or she is perfectly righteous their entire lifetime but rebels at the end, he or she destroys former good deeds, for it is said, 'The righteousness of the righteous shall not deliver him or her in the day of his transgression (Ezekiel 33–12).' And even if one is completely wicked all his or her life but repents at the end, that person is not reproached with his or her wickedness, for it is said, "And as for the wickedness of the wicked, he or she shall not fall thereby in the day that he turns from wickedness (ibid.)."

Kiddushin 40a–b

Why *Zikhronot*?

Why is *Zikhronot* such a key part of the Rosh HaShanah *Musaf*, the key part of the liturgy of the most important of holy days during the year, the *Yamim Norai'im*?

The Baal Shem Tov, founder of Hasidism, who lived from 1700 to 1766 in Ukraine, makes a remarkable and profound statement about remembering that captures the essence of Judaism's emphasis on memory, so much so that his words are inscribed on the entrance to Israel's House of Memorial to the victims of the Holocaust, Yad Vashem:

Redemption lies in remembering.

We remember the good and the bad of what happened before us, so that we can make tomorrow better than today and yesterday.

As we remember, so we begin the slow process of redemption.

D.P.E.

Memory: A Point of Entry to Our Past

The saving grace is that Jews are more attached to memory than to history. In crudest definitional terms, history is our selective record and, necessarily, our interpretation of the past. Memory is even less fixed and more subjective; it is the way we know and recall the past.

If history were our primary guide, then patriarchy might be considered sacrosanct precedent. According to biblical and Rabbinic theology, however, history is only a series of twists and turns controlled by God, leading to lessons along the way, and eventually, to the time of messiah. If Israel is enslaved in Egypt, then the finger of God is at work, and if Israel is freed, the same holds. The details are purely instrumental and of no ultimate importance.

Memory is considered far more significant and sacred. An ever-lasting, renewable resource, it helps us locate ourselves—one of the central purposes of religion—because it relates the present and future with the past. According to traditional understanding, memory provides us access not just to history, but to direct experience. Through memory, the past—recalled in texts and re-enacted in rituals—can be made eternally present. Memory both transcends time and endows it with meaning. Thus, God renews creation each day; Jews of every generation experience the exodus from Egypt; we all receive the Torah at Sinai. Such timeless master-stories—i.e., creation, exodus, and revelation—are sometimes called "Jewish collective memory."

Memory, like midrash (Rabbinic genre of lore often based on biblical texts), is a medium through which we dialogue with the past. The conversation never ends and is never—or perhaps continually—canonized. Generations of experience and interpretation form the holy tradition. Thus, it is never too late for women, or anyone, to join in the conversation.

Rabbi Debra Orenstein

Zikhronot: Remembering Our Noble Heritage

Rabbi Chaim of Zanz was fond of telling the following story:

A prince sinned against his father, the King, and accordingly was banished from the royal palace. As long as he stayed within the villages that bordered on the palace, people recognized him and invited him to their homes for food and drink. But during the course of time, he wandered to the outlying districts of his father's kingdom where people didn't know him. He had nothing to eat, so one by one he sold his handsome garments to purchase food. When he ran out of things to sell, he hired himself out as a shepherd. Like the other shepherds, he sat on the hills grazing his sheep and singing all day. He soon forgot that once he had been a prince with all of the power, privilege and responsibility that being a member of the royal family entails.

Once, he noticed that the other shepherds were building simple straw shelters for protection against the rain. He wanted one too, but didn't have the means to purchase the materials.

Then one day, the king passed through the province. It was an established custom that whenever the king would visit one of his outlying territories, anyone who had a request could write it on a slip of paper and cast it into the royal coach. The prince pressed through the crowds that had gathered and tossed his written request for the straw and other materials into the coach. When the king saw the note, he immediately recognized the handwriting. He became heartsick at the thought that his son had totally forgotten his noble heritage and had no greater aspiration than acquiring a lowly straw shelter.

So, too, claimed the Zanzer Rebbe, is the situation in the real world. Being God's children, all of us are princes. Yet we've forgotten our natural bond to Him. Rather than seeking to return to the palace, we've kept our sights far too low. We commonly ask God for a bit more financial success, less *tsoris,* or a little happiness. While all such requests are fair and appropriate, we should really be even more intent upon asking for the strength and inspiration to become ever more holy.

How beautifully this theme is expressed in our daily prayers: "Restore us, our Father, to thy Torah; draw us near, our Sovereign, to thy service; cause us to return to thee in perfect repentance. Blessed art thou, Lord, who art pleased with return."

Rav Shlomo of Karlin once said that the greatest sin is forgetting that you're a prince. Let us not forget our royal heritage....

Rabbi Bruce Ginsburg

Remembering and Transmitting

Several years ago I was shopping at a local grocery store and when my purchases were tallied, I was surprised and embarrassed to discover that I was ten cents short. I quickly surveyed what I had bought to determine what I could leave behind to buy another day. As I was about to make this decision, the woman behind me suddenly offered me ten cents to cover the shortfall. Now I was also humiliated!

I quickly explained that I couldn't accept her money and that I had no problem leaving something behind. "Oh," she exclaimed, "I'm not giving it to you. Just take it and pass it on." That sounded reasonable, so I accepted the ten cents and left the store with all my purchases, inspired by the whole idea.

Exactly two weeks later, I was in the same store and this time I was second in line when the woman in front of me realized that she was ten cents short. The replay of the episode from my previous visit to the grocery store was uncanny. I offered her the ten cents, which she graciously refused. I explained that I was not giving it to her but that she should take it and pass it on and only then did she agree to accept the money.

I've often wondered how many times that ten cents has traveled the world! The entire experience confirmed for me that even a small gesture of help could have broad consequences. It reinforced the recognition that countless people have assisted me, often in ways unknown to me, and I have an obligation to pass on whatever I can to help others.

Irene Goldfarb

God Remembers Both Mercy and Judgment

How did the Holy One, blessed be God, come to establish the measure of mercy to go with the measure of justice?

R. Haninah said: When the Holy One, blessed be God, wishing to create God's world, observed the doings of the wicked (such as the generation of Enosh, the generation of the flood, the generation of the Tower of Babel and the dispersion of the races of people, the doings of the people of Sodom) God no longer wished to create the world. But then the Holy One, blessed be God, returned and observed the doings of the righteous: the doings of Abraham, Isaac, and Jacob, of Sara, Rebecca, Rachel, and Leah, and of all the other righteous. As God returned and observed them, God said: Should I not create the world because of the wicked? Indeed, I shall create the world and as for the one who sins, it will not be difficult to rebuke him or her.

Nevertheless, when God was about to create the world with the measure of justice alone, God could not bring God's self to do so because of the deeds of the righteous, for whom justice alone would be too severe a measure to have in the world. And when God was about to create it with the measure of mercy alone, God could not bring God's self to do so because of the deeds of the wicked, for whom mercy alone would be too indulgent a measure to only have that in the world.

What did God do? God made partners of the two measures, the measure of justice and the measure of mercy, and created the world, as is said "In the day that the Lord [of mercy and the] God [of justice] made heaven and earth (Genesis 2:4)....

Therefore David said: Master of universes, had You not judged Adam with mercy at the time he ate of the tree, he would not have remained alive for even one hour. And even as You did judge him with mercy, so did You ordain, beginning with him, that this day, New Year's Day, You would judge his children with mercy. "For ever, O God, Your word stands fast" (Psalms 119:89). What is implied by standing fast? Your word that You ordained for Adam still stands: even as You did judge him with mercy, so You judge for ever all the generations after him. As it is said "For ever, O God."

Pesikta Rabbati 40:24

Choosing to Remember

There is an ancient Greek myth of the woman who wanders into the waters of the River Styx where Charon, the guide, was to take her to the region of the departed spirits. Charon reminded her that she could drink of the waters of Lethe and thereby forget all the anguish she had experienced in life.

She said, "I will forget how I have suffered." Charon replied, "You will forget how you rejoiced." The woman challenged, "I shall forget my failures." Charon reminded her, "And also your victories." Again she said, "I shall forget all of the painful memories of life." Charon countered, "You will also forget all the loving and joyful memories of life."

In silence the woman meditated, and ultimately elected not to drink the waters of Lethe. She chose to retain her memories of sadness, of loss and tribulation, rather than surrender the loving memories of her life as well.

Rabbi Steven Carr Reuben

The Dream of Isaac

For Tom and Laya Seghi

It is said that as he grew older, Isaac put the journey to Mount Moriah out of his mind. Even to Rebecca, his wife, he would not speak of what had happened. So circumspect did he become, that by the time of his marriage at the age of forty no one could remember the last time he had spoken on the subject. So it seems likely that during the period in which his wife was expecting a child the old memory came to his mind even less often, for Rebecca had grown ripe with her waiting, which was already much longer than the old wives had estimated.

One such night, while he and Rebecca were sleeping side by side, Isaac dreamed for the first time of the sacrifice that had taken place almost thirty years before. But this dream was even more real than the actual incident, for then his confusion had saved him from his fear, and now all the terror he had not noticed was with him, as a faceless man chained him to a great rock and held a knife against his neck. He felt the blade poised to press down when the sun emerged from behind a cloud and blinded them both, and at the same time they heard the frantic honking of a goose whose gray and white feathers had become entangled in the thorns of a nearby bush. It was then that the fierce and silent man, whom Isaac now saw was his father, put down the blade and pulled the bird free from the thorns and berries, and as he brought it back, Isaac saw how it struggled in his hands. Then, when the goose was pressed firmly to the rock, Isaac watched as his father pulled back the white throat and drew the blade. He saw especially how white was the neck and how cleanly the blade cut through. At last Abraham put down the blade and unbound his son and they embraced. It was then that Isaac opened his eyes, felt the arms of his wife as she tried to wake him, and heard her whispering that the child was about to be born.

When Isaac understood he sat up in bed and hurried from the room to wake the midwife, who had been living with them for almost three weeks. Two hours later Rebecca gave birth, first to one son and then to another, the first who was hairy, his skin red, and the second who came forth with his hand on his brother's heel. Isaac found himself fascinated as he watched the midwife wash the infants in warm water. The first son, whom they came to call Esau, was born with an umbilical cord that was dark purple, the color of blood. But his second son, Jacob, had a cord that was soft and white as pure wax. It was this perfectly woven rope that Isaac found most intriguing, for reasons he could not comprehend. And he sensed a strange terror as he unsheathed a knife and drew the blade to sever this last link between what was and what will be. For it was then the dream of that night came back to him, and he saw in the same instant how the hands of his father had held down the goose, and how the sharp blade had cut across its neck, soft and white, like the severed cord he held in his own hands.

Howard Schwartz

Blessed Are Those Who Hear in the Shofar a Call to Walk by the Light of Your Presence

There are many ways to walk in God's presence. The Talmud tells us that the way we choose for our generation is as valid as the way chosen by the previous generation.

Many centuries ago, two great schools disputed with each other as to whether the Halakhah is according to one or the other. This dispute is reported in *Masechet Eruvin*.

Rabbi Aba said in the name of Shmuel: Beit Shammai and Beit Hillel were in dispute for three years, these saying the Halakhah is according to our opinion and these saying the halakhah is according to our opinion.

A heavenly voice, a *bat kol*, came out and said these and these are the words of the living God, and the Halakhah is according to Bet Hillel.

And indeed since these and these are the words of the living God, why did Beit Hillel merit the Halakhah according to their opinion? Because they were kindly and modest, and they taught both their opinion and the opinions of Bet Shammai, and not only that but they mentioned the opinions of the House of Shammai before their own opinions.

This story from the Talmud clearly illustrates for us that while we generally observe the Halakhah according to Bet Hillel, it is imperative that we understand the opposing view of Bet Shammai as well. This is an example of true plurality. We must stand for who and what we are. At the same time, we must allow those who have a differing view to express it so that we may understand how they have arrived at their opposing viewpoint because there may be more than meets the eye.

Rabbi Yom Tov ibn Ashvilli was a fourteenth-century halakhist from Spain. He comments on *Eruvin* 13b, "These and these are both the words of the living God." The rabbis of France asked: How can it be that both opinions be the word of the living God, since one says that a certain thing is prohibited and the other that it is permitted?

They answered that when Moshe went up to the heavens to receive the Torah he was shown forty-nine ways of prohibiting and forty-nine ways of permitting each thing. When he asked God about this, he was told that this is to be entrusted to the sages of Israel in every generation and the decision will be in their hands.... Each generation must, based upon previous generations, make its own decisions as to what will be allowed and what will be prohibited. As members of this generation we should and must preserve our ability and opportunity to define our own true path to God. This, perhaps, is the meaning of the verse, *B'or panekha y'halaykhun*, in the light of our understanding of God's will must we go.

Rabbi Aaron Gaber

The Sound of the Shofar

R. Abbahu said: "Why do we blow on a ram's horn? For God said: 'Sound before Me a shofar so that I may remember on your behalf the binding of Isaac, the son of Abraham, and Sarah, and credit it to you as if you had bound yourselves before Me.'"

R. Isaac said: "Why do we sound the shofar on Rosh Hashanah? You ask, why do we sound? The All-Merciful has told us to sound!"

Talmud, Rosh Hashanah 16a

Shofar as a Symbol of Transformation

One of the reasons we blow the Shofar is to frighten and confound the evil inclination.

Is it not ironic that in order to accomplish this task, we in turn resort to taking the weapon of an aggressive animal? Indeed, we grasp a weapon used primarily for goring other creatures and transform it into a vehicle that can now serve in the task of elevating ourselves to new and higher levels of holiness.

Rabbi Aryeh Kaplan

Awake You Slumberers from Your Sleep: Shofar and Social Responsibility

Activism pays the rent of being alive and being here on the planet....
If I weren't active politically, I would feel as if I were sitting back eating
at the banquet without washing the dishes or preparing the food. It
wouldn't feel right.

—Alice Walker

How wonderful it is that no one need wait a single moment to start
to improve the world.

—Anne Frank

What begins as the inequality of some, inevitably ends as the inequality of all.

—Rabbi Abraham Joshua Heschel

It has been said that you judge a society by the way it treats the weakest in the dawn of life as children, a nation by the way it deals with the
eldest and the weakest, and you judge America by how it concerns itself
with the homeless, hungry and disabled.

—Rabbi Seymour Cohen

The question is not, "If I stop to help this man in need, what will happen to me?" "If I do not stop to help the sanitation workers what will
happen to them?" That's the question.

—Martin Luther King, Jr.

When will there be justice in the world? When the people who are not
wronged feel just as indignant as those who are.

—Plato

In the beginning I thought I could change man. Today I know I cannot. If I still shout today, if I still scream, it is to prevent man from ultimately changing me.

—Elie Wiesel

If we are able to be involved, but remain indifferent, we are responsible for the consequences.

—Midrash

As life is action and passion, it is required of a man that he should share the passion and action of his time at peril of being judged not to have lived.

—Oliver Wendell Holmes

If you are neutral in a situation of injustice, you have chosen the side of the oppressor. If an elephant has his foot on the tail of a mouse, and you say you are neutral, the mouse will not appreciate your neutrality.

—Bishop Desmond Tutu

Is this not what I require of you as a fast: to loose the fetters of injustice, to untie the cords of lawlessness, to snap every yoke and set free those who have been crushed.

—Isaiah 58:6

Humanity's sole salvation lies in everyone making everything his business.

—Aleksandr Solzhenitsyn

Any religion that professes to be concerned with the souls of people and is not concerned with the slums that damn them and the social conditions that cripple them, is a dry-as-dust religion.

—Martin Luther King, Jr.

I cannot imagine better worship of God than that in His name I should labor for the poor.

—Mahatma Gandhi

It is only in assuming full responsibility for our world, for our lives and for ourselves, that we can be said to live really for God.

—Thomas Merton

If you see what needs to be repaired and how to repair it, then you have found a piece of the world that God has left for you to complete. But if you only see what is wrong and how ugly it is, then it is yourself that needs repair.

—Rabbi Tzvi Freeman

Come, my friends, it is not too late, to seek a better world.

—Alfred Lord Tennyson

And do not think that you have to make big waves in order to contribute. My role model, Sojourner Truth, slave woman, could neither read nor write but could not stand slavery and second-class treatment of women. One day during an anti-slavery speech she was heckled by an old man. "Old woman, do you think that your talk about slavery does any good? Why I don't care any more for your talk than I do for the bite of a flea." "Perhaps not, but the Lord willing, I'll keep you scratching," she replied.

—Marian Wright Edelman

I would unite with anybody to do right and with nobody to do wrong.

—Frederick Douglass

D.P.E.

The Shofar Calls—Something Is Asked of Me

Over and above personal problems, there is an objective challenge to overcome inequity, injustice, helplessness, suffering, carelessness, oppression. Over and above the din of desires there is a calling, a demanding, a waiting, an expectation. There is a question that follows me wherever I turn. What is expected of me? What is demanded of me?

What we encounter is not only flowers and stars, mountains and walls. Over and above all things is a sublime expectation, a waiting for. With every child born a new expectation enters the world.

This is the most important experience in the life of every human being: something is asked of me. Every human being has had a moment in which he senses a mysterious waiting for him. Meaning is found in responding to the demand, meaning is found in sensing the demand.

Rabbi Abraham Joshua Heschel

Shofar

Bend! Dare to bend. The curvature of the Shofar is *kafuf* (bent); it is bent to teach us to bend our stubbornness and our pride. The sound of the Shofar includes *shevarim*, the sobbing staccato of broken notes to remind you that *teshuvah*, repentance, the road to reconciliation, is a process, a series of steps. The sound of the Shofar is broken, for in God's eyes nothing is more whole than a broken heart.

Rabbi Menahem Mendel of Kotzk

Sounding the Shofar

The shofar, like all symbols, has many meanings. In the first place, it reminds us of Abraham's extraordinary loyalty to God and his willingness to sacrifice for his beliefs.

No beliefs are really important to us unless we are willing to make some sacrifice for them. To be sure, the episode of Abraham, in the Torah lesson of the second day of Rosh Hashanah, clearly teaches us, very pointedly, that God goes not want child sacrifice—a practice that was very common in heathen religions. However, though God does not want human sacrifice, we must be ready to sacrifice for that which makes us human.

The shofar has another meaning, too. In ancient days, when a ruler was crowned, the ceremony of coronation would include the blowing of the shofar. On Rosh Hashanah we proclaim the sovereignty of God. We reaffirm our will to serve God and to obey God's laws. In a sense, Rosh Hashanah is the day of God's coronation. Thus, we hear the blast of the shofar.

The shofar has also been interpreted as a signal of alarm or warning. Too frequently we forget our duties and our responsibilities. We become selfish or cruel. We neglect important tasks, and concentrate on goals which are unworthy of us. The sounds of the shofar are meant to shake us up or wake us up, to sound an alert, to remind us how we ought to live in the year that lies ahead.

As we listen to the sounds of the shofar, may its meanings enter into our hearts and shape our actions in the days ahead.

Rabbi Dov Peretz Elkins

Shofar on Shabbat

In ancient times, the sound of the shofar was an everyday experience. Every morning at the Temple in Jerusalem, twenty-one blasts were heard. As the gates opened, three notes rang out, calling the people to worship. Nine blasts accompanied the morning and evening sacrificial offerings. Six notes announced the arrival of Shabbat on Friday afternoon. The sound of the shofar accompanied the people into battle, inaugurated the Jubilee year, proclaimed the new month, and aroused the people to repentance on fast days.

We, on the other hand, wait all year to hear the shofar, and, to many, it is terribly disappointing when Rosh HaShanah coincides with Shabbat and the shofar service is curtailed. According to Rabbi Isaac Klein, writing in the Conservative movement's contemporary *Shulkhan Arukh: A Guide to Jewish Religious Practice,* it is not that the blowing of the shofar is specifically prohibited. Rather, the concern is that it might lead to a violation of Shabbat. For example, someone who wanted to learn how to sound the shofar might inadvertently carry it, and carrying is prohibited on the Sabbath.

The Talmud finds support for this ruling in the fact that the Bible refers to Rosh HaShana both as *Yom Teruah,* the day of the shofar blast, as well as *Zikhron Teruah,* the day of remembering the shofar blast. According to rabbinical interpretation, when the shofar is sounded it is *Yom Teruah,* and when the shofar is not sounded on Shabbat, it is *Yom Zikhron Teruah.*

But, if we cannot hear the actual shofar blasts today, we can hear the message of the shofar, meditating on its meaning in anticipation of tomorrow's shofar service.

Rabbi Isaiah Horowitz, writing in the seventeenth century, comments on the three notes. Each series of blasts begins and ends with *tekiah*—a whole note. In between come *shevarim* and *teruah,* broken notes. So it is, he concludes, with us in our own lives. We begin whole. Along the path of life we become broken, through pain, mistakes, loss, failure, illness and weakness. The end is whole. The lesson, he encourages us to believe, is that there is hope for each of us as we begin the new year, that we can find shalom, peace, a sense of well-being, security and completion in the coming year.

Commentators also call to our attention the fact that the ram's horn cannot be used in its natural state. A great deal of preparation goes into making a ram's horn into a shofar. So it is with repentance. We cannot just show up in shul on the High Holidays and immediately switch in to "penitential mode." Like the ram's horn, *teshuvah* is neither our natural state of being, nor is it easily acquired....

To serve as the *baal t'kiah,* the one who blows the shofar, is among the highest honors the community can bestow. It takes more than the ability to elicit the appropriate notes from the instrument. Many people have the ability to mechanically blow the shofar. That is not enough. The congregation seeks a candidate, however, whose *kavvanah* will blast open the gates of heaven. So, the story is told of the great master, Rabbi Levi Yitzhak of Berditchev, who was besieged by all manner of shofar blowers, each anxious to sound the shofar in the synagogue of the great Rav.

Rabbi Levi Yitzhak tested each applicant with this question, "What goes on in your mind at the very moment of the blast?" They all tried to outdo each other with their mastery of the intricate Kabbalistic interpretations of the shofar. But not one of them satisfied Rabbi Levi Yitzhak.

One day a shofar blower he did not know approached him and said, "My lord, I am one of the common people. I have four daughters, all of whom have reached the age of marriage. At the moment when I sound the shofar there is only one thought in my mind, *'Ribbono shel Olam,* I have bent my will to Yours and fulfilled all Your mitzvot. You, too, then, bend Your will to mine and help me find husbands for my daughters."

Rabbi Levi Yitzhak's heart filled with great joy, and he said, "Your *kavvanah* was a true *kavvanah.* You will blow the shofar in my *Bet Midrash.*"

Rabbi Bonnie Koppell

We Are Like the Shofar

I recently visited the first- and second-grade classes at the local Day School to sound shofar. I brought in a pair of *shofarot* for comparison. As we compared the different horns, these young students were thrilled to have the opportunity to answer my questions that related to the tactile nature of the shofar: hard or soft? hollow or solid? smooth or rough? They "noted" that in regards to the last question, the shofar is both. It is smooth and finished on the outside, but rough and unfinished on the inside. This does not prevent the shofar's voice from carrying our prayers to Heaven. The thought I share with you this morning is that we too are like the shofar. Despite how smooth and polished we might appear externally, all of us have our rough and unfinished insides. One lesson that the shofar comes to teach us is despite our rough and unfinished insides, we too can lift our voices and have our prayers find their way to God.

Rabbi David Greenspoon

Shofar and Judgment

On what day does the Holy One, blessed be God judge the creatures of the world and acquit them? It is on New Year's Day that God judges the world's inhabitants and acquits them. For, God definitely desires to acquit God's creatures, not to hold them guilty, as is said "As I live, says Adonai, I have no pleasure in the death of the wicked (Ezekiel 33:11)," and again "That which God desires is to make people righteous (Isaiah 42:21)," that is, God desires to declare God's creatures righteous. And why does God wish to declare God's creatures righteous? Because, according to R. Judah bar Nahman, "in the name of *Resh Lakish,* the Holy One, blessed be God, reasons as follows: When I win I lose, and when I lose I win. I won out over the generation of the flood and I lost, for I had to destroy all the members of that generation, as is said And God blotted out every living thing (Genesis 7:23). And so it was with the generation of the Tower of Babel and the dispersion of the races of people, and so with the people of Sodom. But at the making of the golden calf, Moses won over Me by asking in entreaty, God why are you so angry? (Exodus 32:11), and I then won for Myself all the generations of the children of Israel. Therefore, I acquit all My creatures in order not to lose them. It is on New Year's Day that I acquit My creatures. Thus when I judge them, let them be sure to lift up shofars and blow them before Me, and I will bring as evidence on their behalf the binding of Isaac and will acquit them at the judgment."

From where do we know that the blowing of the shofar is a reminder to God? From what is read in the Torah reading for the day: "In the seventh month, in the first day of the month ... a time of remembrance proclaimed with the blast of horns" (Leviticus 23:24).

Midrash, *Pesikta Rabbati* **40:1**

TODAY THE WORLD WAS CREATED

A havah refers also to the special and mutual love between God and the soul of each human being. We are created in the *tselem elohim* ("Image of God") as soulful beings, each of us bearing the capacity to know God from within by knowing our own soul or *neshamah*. The soul longs to reflect the fullness of divine radiance, to cause God's light to shine forth to the world around it. This is its response in love to the divine love that gives it life.

The special love of God for the Jewish people, the descendants of Abraham, stands within the context of our *berit* or covenant with God. As we committed ourselves at Sinai to serve as a priestly people, channeling God's love to all who seek it, Israel saw itself as especially beloved by God. That love is, on the one hand, unconditional (for God so loved Abraham that his descendants are beloved forever!) and, on the other hand, entirely conditional, dependent upon the job we do as bearers of God's love-message to the world.

RABBI ARTHUR GREEN, *THESE ARE THE WORDS*

Hayom Harat Olam: Why Not You?

On this Rosh Hashanah, this second chance for change, this birthday of a new year and a new you, I ask, "Why not you?" Why not you, watching the morning mist rise over the mountains of Scotland? Why not you catching a play on the London stage, standing on top of the Eiffel Tower and gazing directly at the *Mona Lisa* in Paris? Why not you, walking the Great Wall in China, riding the Bullet Train in Japan, visiting the outback of Australia to catch a glimpse of a kangaroo? Why not you, sailing the lands of Venice on a gondola with someone you love, catching a sunrise from the top of Masada and gazing down to the austere beauty of the Dead Sea?

And why not you, embracing the Jewish idea of *Tikkun Olam,* taking part in the life task of making whole the broken fragments of the world? Why not you, inventing a new product, creating a new idea, changing someone's life or inspiring another through your own inspiration? Why not you, being happy, joyful, filling your life with loving, giving, sharing, caring, touching, laughter and tenderness? Why not you, wealthy, successful, satisfied, productive, creative, enthusiastic, courageous, energetic, purposeful?

Rabbi Steven Carr Reuben

Recipe for the New Year

Take twelve fine, full grown months, see that they are thoroughly free from all old memories of bitterness, hate and jealousy, cleanse them completely from every clinging spite; pick off all specks of pettiness and littleness; in short see that the months are freed from the past—have them as fresh and clean as when they first came from the storehouse of time.

Cut these months into 30 or 31 equal parts. This batch will keep for just one year. Do not attempt to make the whole batch at one time—so many people spoil their entire lot in this way—but prepare one day at a time as follows:

Into each day put 12 parts of faith, 11 parts of patience, 10 parts of courage, 9 parts of work (some people omit this and so spoil the flavor of the rest), 8 parts of hope, 7 parts of fidelity, 6 parts of liberality, 5 parts of kindness, 4 parts of rest (leaving this out is like leaving the oil

out of a salad), 3 parts prayer, 2 parts meditation and one well selected
resolution.

To the above, add a teaspoon of good spirits, a dash of fun, a pinch
of folly, a sprinkling of play, and a heaped cupful of good humor. Pour
in love and mix together.

Cook thoroughly in a fervent heat; garnish with a few smiles and a
sprig of joy; then serve with quietness, unselfishness and cheerfulness
and a happy new year is a certainty.

Author Unknown

God of Creation

Lord, God of color!
God of yellow dawns and orange dusks,
Of plush green fields and cracked brown river beds,
Of blue skies and gray clouds.
God of rich, black earth and the white snow that covers it,
Of golden sunshine and clear, lucid raindrops.

Lord, God of Shapes!
God of pentagons and hexagons and squares,
Of elliptical orbits and triangular cones,
Of perfect circles and imperfect spheres.
God of trapezoids and rectangles and straight lines and curves.

Lord, God of sizes!
God of giant sequoias and tiny bacteria,
Of bottomless caverns and lofty mountain peaks,
Of mustard seeds and acorns and spores.
God of heights and depth and breadth.

Lord, God of creation!
God of everything that inhabits the earth,
And the earth itself!
Thank You for all Your creation with its endless variety,
And for our senses with which we perceive the myriad of
    Your creation.

Rabbi Roy A. Walter

Knowing Creation

There is a widespread idea in the Jewish community that human beings are partners with God in the completion of Creation. This rabbinic concept has become a major metaphor in Jewish social action theology. But in today's world of technology and science, is it important for Jews to believe in the concept of Creation? Do we really believe in a God who created and sustains the universe? Since Rosh HaShanah is called the "birthday of the world," this is a good time to examine what we think about Creation. We tend to leave the question of the origin of the universe to the scientists, and even then few of us take the time or the mental energy to get to know what it is they are saying. Only fundamentalists seem to be concerned with Creation. When they seek to have it included in the public school curriculum, the Jewish community sees this as an intrusion of religion into the classroom. We say that Creation belongs in the church or synagogue and then we ignore it.

Even more than our intellectual block about creation is our emotional block. In our modern world, we isolate ourselves from any intimate contact with Creation. We cannot see the stars at night unless we travel miles from our homes. The starry night sky should fill us with awe and wonder. Yet the lights of our civilization block the sky, and so our eyes are to the ground. Space does not inspire us now, except in science fiction. The real universe is beyond us, and is for most of us of only passing interest. We have so isolated ourselves from the rhythms of the natural world that even when science itself has provided us with ability to experience the wonder of Creation, we have become blase, because these marvels have become just images on a screen.

If you want to reconnect with Creation, start with what you can see or what you have seen. When you do, you can say, I have experienced Creation. When I was seventeen, I was a counselor at a summer camp, and that summer, on one particular night there was going to be an eclipse of the full moon. Everyone went out to the lake to get a clear view. All of a sudden we heard shouts of surprise and wonder coming. With the moon still bright in the sky, the heavens had exploded in the Aurora Borealis, the northern lights. It was an overwhelming sight, with ripples and waves of light and color dancing in a frenzy across the vault of the sky. That night I experienced Creation. How did I feel? Was it something just to experience and say, "Cool"? Or was it something more? I felt the presence of the numinous, although I did not know that word at the time.

"Numinous" is a word coined by the German Protestant theologian Rudolf Otto in his book *The Idea of the Holy*. Otto wrote that the numinous is that intense experience of the divine that fills us with dread or awe and yet with fascination and wonder. The numinous was what Jacob experienced when, upon waking from his dream of the ladder to heaven he exclaimed, "How awesome is this place! This is none other than the house of God and this is the gateway to heaven!" (Gen. 28:17). It is an experience of our realization that we are creatures.

At this time of year we must remember we are "creatures." The realization of being created is the beginning of spirituality and the foundation of our ethical impulse. Creation checks our arrogance and causes us to reflect on what is our place in the universe. Our theological affirmations of creation as human experience give a sense of dependence and finitude; a response of wonder, trust, gratitude for life, and affirmation of the world; and lastly, a recognition of interdependence, order, and beauty in the world.

And so, if we are to begin a return to God, if we are to become true partners in the work of Creation, if we are going to be motivated to act ethically to our fellow human beings and to the natural world, we must begin with Creation. In sunrise and sunset, in the color of the changing leaves, in the miracle of life pulsing through our veins and in the stars we must see the hand of God. On this Rosh HaShanah, may we open our eyes and truly see Creation.

Rabbi Lawrence Troster

Hayom ... Live in the Presence of God

Living in "the presence of God" does not mean that we have lost self-awareness; we are just too busy being alive to bother reflecting on ourselves. We are so focused on living that we do not have any leftover awareness to remind us that we exist. We are not aware that we are doing anything, because all our consciousness—even the part reserved for self-reflection—is busy being alive. We are so fully present, unbounded, and un-self-aware that we are not even aware we are present.

Rabbi Lawrence Kushner

The Power of Change

On Rosh HaShanah, Jews proclaim that God is creator and ruler of the universe. But while Rosh HaShanah celebrates cosmic Creation, its central message is addressed to the individual: You are not fixed by your past.

Through Creation, the world came into being; it has a beginning and an end. The individual also has a beginning and an end. In the dramatic imagery of the High Holy Days, each person is on trial for his/her life in this period. "On Rosh HaShanah it is written, and on Yom Kippur, it is sealed; who shall live, and who shall die?" Facing death, would you live your life the same way? Or would you be more considerate and loving, more ethical, more adventurous, more creative?

Most people live as if they cannot change. Past habits control us. Each person is trapped by standing obligations or pigeonholed by past career performances. We believe that once we have done wrong, we cannot ever remove that stain of guilt.

The Torah claims otherwise: "See, I place before you today [and every day] life and good and death and evil.... [You can] choose life" (Deut. 30:15, 19). By strict justice, every sinner must be punished. Once done, a wrong can never be wiped out. By the miracle of God's love, however, the past can be erased. Even evil can be left behind.

Repentance goes beyond guilt or sin. As Rabbi Joseph B. Soloveitchik has pointed out, the basis of repentance is that human beings are capable of recreating themselves continually. If we stop growing, if we are prisoners of our past behavior, then we are truly dead-in-life.

Becoming aware of bad or unsatisfactory behaviors is the first step to coming alive. The month before Rosh HaShanah and the ten days of repentance from Rosh HaShanah to Yom Kippur are set aside for this purpose in Jewish tradition. Our subsequent decisions to change and to create new living patterns add up to choosing life.

Rabbi Irving Greenberg

Ayom Ve-kadosh: You Are a Revered and Holy God

Throughout the High Holiday liturgy we find the words *kadosh, m'kadesh*—various forms of the Hebrew word for "holy." These are Days of Awe, days of sanctity and holiness. We are filled with a reverence for God, and for life, as we contemplate the holiness of our universe, and the concomitant obligation to perform deeds of goodness, kindness and righteousness.

While Judaism helps us see the holy in all things, during all 365 days of the year, we feel the special holiness of life during these Ten Days of Awe.

The poet William Wordsworth described this sense of pervasive holiness in one of his poems in these words:

There was a time when meadow, grove, and stream
The earth and every common sight,
To me did seem
Apparelled in celestial light
The glory and the freshness of a dream.

It is our task during the Days of Awe, to see every common sight bathed in divine light, reborn with God's holiness in all its glory.

D.P.E.

Hayom—Today!

And while we live, we should try to make each day a year as far as beauty, nobility, and a warm sense of brotherhood are concerned. In a time when there is so much cruelty abroad, we must generate the oxygen of love to keep the soul of the world still breathing. Religion should summon all of us to treasure each other in the recognition that we do not know how long we shall have each other. The crimes and sins for which there should be little forgiveness are hardheartedness, selfishness, mutual cruelty, lovelessness—all of the little weapons which we use to shorten the lives of others. Our very understanding of each other can serve to deepen life even when we cannot lengthen it.

Rabbi Joshua Loth Leibman

Today Is the Only Day That Counts

Hayom: Today. This word recurs throughout the Rosh Hashanah liturgy. While we often speak about Rosh Hashanah as the "birthday of the world," rabbinic literature was not of one mind on this matter. *Hayom Harat Olam,* does not mean "Today the world was created," but rather, "Today the world is being created." Rosh Hashanah has something to teach us about the present. Each day marks a new beginning, an opportunity to start over; a chance to renew all that has grown old.

"*Hayom Harat Olam,* Today the world is being created." But what does this mean? The world already exists. How can it be created today?

According to one rabbinic tradition, it was not the world but the first human beings who were created on Rosh Hashanah. According to this Midrash, the creation of the world began on the twenty-fifth day of Elul and culminated on Rosh Hashanah, the first of Tishri. Rosh Hashanah then, marks the beginning of humanity, not the beginning of the world.

On Rosh Hashanah, the first human being lived out the entirety of existence. The Midrash tells us what happened on that first day, hour by hour. In the first hour God decided to create humanity; in the second, God consulted with the angels concerning the creation of human beings; and in the third hour, God gathered earth from which humanity was fashioned. In the fourth and fifth hours "God kneaded the dust and jointed the parts" and in the sixth, seventh and eighth hours God stood the first human beings up, breathed life into them and placed them in the garden. What happened in the final hours of that first day? God commanded them not to eat from the tree of life, watched as they disobeyed, and then passed judgment on them in the eleventh hour. Finally in the twelfth hour, the Midrash says, God forgave their trespass. Adam and Eve "went forth from the Holy One's presence free."

In other words birth, formation, rebellion, judgment, repentance and redemption, all of life's transformational moments, took place on Rosh Hashanah. All of life unfolded and took place on this single day. Everything that would matter happened in the first moments of creation.

Imagine thinking about our lives in this way. Each moment has infinite potential. Just as every life is like an entire world, every moment is an eternity. When we awake each day the entire world lies before us: what will we make of it? A wasted day is a wasted life. We have lost an opportunity to heal a broken soul, to comfort the bereaved, to bring the Messiah, to bring redemption to the world. Once the day has passed it is gone forever!

Rosh Hashanah symbolizes all of life. Each day has unlimited potential for good or for evil. Like the first human beings, we are born, we develop, we rebel, we obey, we are judged and we are forgiven. Each day is an opportunity to create a new universe for ourselves and for others. There's no yesterday and no tomorrow, only Hayom, only today. What will we do with this day while it's still here?

Most of us do not think of our lives in this way. We live with regrets and hopes. We dream about the future and ruminate about the past. We spend more time looking back at what we missed or worrying about that which has not yet happened. We buy life insurance and never take advantage of the opportunity to live right now. The High Holy Day liturgy reminds us over and over again. Hayom! Today is the only one that counts.

Rabbi Mark B. Greenspan

God at Work ... Creating the World

Rabbi Harold Kushner, in his beautiful meditation on the Twenty-third Psalm, The Lord Is My Shepherd, relates a conversation he had with a physicist. The subject was "whether Newton's second law, the tendency toward chaos, was an argument for or against the existence of God." Rabbi Kushner writes that after he published something about this conversation, he received a letter from a biologist claiming that he should have spoken to a biologist rather than a physicist. Had he done so, wrote the biologist, he would have had a stronger case for God. Apparently the laws of physics and of biology demonstrate different principles.

Take, for example, wrote the biologist, the case of a jar of marbles. Shake it and the marbles become totally mixed up. On the other hand, if you think about the growth of a human fetus, it starts out as a group of undifferentiated cells, and after some weeks, some of those cells become eyes, some turn into lungs, others fingers, etc., etc. What was totally random becomes totally orderly. This is the opposite of Newton's second law. In the case of a fetus, instead of moving from order toward chaos, it moves from chaos toward order. Isn't this, writes Rabbi Kushner, God's work?

With this compelling argument, it is easy to declare, as we do at the end of each of the *Musaf* sections—*Malkhuyot, Zikhronot,* and *Shofarot, Hayom Harat Olam*—that this is the anniversary on which God created the world.

D.P.E

A Modern Midrash

It has always struck me as a lousy deal that, after all they'd been through together, God wouldn't let Moses enter the Promised Land. Sure, he hit the rock twice and smote the Egyptian, but everything in the last four books has been about Moses leading the Israelites to cross the Jordan. What harm could it do? In some of the most heartrending midrashim, Moses begs for just a few more days of life. And, when even that is denied, he pleads simply to be a bird that could fly over the land and at least view it from the sky. Again, God says no.

But it wasn't until I indulged my fantasy that I understood what Moses and we are being taught. What if God had acceded to Moses' request?

"Okay, Moses, you win. I give you permission to enter the land."

"Oh, thank you, Lord," replies Moses. "For a man one hundred twenty years old, to splash through the Jordan, this is indeed a great gift. Say, I was wondering too, God, if you might also let me visit Majorca before I die. I hear that it's supposed to be beautiful this time of year."

And then I understood. God understands all our humanity and says to Moses (and us, if we want): "Moses, My faithful shepherd, I will bestow on you something even more wonderful than visiting yet another new land. I will take you up on this mountain and let you see with new eyes."

Rabbi Lawrence Kushner

My Script

How do I want to inscribe myself into the Book of Life for the coming year? What do I want my script to be? The Areshet Sefateynu reminds us that we are writing our script in partnership with God. It challenges us to write a good script.

Rabbi Zalman Schachter-Shalomi

The Meaning of Our Lives

What is the Book of Life? It may of course be a prayer for continued physical life. Or, for those of us who believe that the soul survives in some form after death, the Book of Life may be the register of those who merit life in the world to come. But praying to be written into the book of life is much more than a prayer for more life, or even for life in the world to come. It is an assertion that our lives have meaning beyond the limited span of time, however long or short, we've been given.

When asking forgiveness for the people Israel, Moshe says "Write me out of *Your* book." It is God's book, not ours; our goal is to merit to be in it. The book exists without us—it goes beyond our own lives, beyond life as we know it. The idea of a "Book of Life" is an assertion that Creation as a whole has a narrative flow—that any one of our individual lives exists within a broader context, a larger story. We don't really know how our little chapter fits in with the larger story. But suddenly, our lives are not just our own personal concerns—they exist, for Your sake.

What is the Book of Life? In its most meaningful sense, it is the Torah. And looking at the stories in the Torah—especially those in *Bereshit* and *Shemot*—we see that they are not stories of easy life. Often, they are stories of lives that, in some important way, seem too short or incomplete; remember Rachel dying in childbirth; Yaakov, who lamented that his life was not as long as his ancestors'; and Moshe, who died without reaching the Land. But they are stories of *meaningful life*, of lives which have become Torah, teaching. So when we ask to be written into the book of life, what we are really saying is, "may our lives be worthy of being in the Torah; may our deeds be worthy of emulation."

Rabbi Jan R. Uhrbach

Who Made the World

Who made the world?
Who made the swan, and the black bear?
Who made the grasshopper?
This grasshopper, I mean—
the one who has flung herself out of the grass,
the one who is eating sugar out of my hand,
who is moving her jaws back and forth instead of up and
    down—
who is gazing around with her enormous and complicated
    eyes.
Now she lifts her pale forearms and thoroughly washes her
    face.
Now she snaps her wings open, and floats away.
I don't know exactly what a prayer is.
I do know how to pay attention, how to fall down
into the grass, how to kneel down in the grass,
how to be idle and blessed, how to stroll through the fields,
which is what I have been doing all day.
Tell me, what else should I have done?
Doesn't everything die at last, and too soon?
Tell me, what is it you plan to do
with your one wild and precious life?

Mary Oliver

The Creation of Light

Light is the stuff of creation, "And God said: 'Let there be light.'"
The great spiritual paradox consists of this: to our eyes, the world contains both darkness and light. Indeed, the ultimate light of creation
casts ever shifting shadows that appear as antagonistic forces, shades,
and grades of light and darkness. Oftentimes we cannot tell the shadows from true darkness. But our ability to choose is the light that
guides our steps through life. We seek God's light, the light of creation
that transcends the conditions of the moment and partakes of eternity. By consciously choosing love, justice and truth, we draw sustenance from that light and unite with the Source.

Rabbi Sheila Peltz Weinberg

Today ...

Some of the saddest words too frequently spoken at the end of one's life go something like this: "He worked so hard all his life but never took the time to enjoy any pleasures. Now, when he could enjoy life, *nit da kein yoren*, he ran out of years." Whenever I hear this melancholy summary I always ask myself, "Why, why did he postpone the enjoyment of life? Why did he wait? Is it possible to enjoy at sixty the pleasures that are available only at forty? Does financial security enable us to retrace our steps and to do now what should have been done then and could only have been done then? Is there any way of rewinding and replaying the film of life? There is no future joy which can compensate us for the legitimate joys we needlessly deny ourselves today. God, our prayer book reminds us, is waiting—waiting for us to stop waiting and to proceed with all haste to begin to do now, this day, all the things for which this day was made.

Rabbi Sidney Greenberg

ROSH HASHANAH RITUALS AND CUSTOMS

When we bless people, we bestow something upon them. We give them our good wishes as a gift, as something that will offer them strength or consolation. When we ask God to bless us, or bless one another through the priestly blessing *(dukhan)*, we hope to receive of God's gifts. But here, in our most oft-repeated form of prayer, we use the same words, as though we *give* God our blessing. We know full well that God has no need of our offerings. But still, we want to give. To say *barukh* is to say that we want to add something to the wholeness that is God. In return for the endless blessings we receive, we seek, however inadequately, to be active givers in the balance of blessing upon which our universe stands.

RABBI ARTHUR GREEN, *THESE ARE THE WORDS*

A Guide to Greetings

During the month of Elul, the traditional greetings are *Shanah tovah* ("A good year"); or *Leshanah tovah tikatevu* ("May you be inscribed for a good year [in the Book of Life]"); or *Leshanah tovah umetukah tikatevu* ("May you be inscribed for a good and sweet year"); or—less common—*Ketivah tovah* ("A good inscription [in the Book of Life]").

The appropriate response: *Gam leha* (feminine *lakh*)—"The same to you."

Between Rosh Hashanah and Yom Kippur, some people add to the above: *Leshanah tovah tikatevu vetehatemu* ("May you be inscribed and sealed for a good life"). Others use these greetings only through the first night of Rosh Hashanah; after that, it would be indelicate to suggest that a person is not already inscribed in the Book of Life, for on Rosh Hashanah all the righteous are so inscribed—only those whose records are closely balanced between good and bad have their fate postponed until Yom Kippur.

On Yom Kippur (and until *Hoshana Rabah*) the greeting is *Gemar hatimah tovah* ("A good final sealing [to you]!") or *Hatimah tovah* ("A sealing for good!").

Rabbi Michael Strassfeld

Kiddush: Re-Enactment of Creation

The recitation of *Kiddush*, every Friday night and festival evening, is an act of supreme jubilation and celebration. Through wine we pronounce God's sanctification of time, of holy days, of the people of Israel, and of Shabbat.

In the Rosh Hashanah *Kiddush*, we say the first blessing over wine, and the second blessing over the day—either Shabbat, or Festival, or both.

The Festival *Kiddush* is a reminder that in Judaism, in Abraham Joshua Heschel's felicitous language, time is holy; space is not holy. Six days a week, wrote Rabbi Heschel, we think about the world of creation; on Shabbat we remind ourselves of the creation of the world. The *Kiddush* for Rosh Hashanah is similar in some ways to the Shabbat *Kiddush*, and in some ways different. As a weekly routine, the *Kiddush* on Friday night (and Shabbat afternoon) helps us remember that we, like God, are creators on six days, and "resters" or "restorers" on Shabbat. Our soul is restored, as we re-enact God's rest after the six days of creation.

Each week on Shabbat, and each year on Rosh Hashanah, we bear witness to God's creation and rest, and we partake in the divinity of that very same creation and rest—thus making the *Kiddush* a ritual-ized reminder of a supreme role we play with God in the rhythm of God's world.

D.P.E.

Benediction: Prayers around the Communal Table

The Sephardic custom for the two nights of Rosh Hashanah is after saying the special Kiddush and the *Hamotsi,* every one recites seven prayers around the table.

1. Take a piece of apple, dip it in honey and say: During this coming year, may we all celebrate sweet occasions inside and outside of this synagogue.
2. Take a piece of leek, dip it in honey and say: During this coming year, may there be no leakage to the outside what-ever we decide inside, so we can avoid *Leshon Ha-Ra,* gos-sip and slander.
3. Take a piece of beetroot, dip it in honey and say: During this coming year, may we all re-plant the root of Judaism within this congregation.
4. Take a date and pray: During this coming year, may we all make a date here in this synagogue to pray, to study and to perform good deeds.
5. Take a piece of squash, dip it in honey and say: During this coming year, may all our sins be washed away and thrown into the lake.
6. Take a piece of fish and pray: May the membership of this synagogue multiply like fish in the river.
7. Take a piece of sheep or fish head and pray: May the lead-ership of this congregation be the head of the Jewish orga-nizations in our community and not the tail.

Shanah Tovah U'metukah!

Adapted from Rabbi Abraham Deleon-Cohen

Blessings for a Sweet New Year

> I roused you under the apple tree; there your mother birthed
> you—Song of Songs 8:5.

Love, awakening, and birth are associated with the apple tree. On Rosh
Hashanah, the anniversary of the birthday of the world, we eat apples
to signify our love for God and life, our awakening to our own sins
and potential, the birth of the New Year and the rebirth of our souls.

We dip apples in honey to symbolize the miraculous paradox of the
High Holiday season: sometimes what is ugly or forbidden becomes
the vehicle for delivering what is desirable and holy. Just as unkosher
bees can yield kosher honey, sin can yield repentance. Eating honey-
coated apples, we taste the sweet promise of rebirth and, literally,
embody it.

Apples are already sweet. By dipping them in honey, we implicitly
offer a bold prayer: "God, you have blessed us many times over. Yet we
come before you to ask for even more—another year, a good year, forgiveness, long life. Coat our good, sweet lives with even more sweetness. Let the New Year bring with it new gifts and a renewed sense of
gratitude."

> It is not in heaven, that you should say, "Who shall go up for us to
> heaven, and bring it to us, that we may hear it and do it?" ... But
> [the commandment] is very near to you, in your mouth and in
> your heart, that you may do it—Deuteronomy 30:12, 14.

This is the season when we begin to think about having—and making—a sweet New Year.

A few years back, about a week before Rosh Hashanah, my sister-
in-law phoned me from her car. Her son, my nephew, then about six
years old, had asked her why we dip apples, above all other fruit, into
honey, above all other sweeteners, to celebrate the New Year. She
called for a "professional consultation." It's a good question: Why not
plums into powdered sugar? Or, as some Jews have been campaigning
for, strawberries into chocolate?

There are many interpretations of why apples were chosen. For
example, when Song of Songs 8:5 evokes love and birth under an apple
tree, it reminded the ancient Rabbis of romance and rebirth with

God—a renewal we strive for particularly at this time of year. I asked my nephew, "Did you ever notice that an apple is a big fruit with small seeds? One small apple seed can grow a whole tree and many apples." He answered precociously, "Oh, I get it. Transformation."

And why honey? In general, if an animal is not kosher, its by-products are not kosher, either. However, honey, a product of unkosher bees, is an exception. The fact that honey can be kosher suggests that, sometimes, what is forbidden (an unkosher food or an immoral act) can yield a result that is not only acceptable, but sweet (honey or repentance).

Eating apples dipped in honey sends a message that the opportunities to repent and enjoy a sweet year, like the commandments of the Torah in general, are not far off or obscure, but close and accessible. Saying the blessings, rolling crunchy sweetness dipped in liquid sweetness on our tongues, we remind ourselves of all the gifts we hold close, ready to enjoy: life, family, community, and, especially important this time of year, transformation: the ability to learn and grow. When you think of the alternative—being trapped in doing what we have always done or being only what we have been until now—the opportunity for awareness and correction seems very sweet indeed. Let us notice and pay attention. Let us act on what we know. Let us make it a good, sweet year.

Rabbi Debra Orenstein

Rosh Hashana Symbols Revealed

Apples and Honey

Though the Torah never identifies the fruit eaten by Eve and Adam, in our culture that fruit has become an apple. And given the ubiquitous nature of Christian symbolism in our society most people also identify that first fruit with original sin, and more specifically with the sin of Eve. It is therefore important for us to reclaim the apple for what it is in our own tradition, not a symbol of women's sin but of our initiative, our active sexuality, and our role in saving the Jewish people.

Janet Zimmern notes that when the Babylonian Talmud (Sotah 11b) depicts God as the original midwife of Israel, this Divine birthing takes place under apple trees. According to the tale recounted in this section of the Talmud, when the Israelites were in Egypt, the women seduced their husbands, conceived and gave birth in apple orchards. As there were no midwives in these fields God served as midwife to the Israelite women. Thus, apples can be seen as a symbol of women's insistence on their sexuality and their claim to the future, even in times of enslavement. To see apples in this light helps move us away from associations of women's sexuality as sinful. This is especially important at this time of the year when we must remain attuned to the difference between repenting for things we feel we have done wrong and remaining insistent that certain culturally defined sins are in fact not sinful at all.

Raisin Challah

According to Judith Solomon, the Ashkenazi custom of eating raisin challah on Rosh Hashana is tied to the biblical story of Abigail. Abigail, one of the seven women considered a prophet by the rabbis of the Talmud, appears in the early chapters of the First Book of Samuel. She is portrayed in this story as a smart woman who recognizes the importance of the soon-to-be-king David. She overturns her boorish husband's snub of David and presents David with many gifts including two hundred loaves of bread and one hundred clusters of raisins. Her speech to David is a richly nuanced, strategically brilliant display of foresight and cunning. It is also a carefully articulated request for forgiveness for the previous wrongdoings of her household toward David and his party. David, won over by Abigail's speech and gifts, decides to spare her and her household. Ten days later her husband dies, and she becomes a wife of the first king of Israel.

What does this story have to do with the High Holidays? The hint is the ten days. Which ten days pass between Abigail's speech and the miraculous death of her husband? According to the commentators, the ten days of repentance. Thus it was on Rosh Hashana that Abigail came to David with bread and raisins, taking her future into her own hands and changing the course of her life. Let us all tell this story around our own tables as we enjoy raisin challah and pledge to speak out on our own behalf as the prophet Abigail did on a Rosh Hashana long ago.

More Shofar Symbolism

The horn, a very ancient symbol of the new moon, has long been connected to women and their menstrual cycles. At the entrance of a cave in southern France there is a wall carving from 25,000–20,000 BCE of a Paleolithic goddess holding a bison horn in one hand while she rests the other on her round belly. In the Song of Hannah, read on Rosh Hashana, the horn is mentioned twice, in the first and last verses. According to Rabbi Lisa Edwards, the reference to "a horn exalted by God's annointed" in the first verse of Hannah's song makes new sense in the context of Rosh Hashana. Edwards points out that the shofar is further connected with Hannah by midrashim that associate the number of benedictions recited during the shofar service with the number of times Hannah mentions the name of God in her song.

The other matriarch who is tied by midrashic literature to the sounds of the shofar is Sarah. According to diverse rabbinic commentaries, Sarah cries out at the discovery of the deed of the Binding of Isaac. Her cries are the sounds of the shofar.

Tamara R. Cohen

Culinary Prayers—*Yehi Ratzon*

Historically, the prayers of Jewish women were not included in the official Rosh Hashanah liturgy, yet this did not stop them from expressing their desires. With a great deal of creativity, they literally cooked up their own efforts to shape the year ahead. Traditionally it was women's responsibility to prepare the special Rosh Hashanah foods that give new meaning to the saying "you are what you eat!"

The best known examples of these culinary prayers are apples and round challah. The sweet fall apple, made sweeter still by the addition of honey, symbolizes the sweetness we hope fills the new year. The challah is round like the circle of life we hope to continue living. Its sweetness is enhanced by the addition of raisins. As we eat these foods and make them part of us, we hope to realize their symbolic meaning in the year ahead.

From the time of the Talmud, a fanciful combination of word play, visual association and flavors designated a whole series of foods as totems for the year to come. The head of a sheep or fish, like the round challah, was traditionally eaten because of its physical form. It symbolizes our desire to come out "ahead" in the coming year. Dates, fenugreek, pumpkins and leeks were all eaten because of linguistic links between the Hebrew names of these foods and requests for the year to come. The puns are subtle and often stretch meaning and pronunciation. Though not a direct translation of the original, this version of the leek blessing by Gilda Angel suggests the possibilities of the genre: "Like as we eat this leek may our luck never lack in the year to come."

The word plays, however, were not limited to Hebrew. European Jews are fond of eating dishes with carrots. The German and Yiddish words for carrot sound like the word *mehr* meaning more. Add to this the golden color and round shape of cooked carrots cut on the diameter and we have a dish that brings together in sound and sight the wish for more gold pieces—money—in the year to come.

The potential of this tradition can be seen best in the homes of Jews from North Africa and the Levant. Women in these communities developed whole menus which bring together foods and prayer. In many places the everyday savory spices were replaced entirely by sweet ones. Others forbade the use of black foods. Unique Rosh Hashanah recipes abound. One example is pumpkin phyllo rounds. Though spelled differently, the Hebrew word for pumpkin sounds the same as the verb "to rip." Thus, snail-shaped pastries filled with sweetly spiced pumpkin are a tasty start to a meal and a plea for God to tear out the pages from our book of sins, allowing us to continue sweetly in the round circle of life.

As many of our foremothers have done, we too can give significance to our holiday table. Traditional Mediterranean dishes for Rosh Hashanah can be found in many Jewish cookbooks and incorporated into a meal. Using this traditional genre we can also serve innovative menus that reflect our contemporary needs. A wish for peace might be invoked by a first course of "peas" soup. The pomegranate with its many seeds may be eaten with an eye towards having a fertile or productive year. Consider eating fresh figs cut in half lengthwise. Visually and biblically, this fruit is linked with women's sexuality; dip it in honey and bless the physical fulfillment of the year to come. Serve a sweet multi-grain challah that celebrates the diversity of the world around us. Invite family members and friends to consider the year ahead and come up with dishes that reflect their concerns.

All the traditional blessings over these meaningful foods begin with the same phrase that is recited before eating the apple and honey: "May it be your will, our God and the God of our ancestors that ... "

Whether your own additions finish this phrase with the serious or the sublime, the gourmet or "Chef Boyardee," the traditional or the

innovative, this is a women's tradition that provides a tasty counter-
point to the traditional male liturgy. It also provides an opportunity for
celebrating Jewish women's relationship to food as a historic source of
creativity and spirituality.

Ruth Abusch-Magder

Apples and Honey

> Do not eat the apple, study it.
> Seeds stir inside its womb, inside its heart
> Ready to give birth if allowed.
> We devour it before its time
> With sweet, glistening honey
> Swirling over a matrix split,
> Open, pulsing with force.
> The honey, the seed together
> Create new worlds that blossom
> After songs and psalms fade away.
> We will nurture the seed another season.
> Another year will pass.
> Time to study the apple,
> Split for seeds to emerge
> Another year.

Michael Halperin

Honey on Rosh Hashanah

Tradition, Tradition! are the familiar words of the song from *Fiddler
on the Roof.* How true it is that tradition and family customs endure,
even when fundamental Jewish laws and mitzvot are ignored. Covering
mirrors at a shiva house, moving to a new home on Tuesday and eating
bagels and lox at the post–Yom Kippur "Break the fast" meal are often
more rigorously observed than more essential Jewish practices.

Since these traditions are so entrenched, it is important that rabbis
reinterpret and give contemporary meanings to these rituals so that
they will be viewed with unique Jewish insights and ethical values. The
tradition of eating apples and/or hallah dipped in honey can provide
living thoughts and special lessons for life: Why honey? Why not candy,

M&M's, Sweet'n Low (especially, if you are calorie conscious) or some other sweetener?

One answer is that, while all of the above infuse sweetness, honey has one additional special characteristic. It is sticky. Symbolically, we are saying that our noble resolutions and affirmations for the year ahead will not fade like a spiritual suntan, but will "stick with us" throughout the year.

A second interpretation on the use of honey as expressive of our wish for a sweet New Year, is more realistic and practical. Yes, honey is indeed sweet. But, it comes from bees and they often sting. The sweetness you are praying for can be accompanied by a sting, some form of pain and anguish that is an inevitable part of every life.

Dipping apples/hallah in honey acknowledges that, while we ask for sweetness, we must be prepared to deal with stings that are also part of everyone's life. The American approach to life is total confidence, and self-esteem: "I can do it." In fact, the last four letters of the word American, are "I can." As Jews, we are more humble and realize that we need God's help for the fulfillment of our wishes. The last four letters of the word Jewish are "wish."

The bottom line is that eating apples/challah dipped in honey is only a symbol. Each of us must, everyday, in every way, bring sweetness and kindness into the lives of every person we relate to. That will certainly make *Shana Tova U'metuka* not just a wish but a reality.

Rabbi Joseph L. Braver

Simplicity

*"May it be your will Adonai our God and God of our
ancestors to renew us for a good and sweet year."*
ON EATING AN APPLE ON ROSH HASHANAH

There is something so profoundly simple about apples and honey on New Year. It's so basic. For me, it is a prayer of thanksgiving and hope rolled in one. All of my life's aspirations brought into focus. I humbly recognize where I have come from and where I need to go, what I have yet to do to make my life holy. No glitz, no glitter. I simply savor the sweet juices of the fruits of God's world as I prepare myself for the spiritual renewal I yearn for all year long. I know it's possible at any time, but there is something special about the Holy Day season that makes it seem ever the more possible for me.

For me, apples are symbols that I call return. So I get ready for my return with a modest prayer and an unadorned act. According to tradition, when children are born, trees are to be planted—their branches to be used for a *chuppah* (bridal canopy) much later in that person's life. In recovery, through spiritual renewal, we are all as children who take that first breath in the world.

For growth and renewal: Share some apples and honey with a friend. Then take a seed and plant it so that you may watch it grow as you do.

Rabbi Kerry M. Olitzky

Joy on Rosh Hashanah

One of the great joys of the High Holidays, apart from their profound religious meaning, is the opportunity to re-connect with so many people we truly care about, have shared so many experiences with, and just don't get to see enough of during the year. I'd like you to take a moment right now and look around the room and appreciate all the people who care about you and bring blessing to your life. The shul is, ideally, the place, "where everybody knows your name." It is a safe haven for us in a troubled world. I'd like to challenge you in the year ahead to make that effort to stay in touch. Schedule regular times to get together, communicate via e-mail, pick up the phone when you need to talk. I hope that we won't meet again a year from now asking ourselves the question, "Where has the time gone and why have I not made time for the people I care about?" "A person without a friend," one sage taught, "is like a left hand without a right." May we all be blessed in the coming year to extend the hand of friendship to others and to find comfort and sustenance in the hands of our friends.

Rabbi Bonnie Kopell

Casting Away Our Sins *(Tashlikh)*

On Rosh Hashanah, I was walking my dog with a regular nighttime dog-walking companion who is not Jewish. He remarked: "Late this afternoon, as I was getting off the Westside Highway, I saw hundreds of people—I think they were Jewish—assembled by the edge of the Hudson River. They were throwing things into the river. What on earth were they doing?" How would I explain *tashlikh*, the ritual of throwing bread crumbs into a body of water, to my friend? "We are symbolically casting away our sins," I said, laughing to myself, imagining the sins of Manhattan cast off, floating towards Jersey. After the laughter, I began to think about the deeper meaning of the practice, the serious self-reflection that happens at the water's edge.

"You shall cast your sins into the depths of the sea."

Meditation
On this Day of Judgment, I take account of my life and relationships during the last year. Of some things I am proud, of others disappointed or ashamed. I resolve to strengthen and sustain the many mitzvot I have performed—love in relationships, honesty in business, engagement in the repair of the world—and I resolve to cast off those actions or words that I regret. Help me to keep preserving what is good and to keep casting off what is bad. May this be a year of goodness and blessing.

Ritual
On the afternoon of the first day of Rosh Hashanah (the second day, if the first day falls on Shabbat), go to a body of water and cast away your sins symbolically by reaching into your pockets and throwing out "sins."

Blessing
(Before casting out your "sins"):
May You cast out all the sins of Your people Israel into a place where they will not be remembered, nor counted, nor ever again be minded. Blessed are You who enables me to distinguish between good and bad.

Teaching
You shall cast out our sins into the depths of the sea (Micah 7:19).
Yom Kippur atones only for transgressions between human beings and God. For transgressions between one individual and another, atonement is achieved only by reconciling with the person who has been offended (*Mishnah Yoma* 8:9).

When one forgets the essence of one's own soul, when one distracts one's mind from attending to the substantive content of one's own inner life, everything becomes confused and uncertain. The primary role of penitence, which at once sheds light on the darkened zone, is for one to return to oneself, to the root of one's soul. Then one will at once return to God, the Soul of all souls (Avraham Isaac Kook, *The Lights of Penitence*).

What should we be throwing into the water? Rabbi Richard Israel, of blessed memory, originated these tongue-in-cheek suggestions:

For ordinary sins—white bread

For exotic sins—French or Italian bread

For dark sins—pumpernickel

For complex sins—multigrain

For truly warped sins—pretzels

For sins of indecision—waffles

For being ill-tempered—sourdough

For excessive use of irony—rye bread

For continual bad jokes—corn bread

For hardening our heart—jelly doughnuts

Rabbi Irwin Kula and Vanessa L. Ochs

Tashlich Thoughts

I watch as some bread-sin crumbs flowing down the stream get stuck against small stones or between the tall grasses that grow there. I see them get soaking wet, those pathetic pieces of what always seems to be leftover challah from the night before. They are just stuck there, bloated and fibrous, spongy and disintegrating as the water washes over them but is not strong enough to move them. Each time the bread dislodges a little I think it will finally pass its stuck spot. "Go, bread, go!" I think to myself. "Come on, water, come on, you can move it!" Sometimes it flows all the way out of sight, and other times it simply moves a little further down and gets stuck somewhere else. Ultimately, I always walk away and trust that the pieces of bread—sins—will somehow find their way to their ocean home where they belong. It seems to me that *teshuva* is like that too. We anxiously try to rid ourselves of things that don't pass away too easily. Even with G-d's help, the old habits die hard, if at all. We may make some movement in a certain area, only to find we get stuck on the same thing months or years later. Ultimately though, we must let go and trust. Once we do the casting of the bread—sins—we must have faith that G-d and/or nature will meet us halfway and help out. The first step though, of course, is the casting.

Rabbi Leah Richman

Bread Crumbs for *Tashlikh*

I was fascinated to read of the rabbinic opposition to casting away bread crumbs, and the triumph of folk wisdom. Perhaps focus on this: the question of the meaning of bread in that context: what are we discarding?

a. Pride of course, as in the *hametz* discussions for Pesah. That is clear. But pride is especially significant on Rosh HaShanah when we celebrate *malkhuyot*. For the root of sin is pride, making yourself and your desires the center of the universe, and in effect dethroning *malkhut shamayim*.

But also:

b. Bread symbolizes the rationalization for a lot of our wrongdoing. Why do I neglect my family? I have to put bread on the table. Why do I cut ethical corners? I have to make a living. Why do I use third-world child labor? The pressures of the market. As it says in the Yom Kippur liturgy: *benafsho yavi lahmo*—he brings home the bacon at the cost of his soul.

c. *Lehem* is connected to *lohem/milhamah*—sins of violence. In front of the Justice Department in Washington is a seven- to eight-floor high sculpture of a plowshare (looks more like a snowplow than a farming plow). When you get closer you see that it is made up entirely of handguns that the D.C. police have collected from the Washington streets.

Thus we symbolically express our desire to discard all these sins: pride, economic wrongdoing, violence.

Rabbi Shamai Kanter

At Water's Edge ... We Seek Your Presence

Our ancestors gathered on this Day of Judgment, at water's
   edge,
To relieve the burden of judgments gone wrong
And moments betrayed, eluding our summons to live them
Again.

They emptied their souls as they turned out their pockets
Trying to cast out the crumbs of last year's leftovers
Greeting the New Year as one who has never eaten the bread of
Remorse.

But we know, looking for places to toss our garbage,
That there is no such place as "out."
Everything has its Place, even our old sins,
And we cannot cleanse ourselves by polluting
Someplace else.

God does not pick up our trash
Unless we have first treated it,
Removing the stench from our sewage and
Runoff, and made it a
Gift.

Adonai, we are not here to cheat You today,
Spoiling Your world with rotten eggs
And tasteless bread. We too seek Your Presence
At water's edge, searching in the vastness of
Your great Sea, in the faces of our friends,
In the joy of Your children, come together to
Speak Your Name and share their gifts with each other
And with You.

Take our sins, then, as reminders of last year's efforts;
Cleanse them, as we have tried to do; let our failures
Feed Your creatures, strengthening Your world,
Binding us to all that lives and grows.
Let them be a picnic for Your fishes,
A blessing to Your planet.
We have spoken their names,

Broken their power,
And redeemed them with our prayers
And Your forgiveness.

Rabbi Dan Shevitz

Guided Meditation for *Tashlich*

We begin this meditation by standing in mountain pose. So, make sure that:

1. Your feet are about shoulder-width apart
2. Your feet are pressing evenly into the floor
3. Your knees are relaxed
4. Your shoulders are loose and your arms are dangling by your sides
5. Your facial muscles are softened
6. Your spine makes a straight line from your stomach to your neck, pulling up to a point above your head
7. Your arms are stretched straight by your sides

Take a deep breath in through your nose and out through your mouth to secure this position. With each breath afterwards, see if you can notice tiny adjustments you can make to deepen the posture.

In these next breaths, begin to imagine roots growing from all different parts of your feet, reaching deep into the ground. Imagine that these roots are pulling your feet down flat into the soil, supporting you—see if you can feel them from your toes, your heels, your arches and the balls of your feet. Relax your arms, straighten your spine and breathe.

Now that we're in a relaxed position, start to think back through this past year. Let images enter and exit your mind—small moments, meaningful moments, smells, pictures and faces. Think back now to last Elul, last September: where were you at the last High Holiday cycle? What promises had you made? What goals did you have for the coming year?

Move now into late September and October, the middle of fall, the Hebrew month of Tishrei, the holiday of Sukkot and the time for harvesting. What kinds of benefits did you reap this year? Financial? Educational? Experiential? See if you can recall them now.

Think now about last November, roughly the Hebrew month of Heshvan. Late fall, colder weather. The natural world slowly moving from bountiful to barren as the winter moves in, so that the cycle can begin again in the spring. Think now about changes that you made in your life this year. What patterns did you break? What new work did you take on?

Move slowly from November into December, the Hebrew month of Kislev, the month that holds Hanukkah, the holiday of lights and miracles. In what ways did you bring light or goodness into the world this year? What miracles happened in your life this year?

Then think back to last January and February; first, the Hebrew month of Tevet, the conclusion of Hanukkah. Then, the month of Shevat, the month that contains Tu B'Shevat, the festival of the trees, a time for planting. Think about new projects that you started this year, new plans that you made, "seeds" that you planted for your or your family's future.

Move from late February into March, the Hebrew month of Adar and the ending of winter. During Adar, we celebrate Purim, a festival of fun and revelry. Think about the joy that came into your life this year? In what ways were you silly? Can you think of moments when you laughed?

From March to April, from Adar to Nisan, the month of spring. The time we celebrate Pesach and think about renewal, rebirth and newfound freedom. What struggles concluded in your life this year? Were there issues or difficulties in your life that you were able to overcome?

Next, think back to last May, the Hebrew month of Iyar. In the secular year, a time for closings and endings. Think about endings that occurred in your life this year. What issues, relationships, situations came to a close during the past twelve months?

Move from May into June and into the month of Sivan, the month that holds the holiday of Shavuot, the holiday that celebrates our receiving of the Torah. Think about learning that you did during the year. What new things did you learn this year, and what effect did they have on you?

From June into July and August; through the Hebrew months of Tammuz and Av; hot and humid weather; slowing of activity and some time for rest; in the Hebrew calendar, these months are a time to think about history and loss; think about losses in your life this past year. In what ways did you grieve?

And here we are in the new year, making new promises and setting new goals. So before we do that, take a few moments and deep breaths to remember the journey of the past year.

Erika Katske

Tashlich

One of my favorite parts of Rosh Hashanah is *tashlich*. *Tashlich* is a personal ritual of repentance, outside the forum of the synagogue, in which we appeal to God's side of mercy, in which we remind God of the divine ability to release us from what we have done wrong through an act of compassion. *Tashlich* should never be seen as the beginning stage of *teshuvah*, but rather as the end stage. It is an act of letting go.

It's very physical and very real, watching all of our sins represented by bread floating away. Letting go is not something you can do by proxy. You can identify for yourself what you need to release into the water. *Tashlich* becomes an act of closure, the Jewish way of burning up a letter you've never sent. There is strength to be taken from the presence of others during prayer. But I think we can't obscure in this the need to take time for personal reflection, for individual pleas of *teshuvah*. We must all take the time to release before God what our lives have been like. And in doing so, we can begin to forgive ourselves.

We must learn to let go and forgive ourselves for the wrongs we are expressing. This is not something we necessarily ask for in our fixed prayers. And yet we are often one of the people we have most wronged. Moreover, as we ask others for forgiveness for having hurt them, or as we promise God to be better in God's eyes in the coming year, we can dredge up a lot of personal resentment for not having lived up to our promises. That type of self-knowledge is important, because it gives our *teshuvah* depth and meaning, but there is a point at which we have to stop beating ourselves up mentally and acknowledge that we need to give ourselves permission to try again. If God can forgive us, so can we. That is a necessary part of sincere *teshuvah*.

If this is our goal, then *tashlich* is an integral part of our process of letting go. We physically release what we have been holding onto. Think about the parts of yourself that you are sending down into the water, the events from the past year, the interactions with people that you can never recover. The events become memories, like the bread soaking up the water and floating away. They don't disappear but they are transformed into something new, something further away and less painful. This is a moment for you as an individual to make sure that nothing is forgotten. That everything you need to say is said. But also, a chance to forgive yourself and admit that a new year has begun. If, as we throw the bread, we ask God for compassion, then we also can learn in that moment to have compassion for ourselves.

Rachel Kahn-Troster

Tashlich: Casting-Off Sinprints

Many people carry around the footprints of people who have walked all over them. These sinprints often stay on us for years after the original events. They usually weigh us down and often keep us from growing. How can we reduce the weight of these sinprints? Reconciliation is the best way, but it takes two to effect a reconciliation. If the person whose sinprints still burden us is unrepentant (or deceased) what can we do on our own to lighten the load?

Jewish tradition provides a way called *Tashlich.* This ceremony developed in the Middle Ages in connection with Rosh Hashanah—the Jewish New Year. If one wants to make the New Year better than the last year, one has to change some of the things that led us to hurt people and also to rid ourselves of things that make us vulnerable to the sins of others. The High Holy Days concentrate our attention on the need to change our behavior. *Tashlich* focuses our attention on the need to change our attitudes by visibly casting off the sinprints of others.

After the Rosh Hashanah morning service, people would walk to a nearby stream or river, take bread crumbs from their pockets, cast *(Tashlich)* the crumbs into the water and watch the current carry away the sinprints, i.e., the many crummy things that had happened to them in the past. To have a better year we need to purify ourselves of our sinprints as well as our sins.

At Temple Akiba, in Culver City, California, we have developed a worksheet to help people focus on the hurtful sinprints they need to cast off. The worksheet is distributed after the Rosh Hashanah evening service. (A copy of the worksheet is found on the following page.) People are asked to fill out the worksheet that night or the next morning. Then they crush the worksheet up with a five- or ten-dollar bill inside, and prior to or subsequent to the Rosh Hashanah morning service they cast the crushed up ball of paper into a large cardboard box. The money is donated to a shelter for battered women. The alleviation of one's own troubles should always be combined with helping others.

During the last few years when we have done *Tashlikh* in this way, people have often told me that the process had made them feel somewhat less burdened by the sinprints of the past.

Tashlich: Let Go of Hurt Worksheet

Name of the person who hurt me:

Name the pain he or she said/did:

Face the hurt. I felt:

What results did this have on my life?

Are there any aspects of this situation that are my responsibility?

What did I learn from this negative experience that helped me avoid or minimize being victimized again?

How long has this pain bothered me and what have I done about it?

In order to free myself from this pain I will cast off (let go) by ...

Wrap this *Tashlich* paper around some money and deposit it in a donation box. The money will help others.

Rabbi Allen S. Maller

Tashlikh

On Rosh ha-Shanah *TASHLIKH* standing by the water,
Emptying our pockets of the remaining crumbs of sin, We
    turn to You, O God,
Creator of heaven and earth, Creator of the water. We pour out
    like water the confession of our sin. Hear our prayer, and
"Tashlikh, cast all our sins into the ocean's depths."
As You appeared to grieving, exiled Hagar (Who, in desperation,
Had cast her thirsting lad under the bushes) And assured her
    at the well of water

That You, the Living God, look mercifully upon the
   afflicted—Look upon us in our affliction, and
"Tashlikh, cast all our sins into the ocean's depths."
As Abraham and Isaac, on their way to Mount Moriah, Con-
   fronted by an impassable river (The guise that Satan took
To deter them from fulfilling the command of Your dread
   test), Marched boldly into the water—So strengthen our
   faith and trust,
That we may pass whatever test You set for us, and
"Tashlikh, cast all our sins into the ocean's depths."
As You sustained our people Israel, Your people Israel, With
   the never-failing well of water
That accompanied them (through "ram's merit") In their
   desert wanderings—
So save us and sustain us with your living water, and
"Taslilikh, cast all our sins into the ocean's depths."

As fish in water are ever in danger
Of being caught and then devoured, So are we in peril
   constantly.
We turn to You, our only sure protection. Shelter us, and
"Tashlikh, cast all our sins into the ocean's depths."
As in days of yore
A king was crowned at river's edge,
So too do we at water's edge renew Your coronation, O Sov-
   ereign of the Universe,
And take upon ourselves anew
The blessed yoke of Your sovereignty. Accept us as Your loyal
   servants, and *"Tashlikh,* cast all our sins into the ocean's
   depths."
As You promised through Your prophet Ezekiel To sprinkle
   upon the people Israel Your pure and purifying water, Do
   so now, we pray,
As we turn our hearts in penitence to You, and *"Tashlikh,* cast
   all our sins into the ocean's depths."
Let these waters be a token of Your covenant promise: "As I
   swore that Noah's waters
Never again would flood the earth,
So I swear that I will not be angry with you or rebuke you.
   For though the mountains may move and the hills be

shaken My steadfast love shall never move from you, Nor
My covenant of shalom be shaken,"
Says *Ha-Shem*, your Compassionate One. So
"*Tashlikh*, cast all our sins into the ocean's depths."

Author Unknown

Tashlich

And I plod gently, cautiously
Through the Santa Monica sands.
Toward the shoreline;
Toward the separation
Between Who I am and Who I want to be.
I carry my compact *Art Scroll* in hand
Like a flotation device,
Like a mother grasping her child in stormy winds.
I read the words and I inhale their meaning.

As I approach the water's edge,
From my pocket I pull the
Crumbs of my sins and cast them
Into the September waters.

I then cast the stones and pebbles
The Rabbi said weigh us down.
Regret. Anxiety. Sadness.
Sadness.

I watch the crumbs float.
I watch the stones sit in the sand,
As the waters reside.
After moments I sacrilegiously turn
My back on the ocean and retreat.

I never see the stones, the pebbles, the crumbs
Returned by the water to the place I stood.

Jeff Bernhardt

Acknowledgments

My deepest thanks are extended to the entire staff of Jewish Lights Publishing; they are an amazing team, and a pleasure to work with. For this book, the guidance, attention to detail, cooperation and encouragement of Lauren Seidman was indispensable. In the midst of a busy rabbinate I could not have completed this book on time, and with such high quality, without the able and competent assistance of Rachel Kahn-Troster, who also helped me with the first book in this set, *Yom Kippur Readings*. My wife, Maxine, is always supportive and loving, and is my best reader, most effective critic and wisest adviser.

Sources

"Personal correspondence" includes e-mails, postings on rabbinic message boards and other nonarchived electronic communications.

Abusch-Magder, Ruth. "Culinary Prayers—*Yehi Ratzon,*" from *Ma'yan's Journey,* Fall 1998. 8–9.

Adler, Morris. "Rosh Hashanah on Shabbat: *Retzay Bimenuhatenu* ... Accept Our Rest," from *May I Have a Word With You?* New York: Crown, 1967.

Agus, Jacob. "There Is Hope for Your Future, Declares God (Jeremiah 31:17)." Personal correspondence.

Ariel, David S. "As We Begin Our Prayers Tonight," from *Spiritual Judaism: Restoring Heart and Soul to Jewish Life.* New York: Hyperion, 1998.

———. "Why We Pray," from *Spiritual Judaism: Restoring Heart and Soul to Jewish Life.* New York: Hyperion, 1998.

Artson, Bradley Shavit. *"Akedah."* Personal correspondence.

Bernhardt, Jeff. *"Tashlich."* Personal correspondence.

Berner, Leila Gal. "A New Year," from *Kol Haneshama: Mahzor Leyamim Nora'im (Prayerbook for the Days of Awe),* Elkins Park, PA: Reconstructionist Press, 1999.

Bingham, June. *"Aseh Imanu Tzedakah Va-Chesed:* Deal with Us Charitably and Lovingly," in "The Living Pulpit." Roth Advertising, Inc. PO Box 96, Sea Cliff, NY 11579; 516-674-8603. Fax: 516-674-8606.

Blanchard, Tsvi. *"Ga'al Yisrael:* Redemption as Social Redemption," from *Sacred Days,* 1995–1996. New York: CLAL, The National Center for Jewish Learning and Leadership, 1995.

Blumenthal, Rena. "Are You an Abraham or a Hannah?" Personal correspondence.

Bockman, David. "The Meaning of Elul," adapted from Breslov Research Institute. Personal correspondence.

Bokser, Ben Zion. "The Song of God's Presence." Personal correspondence.

Braver, Joseph L. "Honey on Rosh Hashanah." Personal correspondence.

———. *"Zokhrenu Le-Hayim:* To Life!" Personal correspondence.

Buber, Martin. *"Kadosh Atah V'nora Sh'mekha:* You Are Holy and Awesome," in On Zion: *The History of an Idea.* New York: Schocken Books, 1973.

Buckman, Lee. *"Ve-khol Ma-minim She-hu Tamim Po-olo: God is Wholehearted, So Must We Be."* Personal correspondence.

Bulka, Reuven. "The *Akedah:* A Test within a Test," from *More Torah Therapy: Further Reflections on the Weekly Sidrah and Special Occasions."* Hoboken, N.J.: KTAV, 1993.

Cardin, Nina Beth. "And God Remembered Sarah: Prayers and Rituals for an Infertile Couple on Rosh Hashanah," in *Tears of Sorrow, Seeds of Hope: A Jewish Spiritual Companion for Infertility and Pregnancy Loss.* Woodstock, VT: Jewish Lights, 1999.

———. "Prayer for an Expecting Couple during the Days of Awe," in *Tears of Sorrow, Seeds of Hope: A Jewish Spiritual Companion for Infertility and Pregnancy Loss.* Woodstock, VT: Jewish Lights, 1999.

Cohen, Diane. *"Hineni:* Here I am!" Personal correspondence.

———. *"L'El Orekh Din:* Justice Tempered with Mercy." Personal correspondence.

———. *"Malkhuyot, Zikhronot, Shofarot."* Personal correspondence.

Cohen, Jeffrey M. "Consequences of *Akedah,"* from *Prayer and Penitence: A Commentary on the High Holy Day Machzor.* Northvale, N.J.: Jason Aronson, 1994.

Cohen, Kenneth L. "And Abraham Grew Big—Like God." Personal correspondence.

Cohen, Tamara R. "Rosh Hashana Symbols Revealed." *Ma'yan's Journey,* Fall 2000. 13–14.

Cohler-Esses, Dianne. "The *Akedah:* Giving Freely." Personal correspondence.

Cooper, David A. "Mending the Soul, Mending the World," from *God Is a Verb: Kabbalah and the Practice of Mystical Judaism.* New York: Riverhead Books, 1997.

Deleon-Cohen, Abraham. "Benediction: Prayers around the Communal Table." Personal correspondence.

Diamond, James S. "How 'High' Are the High Holidays?" Personal correspondence.

Dorff, Elliot N. *"U'Tefilah:* Like Baseball, Prayer Needs Practice," from *Knowing God: Jewish Journeys to the Unknowable.* Northvale, N.J.: Jason Aronson, 1992.

Durlester, Adrian A. "Holiness and Righteousness," from *Random Musings for Shabbat-Shoftim 5758-Tzedek Tzedek.* Personal correspondence.

Edelman, Marian Wright. "Prayer for the Gift and Raising of Children," from *Guide My Feet: Prayers and Meditations on Loving and Working for Children.* Boston: Beacon Press, 1995.

Elcott, David. "To Be Human Is to Be Capable of Change." Personal correspondence.

Elliot, Diane. "Hannah's Tears." Personal correspondence.

Eron, Lewis John. "The Confessions of Elul." Personal correspondence.

———. "Elul." Personal correspondence.

Feld, Edward. "The Wailing of the Shofar: Feeling the Other's Pain." Originally written for and published by Rabbis for Human Rights.

Fine, David J. "Genesis 21 and 22: Two Versions of the Same Story." Personal correspondence.

Forman, Lori. *Oseh Shalom Bim'romav."* Personal correspondence.

———. "Who Gains Most from *Tzedakah?"* Personal correspondence.

Frankiel, Tamar, and Judy Greenfeld. "Forgive Yourself: A Guided Imagery Meditation," from *Entering the Temple of Dreams: Jewish Prayers, Movements and Meditations for the End of the Day.* Woodstock, VT: Jewish Lights, 2000.

Friedman, Edward M. *"Tik'u Va-Chodesh* Shofar: Linking Our Lives Below with the Unknowable Above." Personal correspondence.

Friedman, Michelle. "Memory and New Beginnings." Personal correspondence.

Gaber, Aaron. "Blessed Are Those Who Hear in the Shofar a Call to Walk by the Light of Your Presence." Personal correspondence.

Geduld, Herb. "The Trumpets of Rosh Hashanah." *Cleveland Jewish News,* September 25, 1992.

Gellman, Marc. "After These Things." *Moment Magazine,* May/June 1976.

Gillman, Neil. "On That Day, God Will Be One and God's Name One," from *Sacred Fragments.* Philadelphia: Jewish Publication Society, 1990.

———. *"V'khol Ma'aminim:* Seeing the Invisible," from *The Jewish Lights Spirituality Handbook: A Guide to Understanding, Exploring and Living a Spiritual Life.* Edited by Stuart M. Matlins. Woodstock, VT: Jewish Lights, 2001.

Ginsburg, Bruce. *"Zikhronot:* Remembering Our Noble Heritage." Personal correspondence.

Gold, Michael. "The Righteous Will See and Be Glad, the Pious Will Rejoice in Song." Personal correspondence.

———. "When God Answers Yes." Personal correspondence.

Goldfarb, Daniel C. "Abraham the Fundamentalist?" Personal correspondence.

Goldfarb, Irene. "Remembering and Transmitting." Personal correspondence.

Goldstein, Elyse. *"U'netaneh Tokef."* Personal correspondence.

Goldstein, H. Rafael. "Moving Time." Personal correspondence.

———. *"Shema:* Listen." Personal correspondence.

Golinkin, Noah. "Where Are You, God?" from *Say Something New Each Day,* N. Golinkin, 1973.

Goodman, Arnold M. "The Day of Remembering: The Family Reunion." Personal correspondence.

Gore, Al. "Change Begins with Me," from *Earth In The Balance.* New York: Houghton Mifflin, 1992.

Green, Arthur. All Section Introductions from *These Are the Words: A Vocabulary of Jewish Spiritual Life*. Woodstock, VT: Jewish Lights, 1999.

———. *"Hitbodedut:* Praying Separately," from *The Jewish Lights Spirituality Handbook: A Guide to Understanding, Exploring and Living a Spiritual Life*. Edited by Stuart M. Matlins. Woodstock, VT: Jewish Lights, 2001.

———. "Mending the World," from *The Jewish Lights Spirituality Handbook: A Guide to Understanding, Exploring and Living a Spiritual Life*. Edited by Stuart M. Matlins. Woodstock, VT: Jewish Lights, 2001.

Greenberg, Irving. "Jewish Courage to Hope for Redemption," from *The Jewish Way*. New York: Touchstone, 1988.

———. "The Power of Change," from *Sacred Days, 1995–1996*. New York: CLAL, The National Center for Jewish Learning and Leadership, 1995.

———. *"Teshuvah:* Tilt the World to the Side of Good." Personal correspondence.

———. *"Tikkun Olam,"* from *Sacred Days, 1995–1996*. New York: CLAL, The National Center for Jewish Learning and Leadership, 1995.

Greenberg, Sidney. "A Prayer for Life." Personal correspondence.

———. "Today ..." Personal correspondence.

Greenfield, Meg. *"Teshuvah:* Forgiveness and Exoneration Require Acknowledging Our Wrongdoing," from *Newsweek*, June 24, 1991. 72.

Greenspan, Mark B. *"Hamelekh:* Prayer and Worship, *Keva* and *Kavannah."* Personal correspondence.

———. "The Metaphor of Parenthood." Personal correspondence.

———. "Today Is the Only Day That Counts." Personal correspondence.

Greenspoon, David. "We Are Like the Shofar." Personal correspondence.

Gutterman, David. *"Akedah:* Sinai or Moriah?" Personal correspondence.

———. "The Past Lives in Me." Personal correspondence.

———. *"Teshuvah:* I Am Still Growing." Personal correspondence.

Halperin, Michael. "Apples and Honey." Personal correspondence.

———. "Sarah's Song." Personal correspondence.

Heller, Joshua. *"Akedah."* Personal correspondence.

Heschel, Abraham Joshua. *"Le-taken Olam B'malkhut Shaddai,"* from *The Insecurity of Freedom: Essays on Human Existence*. New York: Farrar, Straus & Giroux, 1966.

———. "The Shofar Calls—Something Is Asked of Me," from *Who is Man?* Stanford, CA: Stanford University Press, 1965.

———. *"Tefilah:* Prayer Is Spiritual Ecstasy," from *Man's Quest for God*. New York: Scribner, 1954.

Holden, Karen. *"Ve-Taher Leebenu:* Kindness." Personal correspondence.

Horwitz, Danny. *"Shema:* With All Your Heart," from United Synagogue for Conservative Judaism's "Torah Sparks."

Jacobs, Louis. "Yitzhak—He Laughed," from *The Book of Jewish Belief*. New York: Behrman House, 1984.

Jacobson, Simon. "Blowing God's Breath into the Shofar," originally published by The Meaningful Life Center (www.meaningfullife.com), 2005.

Jacoby, Jeff. *"U'Tzedakah:* Kindness and Compassion," from the *Boston Globe*, September 21, 1998.

Jewish Theological Seminary. *"Tefilah:* Will You Say a Prayer for Me?" from a 1991 mailing and advertisement campaign.

Johnson, Gershon. *"Selihot* Meditation." Personal correspondence.

Kahn-Troster, Rachel. "Demanding God's Presence." Personal correspondence.

———. "God Is a Source of Comfort." Personal correspondence.

———. "Naming Our Relationship with God." Personal correspondence.

———. *"Tashlich."* Personal correspondence.

Kamens, Sylvan D. *"Ve-ten Helkenu be-Toratekha:* The Lesson of Nature." Personal correspondence.

Kanter, Shamai. "Bread Crumbs for *Tashlikh."* Personal correspondence.

———. *"Teshuvah:* Making a U-turn." Personal correspondence.

———. *"V'kol D'mama Dakah Yishama:* God's Presence in the Silence." Personal correspondence.

Kaplan, Aryeh. "Shofar as a Symbol of Transformation," from *The Aryeh Kaplan Reader: The Gift He Left Behind: Collected Essays on Jewish Themes from the Noted Writer and Thinker*. Brooklyn, N.Y.: Mesorah Publications, 1983.

Kaplan, Mordecai M. *"Yom Hazikaron,"* from *Communings of the Spirit: The Journals of Mordecai M. Kaplan*. Detroit: Wayne State University Press and The Reconstructionist Press, 2001.

Katske, Erika. "Guided Meditation for *Tashlich,"* from "Women Welcoming the New Year: *Ma'yan* (Pre-Holiday) *Tashlich* and Study," September 25, 2000.

Kedar, Karyn D. "Fragments of Memory," from *The Dance of the Dolphin: Finding Prayer, Perspective and Meaning in the Stories of Our Lives*. Woodstock, VT: Jewish Lights Publishing, 2004.

———. "Think before You Speak," from *God Whispers: Stories of the Soul, Lessons of the Heart*. Woodstock, VT: Jewish Lights, 2000.

Kimelman, Reuven. "A Story of Consolation (1 Samuel 1:1–2:10)" Personal correspondence.

Kipling, Rudyard. "And the Two of Them Walked Together: A Parent's Advice to a Child," from *Rewards and Fairies*. Garden City, N.Y.: Doubleday, Page and Company, 1910.

Koppell, Bonnie. *"Avinu Malkenu."* Personal correspondence.

———. "Joy on Rosh Hashanah." Personal correspondence.

———. "A *Shanah Tovah."* Personal correspondence.

———. "Shofar on Shabbat." Personal correspondence.

———. "Silence as Prayer." Personal correspondence.

———. *"Zokhrenu L'hayim."* Personal correspondence.

Kraemer, David. "Remember." *Sh'ma: A Journal of Jewish Responsibility,* 26/513, April 26, 1996.

Kraiem, Elizabeth Leiman. "Opening the New Year." Personal correspondence.

Kula, Irwin. "The *Akedah,"* originally written for CLAL–The National Jewish Center for Learning and Leadership, 1992.

———, and Vanessa L. Ochs. "Casting Away Our Sins *(Tashlikh),"* from *The Book of Jewish Sacred Practices.* Woodstock, VT: Jewish Lights, 2001.

———. "Changing Your Fate for the Coming Year," from *The Book of Jewish Sacred Practices.* Woodstock, VT: Jewish Lights, 2001.

Kushner, Lawrence. "Generations," from *God was in this place and I, i did not know.* Woodstock, VT: Jewish Lights, 1994.

———. *"Hayom* ... Live in the presence of God," from *God was in this place and I, i did not know.* Woodstock, VT: Jewish Lights, 1994.

———. "Joining in the Great Return," from *Moment Magazine,* December, 1992. 45–46.

———. "A Modern Midrash," from *Five Cities of Refuge: Weekly Reflections on Genesis, Exodus, Leviticus, Numbers, and Deuteronomy.* With David Mamet. New York: Schocken, 2003.

———. *"Tefilah,"* from *The Book of Words: Talking Spiritual Life, Living Spiritual Talk.* Woodstock, VT: Jewish Lights, 1993.

———. *"Teshuvah:* Coming Home," from *The Book of Words: Talking Spiritual Life, Living Spiritual Talk.* Woodstock, VT: Jewish Lights, 1993.

———. "To Be Forgiven, Learn How to Forgive." Personal correspondence.

Lankin, Eric M. "Do We Really Want to Change?" Personal correspondence.

Levin, Ed. "God Tested Abraham: Our Moral Senses Are Tested Again and Again," from *Sh'ma: A Journal of Jewish Responsibility,* 26/514, May 10, 1996. 7.

Levin, Lynn. "Lines to My Son," from *A Few Questions about Paradise.* Bemidji, MN: Loonfeather Press, 2000.

Lieber, Valerie. "A *Selihot Ritual:* Changing Our Torah Mantles as We Change Ourselves." Personal correspondence.

Lipstadt, Deborah E. "The Days of Awe—or the Daze of Ah," in *The Jewish Spectator,* Fall, 1993.

———. "God Accepts Our Newer Selves: Genesis 21:1," in *The Jewish Spectator,* Fall, 1993.

———. "The Power of Our Most Banal Acts." *The Jewish Spectator,* Fall, 1993

———. *"U'teshuvah: Teshuvah* Affects Our Relationships, but Even More So, Ourselves," in *The Jewish Spectator,* Fall, 1993.

Lubliner, Immanuel. "Introduction to the Silent *Amidah,"* from *Siddur Sim Shalom.* Edited by Rabbi Jules Harlow. New York: The Rabbinical Assembly, 1985.

Mallach, Mark. *"Teshuvah."* Personal correspondence.

Maller, Allen S. "Forgiveness: A Bag of Nails." Personal correspondence.

———. *"Tashlich:* Casting-Off Sinprints." Personal correspondence.

Matt, Hershel. "Why the Shofar?" from *Walking Humbly with God: The Life and Writings of Rabbi Hershel Jonah Matt*. Edited by Daniel C. Matt. Hoboken, N.J.: Ktav, 1993.

Meir, Aryeh. "Amidah: Prayer Lifts Creation." Personal correspondence.

Meier, Levi S. "Trying to Believe," from *Seven Heavens: Inspirational Stories to Elevate Your Soul*. New York: Pitspopany Press, 2002.

Metzger, Laura. "Shofar: Because It's Imperfect." Personal correspondence.

Meyer, Marshall T. "Begin," from *You Are My Witness: The Living Words of Rabbi Marshall T. Meyer*. Edited by Jane Isay. New York: St. Martin's Press, 2004.

———. "Shofar: Awaken Our Slumbering Hearts," from *You Are My Witness: The Living Words of Rabbi Marshall T. Meyer*. Edited by Jane Isay. New York: St. Martin's Press, 2004.

Moline, Jack. "Shofar Ceremony." Personal correspondence.

Nathan, Steven. *"Avinu Malkeinu,* Graciously Answer Us, Even Though We Are Without Merit." Personal correspondence.

Olitzky, Kerry M. "A Fresh Start," from *100 Blessings Every Day: Daily Twelve Step Recovery Affirmations, Exercises for Personal Growth and Renewal Reflecting Seasons of the Jewish Year*. Woodstock, VT: Jewish Lights Publishing, 1993.

———. "Gratitude," from *100 Blessings Every Day: Daily Twelve Step Recovery Affirmations, Exercises for Personal Growth and Renewal Reflecting Seasons of the Jewish Year*. Woodstock, VT: Jewish Lights Publishing, 1993.

———. "Simplicity," from *100 Blessings Every Day: Daily Twelve Step Recovery Affirmations, Exercises for Personal Growth and Renewal Reflecting Seasons of the Jewish Year*. Woodstock, VT: Jewish Lights Publishing, 1993.

Oliver, Mary. "Who Made the World?" from *Kol Haneshama: Mahzor Leyamim Nora'im (Prayerbook for the Days of Awe)*, Elkins Park, PA: Reconstructionist Press, 1999.

Orenstein, Debra. *"Avinu Malkeynu*—Our Father, Our King." Personal correspondence.

———. "The Binding of Sarah," from *Lifecylces, Vol. 2: Jewish Women on Biblical Themes in Contemporary Life*. Edited by Debra Orenstein and Jane Rachel Litman. Woodstock, VT: Jewish Lights, 2000.

———. "Blessings for a Sweet New Year." Personal correspondence.

———. "Memory: A Point of Entry to Our Past," from *Lifecylces, Vol. 2: Jewish Women on Biblical Themes in Contemporary Life*. Edited by Debra Orenstein and Jane Rachel Litman. Woodstock, VT: Jewish Lights, 2000.

Parnes, Stephan O. *"Kol ha-Shofar:* The Voice of the Shofar." Personal correspondence.

Pearce, Stephen S. "Shofar: The Clarion Call of Hope." Personal correspondence.

Pincus, Helen Weiss. "My Father's Shofar." Personal correspondence.

Prager, Marcia. "Blessing God," from *The Path of Blessing: Experiencing the Energy and Abundance of the Divine.* Woodstock, VT: Jewish Lights, 2003.

Pressman, Jacob. "Prayer for a Happy New Year." Personal correspondence.

Raskas, Bernard Solomon. *"Akedah:* The Two of Them Went Together." Personal correspondence.

Raz, Simcha. "Psalm 27:4 " … Dwell in the House of the Lord All the Days of My Life." Personal correspondence.

Remen, Rachel Naomi. *"Teshuvah:* Is My Life Tuned to My Own Note?" from *My Grandfather's Blessings: Stories of Strength, Refuge, and Belonging.* New York: Riverhead Books, 2000.

Reuben, Steven Carr. "Choosing to Remember." Personal correspondence.

———. *"Hayom Harat Olam:* Why Not You?" Personal correspondence.

Richman, Leah. *"Tashlich* Thoughts." Personal correspondence.

Roiphe, Anne. "Memory," from *Generation Without Memory.* New York: Simon and Schuster, 1981.

Rosen, David. *"Teshuvah:* Why Should I Go Elsewhere?" Personal correspondence.

Rubin, Yehoshua. *"U'teshuvah:* How Do People Change—Through Honey or Vinegar?" Personal correspondence.

Sacks, Jonathan. "Can Faith Be Justified?" from *Radical Then, Radical Now.* London: Continuum International Publishing Group, 2003.

———. "The Importance of Children." From the BBC Rosh Hashanah Broadcast "Remembering for the Future." BBC: September 12, 2004.

Schachter-Shalomi, Zalman. *"Alenu:* Is Judaism then Asserting Itself as the One 'True' Religion?" from *Broken Tablets: Restoring the Ten Commandments and Ourselves.* Edited by Rachel S. Mikva. Woodstock, VT: Jewish Lights, 1999.

———. "Getting Rid of the Mud," in *Wrapped in a Holy Flame: Teachings and Tales of the Hasidic Masters.* San Francisco: Jossey-Bass, 2003.

———. "My Script." *Kol Haneshama: Mahzor Leyamim Nora'im (Prayerbook for the Days of Awe).* Elkins Park, PA: Reconstructionist Press, 1999.

———. "Shofar: The Primal Scream," in *Wrapped in a Holy Flame: Teachings and Tales of the Hasidic Masters.* San Francisco: Jossey-Bass, 2003.

Scheinberg, Robert. "The *Akedah* from Isaac's Point of View." Personal correspondence.

Schulweis, Harold M. "It Is Never Too Late." Personal correspondence.

Schwartz, Dannel I. *"Amidah:* Purify Our Hearts to Serve You in Truth." Personal correspondence.

Schwartz, Howard. "The Dream of Isaac." Personal correspondence.

Schwartz, Rachel. "Sacred Questions." Personal correspondence.

Shapiro, Rami. "Opening Our Eyes," from *Kol Haneshama: Mahzor Leyamim Nora'im (Prayerbook for the Days of Awe)*. Elkins Park, PA: Reconstructionist Press, 1999.

———. "Our Goal: Shalom." Personal correspondence.

Shendelman, Sara, and Avram Davis. "Allowing the Hand of God to Worth through Us," from *Traditions: The Complete Book of Prayers, Rituals, and Blessings for Every Jewish Home*. New York: Hyperion, 1998.

Shevitz, Dan. "At Water's Edge …We Seek Your Presence." Personal correspondence.

Siegel, Bernie. "God Remembers Everything You Forget." Personal correspondence.

Siegel, Danny. "A Blessing," from *Danny Siegel's Bar and Bat Mitzvah Book*. Pittsboro, N.C.: The Town Hall Press, 2004.

———. "With a Kiss," from *The Meadow Bevond the Meadow*. Pittsboro, N.C.: The Town House Press, 1991.

Siegel, Michael S. "Teaching Children Jewish Ethics." Personal correspondence.

Silverman, Hillel E. "Debtors Are We All." Personal correspondence.

Silverstein, Mordechai. "We Are Dear Children to God." Personal correspondence.

Singer, Isaac Bashevis. "*Tefilah:* Why We Praise God," from *The Death of Methuselah and Other Stories*. New York: New American Library, 1989.

Spielberg, Steven. "*Shema:* Those Little Whispers." Interview by James Lipton, *Inside the Actor's Studio*, Bravo! March 5, 1999.

Stephen S. Wise Temple. "Meaning of the Blasts: One, Three, Nine, Longest," from *High Holy Day Family Service* of Stephen S. Wise Temple. Los Angeles, CA, 1992.

Strassfeld, Michael. "A Guide to Greetings," from *Kol Haneshama: Mahzor Leyamim Nora'im (Prayerbook for the Days of Awe)*, Elkins Park, PA: Reconstructionist Press, 1999.

Telushkin, Joseph. "*U'Tefilah,*" from *The Book of Jewish Values*. New York: Bell Tower, 2000.

Teplitz, Saul. "Remembrance: The Key to Redemption," from *The Courage to Change*. Middle Village, N.Y.: Jonathan David Publishers, 1999.

Troster, Lawrence. "Knowing Creation." Personal correspondence.

———. "The Meaning of the Shofar," from the newsletter of the Coalition on the Environment and Jewish Life (COEJL). September, 2004.

———. "*U'teshuvah:* An Environmental Confession." Personal correspondence.

Twerski, Abraham J. "*Avinu Malkenu:* God, Help Us Raise the Level of Your People's Jewish/Spiritual Consciousness," from *Not Just Stories*. Brooklyn, NY: Shaar Press, 2001.

Umansky, Ellen M. *"Zakhor,"* from *Sacred Days, 1995–1996.* New York: CLAL, The National Center for Jewish Learning and Leadership, 1995.

Uhrbach, Jan R. "The Meaning of Our Lives." Personal correspondence.

———. *"Teshuvah*—A Creative Process." Personal correspondence.

Walter, Roy A. "God of Creation," from *Gabriel's Palace: Jewish Mystical Tales.* Selected and retold by Howard Schwartz. New York: Oxford University Press, 1993.

Waskow, Arthur. "Are "Politics" and Prophetic Social Justice the Same?" Personal correspondence.

Waxman, Jonathan. "Like a Fading Flower, a Passing Shadow, a Fugitive Cloud and a Vanishing Dream." Personal correspondence.

Weinberg, Sheila Peltz. "Meditation on Psalm 27," from *Kol Haneshama: Mahzor Leyamim Nora'im (Prayerbook for the Days of Awe),* Elkins Park, PA: Reconstructionist Press, 1999.

———."The Creation of Light." *Kol Haneshama: Mahzor Leyamim Nora'im (Prayerbook for the Days of Awe),* Elkins Park, PA: Reconstructionist Press, 1999.

Weiss, Eric. "Spiritual Flutterings." Personal correspondence.

Wiesel, Elie. "What Being Jewish Means to Me," from the American Jewish Committee advertisement series "What Being Jewish Means to Me." Originally published September 27, 2000.

Wilshire Boulevard Temple. "A Meditation for the New Year," from the Wilshire Boulevard Temple High Holy Day Mahzor. Los Angeles, 1990.

———. "Silent Meditation," from the Wilshire Boulevard Temple High Holy Day Mahzor. Los Angeles, 1990.

———. *"Yom Hazikaron:* This Day of the Year," from the Wilshire Boulevard Temple High Holy Day Mahzor. Los Angeles, 1990.

———. *"Zikhronot* Meditation," from the Wilshire Boulevard Temple High Holy Day Mahzor. Los Angeles, 1990.

Wolf, Arnold Jacob. "The Meaning of Mitzvah." Personal correspondence.

Wolpe, David J. "The *Akedah:* Coming Down the Mountain." Personal correspondence.

———. "Crime and Punishment." Personal correspondence.

———. "Sacred Blessing," in *The Jewish Week,* June 15, 2001.

———. *"Shema:* Awakening a Love of God." Personal correspondence.

———. "Who Will Live and Who Will Die?" Personal correspondence.

Wolpe, Gerald I. *"Hineni:* Send me!" Personal correspondence.

Yehuda, Zvi. "Prayer from the Heart Is Better than Prayer from the Lips," from *Cleveland Jewish News,* December 16, 1999.

Zevin, S.Y. "Cleansed with Tears," from *A Treasury of Chassidic Tales on the Festivals.* New York: Artscroll Mesorah, 1981.

Zevit, Shawn Israel. "Hearing the Silent Scream: And God Heard the Voice of the Boy." Personal correspondence.

———. "Naming the Day." Personal correspondence.

Zimmern, Janet. "A Prayer for Blowing Shofar," from *Ma'yan's Journey,* Fall 2000. 11–12.

Traditional Material

Carlebach, Shlomo. *"Shema Yisrael:* We Close Our Eyes for *Shema* because We're Blind."

De Leon, Moses. "Enlighten Our Eyes in Your Torah: Torah as Unripe Fruit," from Daniel C. Matt, *The Essential Kabbalah: The Heart of Jewish Mysticism* San Francisco: HarperSanFrancisco, 1994.

Frankl, Viktor E. "A Weak Faith, a Strong Faith."

Hafetz Hayyim. *"Avinu Malkenu:* With Compassion and with Favor."

———. "The Power of Groundless Hate."

Kook, Avraham Isaac. "Footsteps of the Messiah."

———. "God Is King."

Loth Leibman, Joshua. "Hayom—Today!"

Luzzatto, Samuel David. "Spontaneity in Prayer." *Mahzor B'nai Roma.*

Pinchas of Koretz. "A Paradox: Praying for Oneself or Praying for the *Shekhinah,"* from *Midrash Pinhas.*

Rokeah, Sholom ben Elazar of Belz. *"Teshuvah* as Ending Self-Exile."

Romero, Oscar. "The Future."

Sanskrit Proverb. "The Promise of This Day," from *Kol Haneshama: Mahzor Leyamim Nora'im (Prayerbook for the Days of Awe),* Elkins Park, PA: Reconstructionist Press, 1999.

Tagore, Rabindranath. "Benediction."

Test, Robert N. "Praise the Lord, O My Soul: Let Every Fiber of My Being Praise God."

"Hold On to What Is Good."

"U'Teshuvah: Changing Ourselves."

Hasidic Tales and Teachings

Baer, Dov of Mezritch. "A Paradox: Praying for Oneself or Praying for the *Shekhinah,"* from *Maggid D'varav L'Ya'akov* 4.

———. "Individual Prayer," in *God in All Moments: Mystical and Practical Spiritual Wisdom from Hasidic Masters.* Edited and translated by Or Rose with Ebn D. Leader. Woodstock, VT: Jewish Lights, 2004.

"Those Who Err Are Closest to God."

Mendel, Menahem of Kotzk. "Shofar."

Nahum, Menachem of Chernobyl. "Nightly Teshuvah," in *God in All Moments: Mystical and Practical Spiritual Wisdom from Hasidic Masters.* Edited and translated by Or Rose with Ebn D. Leader. Woodstock, VT: Jewish Lights, 2004.

———. *"Tzedakah:* The Root of Life," in *God in All Moments: Mystical and Practical Spiritual Wisdom from Hasidic Masters.* Edited and translated by Or Rose with Ebn D. Leader. Woodstock, VT: Jewish Lights, 2004.

Sources from the Apochrypha

"Confession."
"Forgive Your Neighbors."

Sources from Midrash

"You and Your Neighbor."
"The Torah Was Given with the Sound of the Shofar."
"Thy Children Shall Return to Their Own Borders," quoted in Nahum N. Glatzer *Hammer on the Rock.* Translated by Jacob Sloan. New York: Schocken, 1948.
"The First Day of the Year."
"The Lesson of Abraham."
"Passing before God."
"Four Results of Sin."
"God Remembers Both Mercy and Judgment."
"Shofar and Judgment."
"The Original Shofar."
"Ahavah Rabbah: Enlighten Our Eyes in Your Torah."

Sources from Talmud

"How to Remember Yourself."
"A New Year for Years."
"Not Just Today, But Every Day."
"Standing in Our Defense"
"The Sound of the Shofar."

Sources from Torah

"Avinu Malkenu, Judge us according to Our Actions."
"Choose Life That You May Live."

"A Clean Heart."
"God Is Merciful."
"A Sacred Occasion."
"Sound the Shofar."

Sources from Unknown Authors

"Forgiveness."
"God's Boxes."
"How Can I Sound the Shofar?"
"It Is Not Enough to Repent."
"The Kindness of Your Youth."
"Prayer for Rosh Hashanah Evening."
"Recipe for a New Year."
"*Selihah:* Forgiveness."
"The Shofar Is Not Magic."
"*Shofarot.*"
"*Tashlikh.*"
"*U'Tefilah:* The Prayer of an Anonymous Confederate Soldier."
"*Ve-yay-asu Kulam Agudah* Ehat ... The Need for Community."

Previously Existing Material Adapted by Rabbi Dov Peretz Elkins (Attributed to D.P.E.)

"*Adam Yesodo Me-Afar:* Our Origin Is Dust and Our End Is Dust."
"*Alenu: Le-takken Olam:* 'To Bring Healing Perspective.'"
"*Alenu:* Perfecting Society through Reduced Consumption."
"*Aleinu:* The Particular and the Universal."
"*Al Neesekha She-be-khol Yom Imanu.*"
"*Amidah:* Saying Grace."
"Avinu Malkenu: Become a Ruler over Yourself."
"*Avinu Malkeinu:* Graciously Answer Us, Even Though We Are Without Merits."
"Awake You Slumberers from Your Sleep: Shofar and Social Responsibility."
"*Ayom Ve-kadosh:* You Are a Revered and Holy God."
"The Call to Battle."
"The Day of Remembrance."
"The Divinity Inside You."
"Faith Comes Slowly, Gradually."
"God at Work ... Creating the World."

"How We Become Wise, How We Change."
"Kiddush: Re-Enactment of Creation."
"L'El Orekh Din: God Searches All Hearts on the Day of Judgment."
"Maimonides' Five Steps to True *Teshuvah.*"
"Melekh Hafetz Ba-Hayyim: God Desires Life."
"A New Year—Turning Stone into Light."
"Our Lives Are in the Balance: Who Shall Live and Who Shall Die?"
"Sanctify Us through Your Mitzvot."
"Shofar: Cleaning the Earth for Those Who Come after Us."
"Sim Shalom: Grant Peace, Goodness, Kindness to All Your People."
"Sim Shalom: Thoughts on War and Peace."
"Sim Shalom: You Have Revealed to Us Your Life-Giving Torah."
"Teshuvah: Taking Care of Others."
"Teshuvah: Lessons from a Fish."
"Three Lessons about the High Holy Days from the Musar Movement."
"U'Tefilah: Thanking God for God's World."
"U'teshuvah: Much More than Repentance."
"Ve-khol Ma-aminim: Permanent Trust or Permanent Mistrust."
"V'khol Ma'aminim: We Believe, We Hope."
"Ve-khol Ma-aminim: What Is True Faith?"
"We Pass By God, One by One, Like a Flock of Sheep."
"Who Is Holding Whom?"
"Why *Zikhronot?*"
"You Record and Seal, Count and Measure."
"Zikhronot: Memory Transfigures."

About the Contributors

Ruth Abusch-Magder received her rabbinic ordination from Hebrew Union College–Jewish Institute of Religion in 2006. Her doctorate in religious studies from Yale is called *Home-made Judaism: Food and Domestic Judaism in Germany and America, 1850-1914.*

Rabbi Jacob Agus was spiritual leader of Beth El Congregation in Baltimore, Maryland, author of many books, and a leading philosopher in the Conservative Movement in Judaism.

Rabbi Morris Adler was spiritual leader of Shaarey Zedek Congregation in Southfield, Michigan.

Dr. David S. Ariel is the president of Siegal College in Cleveland, Ohio.

Rabbi Bradley Shavit Artson is the dean of the Zigler School of Rabbinic Studies at the University of Judaism, where he is vice president. He is the author of *The Bedside Torah: Wisdom, Dreams, and Visions.*

Rabbi Dov Baer of Mezritch, 1710–1772, was the successor to the Baal Shem Tov as leader of the Hasidic movement.

Rabbi Leila Gal Berner received her ordination from the Reconstructionist Rabbinical College and a doctorate in medieval Jewish Studies from UCLA. She is spiritual leader of Kol Ami, The Northern Virginia Reconstructionist Community.

Jeff Bernhardt is a Jewish communal professional, licensed clinical social worker, educator, and writer living in Los Angeles. His work can be found in the anthology *Mentsh*, and he is the author of the High Holiday themed play *Who Shall Live…?*

June Bingham is an author and playwright listed in *Who's Who in America*. She has thirteen grandchildren.

Dr. Tsvi Blanchard is the director of organizational development of CLAL and a psychotherapist in private practice. In addition to his work in Jewish thought, his parables and stories have been widely anthologized.

Rabbi Rena Blumenthal is the Rose and Irving Rachlin Advisor to Students at Vassar College.

David Bockman, originally from California, was ordained at the Jewish Theological Seminary in 1986. He has played trumpet, cooked kosher jambalaya, and taught Torah in a number of great jazz cities, including Kansas City, New Orleans, and Bergenfield, New Jersey.

Rabbi Ben Zion Bokser was spiritual leader of the Forest Hills Jewish Center, author of many books, and a leading philosopher in the Conservative Movement.

Rabbi Joseph L. Braver was a Jewish educator, filling key positions of leadership in national and local Jewish educational organizations.

Martin Buber, born in Germany, was a philosopher, author and professor at the Hebrew University in Jerusalem until his death in 1965.

Rabbi Lee Buckman works at the Jewish Academy of Metro Detroit.

Rabbi Reuven Bulka is spiritual leader of Congregation Machzikei Hadas in Ottawa, Ontario, Canada, and is past chair of the Rabbinic Cabinet of Israel Bonds.

Rabbi Nina Beth Cardin is director of Jewish life at the Jewish Community Center of Baltimore. She is the author of *Tears of Sorrow, Seeds of Hope: A Jewish Spiritual Companion for Infertility and Pregnancy Loss.*

Rabbi Shlomo Carlebach was a songwriter, storyteller, traveling minstrel and teacher whose spirituality influenced thousands throughout the world.

Rabbi Diane Cohen was ordained by the Jewish Theological Seminary of America in 1993 and has served a variety of congregations. Her work includes an exploration of the spiritual dimension of observance as well as the writing of children's stories for her grandchildren.

Rabbi Jeffrey M. Cohen is the author of some eighteen books on the festivals and liturgy. He is the retired rabbi of the largest Orthodox congregation in Britain, and former lecturer at Jews' College of London.

Rabbi Kenneth L. Cohen is director of American University Hillel in Washington, D.C.

Tamara L. Cohen teaches at the University of Florida.

Rabbi Dianne Cohler-Esses is the first woman from the Syrian Jewish community to become a rabbi, ordained in 1995 by the Jewish Theological Seminary. She currently serves as a scholar in residence at UJA Federation. She lives in New York City with her husband and three children.

Rabbi David A. Cooper is author of *God Is a Verb, The Handbook of Jewish Meditation Practices: A Guide to Enriching the Sabbath and Other Days of Your Life* and *Ecstatic Kabbalah,* and leads spiritual retreats all over the world.

Avram Davis is a teacher of Jewish meditation and spirituality, and founder and codirector of an independent center for Jewish learning and meditation, Chochmat HaLev in Berkeley, California. He is the author of *The Way of Flame: A Guide to the Forgotten Mystical Tradition of Jewish Meditation.*

Moses deLeon, a thirteenth century rabbi, is traditionally thought of as the author of the Zohar.

Abraham Deleon-Cohen is spiritual leader of Temple Benarroch in Miami Beach, Florida.

Rabbi James S. Diamond was director of the Center for Jewish Life/Princeton Hillel from 1995–2004. He teaches in the Program in Judaic Studies at Princeton University.

Rabbi Elliot N. Dorff is rector and Distinguished Professor of Philosophy at the University of Judaism in Los Angeles. He is the author of *Knowing God: Jewish Journeys to the Unknowable, The Way Into* Tikkun Olam *(Repairing the World)* and many other books.

Adrian A. Durlester is a Jewish educator in the Greater Washington, D.C. metro area.

Marion Wright Edelman is president of the Children's Defense Fund.

Dr. David Elcott is United States director of interreligious affairs of the American Jewish Committee.

Diane Elliot, senior rabbinical student at the Academy for Jewish Religion, California, is active in the Jewish renewal movement and has served as student rabbi with both the Elijah Minyan and Havurat Shir Ha-Yam in San Diego. Trained as a dancer, choreographer, and teacher of body-mind centering, she has been in private practice as a somatic movement therapist for the past twenty years.

Rabbi Lewis John Eron, PhD, is currently the Jewish community chaplain for the Jewish Federation of Southern New Jersey and the rabbi at the Jewish Geriatric Home in Cherry Hill, New Jersey. He enjoys reading and writing stories, poems, and theology, and cooking for his family.

Rabbi Edward Feld is rabbi-in-residence at the Jewish Theological Seminary of America and author of *The Spirit of Renewal: Finding Faith after the Holocaust.* He also serves on the executive committee of Rabbis for Human Rights.

Rabbi David J. Fine is rabbi of Shaarei Tikvah, The Scarsdale Conservative Congregation, and is a PhD candidate in modern European history at the graduate center, City University of New York.

Rabbi Lori Forman is assistant principal of Bergen County School of Jewish Studies in New Jersey. She is coauthor of *Restful Reflections: Nighttime Inspiration to Calm the Soul, Based on Jewish Wisdom* and *Sacred Intentions: Daily Inspiration to Strengthen the Spirit, Based on Jewish Wisdom.*

Tamar Frankiel, PhD, teaches at the University of California, Riverside, and lectures frequently on topics of Jewish mysticism. She is the author of *The Gift of Kabbalah: Discovering the Secrets of Heaven, Renewing Your Life on Earth* and *Kabbalah: A Brief Introduction for Christians.*

Viktor E. Frankl (1905–1997) was a leading psychotherapist in Vienna.

Rabbi Edward M. Friedman has served pulpits in Bloomfield, Connecticut, Charleston, South Carolina, Northampton, Massachusetts, and Dallas, Texas. He is co-chair of the Greater Carolinas Association of Rabbis Wilderness Interfaith Institute held annually in North Carolina.

Michelle Friedman, MD, is director of pastoral counseling, Yeshivat Chovevei Torah Rabbinical School and assistant professor of clinical psychiatry, Mt. Sinai Hospital and Medical Center. She has a private practice of psychiatry and psychoanalysis in Manhattan.

Rabbi Aaron Gaber is a graduate of the Jewish Theological Seminary and is the spiritual leader of Congregation Beth Judah in Ventnor, New Jersey. He is married to Sharon Bromberg and they have four children.

Herb Geduld is a writer who lives in Cleveland, Ohio.

Rabbi Marc Gellman is spiritual leader of Temple Beth Torah, Melville, New York, and a well known media personality. He writes a weekly column for *Newsweek.*

Rabbi Neil Gillman is professor of Jewish Philosophy at the Jewish Theological Seminary in New York, where he has also served as chair of the department of Jewish philosophy and dean of the Rabbinical School. He is the author of *Traces of God: Seeing God in Torah, History and Everyday Life, The Way Into Encountering God in Judaism,* and other books.

Rabbi Bruce Ginsburg is the spiritual leader of Congregation Sons of Israel, Woodmere, New York, and president of the Union for Traditional Judaism.

Rabbi Michael Gold is the spiritual leader of Temple Beth Torah, Tamarac, Florida. His newest book is *The Ten Journeys of Life.*

Rabbi Daniel C. Goldfarb is the director of the Conservative Yeshiva of the United Synagogue of Conservative Judaism in Jerusalem. A native of Boston, he made *aliyah* to Israel in 1976 and worked as a lawyer for the government of Israel and in private practice until 2000.

Irene Goldfarb is a wife (1 husband), mother (4 children), grandmother (3 grandsons), retired certified financial planner, and graduate of Douglass College. Her degrees are from Rutgers University (BS) and the Wharton School, University of Pennsylvania (MBA).

Rabbi Elyse Goldstein is the author of *ReVisions: Seeing Torah through a Feminist Lens* and the editor of *The Women's Torah Commentary* and *The Women's Haftarah Commentary.*

Rabbi H. Rafael Goldstein is vice president for Jewish affairs of the Jewish Family and Children's Service of Phoenix, Arizona, and the rabbi of Congregation Kol Haneshamah in Irvine, California.

Rabbi Noah Golinkin was rabbi emeritus at Beth Shalom Congregation in Columbia, Maryland, and was the founder of the Institute for Jewish Literacy.

Rabbi Arnold M. Goodman is the senior rabbinic scholar and rabbi emeritus of the Ahavath Achim Synagogue in Atlanta, Georgia. He and his wife now live in Jerusalem. He is a past president of the Rabbinical Assembly.

Al Gore was the vice president of the United States and has written several books on the environment.

Rabbi Arthur Green is professor of Jewish philosophy and religion at Hebrew College, Boston, and rector of the rabbinical school. He is the author of *Ehyeh: A Kabbalah for Tomorrow, Seek My Face: A Jewish Mystical Theology,* and other books.

Rabbi Irving Greenberg is president of Jewish Life Network/Steinhardt Foundation, and author of several books. Jewish Life Network's mission is to create new institutions and initiatives to enrich the inner life (religious, cultural, institutional) of American Jewry. Rabbi Greenberg also served as Chairman of the United States Holocaust Memorial Council from 2000–2002.

Rabbi Sidney Greenberg was rabbi emeritus at Temple Sinai, Dresher, Pennsylvania, and author or editor of over thirty-five books.

Judy Greenfeld is the second invested cantor at Temple Emanuel in Beverly Hills, California. She leads the New Emanuel *minyan,* a weekly progressive prayer service.

Meg Greenfield was a *Washington Post* and *Newsweek* editorial writer.

Rabbi Mark B. Greenspan lights fires in his congregation and puts them out in his home town of Oceanside. He is the spiritual leader of the Oceanside Jewish Center on Long Island and also a volunteer firefighter in the Oceanside Fire Department.

Rabbi David Greenspoon serves Congregation Knesset Israel in Pittsefield, Massachusetts.

Rabbi David Gutterman is a graduate of Yeshiva University, Mirrer Yeshiva, Sacred Heart University, and holds two *semichot.* He is currently a doctoral student in Talmud and rabbinics. He is a rabbi with the Jewish Federation of Greater Philadelphia and executive director of VAAD: Board of Rabbis of Greater Philadelphia.

Hafetz Hayyim (Rabbi Yisrael Meir Kagan HaKohen) 1838–1933, was a great rabbinic scholar in Poland.

Michael Halperin is an author, playwright, screen and television writer. He holds a BA degree from the University of Southern California Annenberg School of Communication, a PhD in film studies and teaches in the School of Film and Television at Loyola Marymount University, Los Angeles, California.

Rabbi Joshua Heller, a ninth generation rabbi, serves as spiritual leader of Congregation Bnai Torah in Sandy Springs, Georgia. He previously served as director of distance learning for the Jewish Theological Seminary.

Rabbi Abraham Joshua Heschel was professor of Jewish mysticism and philosophy at the Jewish Theological Seminary, and author of many books on Jewish thought.

Karen Holden is a poet, artist, and teacher. A native of Los Angeles, she currently works in development at the USC School of Business.

Rabbi Danny Horwitz serves Congregation Brith Shalom, Bellaire, Texas.

Rabbi Simon Jacobson is the author of the best-selling book *Toward a Meaningful Life.* He heads The Meaningful Life Center, presenting the teachings of Torah to people of all backgrounds, in accessible and relevant language, enabling them to lead more meaningful lives. He is a sought-after scholar and lecturer on Jewish thought and its contemporary application, speaking to diverse audiences worldwide.

Rabbi Dr. Louis Jacobs is rabbi emeritus at New London Synagogue, London, England, and author of many books on Jewish thought.

Jeff Jacoby is a syndicated columnist for the *Boston Globe.*

Rabbi Gershon Johnson has served Temple Beth Haverim in Agoura, Califronia since 1988. He is married to Sharene, and they are parents to Gavriel (and Shalvi), Rachel, and Aliza, and grandparents to Noson and Sarah.

Rachel Kahn-Troster is a rabbinical student at the Jewish Theological Seminary. She lives in New York, where she teaches midrash to Jews of all ages.

Rabbi Sylvan D. Kamens is a retired Conservative rabbi who served over forty years in the pulpit. He has written a number of liturgical poems and prayers.

Rabbi Shamai Kanter, retired rabbi of Temple Beth El, Rochester, New York, and past editor of *Conservative Judaism,* is the author of *Rabban Gamliel: The Legal Traditions.*

Rabbi Aryeh Kaplan was a scientist, scholar and author of many books.

Rabbi Mordecai M. Kaplan was a graduate of the Jewish Theological Seminary where he taught philosophy and homiletics for many years. He is the founder of Reconstructionist Judaism.

Erika Katske has been writing about, teaching, speaking on and organizing Jewish, feminist and lesbian, gay, bisexual and transgender social justice issues for more than ten years. She currently works as an interfaith community organizer in San Francisco with the San Francisco Organizing Project, a member of the PICO National Network.

Rabbi Karyn D. Kedar is senior rabbi at B'nai Jehoshua Beth Elohim in Glenview, Illinois. She is the author of *God Whispers: Stories of the Soul, Lessons of the Heart* and *Our Dance with God: Finding Prayer, Perspective and Meaning in the Stories of Our Lives.*

Reuven Kimelman is a professor of classical Judaica at Brandeis University.

Rudyard Kipling (1865–1936) was a British writer, and recipient of the Nobel Prize in Literature in 1907.

Rabbi Avraham Isaac Kook was first chief rabbi of the Land of Israel. He died in Jerusalem in 1935.

Rabbi Bonnie Koppell serves as a rabbi in the greater Phoenix Jewish community. An army reserve chaplain, holding the rank of colonel, Rabbi Koppell was the first female rabbi in the U.S. military.

David Kraemer is Joseph J. and Dora Abbell Librarian and Professor of Talmud and Rabbinics at the Jewish Theological Seminary. His most recent book is *The Gastronomic Jew: A History of Jewish Eating.*

Elizabeth Leiman Kraiem studies at the Drisha Institute, and is a member of Congregation B'nai Jeshurun in Manhattan.

Rabbi Irwin Kula is president of CLAL–The National Jewish Center for Learning and Leadership, author of *Yearning: Finding Wisdom in our Deepest Desires* and coeditor of *The Book of Jewish Sacred Practices: CLAL's Guide to Everyday and Holiday Rituals and Blessings.*

Rabbi Lawrence Kushner is Emanu-El Scholar at Congregation Emanu-El in San Francisco and author of *The Book of Words: Talking Spiritual Life, Living Spiritual Talk, The Way Into Jewish Mystical Tradition,* and many other books on Jewish spirituality.

Rabbi Eric M. Lankin, DMin, is chief, institutional advancement and education, of the Jewish National Fund.

Ed Levin has contributed to *Sh'ma: A Journal of Jewish Responsibility*.

Lynn Levin is the author of two poetry collections, *Imaginarium and A Few Questions about Paradise*. She teaches creative writing at the University of Pennsylvania and at Drexel University, where she is also executive producer of the cable TV show, *The Drexel InterView*.

Rabbi Valerie Lieber serves Temple Israel of Jamaica in Queens, New York.

Dr. Deborah E. Lipstadt is Dorot Professor of Modern Jewish History and Holocaust Studies at Emory University. She is the author most recently of *History on Trial: My Day in Court with Holocaust Denier David Irving*, which is the story of her successful libel defense in the British High Court of Justice.

Rabbi Joshua Loth Leibman was a well known reform rabbi in the Boston area.

Rabbi Immanuel Lubliner was rabbi emeritus of the Greenburgh Hebrew Center in Dobbs Ferry, New York.

Samuel David Luzzatto (1800–1865) was a well known Italian Hebraist and biblical commentator.

Rabbi Mark Mallach serves at Temple Beth Ahm, Springfield, New Jersey.

Rabbi Allen S. Maller recently retired as rabbi of Temple Akiva of Culver City after thirty-nine years. He is the author of *God, Sex, and Kabbalah* and editor of the Tikkun Series of High Holiday Prayer Books.

Rabbi Hershel Matt was a beloved spiritual leader, passionate about serving God through the power of prayer and the enhancement of ritual, and passionate about serving the Jewish people.

Rabbi Aryeh Meir is dean of admissions and is on the faculty of the Academy for Jewish Religion in Riverdale, New York.

Rabbi Menachem Mendel of Kotzk, better known as the Kotzker Rebbe (1787–1859), was a Hasidic leader.

Rabbi Laura Metzger is an independent rabbi in Louisville, Kentucky, where she serves as a spiritual resource to the unaffiliated, works with the residents of the Jewish nursing home, and teaches in Jewish and interfaith settings. With husband Cantor David Lipp and daughter Natania, she is surrounded with music, books and love.

Rabbi Levi Meier, PhD, is Jewish chaplain of Cedars-Sinai Medical Center in Los Angeles. He is a licensed clinical psychologist and a marriage, family, and child therapist.

Rabbi Marshall T. Meyer was a rabbi in Argentina for twenty-five years and a staunch fighter for human rights during the military regime there. He founded the Seminario Rabinico in Buenos Aires and upon his return to the United States, he rebuilt Congregation Bnai Jeshurun on the Upper West Side in New York City.

Rabbi Jack Moline has been rabbi of Agudas Achim Congregation in Alexandri, Virginia since 1987.

Rabbi Menachem Nahum of Chernobyl was born in Garinsk, Volhynia, 1730, and died in Chernobyl, Ukraine, 1797. He was a student of the Baal Shem Tov and the Maggid of Mezritch, and was one of the pioneers of the Hasidic movement.

Rabbi Steven Nathan, spiritual leader of Temple Menorah Kneseth Chai in Philadelphia, was ordained from the Reconstructionist Rabbinical College and trained with Peninnah Schramm at the Institute for Contemporary Midrash. He is also a graduate of the Meditation Leadership Training Program at Elat Chayyim. His weekly Torah commentaries can be found at www.groups.yahoo.com/group/mindfultorah.

Vanessa L. Ochs, PhD, is director of Jewish studies at the University of Virginia, and associate professor of religious studies. She is coeditor of *The Book of Jewish Sacred Practices: CLAL's Guide to Everyday and Holiday Rituals and Blessings* and author of *The Jewish Dream Book: The Key to Opening the Inner Meaning of Your Dreams.*

Rabbi Kerry M. Olitzky is executive director of the Jewish Outreach Institute in New York City. He has written and edited a number of books on Jewish life, including *Jewish Holidays: A Brief Introduction for Christians* and *The Rituals and Practices of a Jewish Life: A Handbook for Personal Spiritual Renewal.*

Mary Oliver is an award-winning poet. She holds the Catharine Osgood Foster Chair for Distinguished Teaching at Bennington College.

Rabbi Debra Orenstein is spiritual leader of Makom Ohr Shalom in Tarzana, California and a sought-after scholar-in-residence across North America. She is editor of *Lifecycles I: Jewish Women on Life Passages and Personal Milestones* and coeditor of *Lifecycles II: Jewish Woman on Biblical Themes in Contemporary Life.*

Rabbi Stephan O. Parnes, editor of *The Jewish Book of Days* and *The Art of Passover,* has edited several prayer books and writes liturgical poetry.

Rabbi Stephen S. Pearce, PhD, is senior rabbi of Congregation Emanu-El of San Francisco and author of *Flash of Insight: Metaphor and Narrative in Therapy.*

Rabbi Pinchas of Koretz (1726–1791) was considered to be one of the two most preeminent followers of Hasidism's founder, the Baal Shem Tov, along with his successor, the Maggid of Mezritch.

Helen Weiss Pincus is the program coordinator at the Simon Senior Center of the Riverdale YM-YHWA. A freelance writer and award-winning journalist, she was the associate editor of the *New Jersey Jewish Standard.* She grew up in her parents' hotel, Weisses' Farms, which was a gathering place for Jewish intellectuals and dreamers.

Rabbi Marcia Prager is a teacher, storyteller, artist and therapist. She is the author of *The Path of Blessing: Experiencing the Energy and Abundance of the Divine.*

Rabbi Jacob Pressman has been senior rabbi and rabbi emeritus at Temple Beth Am in Los Angeles, California, for over fifty-six years. He is a founder of the Brandeis Bardin Institute, Los Angeles Hebrew High, University of Judaism, Camp Ramah at Ojai, Herzl Academy, Akiba Academy, Rabbi Jacob Pressman Academy, Beverly Hills Maple Counseling Center, author and columnist.

Rabbi Bernard Solomon Raskas is rabbi laureate at Temple of Aaron and Professor Emeritus at Macalaster College.

Rabbi Simcha Raz is an Israeli author and educator. He has written and edited dozens of books on Aggadic and Hasidic themes, many of which have been translated into English. He lives with his family in Jerusalem.

Rachel Naomi Remen, MD, is founder and director of the Institute for the Study of Health and Illness, and clinical professor of family and community medicine at the UCSF School of Medicine. She is the author of *Kitchen Table Wisdom and My Grandfather's Blessings*.

Rabbi Leah Richman is rabbi at the Oheb Zedeck Synagogue in Pottsville, Pennsylvania. She is a graduate of the Reconstructionist Rabbinical College.

Anne Roiphe is a novelist living in Jerusalem.

Rabbi Sholom ben Elazar Rokeah of Belz (1779–1867). was founder of Belz Hasidic movement.

Rabbi Steven Carr Reuben, PhD, is the senior rabbi of Kehillat Israel Reconstructionist Congregation of Pacific Palisades, California, and the author of several books, including *Children of Character: Leading Your Children to Ethical Choices in Everyday Life*.

Oscar Romero was archbishop of San Salvador, El Salvador.

Rabbi David Rosen is the senior rabbi of Congregation Beth Yeshurun, Houston, Texas.

Rabbi Yehoshua Rubin is an Israeli teacher, storyteller, workshop leader, author, and minstrel.

Rabbi Jonathan Sacks is chief rabbi of Great Britain and author of many books.

Rabbi Zalman Schachter-Shalomi is the "guru" and founder of the Jewish Renewal Movement. Currently he teaches at the Nairopa Institute of Boulder, Colorado.

Rabbi Robert Scheinberg is the rabbi of United Synagogue of Hoboken, New Jersey, and adjunct instructor of liturgy at the Jewish Theological Seminary and the Academy for Jewish Religion.

Rabbi Harold M. Schulweis, of Temple Valley Beth Shalom in Encino, California, is the founder of Jewish Foundation for Rescuers, a group which raises and distributes money to Christians who risked their lives during the Holocaust. Rabbi Schulweis is also the founder of Jewish World Watch, concerned about genocide, especially in Darfur. He is the author of many books, including *For Those Who Can't Believe*.

Rabbi Dannel I. Schwartz is the founding rabbi of Temple Shir Shalom in West Bloomfield, Michigan. He is the author of *Finding Joy: A Practical Spiritual Guide to Happiness* and *On Wings of Healing: A Hospital Prayer Book for all Faiths* and has served as a technical consultant on Jewish mystical practices on the television show *The X-Files*.

Rachel Schwartz is a rabbinical student at the Jewish Theological Seminary.

Rabbi Rami Shapiro is the president of the One River Foundation for Interspiritual Studies and author of a dozen books, including *The Sacred Art of Lovingkindness: Preparing to Practice*.

Sara Shendelman is a cantor and songwriter. She serves as spiritual leader for B'nai Harim, a congregation in Placerville, California.

Rabbi Dan Shevitz serves Congregation Mishkon Tephilo in Venice, California, and teaches Talmud in the Rabbinical School of the University of Judaism. His poem is part of the congregation's *tashlich* service on Venice Beach.

Bernie Siegel, MD, is a retired surgeon who is still trying to heal lives. He is also an outside consultant to the board of directors of heaven.

Danny Siegel, poet, author, and lecturer, is the founder of Ziv Tzedakah Fund.

Rabbi Michael S. Siegel serves at The Anshe Emet Synagogue in Chicago, Illinois.

Rabbi Hillel E. Silverman is rabbi emeritus of Temple Shalom, Greenwich, Connecticut, and author of several books.

Rabbi Mordechai Silverstein teaches at the Conservative Yeshiva and writes on the weekly Haftarah for the internet.

Isaac Bashevis Singer (1904–1991) was a Yiddish writer of novels and short stories, and the recipient of the Nobel Prize in Literature in 1978.

Steven Spielberg produces movies in Hollywood, California, and has several Jewish charity foundations including The Shoah Foundation and the Righteous Persons Foundation.

Rabbi Michael Strassfeld serves as spiritual leader at the Society for the Advancement of Judaism in New York City.

Rabindranath Tagore is to the Indian subcontinent what Shakespeare is to the English-speaking world. A poet, playwright, painter, and educator, Tagore was awarded the Nobel Prize for Literature in 1913.

Rabbi Joseph Telushkin is a lecturer and author of many best-selling books. He lives with his family in New York City.

Rabbi Saul Teplitz is rabbi emeritus at Congregation Sons of Israel, Woodmere, New York.

Robert N. Test was a writer whose poignant 1976 essay, "To Remember Me...," elevated the issue of organ donation into the public consciousness.

Rabbi Lawrence Troster is the Jewish chaplain and associate of the Institute of Advanced Theology at Bard College, Annandale-on-Hudson, New York, as well as the rabbinic fellow at the Coalition on the Environment and Jewish Life and at GreenFaith: Interfaith Partners for the Environment. He is the author of numerous articles on Jewish theology, environmentalism, liturgy, bio-ethics and Judaism, and modern cosmology.

Rabbi Abraham J. Twerski, MD, is a psychiatrist who specializes in substance abuse, and is the author of dozens of books on Judaism and psychology.

Rabbi Jan R. Uhrbach is the rabbi of the Conservative Synagogue of the Hamptons, a congregation that she helped found. She is adjunct lecturer of professional and pastoral skills at the Jewish Theological Seminary Rabbinical School, a member of the Wexner Heritage faculty, and a teacher of Torah in the New York area.

Dr. Ellen M. Umansky serves as the Carl and Dorothy Bennett Professor of Judaic Studies at Fairfield University. The author of many articles and books on modern Jewish history and thought and women's spirituality, her most recent work is *From Christian Science to Jewish Science: Spiritual Healing and American Jews.*

Rabbi Roy A. Walter is senior rabbi of Congregation Emanu El in Houston, Texas.

Rabbi Arthur Waskow is director of The Shalom Center (www.shalomctr.org), which voices a new prophetic agenda in Jewish, multireligious, and American life, by seeking peace, justice, and healing of the earth. He is the author of many books on public policy and on spiritual renewal, available from the Shalom Center by writing Office@shalomctr.org.

Rabbi Jonathan Waxman currently serves Congregation Beth El of Massapequa, New York. Previously, he was the rabbi of Congregation B'nai Shalom of Westend, New Jersey.

Rabbi Sheila Peltz Weinberg is a Reconstructionist rabbi, teacher of meditation to Jews, outreach director and senior faculty member of the Institute for Jewish Spirituality.

Rabbi Eric Weiss is the executive director of the Bay Area Jewish Healing Center in San Francisco.

Elie Wiesel is the Andrew W. Mellon Professor in the Humanities at Boston University, and the author of more than forty books. He was the recipient of the Nobel Peace Prize in 1986.

Rabbi Arnold Jacob Wolf is a rabbi, teacher, chaplain, author, and has been called "the conscience of liberal Judaism."

Rabbi David J. Wolpe is the rabbi of Sinai Temple in Los Angeles and the author of several books, including *Floating Takes Faith: Ancient Wisdom for a Modern World.*

Rabbi Gerald I. Wolpe is rabbi emeritus at Har Zion Temple, Penn Valley, Pennsylvania.

Rabbi Zvi Yehuda was a teacher and writer at the Siegel College of Jewish Studies in Cleveland, Ohio, and is now retired in Boca Raton, Florida.

Rabbi S.Y. Zevin was a prolific writer on Jewish themes.

Rabbi Shawn Israel Zevit is the director of outreach and *tikkun olam* for the Jewish Reconstructionist Federation, a spiritual director, author, recording artist, and co-director of the Davening Leaders Training Institute.

Janet Zimmern teaches and writes about Jewish spirituality and is a psychotherapist living in Cambridge, Massachusetss.

Credits

This page constitutes a continuation of the copyright page. Every effort has been made to trace and acknowledge copyright holders of all the material included in this anthology. The editor apologizes for any errors or omissions that may remain and asks that any omissions be brought to his attention so that they may be corrected in future editions.

Grateful acknowledgement is given to the following sources for permission to use material:

Dov Baer of Mezeritch, "Individual Prayer," from *God In All Moments: Mystical & Practical Spiritual Wisdom from Hasidic Masters* © 2004 by Or Rose with Ebn D. Leader (Woodstock, VT: Jewish Lights Publishing). $16.95+$3.95 s/h. Order by mail or call 800-962-4544 or on-line at www.jewishlights.com. Permission granted by Jewish Lights Publishing, P.O. Box 237, Woodstock, VT 05091.

Leila Gal Berner, "A New Year," from *Kol Haneshamah: Mahzor Leyamim Nora'im (Prayerbook for the Days of Awe)*, 1999 Reconstructionist Press, Elkins Park, PA.

June Bingham, *"Aseh Imanu Tzedakah Va-Chesed:* Deal with Us Charitably and Lovingly," courtesy of The Living Pulpit.

Tsvi Blanchard, *"Ga'al Yisrael:* Redemption as Social Redemption," © Tsvi Blanchard.

Ben Zion Bokser, "The Song of God's Presence," © Kallia H. Bokser.

Lee Buckman, *"Ve-khol Ma-minim She-hu Tamim Po-olo:* Wholehearted, So Must We Be," © Lee Buckman.

Reuven Bulka, *"The Akedah:* A Test Within a Test," from *More Torah Therapy: Further Reflections on the Weekly Sidrah and Special Occasions*, Hoboken, New Jersey: KTAV Publishing House, 1993.

Nina Beth Cardin, "And God Remembered Sarah: Prayers and Rituals for an Infertile Couple on Rosh Hashanah" and "Prayer for an Expecting Couple During the Days of Awe," from *Tears of Sorrow, Seeds of Hope: A Jewish Spiritual Companion for Infertility and Pregnancy Loss* © 1999 by Nina Beth Cardin (Woodstock, VT: Jewish Lights Publishing). $19.95+$3.95 s/h. Order by mail

Credits

by Jewish Lights Publishing, P.O. Box 237, Woodstock, VT 05091.

Diane Cohen, *"Hineni: Here I Am!" "L'El Orekh Din:* Justice Tempered with
Mercy" and *"Malkhuyot, Zikhronot, Shofarot,"* © Diane Aronson Cohen.

Kenneth Cohen, "And Abraham Grew Big—Like God," © 1997 Kenneth L.
Cohen.

Abraham Deleon-Cohen, "Benediction: Prayers around the Communal Table,"
© Abraham Deleon-Cohen, PhD.

James Diamond, "How 'High' Are the High Holidays?" © James S. Diamond.

Elliot N. Dorff, *"U'Tefilah:* Like Baseball, Prayer Needs Practice," © 1992 Elliot
N. Dorff. From *Knowing God: Jewish Journeys to the Unknowable,* Jason Aronson,
1992. Jason Aronson is an imprint of Rowman & Littlefield Publishers, Inc.,
Lanham, Maryland.

Adrian A. Durlester, "Holiness and Righteousness," © 1998 Adrian A.
Durlester.

Lewis John Eron, "Elul," © Lewis John Eron 2005.

Tamar Frankiel and Judy Greenfeld, "Forgiving Yourself: A Guided Imagery
Meditation," from *Entering the Temple of Dreams: Jewish Prayers, Movements
& Meditations for the End of the Day* © 2000 by Tamar Frankiel and Judy
Greenfeld (Woodstock, VT: Jewish Lights Publishing). $16.95+$3.95 s/h.
Order by mail or call 800-962-4544 or on-line at www.jewishlights.com. Per-
mission granted by Jewish Lights Publishing, P.O. Box 237, Woodstock,
VT 05091.

Neil Gillman, *"V'khol Ma'aminim:* Seeing the Invisible," from T*he Jewish Lights
Spirituality Handbook: A Guide to Understanding, Exploring & Living a Spir-
itual Life* © 2001 by Jewish Lights Publishing (Woodstock, VT: Jewish
Lights Publishing). $19.99+$3.95 s/h. Order by mail or call 800-962-4544
or on-line at www.jewishlights.com. Permission granted by Jewish Lights
Publishing, P.O. Box 237, Woodstock, VT 05091.

Noah Golinkin, "Where Are You, God?" from *Say Something New Each Day.*
© 1973 by Noah Golinkin. Reprinted by permission of Mrs. Noah Golinkin.
Prayer revisions by Cantor Abe Golinkin.

Arthur Green, *"Hitbodedut:* Praying Separately" and "Mending the World,"
from *The Jewish Lights Spirituality Handbook: A Guide to Understanding,
Exploring & Living a Spiritual Life* © 2001 by Jewish Lights Publishing
(Woodstock, VT: Jewish Lights Publishing). $19.99+$3.95 s/h. Order by
mail or call 800-962-4544 or on-line at www.jewishlights.com. Permission
granted by Jewish Lights Publishing, P.O. Box 237, Woodstock, VT 05091.

Arthur Green Section Introductions excerpted from *These Are the Words: A
Vocabulary of Jewish Spiritual Life* © 1999 Arthur Green (Woodstock, VT:
Jewish Lights Publishing). $18.95+$3.95 s/h. Order by mail or call 800-962-

354

Lawrence Kushner, "Generations" and *"Hayom ... Live in the Presence of God,"* from *God Was In This Place and I, i Did Not Know: Finding Self, Spirituality and Ultimate Meaning* © 1994 by Lawrence Kushner (Woodstock, VT: Jewish Lights Publishing). $16.95+$3.95 s/h. Order by mail or call 800-962-4544 or on-line at www.jewishlights.com. Permission granted by Jewish Lights Publishing, P.O. Box 237, Woodstock, VT 05091.

Lawrence Kushner, *"Tefilah"* and *"Teshuvah:* Coming home," from *The Book of Words: Talking Spiritual Life, Living Spiritual Talk* © 1993 by Lawrence Kushner (Woodstock, VT: Jewish Lights Publishing). $16.95+$3.95 s/h. Order by mail or call 800-962-4544 or on-line at www.jewishlights.com. Permission granted by Jewish Lights Publishing, P.O. Box 237, Woodstock, VT 05091.

Ed Levin, "God Tested Abraham: Our Moral Senses Are Tested Again and Again," reprinted with permission from *Sh'ma: A Journal of Jewish Responsibility* May 1996 (www.shma.com).

Lynn Levin, Lines to My Son," from *A Few Questions about Paradise* (Loonfeather Press). © 2000 by Lynn Levin. Reprinted by permission of the author.

Immanuel Lubliner, "Introduction to the Silent *Amidah,"* originally titled "The Whispered Prayer," reprinted with permission from *Siddur Sim Shalom,* edited by Rabbi Jules Harlow, The Rabbinical Assembly, © 1985, p. 802.

Levi Meier, "Trying to Believe," © 2002 by Levi Meier. Excerpted from *Seven Heavens,* published by Pitspopany Press.

Marshall T. Meyer, "Begin" and "Shofar: Awaken Our Slumbering Hearts," from *The Living Words of Rabbi Marshall T. Meyer,* ed. Jane Isay, publ: St. Martin's Press. © Naomi Meyer.

Menahem Nahum of Chernobyl, "Nightly *Teshuvah"* and "Tzedakah: The Root of Life," from *God In All Moments: Mystical & Practical Spiritual Wisdom from Hasidic Masters* © 2004 by Or Rose with Ebn D. Leader (Woodstock, VT: Jewish Lights Publishing). $16.95+$3.95 s/h. Order by mail or call 800-962-4544 or on-line at www.jewishlights.com. Permission granted by Jewish Lights Publishing, P.O. Box 237, Woodstock, VT 05091.

Kerry M. Olitzky, "A Fresh Start," "Gratitude," and "Simplicity," from *100 Blessings Every Day: Daily Twelve Step Recovery Affirmations, Exercises for Personal Growth & Renewal Reflecting Seasons of the Jewish Year* © 1993 by Kery M. Olitzky (Woodstock, VT: Jewish Lights Publishing). $15.99+$3.95 s/h. Order by mail or call 800-962-4544 or on-line at www.jewishlights.com. Permission granted by Jewish Lights Publishing, P.O. Box 237, Woodstock, VT 05091.

Mary Oliver, "Who Made the World," from *Kol Haneshamah: Mahzor Leyamim Nora'im (Prayerbook for the Days of Awe),* 1999 Reconstructionist Press, Elkins Park, PA.

Debra Orenstein, *"Avinu Malkeynu*—Our Father, Our King" and "Blessings for a Sweet New Year" © by Debra Orenstein 2006.

Debra Orenstein, "The Binding of Sarah," from *Lifecycles V. 2: Jewish Women on Biblical Themes in Contemporary Life* © 1997 by Debra Orenstein and Jane Rachel Litman (Woodstock, VT: Jewish Lights Publishing). $19.95+$3.95 s/h. Order by mail or call 800-962-4544 or on-line at www.jewishlights.com. Permission granted by Jewish Lights Publishing, P.O. Box 237, Woodstock, VT 05091.

Stephan O. Parnes, *"Kol ha-Shofar:* The Voice of the Shofar," reprinted by permission of Stephan Owen Parnes.

Marcia Prager, "Blessing God," from *The Path of Blessing: Experiencing the Energy and Abundance of the Divine* © 1998 by Marcia Prager (2003 first Jewish Lights Publishing). $16.95+$3.95 s/h. Order by mail or call 800-962-4544 or on-line at www.jewishlights.com. Permission granted by Jewish Lights Publishing, P.O. Box 237, Woodstock, VT 05091.

Rachel Naomi Remen, *"Teshuvah:* Is My Life Tuned to My Own Note?" from *My Grandparents Blessings,* Riverhead, 2000, Rachel Naomi Remen, MD.

Jonathan Sacks, "Can Faith Be Justified?" from *RADICAL THEN, RADICAL NOW; On Being Jewish* (LONDON: Continuum International Publishing Group, 2003).

Jonathan Sacks, "The Importance of Children," from BBC Rosh HaShanah Broadcast: "Remembering for the Future" BBC1 12 September 2004 (5765).

Zalman Schachter-Shalomi, "Shofar: The Primal Scream" and "Getting Rid of the Mud," from *Wrapped in a Holy Flame: Teachings and Tales of the Hasidic Masters* © 2003 Zalman Schachter-Shalomi. Reprinted with permission of John Wiley & Sons, Inc.

Zalman Schachter-Shalomi, *"Alenu:* Is Judaism Then Asserting Itself as the One 'True' Religion?" from *Broken Tablets: Restoring the Ten Commandments and Ourselves* © edited by Rachel S. Mikva (Woodstock, VT: Jewish Lights Publishing, 1999). $16.95+$3.95 s/h. Order by mail or call 800-962-4544 or on-line at www.jewishlights.com. Permission granted by Jewish Lights Publishing, P.O. Box 237, Woodstock, VT 05091.

Zalman Schachter-Shalomi, "My Script," from *Kol Haneshamah: Mahzor Leyamim Nora'im (Prayerbook for the Days of Awe),* 1999 Reconstructionist Press, Elkins Park, PA.

Harold Schulweis, "It Is Never Too Late," © 2005 Valley Beth Shalom, a California non-profit corporation. All rights reserved.

Rachel Schwartz, "Sacred Questions," © 2005 Rachel Schwartz.

Rami Shapiro, "Opening Our Eyes," from *Kol Haneshamah: Mahzor Leyamim Nora'im (Prayerbook for the Days of Awe),* 1999 Reconstructionist Press, Elkins Park, PA.

Bar/Bat Mitzvah

The JGirl's Guide: The Young Jewish Woman's Handbook for Coming of Age
By Penina Adelman, Ali Feldman, and Shulamit Reinharz
An inspirational, interactive guidebook designed to help pre-teen Jewish girls address the spiritual, educational, and psychological issues surrounding coming of age in today's society.   6 x 9, 240 pp, Quality PB, 978-1-58023-215-9 **$14.99**

  Also Available: **The JGirl's Teacher's and Parent's Guide**
  8½ x 11, 56 pp, PB, 978-1-58023-225-8 **$8.99**
Bar/Bat Mitzvah Basics: A Practical Family Guide to Coming of Age Together
  Edited by Cantor Helen Leneman   6 x 9, 240 pp, Quality PB, 978-1-58023-151-0 **$18.95**
The Bar/Bat Mitzvah Memory Book, 2nd Edition: An Album for Treasuring the
  Spiritual Celebration *By Rabbi Jeffrey K. Salkin and Nina Salkin*
  8 x 10, 48 pp, Deluxe HC, 2-color text, ribbon marker, 978-1-58023-263-0 **$19.99**
For Kids—Putting God on Your Guest List: How to Claim the Spiritual Meaning
  of Your Bar or Bat Mitzvah *By Rabbi Jeffrey K. Salkin*
  6 x 9, 144 pp, Quality PB, 978-1-58023-015-5 **$14.99** *For ages 11–13*

Putting God on the Guest List, 3rd Edition: How to Reclaim the Spiritual
  Meaning of Your Child's Bar or Bat Mitzvah *By Rabbi Jeffrey K. Salkin*
  6 x 9, 224 pp, Quality PB, 978-1-58023-222-7 **$16.99**; HC, 978-1-58023-260-9 **$24.99**
  Also Available: **Putting God on the Guest List Teacher's Guide**
  8½ x 11, 48 pp, PB, 978-1-58023-226-5 **$8.99**
Tough Questions Jews Ask: A Young Adult's Guide to Building a Jewish Life
  By Rabbi Edward Feinstein   6 x 9, 160 pp, Quality PB, 978-1-58023-139-8 **$14.99** *For ages 12 & up*
  Also Available: **Tough Questions Jews Ask Teacher's Guide**
  8½ x 11, 72 pp, PB, 978-1-58023-187-9 **$8.95**

Bible Study/Midrash

**Abraham's Bind & Other Bible Tales of Trickery, Folly, Mercy
and Love** *By Michael J. Caduto*
Re-imagines many biblical characters, retelling their stories and highlighting their foibles and strengths, their struggles and joys. Readers will learn that God has a way of working for them and through them, even today.
6 x 9, 224 pp, HC, 978-1-59473-186-0 **$19.99** *(A SkyLight Paths book)*
Ancient Secrets: Using the Stories of the Bible to Improve Our Everyday Lives
  By Rabbi Levi Meier, PhD 5½ x 8½, 288 pp, Quality PB, 978-1-58023-064-3 **$16.95**

The Genesis of Leadership: What the Bible Teaches Us about Vision,
Values and Leading Change *By Rabbi Nathan Laufer; Foreword by Senator Joseph I. Lieberman*
Unlike other books on leadership, this one is rooted in the stories of the Bible, and teaches the values that the Bible believes are prerequisites for true leadership.
6 x 9, 288 pp, HC, 978-1-58023-241-8 **$24.99**

Hineini in Our Lives: Learning How to Respond to Others through 14 Biblical Texts and
  Personal Stories *By Norman J. Cohen* 6 x 9, 240 pp, Quality PB, 978-1-58023-274-6 **$16.99**
Moses and the Journey to Leadership: Timeless Lessons of Effective Management from
  the Bible and Today's Leaders *By Dr. Norman J. Cohen* 6 x 9, 250 pp, HC, 978-1-58023-227-2 **$21.99**
Self, Struggle & Change: Family Conflict Stories in Genesis and Their Healing Insights for
  Our Lives *By Norman J. Cohen* 6 x 9, 224 pp, Quality PB, 978-1-879045-66-8 **$18.99**
The Triumph of Eve & Other Subversive Bible Tales *By Matt Biers-Ariel*
  5½ x 8½, 192 pp, HC, 978-1-59473-040-5 **$19.99** *(A SkyLight Paths book)*
Voices from Genesis: Guiding Us through the Stages of Life *By Norman J. Cohen*
  6 x 9, 192 pp, Quality PB, 978-1-58023-118-3 **$16.95**

Congregation Resources

The Art of Public Prayer, 2nd Edition: Not for Clergy Only *By Lawrence A. Hoffman*
6 x 9, 272 pp, Quality PB, 978-1-893361-06-5 **$19.99** *(A SkyLight Paths book)*

Becoming a Congregation of Learners: Learning as a Key to Revitalizing
Congregational Life *By Isa Aron, PhD; Foreword by Rabbi Lawrence A. Hoffman*
6 x 9, 304 pp, Quality PB, 978-1-58023-089-6 **$19.95**

Finding a Spiritual Home: How a New Generation of Jews Can Transform the
American Synagogue *By Rabbi Sidney Schwarz*
6 x 9, 352 pp, Quality PB, 978-1-58023-185-5 **$19.95**

Jewish Pastoral Care, 2nd Edition: A Practical Handbook from Traditional &
Contemporary Sources *Edited by Rabbi Dayle A. Friedman*
6 x 9, 528 pp, HC, 978-1-58023-221-0 **$40.00**

Jewish Spiritual Direction: An Innovative Guide from Traditional and Contemporary
Sources *Edited by Rabbi Howard A. Addison and Barbara Eve Breitman*
6 x 9, 368 pp, HC, 978-1-58023-230-2 **$30.00**

The Self-Renewing Congregation: Organizational Strategies for Revitalizing
Congregational Life *By Isa Aron, PhD; Foreword by Dr. Ron Wolfson*
6 x 9, 304 pp, Quality PB, 978-1-58023-166-4 **$19.95**

Spiritual Community: The Power to Restore Hope, Commitment and Joy
By Rabbi David A. Teutsch, PhD 5½ x 8½, 144 pp, HC, 978-1-58023-270-8 **$19.99**

The Spirituality of Welcoming: How to Transform Your Congregation into a
Sacred Community *By Dr. Ron Wolfson* 6 x 9, 224 pp, Quality PB, 978-1-58023-244-9 **$19.99**

Rethinking Synagogues: A New Vocabulary for Congregational Life
By Rabbi Lawrence A. Hoffman 6 x 9, 240 pp, Quality PB, 978-1-58023-248-7 **$19.99**

Children's Books

What You Will See Inside a Synagogue
By Rabbi Lawrence A. Hoffman and Dr. Ron Wolfson; Full-color photos by Bill Aron
A colorful, fun-to-read introduction that explains the ways and whys of Jewish
worship and religious life.
8½ x 10½, 32 pp, Full-color photos, HC, 978-1-59473-012-2 **$17.99** *For ages 6 & up (A SkyLight Paths book)*

The Kids' Fun Book of Jewish Time
By Emily Sper 9 x 7½, 24 pp, Full-color illus., HC, 978-1-58023-311-8 **$16.99**

In God's Hands
By Lawrence Kushner and Gary Schmidt 9 x 12, 32 pp, HC, 978-1-58023-224-1 **$16.99**

Because Nothing Looks Like God
By Lawrence and Karen Kushner
Introduces children to the possibilities of spiritual life.
11 x 8½, 32 pp, Full-color illus., HC, 978-1-58023-092-6 **$16.95** *For ages 4 & up*

Also Available: **Because Nothing Looks Like God Teacher's Guide**
8½ x 11, 22 pp, PB, 978-1-58023-140-4 **$6.95** *For ages 5–8*
> **Board Book Companions to** *Because Nothing Looks Like God*
> 5 x 5, 24 pp, Full-color illus., SkyLight Paths Board Books *For ages 0–4*

What Does God Look Like? 978-1-893361-23-2 **$7.99**
How Does God Make Things Happen? 978-1-893361-24-9 **$7.95**
Where Is God? 978-1-893361-17-1 **$7.99**

The Book of Miracles: A Young Person's Guide to Jewish Spiritual Awareness
By Lawrence Kushner. All-new illustrations by the author
6 x 9, 96 pp, 2-color illus., HC, 978-1-879045-78-1 **$16.95** *For ages 9 and up*

In Our Image: God's First Creatures
By Nancy Sohn Swartz 9 x 12, 32 pp, Full-color illus., HC, 978-1-879045-99-6 **$16.95** *For ages 4 & up*

Also Available as a Board Book: **How Did the Animals Help God?**
5 x 5, 24 pp, Board, Full-color illus., 978-1-59473-044-3 **$7.99** *For ages 0–4 (A SkyLight Paths book)*

Children's Books
by Sandy Eisenberg Sasso

Adam & Eve's First Sunset: God's New Day
Engaging new story explores fear and hope, faith and gratitude in ways that will delight kids and adults—inspiring us to bless each of God's days and nights.
9 x 12, 32 pp, Full-color illus., HC, 978-1-58023-177-0 **$17.95** *For ages 4 & up*

Also Available as a Board Book: **Adam and Eve's New Day**
5 x 5, 24 pp, Full-color illus., Board, 978-1-59473-205-8 **$7.99** *For ages 0–4 (A SkyLight Paths book)*

But God Remembered
Stories of Women from Creation to the Promised Land
Four different stories of women—Lillith, Serach, Bityah, and the Daughters of Z—teach us important values through their faith and actions.
9 x 12, 32 pp, Full-color illus., HC, 978-1-879045-43-9 **$16.95** *For ages 8 & up*

Cain & Abel: Finding the Fruits of Peace
Shows children that we have the power to deal with anger in positive ways. Provides questions for kids and adults to explore together.
9 x 12, 32 pp, Full-color illus., HC, 978-1-58023-123-7 **$16.95** *For ages 5 & up*

God in Between
If you wanted to find God, where would you look? This magical, mythical tale teaches that God can be found where we are: within all of us and the relationships between us.
9 x 12, 32 pp, Full-color illus., HC, 978-1-879045-86-6 **$16.95** *For ages 4 & up*

God's Paintbrush: Special 10th Anniversary Edition
Wonderfully interactive, invites children of all faiths and backgrounds to encounter God through moments in their own lives. Provides questions adult and child can explore together.
11 x 8½, 32 pp, Full-color illus., HC, 978-1-58023-195-4 **$17.95** *For ages 4 & up*

Also Available: **God's Paintbrush Teacher's Guide**
8½ x 11, 32 pp, PB, 978-1-879045-57-6 **$8.95**

God's Paintbrush Celebration Kit
A Spiritual Activity Kit for Teachers and Students of All Faiths, All Backgrounds
Additional activity sheets available:
8-Student Activity Sheet Pack (40 sheets/5 sessions), 978-1-58023-058-2 **$19.95**
Single-Student Activity Sheet Pack (5 sessions), 978-1-58023-059-9 **$3.95**

In God's Name
Like an ancient myth in its poetic text and vibrant illustrations, this award-winning modern fable about the search for God's name celebrates the diversity and, at the same time, the unity of all people.
9 x 12, 32 pp, Full-color illus., HC, 978-1-879045-26-2 **$16.99** *For ages 4 & up*

Also Available as a Board Book: **What Is God's Name?**
5 x 5, 24 pp, Board, Full-color illus., 978-1-893361-10-2 **$7.99** *For ages 0–4 (A SkyLight Paths book)*

Also Available: **In God's Name video and study guide**
Computer animation, original music, and children's voices. 18 min. **$29.99**

Also Available in Spanish: **El nombre de Dios**
9 x 12, 32 pp, Full-color illus., HC, 978-1-893361-63-8 **$16.95** *(A SkyLight Paths book)*

Noah's Wife: The Story of Naamah
When God tells Noah to bring the animals of the world onto the ark, God also calls on Naamah, Noah's wife, to save each plant on Earth. Based on an ancient text.
9 x 12, 32 pp, Full-color illus., HC, 978-1-58023-134-3 **$16.95** *For ages 4 & up*

Also Available as a Board Book: **Naamah, Noah's Wife**
5 x 5, 24 pp, Full-color illus., Board, 978-1-893361-56-0 **$7.95** *For ages 0–4 (A SkyLight Paths book)*

For Heaven's Sake: Finding God in Unexpected Places
9 x 12, 32 pp, Full-color illus., HC, 978-1-58023-054-4 **$16.95** *For ages 4 & up*

God Said Amen: Finding the Answers to Our Prayers
9 x 12, 32 pp, Full-color illus., HC, 978-1-58023-080-3 **$16.95** *For ages 4 & up*

Current Events/History

The Story of the Jews: A 4,000-Year Adventure—A Graphic History Book
Written & illustrated by Stan Mack
Witty, illustrated narrative of all the major happenings from biblical times to the twenty-first century. 6 x 9, 288 pp, illus., Quality PB, 978-1-58023-155-8 **$16.95**

Hannah Senesh: Her Life and Diary, the First Complete Edition
By Hannah Senesh; Foreword by Marge Piercy; Preface by Eitan Senesh
6 x 9, 352 pp, HC, 978-1-58023-212-8 **$24.99**

The Jewish Prophet: Visionary Words from Moses and Miriam to Henrietta Szold and A. J. Heschel *By Rabbi Dr. Michael J. Shire*
6½ x 8½, 128 pp, 123 full-color illus., HC, 978-1-58023-168-8
Special gift price $14.95

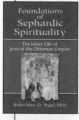

Foundations of Sephardic Spirituality: The Inner Life of Jews of the Ottoman Empire
By Rabbi Marc D. Angel, PhD 6 x 9, 224 pp, HC, 978-1-58023-243-2 **$24.99**

Judaism and Justice: The Jewish Passion to Repair the World
By Rabbi Sidney Schwarz; Foreword by Elie Wiesel
6 x 9, 250 pp, HC, 978-1-58023-312-5 **$24.99**

Ecology

Ecology & the Jewish Spirit: Where Nature & the Sacred Meet
Edited by Ellen Bernstein 6 x 9, 288 pp, Quality PB, 978-1-58023-082-7 **$16.95**

Torah of the Earth: Exploring 4,000 Years of Ecology in Jewish Thought
Vol. 1: Biblical Israel: One Land, One People; Rabbinic Judaism: One People, Many Lands
Vol. 2: Zionism: One Land, Two Peoples; Eco-Judaism: One Earth, Many Peoples
Edited by Arthur Waskow
Vol. 1: 6 x 9, 272 pp, Quality PB, 978-1-58023-086-5 **$19.95**
Vol. 2: 6 x 9, 336 pp, Quality PB, 978-1-58023-087-2 **$19.95**

The Way Into Judaism and the Environment
By Jeremy Benstein 6 x 9, 224 pp, HC, 978-1-58023-268-5 **$24.99**

Grief/Healing

Against the Dying of the Light: A Parent's Story of Love, Loss and Hope
By Leonard Fein
5½ x 8½, 176 pp, Quality PB, 978-1-58023-197-8 **$15.99**

Grief in Our Seasons: A Mourner's Kaddish Companion *By Rabbi Kerry M. Olitzky*
4½ x 6½, 448 pp, Quality PB, 978-1-879045-55-2 **$15.95**

Healing of Soul, Healing of Body: Spiritual Leaders Unfold the Strength & Solace in Psalms *Edited by Rabbi Simkha Y. Weintraub, CSW*
6 x 9, 128 pp, 2-color illus. text, Quality PB, 978-1-879045-31-6 **$14.99**

Jewish Paths toward Healing and Wholeness: A Personal Guide to Dealing with Suffering *By Rabbi Kerry M. Olitzky; Foreword by Debbie Friedman.*
6 x 9, 192 pp, Quality PB, 978-1-58023-068-1 **$15.95**

Mourning & Mitzvah, 2nd Edition: A Guided Journal for Walking the Mourner's Path through Grief to Healing *By Anne Brener, LCSW*
7½ x 9, 304 pp, Quality PB, 978-1-58023-113-8 **$19.99**

The Perfect Stranger's Guide to Funerals and Grieving Practices
A Guide to Etiquette in Other People's Religious Ceremonies *Edited by Stuart M. Matlins*
6 x 9, 240 pp, Quality PB, 978-1-893361-20-1 **$16.95** *(A SkyLight Paths book)*

Tears of Sorrow, Seeds of Hope: A Jewish Spiritual Companion for Infertility and Pregnancy Loss *By Rabbi Nina Beth Cardin*
6 x 9, 192 pp, HC, 978-1-58023-017-9 **$19.95**

A Time to Mourn, A Time to Comfort, 2nd Edition: A Guide to Jewish Bereavement *By Dr. Ron Wolfson*
7 x 9, 384 pp, Quality PB, 978-1-58023-253-1 **$19.99**

When a Grandparent Dies: A Kid's Own Remembering Workbook for Dealing with Shiva and the Year Beyond *By Nechama Liss-Levinson, PhD*
8 x 10, 48 pp, 2-color text, HC, 978-1-879045-44-6 **$15.95** *For ages 7–13*

Holidays/Holy Days

Rosh Hashanah Readings: Inspiration, Information and Contemplation
Yom Kippur Readings: Inspiration, Information and Contemplation
Edited by Rabbi Dov Peretz Elkins with Section Introductions from Arthur Green's These Are the Words
An extraordinary collection of readings, prayers and insights that enable the modern worshiper to enter into the spirit of the High Holy Days in a personal and powerful way, permitting the meaning of the Jewish New Year to enter the heart.
RHR: 6 x 9, 400 pp, HC, 978-1-58023-239-5 **$24.99**
YKR: 6 x 9, 368 pp, HC, 978-1-58023-271-5 **$24.99**

Jewish Holidays: A Brief Introduction for Christians
By Rabbi Kerry M. Olitzky and Rabbi Daniel Judson
5½ x 8½, 144 pp, Quality PB, 978-1-58023-302-6 **$16.99**

Leading the Passover Journey: The Seder's Meaning Revealed, the Haggadah's Story Retold *By Rabbi Nathan Laufer*
Uncovers the hidden meaning of the Seder's rituals and customs.
6 x 9, 224 pp, HC, 978-1-58023-211-1 **$24.99**

Reclaiming Judaism as a Spiritual Practice: Holy Days and Shabbat
By Rabbi Goldie Milgram
7 x 9, 272 pp, Quality PB, 978-1-58023-205-0 **$19.99**

7th Heaven: Celebrating Shabbat with Rebbe Nachman of Breslov
By Moshe Mykoff with the Breslov Research Institute
5⅛ x 8¼, 224 pp, Deluxe PB w/flaps, 978-1-58023-175-6 **$18.95**

The Women's Passover Companion: Women's Reflections on the Festival of Freedom *Edited by Rabbi Sharon Cohen Anisfeld, Tara Mohr, and Catherine Spector*
Groundbreaking. A provocative conversation about women's relationships to Passover as well as the roots and meanings of women's seders.
6 x 9, 352 pp, Quality PB, 978-1-58023-231-9 **$19.99**

The Women's Seder Sourcebook: Rituals & Readings for Use at the Passover Seder *Edited by Rabbi Sharon Cohen Anisfeld, Tara Mohr, and Catherine Spector*
Gathers the voices of more than one hundred women in readings, personal and creative reflections, commentaries, blessings, and ritual suggestions that can be incorporated into your Passover celebration.
6 x 9, 384 pp, Quality PB, 978-1-58023-232-6 **$19.99**

Creating Lively Passover Seders: A Sourcebook of Engaging Tales, Texts & Activities
By David Arnow, PhD 7 x 9, 416 pp, Quality PB, 978-1-58023-184-8 **$24.99**

Hanukkah, 2nd Edition: The Family Guide to Spiritual Celebration
By Dr. Ron Wolfson. Edited by Joel Lurie Grishaver.
7 x 9, 240 pp, illus., Quality PB, 978-1-58023-122-0 **$18.95**

The Jewish Family Fun Book: Holiday Projects, Everyday Activities, and Travel Ideas with Jewish Themes *By Danielle Dardashti and Roni Sarig. Illus. by Avi Katz.*
6 x 9, 288 pp, 70+ b/w illus. & diagrams, Quality PB, 978-1-58023-171-8 **$18.95**

The Jewish Gardening Cookbook: Growing Plants & Cooking for Holidays & Festivals *By Michael Brown* 6 x 9, 224 pp, 30+ b/w illus., Quality PB, 978-1-58023-116-9 **$16.95**

The Jewish Lights Book of Fun Classroom Activities: Simple and Seasonal Projects for Teachers and Students *By Danielle Dardashti and Roni Sarig*
6 x 9, 240 pp, Quality PB, 978-1-58023-206-7 **$19.99**

Passover, 2nd Edition: The Family Guide to Spiritual Celebration
By Dr. Ron Wolfson with Joel Lurie Grishaver 7 x 9, 352 pp, Quality PB, 978-1-58023-174-9 **$19.95**

Shabbat, 2nd Edition: The Family Guide to Preparing for and Celebrating the Sabbath
By Dr. Ron Wolfson 7 x 9, 320 pp, illus., Quality PB, 978-1-58023-164-0 **$19.99**

Sharing Blessings: Children's Stories for Exploring the Spirit of the Jewish Holidays
By Rahel Musleah and Rabbi Michael Klayman
8½ x 11, 64 pp, Full-color illus., HC, 978-1-879045-71-2 **$18.95** For ages 6 & up

Inspiration

God's To-Do List: 103 Ways to Live Your Purpose for Doing God's Work on Earth
By Dr. Ron Wolfson 6 x 9, 150 pp, Quality PB, 978-1-58023-301-9 **$15.99**

God in All Moments: Mystical & Practical Spiritual Wisdom from Hasidic Masters
Edited and translated by Or N. Rose with Ebn D. Leader
5½ x 8½, 192 pp, Quality PB, 978-1-58023-186-2 **$16.95**

Our Dance with God: Finding Prayer, Perspective and Meaning in the Stories of Our
Lives *By Karyn D. Kedar* 6 x 9, 176 pp, Quality PB, 978-1-58023-202-9 **$16.99**
Also Available: **The Dance of the Dolphin** (HC edition of *Our Dance with God*)
6 x 9, 176 pp, HC, 978-1-58023-154-1 **$19.95**

The Empty Chair: Finding Hope and Joy—Timeless Wisdom from a Hasidic Master,
Rebbe Nachman of Breslov *Adapted by Moshe Mykoff and the Breslov Research Institute*
4 x 6, 128 pp, 2-color text, Deluxe PB w/flaps, 978-1-879045-67-5 **$9.95**

The Gentle Weapon: Prayers for Everyday and Not-So-Everyday Moments—
Timeless Wisdom from the Teachings of the Hasidic Master, Rebbe Nachman of Breslov
Adapted by Moshe Mykoff and S. C. Mizrahi, together with the Breslov Research Institute
4 x 6, 144 pp, 2-color text, Deluxe PB w/flaps, 978-1-58023-022-3 **$9.99**

God Whispers: Stories of the Soul, Lessons of the Heart *By Karyn D. Kedar*
6 x 9, 176 pp, Quality PB, 978-1-58023-088-9 **$15.95**

An Orphan in History: One Man's Triumphant Search for His Jewish Roots
By Paul Cowan; Afterword by Rachel Cowan. 6 x 9, 288 pp, Quality PB, 978-1-58023-135-0 **$16.95**

Restful Reflections: Nighttime Inspiration to Calm the Soul, Based on Jewish Wisdom
By Rabbi Kerry M. Olitzky & Rabbi Lori Forman 4½ x 6½, 448 pp, Quality PB, 978-1-58023-091-9 **$15.95**

Sacred Intentions: Daily Inspiration to Strengthen the Spirit, Based on Jewish Wisdom
By Rabbi Kerry M. Olitzky and Rabbi Lori Forman 4½ x 6½, 448 pp, Quality PB, 978-1-58023-061-2 **$15.95**

Kabbalah/Mysticism/Enneagram

Awakening to Kabbalah: The Guiding Light of Spiritual Fulfillment
By Rav Michael Laitman, PhD 6 x 9, 192 pp, HC, 978-1-58023-264-7 **$21.99**

Seek My Face: A Jewish Mystical Theology *By Arthur Green*
6 x 9, 304 pp, Quality PB, 978-1-58023-130-5 **$19.95**

Zohar: Annotated & Explained
Translation and annotation by Daniel C. Matt; Foreword by Andrew Harvey
5½ x 8½, 176 pp, Quality PB, 978-1-893361-51-5 **$15.99** *(A SkyLight Paths book)*

Cast in God's Image: Discover Your Personality Type Using the Enneagram and Kabbalah
By Rabbi Howard A. Addison
7 x 9, 176 pp, Quality PB, Layflat binding, 20+ journaling exercises, 978-1-58023-124-4 **$16.95**

Ehyeh: A Kabbalah for Tomorrow
By Arthur Green 6 x 9, 224 pp, Quality PB, 978-1-58023-213-5 **$16.99**

The Enneagram and Kabbalah, 2nd Edition: Reading Your Soul
By Rabbi Howard A. Addison 6 x 9, 192 pp, Quality PB, 978-1-58023-229-6 **$16.99**

Finding Joy: A Practical Spiritual Guide to Happiness *By Dannel I. Schwartz with Mark Hass*
6 x 9, 192 pp, Quality PB, 978-1-58023-009-4 **$14.95**

The Flame of the Heart: Prayers of a Chasidic Mystic *By Reb Noson of Breslov. Translated by
David Sears with the Breslov Research Institute* 5 x 7¼, 160 pp, Quality PB, 978-1-58023-246-3 **$15.99**

The Gift of Kabbalah: Discovering the Secrets of Heaven, Renewing Your Life on Earth
By Tamar Frankiel, PhD 6 x 9, 256 pp, Quality PB, 978-1-58023-141-1 **$16.95;**
HC, 978-1-58023-108-4 **$21.95**

Kabbalah: A Brief Introduction for Christians
By Tamar Frankiel, PhD 5½ x 8½, 176 pp, Quality PB, 978-1-58023-303-3 **$16.99**

The Lost Princess and Other Kabbalistic Tales of Rebbe Nachman of Breslov
The Seven Beggars and Other Kabbalistic Tales of Rebbe Nachman of Breslov
Translated by Rabbi Aryeh Kaplan; Preface by Rabbi Chaim Kramer
Lost Princess: 6 x 9, 400 pp, Quality PB, 978-1-58023-217-3 **$18.99**
Seven Beggars: 6 x 9, 192 pp, Quality PB, 978-1-58023-250-0 **$16.95**

See also *The Way Into Jewish Mystical Tradition* in Spirituality / The Way Into… Series

Life Cycle
Marriage / Parenting / Family / Aging

Jewish Fathers: A Legacy of Love
Photographs by Lloyd Wolf. Essays by Paula Wolfson. Foreword by Rabbi Harold Kushner.
Honors the role of contemporary Jewish fathers in America. Each father tells in his own words what it means to be a parent and Jewish, and what he learned from his own father. Insightful photos.
10¾ x 9⅞, 144 pp with 100+ duotone photos, HC, 978-1-58023-204-3 **$30.00**

The New Jewish Baby Album: Creating and Celebrating the Beginning of a Spiritual Life—A Jewish Lights Companion
By the Editors at Jewish Lights. Foreword by Anita Diamant. Preface by Rabbi Sandy Eisenberg Sasso.
A spiritual keepsake that will be treasured for generations. More than just a memory book, *shows you how—and why it's important*—to create a Jewish home and a Jewish life. 8 x 10, 64 pp, Deluxe Padded HC, Full-color illus., 978-1-58023-138-1 **$19.95**

The Jewish Pregnancy Book: A Resource for the Soul, Body & Mind during Pregnancy, Birth & the First Three Months
By Sandy Falk, MD, and Rabbi Daniel Judson, with Steven A. Rapp
Includes medical information, prayers and rituals for each stage of pregnancy, from a liberal Jewish perspective. 7 x 10, 208 pp, Quality PB, b/w photos, 978-1-58023-178-7 **$16.95**

Celebrating Your New Jewish Daughter: Creating Jewish Ways to Welcome Baby Girls into the Covenant—New and Traditional Ceremonies *By Debra Nussbaum Cohen; Foreword by Rabbi Sandy Eisenberg Sasso* 6 x 9, 272 pp, Quality PB, 978-1-58023-090-2 **$18.95**

The New Jewish Baby Book, 2nd Edition: Names, Ceremonies & Customs—A Guide for Today's Families *By Anita Diamant* 6 x 9, 336 pp, Quality PB, 978-1-58023-251-7 **$19.99**

Parenting As a Spiritual Journey: Deepening Ordinary and Extraordinary Events into Sacred Occasions *By Rabbi Nancy Fuchs-Kreimer*
6 x 9, 224 pp, Quality PB, 978-1-58023-016-2 **$16.95**

Parenting Jewish Teens: A Guide for the Perplexed
By Joanne Doades 6 x 9, 200 pp, Quality PB, 978-1-58023-305-7 **$16.99**

Judaism for Two: A Spiritual Guide for Strengthening and Celebrating Your Loving Relationship *By Rabbi Nancy Fuchs-Kreimer and Rabbi Nancy H. Wiener; Foreword by Rabbi Elliot N. Dorff* Addresses the ways Jewish teachings can enhance and strengthen committed relationships. 6 x 9, 224 pp, Quality PB, 978-1-58023-254-8 **$16.99**

Embracing the Covenant: Converts to Judaism Talk About Why & How
By Rabbi Allan Berkowitz and Patti Moskovitz 6 x 9, 192 pp, Quality PB, 978-1-879045-50-7 **$16.95**

The Guide to Jewish Interfaith Family Life: An InterfaithFamily.com Handbook
Edited by Ronnie Friedland and Edmund Case 6 x 9, 384 pp, Quality PB, 978-1-58023-153-4 **$18.95**

Introducing My Faith and My Community
The Jewish Outreach Institute Guide for the Christian in a Jewish Interfaith Relationship
By Rabbi Kerry M. Olitzky 6 x 9, 176 pp, Quality PB, 978-1-58023-192-3 **$16.99**

Making a Successful Jewish Interfaith Marriage: The Jewish Outreach Institute Guide to Opportunities, Challenges and Resources *By Rabbi Kerry M. Olitzky with Joan Peterson Littman*
6 x 9, 176 pp, Quality PB, 978-1-58023-170-1 **$16.95**

The Creative Jewish Wedding Book: A Hands-On Guide to New & Old Traditions, Ceremonies & Celebrations *By Gabrielle Kaplan-Mayer*
9 x 9, 288 pp, b/w photos, Quality PB, 978-1-58023-194-7 **$19.99**

Divorce Is a Mitzvah: A Practical Guide to Finding Wholeness and Holiness When Your Marriage Dies *By Rabbi Perry Netter; Afterword by Rabbi Laura Geller.*
6 x 9, 224 pp, Quality PB, 978-1-58023-172-5 **$16.95**

A Heart of Wisdom: Making the Jewish Journey from Midlife through the Elder Years
Edited by Susan Berrin; Foreword by Harold Kushner
6 x 9, 384 pp, Quality PB, 978-1-58023-051-3 **$18.95**

So That Your Values Live On: Ethical Wills and How to Prepare Them
Edited by Jack Riemer and Nathaniel Stampfer
6 x 9, 272 pp, Quality PB, 978-1-879045-34-7 **$18.99**

Meditation

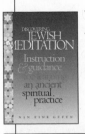

The Handbook of Jewish Meditation Practices
A Guide for Enriching the Sabbath and Other Days of Your Life
By Rabbi David A. Cooper Easy-to-learn meditation techniques.
6 x 9, 208 pp, Quality PB, 978-1-58023-102-2 **$16.95**

Discovering Jewish Meditation: Instruction & Guidance for Learning an Ancient
Spiritual Practice *By Nan Fink Gefen*
6 x 9, 208 pp, Quality PB, 978-1-58023-067-4 **$16.95**

A Heart of Stillness: A Complete Guide to Learning the Art of Meditation
By David A. Cooper 5½ x 8½, 272 pp, Quality PB, 978-1-893361-03-4 **$16.95** *(A SkyLight Paths book)*

Meditation from the Heart of Judaism: Today's Teachers Share Their
Practices, Techniques, and Faith *Edited by Avram Davis*
6 x 9, 256 pp, Quality PB, 978-1-58023-049-0 **$16.95**

Silence, Simplicity & Solitude: A Complete Guide to Spiritual Retreat at Home
By David A. Cooper 5½ x 8½, 336 pp, Quality PB, 978-1-893361-04-1 **$16.95**
(A SkyLight Paths book)

The Way of Flame: A Guide to the Forgotten Mystical Tradition of Jewish
Meditation *By Avram Davis* 4½ x 8, 176 pp, Quality PB, 978-1-58023-060-5 **$15.95**

Ritual/Sacred Practice/Journaling

The Jewish Dream Book: The Key to Opening the Inner Meaning of
Your Dreams *By Vanessa L. Ochs with Elizabeth Ochs; Full-color illus. by Kristina Swarner*
Instructions for how modern people can perform ancient Jewish dream practices
and dream interpretations drawn from the Jewish wisdom tradition.
8 x 8, 128 pp, Full-color illus., Deluxe PB w/flaps, 978-1-58023-132-9 **$16.95**

The Jewish Journaling Book: How to Use Jewish Tradition to Write
Your Life & Explore Your Soul *By Janet Ruth Falon*
Details the history of Jewish journaling throughout biblical and modern times, and
teaches specific journaling techniques to help you create and maintain a vital journal,
from a Jewish perspective. 8 x 8, 304 pp, Deluxe PB w/flaps, 978-1-58023-203-6 **$18.99**

The Book of Jewish Sacred Practices: CLAL's Guide to Everyday & Holiday
Rituals & Blessings *Edited by Rabbi Irwin Kula and Vanessa L. Ochs, PhD*
6 x 9, 368 pp, Quality PB, 978-1-58023-152-7 **$18.95**

Jewish Ritual: A Brief Introduction for Christians
By Rabbi Kerry M. Olitzky and Rabbi Daniel Judson
5½ x 8½, 144 pp, Quality PB, 978-1-58023-210-4 **$14.99**

The Rituals & Practices of a Jewish Life: A Handbook for Personal Spiritual
Renewal *Edited by Rabbi Kerry M. Olitzky and Rabbi Daniel Judson*
6 x 9, 272 pp, illus., Quality PB, 978-1-58023-169-5 **$18.95**

The Sacred Art of Lovingkindness: Preparing to Practice
By Rabbi Rami Shapiro 5½ x 8½, 176 pp, Quality PB, 978-1-59473-151-8 **$16.99**
(A SkyLight Paths book)

Science Fiction/Mystery & Detective Fiction

Mystery Midrash: An Anthology of Jewish Mystery & Detective Fiction
Edited by Lawrence W. Raphael; Preface by Joel Siegel
6 x 9, 304 pp, Quality PB, 978-1-58023-055-1 **$16.95**

Criminal Kabbalah: An Intriguing Anthology of Jewish Mystery & Detective Fiction
Edited by Lawrence W. Raphael; Foreword by Laurie R. King
6 x 9, 256 pp, Quality PB, 978-1-58023-109-1 **$16.95**

Wandering Stars: An Anthology of Jewish Fantasy & Science Fiction
Edited by Jack Dann; Introduction by Isaac Asimov
6 x 9, 272 pp, Quality PB, 978-1-58023-005-6 **$16.95**

More Wandering Stars: An Anthology of Outstanding Stories of Jewish Fantasy and
Science Fiction *Edited by Jack Dann; Introduction by Isaac Asimov*
6 x 9, 192 pp, Quality PB, 978-1-58023-063-6 **$16.95**

Spirituality

The Adventures of Rabbi Harvey: A Graphic Novel of Jewish
Wisdom and Wit in the Wild West *By Steve Sheinkin*
Jewish and American folktales combine in this witty and original graphic novel
collection. Creatively retold and set on the western frontier of the 1870s.
6 x 9, 144 pp, Full-color illus., Quality PB, 978-1-58023-310-1 **$16.99**

Ethics of the Sages: *Pirke Avot*—Annotated & Explained
Translation and Annotation by Rabbi Rami Shapiro
5½ x 8½, 192 pp, Quality PB, 978-1-59473-207-2 **$16.99** *(A SkyLight Paths book)*

A Book of Life: Embracing Judaism as a Spiritual Practice
By Michael Strassfeld 6 x 9, 528 pp, Quality PB, 978-1-58023-247-0 **$19.99**

Meaning and Mitzvah: Daily Practices for Reclaiming Judaism through Prayer, God,
Torah, Hebrew, Mitzvot and Peoplehood *By Rabbi Goldie Milgram*
7 x 9, 336 pp, Quality PB, 978-1-58023-256-2 **$19.99**

The Soul of the Story: Meetings with Remarkable People
By Rabbi David Zeller 6 x 9, 288 pp, HC, 978-1-58023-272-2 **$21.99**

Aleph-Bet Yoga: Embodying the Hebrew Letters for Physical and Spiritual Well-Being
By Steven A. Rapp. Foreword by Tamar Frankiel, PhD and Judy Greenfeld. Preface by Hart Lazer.
7 x 10, 128 pp, b/w photos, Quality PB, Layflat binding, 978-1-58023-162-6 **$16.95**

Entering the Temple of Dreams
Jewish Prayers, Movements, and Meditations for the End of the Day
By Tamar Frankiel, PhD, and Judy Greenfeld
7 x 10, 192 pp, illus., Quality PB, 978-1-58023-079-7 **$16.95**

Does the Soul Survive? A Jewish Journey to Belief in Afterlife, Past Lives & Living
with Purpose *By Rabbi Elie Kaplan Spitz; Foreword by Brian L. Weiss, MD*
6 x 9, 288 pp, Quality PB, 978-1-58023-165-7 **$16.99**

First Steps to a New Jewish Spirit: Reb Zalman's Guide to Recapturing the
Intimacy & Ecstasy in Your Relationship with God *By Rabbi Zalman M. Schachter-Shalomi
with Donald Gropman* 6 x 9, 144 pp, Quality PB, 978-1-58023-182-4 **$16.95**

God in Our Relationships: Spirituality between People from the Teachings of Martin
Buber *By Rabbi Dennis S. Ross* 5½ x 8½, 160 pp, Quality PB, 978-1-58023-147-3 **$16.95**

Judaism, Physics and God: Searching for Sacred Metaphors in a Post-Einstein World
By Rabbi David W. Nelson 6 x 9, 368 pp, Quality PB, inc. reader's discussion guide, 978-1-58023-306-4 **$18.99**;
HC, 352 pp, 978-1-58023-252-4 **$24.99**

The Jewish Lights Spirituality Handbook: A Guide to Understanding,
Exploring & Living a Spiritual Life *Edited by Stuart M. Matlins*
What exactly is "Jewish" about spirituality? How do I make it a part of my life?
Fifty of today's foremost spiritual leaders share their ideas and experience with us.
6 x 9, 456 pp, Quality PB, 978-1-58023-093-3 **$19.99**

Bringing the Psalms to Life: How to Understand and Use the Book of Psalms
By Daniel F. Polish 6 x 9, 208 pp, Quality PB, 978-1-58023-157-2 **$16.95**;
HC, 978-1-58023-077-3 **$21.95**

God & the Big Bang: Discovering Harmony between Science & Spirituality
By Daniel C. Matt 6 x 9, 216 pp, Quality PB, 978-1-879045-89-7 **$16.99**

Minding the Temple of the Soul: Balancing Body, Mind, and Spirit through Traditional
Jewish Prayer, Movement, and Meditation *By Tamar Frankiel, PhD, and Judy Greenfeld*
7 x 10, 184 pp, illus., Quality PB, 978-1-879045-64-4 **$16.95**
Audiotape of the Blessings and Meditations: 60 min. **$9.95**
Videotape of the Movements and Meditations: 46 min. **$20.00**

One God Clapping: The Spiritual Path of a Zen Rabbi *By Alan Lew with Sherril Jaffe*
5½ x 8½, 336 pp, Quality PB, 978-1-58023-115-2 **$16.95**

There Is No Messiah ... and You're It: The Stunning Transformation of Judaism's
Most Provocative Idea *By Rabbi Robert N. Levine, DD*
6 x 9, 192 pp, Quality PB, 978-1-58023-255-5 **$16.99**

These Are the Words: A Vocabulary of Jewish Spiritual Life
By Arthur Green 6 x 9, 304 pp, Quality PB, 978-1-58023-107-7 **$18.95**

Spirituality/Lawrence Kushner

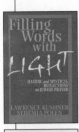

Filling Words with Light: Hasidic and Mystical Reflections on Jewish Prayer
By Lawrence Kushner and Nehemia Polen
5½ x 8½, 176 pp, HC, 978-1-58023-216-6 **$21.99**

The Book of Letters: A Mystical Hebrew Alphabet
Popular HC Edition, 6 x 9, 80 pp, 2-color text, 978-1-879045-00-2 **$24.95**
Collector's Limited Edition, 9 x 12, 80 pp, gold foil embossed pages, w/limited edition silkscreened print, 978-1-879045-04-0 **$349.00**

The Book of Miracles: A Young Person's Guide to Jewish Spiritual Awareness
6 x 9, 96 pp, 2-color illus., HC, 978-1-879045-78-1 **$16.95** For ages 9 and up

The Book of Words: Talking Spiritual Life, Living Spiritual Talk
6 x 9, 160 pp, Quality PB, 978-1-58023-020-9 **$16.95**

Eyes Remade for Wonder: A Lawrence Kushner Reader Introduction by Thomas Moore
6 x 9, 240 pp, Quality PB, 978-1-58023-042-1 **$18.95**

God Was in This Place & I, i Did Not Know: Finding Self, Spirituality and Ultimate Meaning   6 x 9, 192 pp, Quality PB, 978-1-879045-33-0 **$16.95**

Honey from the Rock: An Introduction to Jewish Mysticism
6 x 9, 176 pp, Quality PB, 978-1-58023-073-5 **$16.95**

Invisible Lines of Connection: Sacred Stories of the Ordinary
5½ x 8½, 160 pp, Quality PB, 978-1-879045-98-9 **$15.95**

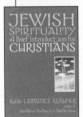

Jewish Spirituality—A Brief Introduction for Christians
5½ x 8½, 112 pp, Quality PB, 978-1-58023-150-3 **$12.95**

The River of Light: Jewish Mystical Awareness
6 x 9, 192 pp, Quality PB, 978-1-58023-096-4 **$16.95**

The Way Into Jewish Mystical Tradition
6 x 9, 224 pp, Quality PB, 978-1-58023-200-5 **$18.99**; HC, 978-1-58023-029-2 **$21.95**

Spirituality/Prayer

Pray Tell: A Hadassah Guide to Jewish Prayer
By Rabbi Jules Harlow, with contributions from many others
8¼ x 11, 400 pp, Quality PB, 978-1-58023-163-3 **$29.95**

Witnesses to the One: The Spiritual History of the Sh'ma By Rabbi Joseph B. Meszler; Foreword by Rabbi Elyse Goldstein 6 x 9, 176 pp, HC, 978-1-58023-309-5 **$19.99**

My People's Prayer Book Series

Traditional Prayers, Modern Commentaries   Edited by Rabbi Lawrence A. Hoffman
Provides diverse and exciting commentary to the traditional liturgy, helping modern men and women find new wisdom in Jewish prayer, and bring liturgy into their lives. Each book includes Hebrew text, modern translation, and commentaries from all perspectives of the Jewish world.

Vol. 1—The Sh'ma and Its Blessings
7 x 10, 168 pp, HC, 978-1-879045-79-8 **$24.99**
Vol. 2—The Amidah
7 x 10, 240 pp, HC, 978-1-879045-80-4 **$24.95**
Vol. 3—P'sukei D'zimrah (Morning Psalms)
7 x 10, 240 pp, HC, 978-1-879045-81-1 **$24.95**
Vol. 4—Seder K'riat Hatorah (The Torah Service)
7 x 10, 264 pp, HC, 978-1-879045-82-8 **$23.95**
Vol. 5—Birkhot Hashachar (Morning Blessings)
7 x 10, 240 pp, HC, 978-1-879045-83-5 **$24.95**
Vol. 6—Tachanun and Concluding Prayers
7 x 10, 240 pp, HC, 978-1-879045-84-2 **$24.95**
Vol. 7—Shabbat at Home
7 x 10, 240 pp, HC, 978-1-879045-85-9 **$24.95**
Vol. 8—Kabbalat Shabbat (Welcoming Shabbat in the Synagogue)
7 x 10, 240 pp, HC, 978-1-58023-121-3 **$24.99**
Vol. 9—Welcoming the Night: Minchah and Ma'ariv (Afternoon and Evening Prayer) 7 x 10, 272 pp, HC, 978-1-58023-262-3 **$24.99**
Vol. 10—Shabbat Morning: Shacharit and Musaf (Morning and Additional Services) 7 x 10, 240 pp, HC, 978-1-58023-240-1 **$24.99**

Spirituality/Women's Interest

The Quotable Jewish Woman: Wisdom, Inspiration & Humor from the Mind & Heart
Edited and compiled by Elaine Bernstein Partnow
6 x 9, 496 pp, HC, 978-1-58023-193-0 **$29.99**

The Knitting Way: A Guide to Spiritual Self-Discovery *By Linda Skolnick and Janice MacDaniels* 7 x 9, 240 pp, Quality PB, 978-1-59473-079-5 **$16.99** *(A SkyLight Paths book)*

The Quilting Path: A Guide to Spiritual Self-Discovery through Fabric, Thread and Kabbalah
By Louise Silk 7 x 9, 192 pp, Quality PB, 978-1-59473-206-5 **$16.99** *(A SkyLight Paths book)*

The Divine Feminine in Biblical Wisdom Literature: Selections Annotated &
Explained *Translated and Annotated by Rabbi Rami Shapiro*
5½ x 8½, 240 pp, Quality PB, 978-1-59473-109-9 **$16.99** *(A SkyLight Paths book)*

Lifecycles, Vol. 1: Jewish Women on Life Passages & Personal Milestones
Edited and with Introductions by Rabbi Debra Orenstein
6 x 9, 480 pp, Quality PB, 978-1-58023-018-6 **$19.95**

Lifecycles, Vol. 2: Jewish Women on Biblical Themes in Contemporary Life
Edited and with Introductions by Rabbi Debra Orenstein and Rabbi Jane Rachel Litman
6 x 9, 464 pp, Quality PB, 978-1-58023-019-3 **$19.95**

Moonbeams: A Hadassah Rosh Hodesh Guide *Edited by Carol Diament, PhD*
8½ x 11, 240 pp, Quality PB, 978-1-58023-099-5 **$20.00**

ReVisions: Seeing Torah through a Feminist Lens *By Rabbi Elyse Goldstein*
5½ x 8½, 224 pp, Quality PB, 978-1-58023-117-6 **$16.95**

The Women's Haftarah Commentary: New Insights from Women Rabbis on the
54 Weekly Haftarah Portions, the 5 Megillot & Special Shabbatot
Edited by Rabbi Elyse Goldstein 6 x 9, 560 pp, HC, 978-1-58023-133-6 **$39.99**

The Women's Torah Commentary: New Insights from Women Rabbis on the 54
Weekly Torah Portions *Edited by Rabbi Elyse Goldstein*
6 x 9, 496 pp, HC, 978-1-58023-076-6 **$34.95**

The Year Mom Got Religion: One Woman's Midlife Journey into Judaism
By Lee Meyerhoff Hendler 6 x 9, 208 pp, Quality PB, 978-1-58023-070-4 **$15.95**

See Holidays for *The Women's Passover Companion: Women's Reflections on the Festival of Freedom* and *The Women's Seder Sourcebook: Rituals & Readings for Use at the Passover Seder.* Also see Bar/Bat Mitzvah for *The JGirl's Guide: The Young Jewish Woman's Handbook for Coming of Age.*

Travel

Israel—A Spiritual Travel Guide, 2nd Edition
A Companion for the Modern Jewish Pilgrim
By Rabbi Lawrence A. Hoffman 4¾ x 10, 256 pp, Quality PB, illus., 978-1-58023-261-6 **$18.99**
Also Available: **The Israel Mission Leader's Guide** 978-1-58023-085-8 **$4.95**

12-Step

100 Blessings Every Day: Daily Twelve Step Recovery Affirmations, Exercises for
Personal Growth & Renewal Reflecting Seasons of the Jewish Year
By Rabbi Kerry M. Olitzky; Foreword by Rabbi Neil Gillman
4½ x 6½, 432 pp, Quality PB, 978-1-879045-30-9 **$15.99**

Recovery from Codependence: A Jewish Twelve Steps Guide to Healing Your Soul
By Rabbi Kerry M. Olitzky 6 x 9, 160 pp, Quality PB, 978-1-879045-32-3 **$13.95**

Renewed Each Day: Daily Twelve Step Recovery Meditations Based on the Bible
By Rabbi Kerry M. Olitzky and Aaron Z.
Vol. 1—Genesis & Exodus: 6 x 9, 224 pp, Quality PB, 978-1-879045-12-5 **$14.95**
Vol. 2—Leviticus, Numbers & Deuteronomy: 6 x 9, 280 pp, Quality PB, 978-1-879045-13-2 **$18.99**

Twelve Jewish Steps to Recovery: A Personal Guide to Turning from Alcoholism &
Other Addictions—Drugs, Food, Gambling, Sex...
By Rabbi Kerry M. Olitzky and Stuart A. Copans, MD; Preface by Abraham J. Twerski, MD
6 x 9, 144 pp, Quality PB, 978-1-879045-09-5 **$14.95**

Theology/Philosophy/The Way Into... Series

The Way Into... series offers an accessible and highly usable "guided tour" of the Jewish faith, people, history and beliefs—in total, an introduction to Judaism that will enable you to understand and interact with the sacred texts of the Jewish tradition. Each volume is written by a leading contemporary scholar and teacher, and explores one key aspect of Judaism. *The Way Into...* series enables all readers to achieve a real sense of Jewish cultural literacy through guided study.

The Way Into Encountering God in Judaism
By Neil Gillman
For everyone who wants to understand how Jews have encountered God through-out history and today.
6 x 9, 240 pp, Quality PB, 978-1-58023-199-2 **$18.99**; HC, 978-1-58023-025-4 **$21.95**
Also Available: **The Jewish Approach to God:** A Brief Introduction for Christians
By Neil Gillman
5½ x 8¼, 192 pp, Quality PB, 978-1-58023-190-9 **$16.95**

The Way Into Jewish Mystical Tradition
By Lawrence Kushner
Allows readers to interact directly with the sacred mystical text of the Jewish tradition. An accessible introduction to the concepts of Jewish mysticism, their religious and spiritual significance and how they relate to life today.
6 x 9, 224 pp, Quality PB, 978-1-58023-200-5 **$18.99**; HC, 978-1-58023-029-2 **$21.95**

The Way Into Jewish Prayer
By Lawrence A. Hoffman
Opens the door to 3,000 years of Jewish prayer, making available all anyone needs to feel at home in the Jewish way of communicating with God.
6 x 9, 224 pp, Quality PB, 978-1-58023-201-2 **$18.99**

The Way Into Judaism and the Environment
By Jeremy Benstein
Explores the ways in which Judaism contributes to contemporary social-environmental issues, the extent to which Judaism is part of the problem and how it can be part of the solution.
6 x 9, 224 pp, HC, 978-1-58023-268-5 **$24.99**

The Way Into *Tikkun Olam* (Repairing the World)
By Elliot N. Dorff
An accessible introduction to the Jewish concept of the individual's responsibility to care for others and repair the world.
6 x 9, 320 pp, HC, 978-1-58023-269-2 **$24.99**

The Way Into Torah
By Norman J. Cohen
Helps guide in the exploration of the origins and development of Torah, explains why it should be studied and how to do it.
6 x 9, 176 pp, Quality PB, 978-1-58023-198-5 **$16.99**; HC, 978-1-58023-028-5 **$21.95**

The Way Into the Varieties of Jewishness
By Sylvia Barack Fishman
Explores the religious and historical understanding of what it has meant to be Jewish from ancient times to the present controversy over "Who is a Jew?"
6 x 9, 250 pp, HC, 978-1-58023-030-8 **$24.99**

Theology/Philosophy

Christians and Jews in Dialogue: In the Presence of the Other
By Mary C. Boys and Sara S. Lee; Foreword by Dr. Dorothy Bass
6 x 9, 240 pp, HC, 978-1-59473-144-0 **$21.99** *(A SkyLight Paths book)*

The Death of Death: Resurrection and Immortality in Jewish Thought
By Neil Gillman 6 x 9, 336 pp, Quality PB, 978-1-58023-081-0 **$18.95**

Evolving Halakhah: A Progressive Approach to Traditional Jewish Law
By Rabbi Dr. Moshe Zemer 6 x 9, 480 pp, Quality PB, 978-1-58023-127-5 **$29.95**;
HC, 978-1-58023-002-5 **$40.00**

Hasidic Tales: Annotated & Explained
By Rabbi Rami Shapiro; Foreword by Andrew Harvey
5½ x 8½, 240 pp, Quality PB, 978-1-893361-86-7 **$16.95** *(A SkyLight Paths Book)*

Healing the Jewish-Christian Rift: Growing Beyond our Wounded History
By Ron Miller and Laura Bernstein; Foreword by Dr. Beatrice Bruteau
6 x 9, 288 pp, Quality PB, 978-1-59473-139-6 **$18.99** *(A SkyLight Paths book)*

A Heart of Many Rooms: Celebrating the Many Voices within Judaism
By David Hartman 6 x 9, 352 pp, Quality PB, 978-1-58023-156-5 **$19.95**

The Hebrew Prophets: Selections Annotated & Explained
Translation & Annotation by Rabbi Rami Shapiro; Foreword by Zalman M. Schachter-Shalomi
5½ x 8½, 224 pp, Quality PB, 978-1-59473-037-5 **$16.99** *(A SkyLight Paths book)*

A Jewish Understanding of the New Testament
By Rabbi Samuel Sandmel; Preface by Rabbi David Sandmel
5½ x 8½, 368 pp, Quality PB, 978-1-59473-048-1 **$19.99** *(A SkyLight Paths book)*

Keeping Faith with the Psalms: Deepen Your Relationship with God Using the Book
of Psalms *By Daniel F. Polish* 6 x 9, 320 pp, Quality PB, 978-1-58023-300-2 **$18.99**;
HC, 978-1-58023-179-4 **$24.95**

A Living Covenant: The Innovative Spirit in Traditional Judaism
By David Hartman 6 x 9, 368 pp, Quality PB, 978-1-58023-011-7 **$20.00**

Love and Terror in the God Encounter
The Theological Legacy of Rabbi Joseph B. Soloveitchik
By David Hartman 6 x 9, 240 pp, Quality PB, 978-1-58023-176-3 **$19.95**;
HC, 978-1-58023-112-1 **$25.00**

The Personhood of God: Biblical Theology, Human Faith and the Divine Image
By Dr. Yochanan Muffs; Foreword by Dr. David Hartman
6 x 9, 240 pp, HC, 978-1-58023-265-4 **$24.99**

Tormented Master: *The Life and Spiritual Quest of Rabbi Nahman of Bratslav*
By Arthur Green 6 x 9, 416 pp, Quality PB, 978-1-879045-11-8 **$19.99**

Traces of God: Seeing God in Torah, History and Everyday Life
By Neil Gillman 6 x 9, 240 pp, HC, 978-1-58023-249-4 **$21.99**

We Jews and Jesus: Exploring Theological Differences for Mutual Understanding
By Rabbi Samuel Sandmel; Preface by Rabbi David Sandmel
6 x 9, 176 pp, Quality PB, 978-1-59473-208-9 **$16.99** *(A SkyLight Paths book)*

Your Word Is Fire: The Hasidic Masters on Contemplative Prayer
Edited and translated by Arthur Green and Barry W. Holtz
6 x 9, 160 pp, Quality PB, 978-1-879045-25-5 **$15.95**

I Am Jewish
Personal Reflections Inspired by the Last Words of Daniel Pearl
Almost 150 Jews—both famous and not—from all walks of life, from all around
the world, write about Identity, Heritage, Covenant / Chosenness and Faith,
Humanity and Ethnicity, and *Tikkun Olam* and Justice.
Edited by Judea and Ruth Pearl
6 x 9, 304 pp, Deluxe PB w/flaps, 978-1-58023-259-3 **$18.99**;
HC, 978-1-58023-183-1 **$24.99**
**Download a free copy of the *I Am Jewish Teacher's Guide* at our website:
www.jewishlights.com**

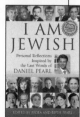

About Jewish Lights

People of all faiths and backgrounds yearn for books that attract, engage, educate, and spiritually inspire.

Our principal goal is to stimulate thought and help all people learn about who the Jewish People are, where they come from, and what the future can be made to hold. While people of our diverse Jewish heritage are the primary audience, our books speak to people in the Christian world as well and will broaden their understanding of Judaism and the roots of their own faith.

We bring to you authors who are at the forefront of spiritual thought and experience. While each has something different to say, they all say it in a voice that you can hear.

Our books are designed to welcome you and then to engage, stimulate, and inspire. We judge our success not only by whether or not our books are beautiful and commercially successful, but by whether or not they make a difference in your life.

For your information and convenience, at the back of this book we have provided a list of other Jewish Lights books you might find interesting and useful. They cover all the categories of your life:

Bar/Bat Mitzvah
Bible Study / Midrash
Children's Books
Congregation Resources
Current Events / History
Ecology
Fiction: Mystery, Science Fiction
Grief / Healing
Holidays / Holy Days
Inspiration
Kabbalah / Mysticism / Enneagram

Life Cycle
Meditation
Parenting
Prayer
Ritual / Sacred Practice
Spirituality
Theology / Philosophy
Travel
12-Step
Women's Interest

Stuart M. Matlins, Publisher

Or phone, fax, mail or e-mail to: **JEWISH LIGHTS Publishing**
Sunset Farm Offices, Route 4 • P.O. Box 237 • Woodstock, Vermont 05091
Tel: (802) 457-4000 • Fax: (802) 457-4004 • www.jewishlights.com
Credit card orders: **(800) 962-4544** (8:30AM–5:30PM ET Monday–Friday)
Generous discounts on quantity orders. SATISFACTION GUARANTEED. Prices subject to change.

For more information about each book, visit our website at www.jewishlights.com